FEMINIST NIGHTMARES

FEMINIST NIGHTMARES

WOMEN AT ODDS

Feminism and the Problem of Sisterhood

EDITED BY
SUSAN OSTROV WEISSER
AND
JENNIFER FLEISCHNER

NEW YORK UNIVERSITY PRESS
New York and London

NEW YORK UNIVERSITY PRESS
New York and London

Library of Congress Cataloging-in-Publication Data
Feminist nightmares : women at odds : feminism and the problem of
sisterhood / edited by Susan Ostrov Weisser and Jennifer Fleischner.
p.   cm.
Includes bibliographical references and index.
ISBN 0-8147-2619-4.—ISBN 0-8147-2620-8 (pbk.)
1. Feminism.   2. Feminism—Moral and ethical aspects.
3. Feminism—United States.   I. Weisser, Susan Ostrov.
II. Fleischner, Jennifer.
HQ1190.F4616   1994
305.42—dc20   94-26606
                     CIP

New York University Press books are printed on acid-free paper,
and their binding materials are chosen for strength and durability.

Manufactured in the United States of America

10   9   8   7   6   5   4   3   2   1

To my children, Cybèle, Amanda, and Billy Weisser

To my sister, Judith Mary Fleischner

CONTENTS

ACKNOWLEDGMENTS

The idea for this book grew from a panel chaired by Susan Ostrov Weisser several years ago at the Northeast Modern Language Association, entitled "Feminist Nightmares: Women against Women." Jennifer Fleischner was one of the participants in the panel. The room in which the 8:00 A.M. session took place was packed, and the heat and interest of the response from the audience were gratifying and thought-provoking: clearly, we felt, here was a subject begging to be explored further. During the ride home, it occurred to one or both of us (we no longer remember which one) to use the panel as a basis for a collection that would put the questions of sisterhood before a wider audience.

Since then we have worked together in ways that suggest the possibilities and difficulties of women's relations with each other. We began with long talks over coffee, during which the personal, the professional, and the political merged seamlessly. Later, when Jennifer began a residence at Harvard University as a Mellon Faculty Fellow, ideas and sentences flew back and forth via fax and phone. During the year-long collaboration, mutual sympathy and respect helped us to work out those disagreements and conflicting interests inevitable to a joint project. In the end we developed ways of listening to and learning from each other that have both enriched our individual work and deepened our friendship. Although our book uses experience to contest an unquestioned ideal of sisterhood, *our* experience leaves us wanting to join forces again.

We are grateful to our contributors, whose interests and ideas broadened our own perspectives. We would also like to thank those friends and colleagues who generously offered advice and suggestions, especially Deborah Dorfman, Eugene H. Roth, Karsten Struhl, and Eleanor Skoller. Karla Jay recommended our proposal to Niko Pfund, editor-in-chief at NYU Press, whose enthusiasm for our project never flagged. Laura Reitano gave extra time way beyond the call of duty. Finally, special thanks are due to Paul Mattick, Jr., for his careful and skilled readings.

INTRODUCTION

SUSAN OSTROV WEISSER AND JENNIFER FLEISCHNER

"Though all women are women, *no woman is only a woman*."
— Elizabeth Spelman, *The Inessential Woman*

During the early stages of soliciting essays for this collection, one of the editors encountered the following reaction: "This is a book that shouldn't be written. Feminists should concentrate on how men oppress women, not how bad women are to each other." The very hostility and vigor of the objection to examining "*women* at odds," suggesting that this is a book whose subject touches a nerve, convinced us that such a book ought to be written—and written by feminists.

We do not wish to open the subject of whether women think or act against other women as a question to be answered simply, as a matter of relocating enemies, nor, above all, as a diatribe against feminism—very much to the contrary. The continuing efficacy of feminism as an activist movement depends precisely on its ability to face the ways in which gender identification may be at odds with other modes of identification, say, those grounded in race, class, nationality, or religion. No collective identity based on these, or other, categories can be said to account wholly for each individual's sense of her world. While a common potential for abuse or oppression might unite all women, their diverse locations and situations in the world frequently lead, not only most obviously to differences in the quantity and quality of that abuse, but also to conditions in which the oppressed can themselves be oppressors.

By providing the conceptual tools to map out who we are and want to be, the awareness of difference has been an important originating idea in feminism. But this book seeks to address a difference more often than not obscured in the rhetoric of feminist theory: the differences among women themselves, and specifically those differences born of an inequality in power relations. Academic feminism has relied to such an extent on the theory of the social construction of difference that contemplating a whole substratum of power differentials *within* the oppressed group which are not easily eradicated is particularly threatening. Thus while differences between men and women have been a primary focus for feminists and nonfeminists, the problematics of the relations between women has only recently begun to be addressed.[1]

To engage the question of differential power relations among women is to encounter a deep division within feminism itself over the very meaning of the key term "woman," i.e., its efficacy as a basis of political criticism and change. One important branch of feminism with its roots in a long tradition, that of the cultural or radical feminists, is that there is in fact an authentic female identity based on the shared experience of the biologically female body. "Whatever inequalities may exist among women," Luce Irigaray has written, "they all undergo, even without clearly realising it, the same oppression, the same exploitation of their body, the same denial of their desire."[2] As Irigaray continues, women's consciousness of their own common experience as women is what allows that experience to be politicized into feminism.

But even those feminists who are social constructionists ground their arguments in some notion of sisterhood. That is, they conclude that the "we" of feminism was not born, but created; precisely because "womanhood" does not exist as a natural category, it had to be invented.[3] Feminism as a political enterprise takes as its subject the category (whether seen as natural or socially constructed) "woman," and its founding premise is the redemptive possibilities of the union of minds and bodies in that category. It is no wonder, then, that these bodies and minds have so often been declared as belonging to a unified entity, whose characteristics either constitute the "real" nature of women, or provide the rationale for a "real" feminist program.

Moreover, sisterly relations have been a means for providing comfort, access to insight, and, most importantly, empowerment in the practical realm of social relations. In the United States, for instance, "sisterhood" has been used effectively to enlist the sympathies of women on behalf of a variety of reforming causes (for instance, in the nineteenth century, in movements for abolitionism, temperance, and educational reform) and to enjoin women to activism. It is the recognition of sisterhood as both subject position and object of study that justified the founding of women's studies programs.

Yet the trope of familial relations itself suggests the contradiction inherent in this formulation: in practice many find that familial relations are not always comforting or empowering, and quite frequently just the opposite. Families are often only the most private sites of warfare, of expressions of dominance and fields of hierarchical values, and never more so than when they masquerade as benevolent social extensions of natural relations, of benign patriarchal power, or even of liberal democratic principles. Feminism has long recognized the transmission of oppressive ideology in the institution of motherhood for exactly these reasons; but the mutual nurturance and support attributed to the relation of sisterhood (derived, it is theorized, from motherhood) has proved to be more enduringly mystified. Even the brand of feminism that opposes the essentialist view of women as nurturing, specially endowed creatures, united by their biology, has avoided the implications of looking too closely at the problematics of sisterhood.

While feminist scholars have played a critical role in determining feminism's direction, feminist scholarship has the double task of being a politically prescriptive program as well as a conceptual structure for a description of the world. If anything, it is expedient, perhaps at times necessary, that the first imperative (i.e., of prescription) supersede the second (i.e., description). Placing gender above other categories of identity or causal explanations has been necessary to distinguish feminism from other liberatory projects, while the impetus toward social progress is underwritten by a conceptual apparatus that stresses a clear dichotomy between men and women. It is fine for social constructivists to say that there is no such thing as "woman," but, as several theorists have pointed out (Tania Modleski, for example), the politics of gender are very real and require an immediate and unified response in the real world, and this includes an operating definition of both "women" and "men."[4] As a result, the existence of differential privileges or self-defeating practices *among* women may be particularly disturbing to advocates of social and political change.

Not surprisingly, women of color were among the first to note that all women do not necessarily experience the world in the same way, or share the same political goals, in spite of having in common bodies sexed as female. For many such critics of feminism, the woman's movement was classbound and racebound; that is, it was primarily a movement of and for white, European, middle-class women. A good deal of admirable feminist writing has been directed toward this problem already, and it is not our task here to review or repeat the ways in which these difficult insights have been addressed.[5] We are not unconcerned with this specific topic, but would wish to place it within the larger context of women whose interests are pitted against one another, who are at odds in ways that may in fact be overdetermined and extremely subtle.

There are, we note, two defensive reactions to this disturbing problem: One is an insistence on the accommodation of difference, as if all that is needed is a more generous and inclusive spirit, a talking-to and listening-to, or a sharing of power in the movement itself. The other is an angry denunciation of those who would "criticize" other women, as though such denunciations, without a reasoned exchange, do not themselves reproduce the fragmentation to which we are calling attention. Both of these, we believe, are forms of denial or misdirected hostility that do not serve the interests of women in the long run. Rather, they serve to glamorize the critic or to idealize unity, while preserving the problems in the real world untouched—thereby leaving women more vulnerable than ever to the very conditions against which the mystification was designed to protect.

While we would not wish to deny that identifying with other women and recognizing our importance in each other's lives have been important contributions of feminism, the insistence on sisterhood as a characteristic (rather than ideal) trait of women has led to what we see as a distressing split between theory (and ideal), on the one hand, and the everyday experience of many women, particularly those less privileged in any way. As daughters, mothers, wives, lovers, friends, and workers, we daily encounter and observe instances in which those very attributes that are supposed to unite us do not so often lift us above the tensions of living in a world of multifarious, interlocking oppressions. The female boss who is harder on her female employees, the lover who humiliates her female rival, the mother who abuses her daughter, all belie any positive construction of sisterhood.

Sentimentalizing sisterhood has, also, opened feminists up to charges of parochialism and, ironically, elitism. Thus, identity politics, the basis for feminist politics and one of its strengths, is also its greatest weakness. The realities of everyday life, shaped by unshapely, complex identities, are left to the unnuanced, unanalyzed portrayals in the women's magazine exposé of another "Mommy Dearest," or the sitcom about catty friends, or the popular novel in which the bitch figure appears as a regular feature.

Feminist reluctance to come squarely to grips with women's oppression of other women has virtually handed over the problem to critics unsympathetic to feminism. It doesn't take much insight to note that women are not all good to other women, but many in the media— women and men, both—fairly gloat whenever any particularly flagrant example comes their way. Backlash is a disturbing phenomenon, but should not deter feminists from dissent and self-critique. Instead, feminists are feminism's most appropriate and effective critics.

Feminist theory has introduced the term "feminisms," highlighting the different forms feminisms take; so, for example, for postcolonial women, the structure of any freedom is dictated by freedom from imperialism. The implications for feminist scholarship are profound: thus, field researchers like Daphne Patai (whose essay, "U.S. Academics and Third-World Women: Is Ethical Research Possible?" is included in this volume) have grown uneasy with their previous working assumptions. Do white "first world" and wealthy "third world" women in fact have more in common with one another than with working-class and peasant women of their own worlds? The ethics of doing research based on the supposed commonality of subjective experience between scholar and subject may change when one engages fully with such questions.

Similar dilemmas emerge in the wake of acknowledging political, cultural, intergenerational, and class distinctions among women. An evolving strand in the feminism of the eighties and nineties is the recognition, central to our own collection, that gender is one axis of oppression that does not preclude, and indeed cuts across, multiple others. This holds true whether or not one presumes that woman is an "essential nature," a uniform collection of social attributes with no necessary relation to biological imperatives, or a multiple and contradictory "subject position" within the network of social relations in a culture. Privileging oppression of gender over other forms of oppression erases the complexities and self-contradictions that inhere in any positioning of the socially constructed subject or essential woman. There are still differences within the difference, we say.

The essays gathered here seek to contribute to that growing recognition, with special emphasis on recognizing and engaging with the problematics of female-female relations. Though feminist critics and theorists may postulate a "we" in order to empower women, the authors in this collection acknowledge that this alignment is created at least partly through a cognizance of the conditions that make for difference as *inequality*. All these essays perceive the likenesses between women, but do not necessarily see their experiences or modes of living as qualitatively or quantitatively identical, i.e., in kind or degree of oppression. We *may* argue that the housewife and the whore both serve a male-dominated social, political, and economic order, making them "sisters under the skin," but the suburban matron and the midtown streetwalker who services her husband express the radical divisions our society fosters between women as much as they illustrate the unique tie formed by their biology.

The issue of women's domination over other women is neither transparent nor monolithic, and it extends into all fields of inquiry. This finds reflection in the diversity of topics as well as approaches in our collection. The problems posed by women's relations with other women reach into many areas: textual and nontextual, public and private, historical and contemporary, theoretical and ordinary everyday experience. As editors, our bent is toward texts and the analysis of texts, and thus our collection reflects the bent toward narrative and textuality, but this group of essays is also about social texts and ordinary experience. Surely the experience of oppression is not only in or about language, and to confine ourselves to literary expressions of conflict would be to negate the importance of experience itself as a condition of the oppressed, a point that the feminist philosopher Linda Alcoff makes in her essay on the problem of speaking for others.

Generally, feminist critics have tended to explain (and explain away) the difficulty posed by seemingly antifeminist women in four ways: (1) These women are anomalies (albeit embarrassing ones) whose acts are unnatural, in the same way that women who do not conform to maternal stereotypes are seen as "unnatural mothers," rather than instances that cast doubt on the validity of the premises; (2) Women are human, and humans *all* have the potential for oppressing others, requiring social prescriptions applying equally to both sexes; (3) Women who behave oppressively toward other women operate under a false consciousness, having internalized patriarchal values, including misogyny, a wish for power, competitiveness, aggressiveness, etc.; (4) Women in these cases are bravely behaving the way men do, i.e., exhibiting appropriate behavior (e.g., "striving for excellence") in areas where men are allowed to speak and act against each other's interests and "get away with it." This argument is usually applied selectively, however, to approved behavior such as verbal aggression in a boardroom, rather than to obviously oppressive practices such as racism.

Ironically, the anomalous, the natural, and the socialized as descriptions of women underpin antifeminist accounts of female behavior as well: one thinks, for instance, of the attacks against Mary Wollstonecraft for being "unnatural," one of the "unsex'd females," parodied by such contemporaries as Thomas Taylor, who wrote a *A Vindication of the Rights of Brutes;* or one can go back to such archetypal images of "natural" (i.e., ferocious, terrorizing) women as Medusa, Medea, or a devouring Jocasta; or turn (to choose at random) to Conrad's portrayal of the exquisitely "socialized" Betrothed, or to Twain's embodiment of a strangling domesticity in the "sivilizing" Widow Douglas.

The point here is that feminist discourse on so-called antifeminist women needs to reformulate, not simply recapitulate by mere inversion, the terms and structure of debate. We would like to see the discussions of difference leavened by a thicker description of the ways in which beliefs about feminism are or are not connected to practices in the social sphere, and are enacted within or against these practices. For example, some critics have noted that we expect more in the way of caretaking and kindness from (other) women; therefore, the disappointment and anger generated by their failure to live up to their prescribed gender billing is all the more acute because we are less armored against it, as we are against male hostility or aggression.[6]

But women also learn the ways of the oppressors in dealing with the world, ways of operating within that world which the more privileged do not have to engage in. Confusingly, these may be neither manifest nor distinct from other practices, neither "intentional" nor conscious. It is not surprising that women, whose place in society varies so greatly over time and across cultures, and whose access to power and resources depends so much on their relations to men, should press on each other in such a confounding variety of ways. Womanhood is a category of identity, as Simone de Beauvoir pointed out, that is unique in that it is highly visible, yet so ubiquitous that it melts easily into other categories under the pressure to keep up relations with men and other figures of authority.

Our own way of widening the discussion of women's conflicts with each other is to present multiple forms of conflict for study: theoretical, behavioral, and representational. While there are no simple ways to derive conclusions about actual behavior from textual representations, or to distinguish how the behaviors of "real" women are influenced by their representations in narrative, the continuities and discontinuities of thinking on this difficult issue emerge in juxtaposing the historical with the contemporary, the "real life" narrative with the fictional, theoretical feminist thought with the colorful examples of the problem thrown out by popular culture for mass consumption.

Since many of the essays in this book are analyses of representations, it is interesting to notice the permutations and distinctions among, for example, men's representations of women's relations (as in the Bible); women's representations of women's relations in "high" contemporary literature (by Louise Erdrich and Leslie Silko); in contemporary popular literature (Harlequin romance novels); and in real-life narratives of women who are involved in surrogate-birth relationships, compared to filmed representations revising those narratives (one mainstream and one a feminist alternative video).

Indeed, we were struck by the number of essays in our collection that analyze representations of other representations, both by and about women. Some constitute a series of Chinese boxes in which women essayists write about "other" women (so-called third world subjects of research, an eighteenth-century author, pro-life activists, East German women) at a distance from them (culturally, politically, geographically), who have thought or talked or written about themselves or still *other* "other" women (Turkish women, women considering abortions, West German feminists). Representation, this suggests, may be a distancing device that allows us to look at a problem uncomfortably close to our own experience, while in other instances it constructs a disguise (a "veil," to borrow Devoney Looser's metaphor) for ideology that eases discomfort. A particularly intricate illustration of the ways in which ideology is at once reproduced, concealed, examined, and resisted through representation is Eileen Gillooly's essay, a feminist dissection of the relations among a nineteenth-century female author (Jane Austen), the narrator of her novel *(Mansfield Park)*, the ostensible heroine of the novel (Fanny Price), and the supposed anti-heroine (Mary Crawford), who turns out, Gillooly argues, to be on occasion actually endorsed by the narrator, with subtle and multiple effects on the reader.

Our intent in presenting a wide variety of essays is to explore and complicate the connections, acknowledged or unacknowledged, between the represented and the actual, as well as the ways in which they shape one another. If the Bible represents the ways in which patriarchal culture has thought about women in relation to each other, of what significance is it that the female authors of Harlequin novels, on the one hand, or the actual women at odds in surrogate mother situations, on the other, organize their own narratives along much the same lines? What are we to make of the amazing antiquity and endurance of these plots and characters? What conclusions may we draw about the workings of ideologies of gender in art, in life story, in social theory, in actual behavior?

To the degree that these essays share a common ground, it is in their explicit or implicit call for a revision of feminist thinking on oppression in order to see its multifaceted nature (though our authors in no way arrive at even compatible positions, as is evident, for instance, in the contrast between Daphne Patai's and Linda Alcoff's responses to the feminist practice of speaking on behalf of other women). This revisionary impulse involves reformulating familiar ways of dealing with conflicts within feminism, so that oppression is no longer seen as transferred unproblematically from group to group as object to subject. Even such specific kinds of oppression as those engendered by differences in race, class, or sexuality are multidimensional and dynamic in nature. So, for example, Robin Anne Reid argues that sexual identity should be seen as "process," thereby complicating not only the idea of identity, but that of situating oneself in the margin or center. And in her essay on relations between black and white women under slavery in the United States, Jennifer Fleischner looks at the problematics of identification and difference in the works of white antislavery women who wrote on behalf of enslaved African-American women. Their efforts to establish sisterhood within a profoundly racist culture created overlapping, interlocking, and contradictory identities for both black and white women in North and South.

Moreover, Elizabeth Spelman's observation that "no woman is only a woman" points toward other kinds of problems in dealing with negative relations between women: what is she when she oppresses other women? what is her alliance to the women she oppresses? Even more troubling, what is to be feminism's alliance to women who oppress? This last, in particular, is taken up in several essays. For example, William Thompson attempts to bring such issues to bear upon his discussion of the Société des Citoyennes Républicaines Révolutionnaires, a radical faction of French revolutionary women who, in spite of their mobilization of feminist values (independence, initiative, political activism) were not in fact feminist, if we understand the term to mean someone who supports the emancipation and equality of women in society. Is feminism then not to refer to acting in a liberated way (autonomously, for instance) but rather to a set of prescribed opinions and beliefs? Do women who organize, seek power, and have transgressive agendas necessarily serve the interests of other women?

These questions also pervade Linda C. McClain's analysis of the tactical arguments of Feminists for Life of America, an influential group of activist, anti-abortion women who use traditional feminist arguments to attack abortion rights. McClain's work is a stark example of the troubling notion that there is no agreement about the "equalizing principles" upon which feminism stands. What do we do with the claim of a small group of women who act in the name of feminism in taking a stand repugnant to many American feminists? Rather than dismiss them, McClain takes their arguments seriously, suggesting, as does Patai, that merely accommodating difference may not always be possible in the face of mutually exclusive agendas such as pro-choice and anti-abortion positions. Indeed, Manisha Sinha, using the case of a slaveholding mistress's life and polemical writings, shows how women's historical agency has not always been progressive and that women as a group have not always been on other women's side.

The need to break from the rigidity of searching for identity or difference is implied by Devoney Looser in her essay on the political implications of feminist criticism on Lady Mary Wortley Montagu's *Letters*; the desire to create a bond with women in the past causes some feminist critics to gloss over differences that are potentially oppressive, such as Montagu's misreading of and sense of superiority to Turkish culture. Labeling Montagu (or Austen or Eliot) as "feminist" not only elides other forms of oppression, but merely displaces the question of domination to another level of abstraction.

The presumption of solidarity, and the conflict it blinds us to, is a central concern of Tuzyline Allan, who argues that the commonly held critical view that Alice Walker locates women outside of the sphere of destructive power-play (in her development of womanism) undermines the radical character of the womanist project as an alternative to feminism. What Allan suggestively calls "the lure of domination" affects relationships *among* African-American women (as well as between black and white women), whose solidarity as a group at odds with white women has dominated (we use that word deliberately) black feminist discourse.

Other fruitful critical inquiries might investigate the politics of domination that are played out between women within patriarchal cultures in which female antagonism is presumed. Taking this line, Judith R. Baskin traces the paradigmatic relationships between female figures found in the Hebrew Bible, a collection of documents written and edited by men, in which female conflict is expected. Here we see how the representation of women's collusion in the oppression of their sex results from their position in the "house of the father," whether home of the patriarch or House of God. As Baskin notes , the one exception to this pattern of rivalry (between, say, mistress and maidservant, co-wives, mothers-in-law and daughters-in-law), the positive relationship between a mother and her son's wife (Naomi and Ruth), is significant precisely for its surprising reversal of an anticipated pattern.

Equally "surprising," because unexpected within its apparently patriarchal structure, is the secret and subversive bond of humor that Eileen Gillooly locates in Jane Austen's *Mansfield Park* between the narrator and Mary Crawford (in contrast to the more obvious rivalry between Mary and Fanny Price), constituting an unusual form of sisterhood within an *apparent* conflict among the interests of women, author, and character. Unlike the biblical narratives that all, finally, work to fulfill the imperatives of their form—finding God's (The Father's) marvelous purposes in every human action—Austen's novel provides for Mary and its narrator a linguistic outlet for the frustrations that arise from the hypocrisies and gender biases of their male-dominated culture. These essays suggest that patriarchy not only structurally includes female rivalry, it *requires* it. Other essays, notably by E. Ann Kaplan and Susan Ostrov Weisser, explore this problem further, as they examine the uses of female rivalry in popular culture. Kaplan's essay on narratives of surrogate and adoptive mothers and Weisser's on the bitch figure in popular romance novels discuss ways in which women are played off against one another in pairs as victim-victimizer, in order to privilege gender rivalry over other categories such as class. As in Rosaria Champagne's analysis of female therapists and abusive mothers, Kaplan's research notes the way in which such doubling of women serves patriarchal interests. Popular culture is also the focus of Weisser's essay, in which women construct problematic relations for themselves in order to reconstruct a fantasized, untroubled relationship to men.

Given that many of these essays take as a given that hierarchical relations do structure our culture, issues of collusion come up frequently, and in most of the essays. Rather than propose that women are "better natur'd" or bad-natured, we would suggest that scholars look to the ways in which women actually live, i.e., whether or not women's socialization toward more permeable boundaries makes them more capable of subtle harm as well as greater susceptibility toward being harmed by those with whom they (purportedly) connect most easily. While there are shared bonds based on common experiences of oppression, in other words, the very grounds for social and emotional connection among women also foster the conditions for turning on one another.

Thus Nancy Ries, an anthropologist who has done extensive fieldwork in Russia, discusses the cult of female suffering, embraced by Russian women to justify the drastic double standards under which they labor. Handed down between generations of women, the power of oppression is all the more forceful because it tends to be invisible—i.e., justified by "mother love" and the desire to protect the daughter. Ries's findings illustrate the ways in which women are socialized, not only to take care of and depend on others, but to create dependencies in others which construct the conditions for the (often unwitting) oppression of other women.

In Rosaria Champagne's essay on true crime novels of mother-daughter abuse, "mother love" also serves to veil both crime and cure: playing off good and bad women defuses cultural anxieties about various abuses within the family system, for example. Champagne's study has an additional point to make: what may seem feminist (the heroicization of the good female therapist) sometimes is so at the expense of a category of "other" women (lower-class, noneducated, biological mother).

Jennifer Shaddock deals with two novelists, Louise Erdrich and Leslie Silko, who have examined the ways in which the internalization of masculinist views divide women who share an experience of oppression. Such an analysis may serve more broadly as a radical critique of the notion of "women's culture" as a viable foundational principle for feminism. We may contrast Shaddock's depiction of women's relations in novels by Leslie Silko and Louise Erdrich, i.e., their unwillingness to promote pain and suffering through passivity, with Ries's description of pain, suffering, and passivity among women in Russia.

Interactions between women of East and West (as Nanette Funk shows) reveal that differences (this time in economic and political systems and their effects) are not so easily accommodated, even among those with the "best" of intentions. Such problems return us to Alcoff, exploring tensions of similarities and differences. As Funk's essay demonstrates, feminism itself can become a dividing line and a divisive force among women, to the confusion and dismay of those Western feminists who would like feminism to speak to (and for, to use Alcoff's term) all women. These studies raise a question of great anxiety for feminism: do we really *want* to accommodate or resolve all differences among women?

Linda Alcoff and Muriel Dimen are authors writing in different forms, academic/philosophic and personal/psychoanalytic, respectively, who illustrate the need to deconstruct the discourse of difference in order to struggle with the seemingly insoluble dilemmas presented by women's relations with other women. Both, in very divergent ways, allow for the commonality among women without insisting on universally shared female—or human—traits. Insisting that we should neither justify the problems of difference by the usual rationalizations nor attempt to abandon difference altogether, Alcoff suggests a greater sensitization to the instrumental effects of any act of speaking for others, while Dimen opens possibilities for feminism by asserting the value of ambivalence.

The structure of our collection rests on the metaphor of family relations that has energized much of feminist theory from the nineteenth century on, with a special play on the term "sisterhood." Thus the first section deals directly with the tensions of commonality and difference: How have women worked through a sense of connection to other women when this sameness is at odds with a sense of superiority based on racial, ethnic, or national differences? Or, alternatively, how have commonalities been eroded by internecine conflict? The second section, by contrast, focuses specifically on the institutionalization of "motherhood," as the name for the most potentially intense and problematic bond between women, playing out the political, cultural, and textual manifestations of difference within the mother-daughter bond.

The third section turns to the ways in which women define their relations to each other through males as points of reference or foci of competition. In doing so, these essays address the limits of a concept like sisterhood as it is worked out against the ground of patriarchal hierarchies of authority.

The fourth section considers alternative views of the problem of multiple oppressions: how to cross similarity with difference, to reach a "family relation" that is neither as sentimentalized as sisterhood nor as distant as strangers: a link between theory and experience, likeness rather than sameness.

It has been argued that the divisions which exist among women, in feminism and out, are themselves the result and legend of patriarchy, and that an emphasis on the oppressive nature of women's relations (even some women, some of the time) is to emphasize division at the expense of the loyalty we need to accomplish change in the social order.[7] To point to problems that women have with other women is to point *away* from the cause of resisting male oppression, this argument goes; and further, to do so represents a collusion with the oppressors themselves. Such a charge by other feminists is not seen by us as oppressive to our own thinking; on the contrary, it is a valid concern, and we share it. But we don't agree that the peril to feminism outweighs the opportunity afforded by breaking through mists of sentiment, idealization, and mystification that still surround the name Woman, even among women themselves. Political strategy may require unity, but not at the cost of women reproducing a romantic vision of themselves. We think feminism can take it, should take it in, and moreover can only benefit from it. Ignoring unequal differences can only weaken feminism, as it leaves open the occasion for our exploitation of each other in everyday life, and fuels the argument of those who would reject feminism as an explanatory theory leading to more equitable practices.

It is thus our project, in gathering these essays, not to work against sisterhood or against theory itself but to open up a more fluid notion of what oppression means. The problem of women against other women is part of a much larger picture of oppression and how it works: so, for example, the texts, practices, and ideologies that embody this subject may be seen in light of the ways in which the oppressed often collude with a sensibility of domination. The selfhood of those in any devalued group is developed both in resistance to as well as in cooperation with the oppressor for many reasons; for example, as a means for mastery, or out of a sense of severely limited choices. Furthermore, theories of identity politics, such as feminism, need to speak to the multiple identities within which gender is situated so that the measure of interlocking oppressions may be more fully taken.

We follow the thinking of bell hooks, who argues eloquently (and so, we quote at length) for a feminism that encompasses examining women's capacity for domination:

> Emphasizing paradigms of domination that call attention to woman's capacity to dominate is one way to deconstruct and challenge the simplistic notion that man is the enemy, woman the victim; the notion that men have always been the oppressors. Such thinking enables us to examine our role as women in the perpetuation and maintenance of systems of domination. . . . Even though I speak from the particular experience of living as a Black woman in the United States, a white-supremacist, capitalist, patriarchal society, where small numbers of white men (and honorary "white men") constitute ruling groups, I understand that in many places in the world oppressed and oppressor share the same color. I understand that right here in this room, oppressed and oppressor share the same gender. Right now as I speak, a man who is himself victimized, wounded, hurt by racism and class exploitation is actively dominating a woman in his life—that even as I speak, women who are ourselves exploited, victimized, are dominating children. It is necessary for us to remember, as we think critically about domination, that we all have the capacity to act in ways that oppress, dominate, wound (whether or not that power is institutionalized). It is necessary to remember that it is first the potential oppressor within that we must resist— the potential victim within that we must rescue—otherwise we cannot hope for an end to domination, for liberation.[8]

We believe we will have achieved our goal in this project if we provoke readers to ask difficult questions that have been understandably avoided in the interest of a more purely political striving: what happens when members of an oppressed group become the "oppressors" of others? How do women reproduce power relations through the medium of texts? How might we revise a feminist theory of women's authority to take into account the potential dangers of power? Does "oppression" itself need retheorizing? How important is the gendered body for self-definition, and therefore as a definitive category for political change and action? Is the female body itself always the site for the battle for privilege, or should a theory of change rely more on real alliances forged by those acutely aware of how we are commonly defined by others? These questions, we hope, engage some of the difficult problems underlying feminist theory today.

The problem of women at odds with other women is not a simple one, and therefore it does not admit a single solution or perspective. We have avoided, therefore, essays that present the issue as an unproblematic transfer of devaluation from the bodies or nature of men to those of women. Instead, we have leaned toward inquiry and analysis as the best enemy of that sentimentality which is, we believe, a kind of *human* oppression. Because it caters to fantasy wishes and thus leaves issues unexamined, sentiment and mystification, even within a progressive social force such as feminism, can be the other side of (and the best cover for) a kind of subtle brutality that pervades human relations.

All of our authors reflect conventions of representing social reality that underline some conflicting interest or antagonism between women while obscuring other, less visible agendas. All imply the necessity for a widening of the borders of our understanding on the subject, as part of the work of progressive politics as well as of scholarship. If, in doing so, we risk being misunderstood as encouraging fragmentation among women, or abetting disloyalty, we are willing to risk it. It is our belief that problems must be addressed, and imbalances within groups redressed, in order to make the world what we want it to be.

The more modest hope of the editors is that in identifying and analyzing the complex ways in which women relate (or in some cases, are mythologized as relating) to one another, we might come to a greater understanding of "difference" in feminism. All difference, we might say, is a difference within a context, after all. Rather than see the argument in theoretical feminism as between sameness and difference, or what Ann Snitow calls cultural and radical feminisms, we seek a more complex evaluation of difference—and we call for an unswerving gaze at the range of problems that arise when theory encounters the lived disparities among real women.

NOTES

1. Aside from works specifically addressing issues of the intersection of race and class with gender, some of which are mentioned below, the following books—Helena Michie, *Sororophobia: Differences among Women in Literature and Culture* (New York: Oxford University Press, 1992); Valerie Miner and Helen Longino, eds., *Competition: A Feminist Taboo?* (New York: Feminist Press, 1987); and Marianne Hirsch and Evelyn Fox Keller, eds., *Conflicts in Feminism* (New York: Routledge, 1990)—are three of the most

useful works on various aspects of the subject of women at odds and the implications for feminism of their relations.

2. Luce Irigaray, *This Sex Which Is Not One*, trans. Catherine Porter and Carolyn Burke (Ithaca: Cornell University Press, 1985), 164.

3. For a still useful summary of these distinctions, see Ann Snitow, "A Gender Diary," in Hirsch and Keller, *Conflicts in Feminism*. A more recent contribution is Denise Riley, *"Am I That Name?": Feminism and the Category of "Women" in History* (Minneapolis: University of Minnesota Press, 1988), which questions and considers the efficacy of "woman" as a category of identity for feminism: "That 'women' is indeterminate and impossible," she writes, "is no cause for lament. . . . What makes feminism . . . is a willingness, at times, to shred this 'women' to bits—to develop a speed, foxiness, versatility" (113–14).

4. Tania Modleski, *Feminism without Women: Culture and Criticism in a "Postfeminist" Age* (New York: Routledge, 1991).

5. Angela Y. Davis, *Women, Culture and Politics* (New York: Vintage Books, 1990), focuses on the empowerment of African-American women whose interests are not always aligned with those of white women; bell hooks, *Ain't I a Woman: Black Women and Feminism* (Boston: South End Press, 1981) and *Feminist Theory: From Margins to Center* (Boston: South End Press, 1984); Elizabeth Spelman, *Inessential Woman: Problems of Exclusion in Feminist Thought* (Boston: Beacon Press, 1988); and Diana Fuss, *Essentially Speaking: Feminism, Nature and Difference* (New York: Routledge, 1989) are also pertinent and helpful resources on this question.

6. Luise Eichenbaum and Susie Orbach employ this idea in *Between Women* (New York: Viking, 1988).

7. See the discussion of this point in Miner and Longino, *Competition*, 242; competition, they argue, "amounts to performing for the oppressors the task of keeping us divided and weak."

8. "Feminism: A Transformational Politic," in *Theoretical Perspectives on Sexual Difference*, ed. Deborah L. Rhode (New Haven: Yale University Press, 1990).

I.

SISTERS UNDER THE SKIN?

1.

U.S. ACADEMICS AND THIRD-WORLD WOMEN: IS ETHICAL RESEARCH POSSIBLE?

DAPHNE PATAI

The short answer to the question posed by my subtitle is, in my view, "No." But much more than that needs to be said. To which "U.S. academics" am I referring? What is meant by "third-world women"? What is "ethical" research? Before addressing these questions, I must make explicit a term that, though not named in my title, frames the comments that follow: my concern is above all with feminist academics and with the meaning of feminism in research situations governed by inequalities and hierarchies—situations, in other words, that routinely unfold in the real world. These inequalities, which may also occur in many other settings, are readily apparent when one considers the average U.S. female academic—white and middle-class—in contrast to her average "third world" object of research: nonwhite and/or poor. Although exploitation and unethical behavior are always a possibility when research is conducted with living persons, this danger is increased when the researcher is interviewing "down," that is, among groups less powerful (economically, politically, socially) than the researcher herself.[1]

In the discussion that follows, I use the image of the North American academic researcher interviewing women from the so-called third world to epitomize an interaction typically characterized by systemic inequality. In such situations, it is the very existence of privilege that allows the research to be undertaken.

Academics who are not feminists also experience moral dilemmas as they conduct research with living persons, which is why ethical guidelines delineating proper procedures exist in many disciplines. These guidelines generally follow the medical injunction: do no harm. Yet even such a minimal directive, if taken seriously, would paralyze researchers, for we are usually unable to gauge, let alone control, the potential consequences of our procedures and of the research products in which they result. But I would go beyond this minimal directive and set instead a maximalist feminist ethic, for while questions about ethics occur in many contexts, they take on special urgency in the case of women—feminists—doing research with women. In practice, at this particular historical moment, such questions seem to demand special attention from feminists. As I see it, the goals and procedures of feminism ought to be the generally human ones. But they are not; at least not yet. Hence feminists—because we are among the few who articulate commitments and political priorities—must invoke that better human model of behavior that is as yet nowhere to be found. In an ideal world there would be no feminist ethics, because "feminism" arises precisely due to the fact of patriarchy and oppression in the real world. In this sense our concerns are indeed uniquely feminist—with the proviso that "feminism" ought to be viewed not as an absolute but as a time-bound concept and movement, appearing in many guises and variations.

Some scholars, however, may take amiss any suggestion that we need to be concerned about the ethical implications of our research. Mere discussion of this issue threatens to raise the specter of norms imposed on all researchers, which would necessarily interfere with the autonomy of the individual researcher, an autonomy that is perhaps the prime value in contemporary western culture. Gail Webber encountered such views in a small minority of those replying to a questionnaire in which she asked respondents to choose from among fourteen items the kind of statement on ethics they considered most important for feminists. The majority selected as their first choice the statement: "Feminists seek social, political, and economic equality for all women." But the very word "ethics" had negative connotations for some. Webber cites a few such comments: "I think the whole idea [of ethical guidelines] is bizarre and even dangerous. When do we get the feminist mind police uniforms?

It's bad enough as it is." "One person's dogma is another's repression. When will we schedule the inquisition? I object to the whole idea of ethical behavior guidelines." "Sounds like the '14 commandments.'"[2] It is instructive that, in these reactions, "guidelines" have been construed to suggest "dogma" and institutionally imposed control. My own starting point is somewhat different. I assume that we are doing something other than merely pursuing our own careers and adding knowledge to the world, and that we must raise questions about the ethics of our behavior in relation to those on and with whom we do our research. I also take it as a given that most women doing research on women are moved by commitments to women. Such research is *for* women, as the popular formula has it, not merely by or about them. But because "women," gender notwithstanding, are not a monolithic block, ethical questions about our actions and the implications of those actions are especially appropriate.

Whether we adopt a broad or a narrow definition of feminism, if the term is to have any meaning it must involve a critique of traditional concepts and structures that have marginalized women materially and psychologically, in the world and even in their own souls. It must also ultimately aim at social transformation. Because feminism has challenged the pose of neutrality and objectivity that for so long governed positivist social science, it has forced us to scrutinize, as well, our own practice as scholars. One result is that the ethical problems of using other women as the subjects of our research become an immediate source of tension. For it is a fact that we are confronted by dual allegiances. On the one hand, we are obligated to our academic disciplines and institutions, within which we must succeed if we are to have any impact on the academy (and this in itself involves us in numerous contradictions, as part of our project entails transforming those very disciplines and institutions). On the other hand, if we take feminism seriously, it commits us to a transformative politics. In other words, most of us do not want to bite the hand that feeds us; but neither do we want to caress it too lovingly.

As I see it, the problem for us academics, who are already leading privileged existences, resides in the obvious fact that our enjoyment of research and its rewards constantly compromises the ardor with which we promote social transformation. At the very least, it dilutes our energy; at the most, it negates our ability to work for change. I do not think the current emphasis on "empowering" or "dialogic" research designs, as promising as these are, has done much to mitigate this fundamental contradiction.[3] E. B. White expressed the conflict I am alluding to in a pointed phrase: "I arise in the morning," he wrote, "torn between a desire to improve (or save) the world and a desire to enjoy (or savor) the world. This makes it hard to plan the day."[4] White's subversive humor should be taken to heart by feminist scholars who often claim the moral, even as they occupy the material, high ground.

The dilemma of feminist researchers working on groups less privileged than themselves can be succinctly stated as follows: is it possible— not in theory, but in the actual conditions of the real world today—to write about the oppressed without becoming one of the oppressors? In an absolute sense, I think not, and that is the meaning of the "No" with which I began this essay. In addition to the characteristic privileges of race and class, the existential or psychological dilemmas of the split between subject and object on which all research depends (even that of the most intense "participant observer") imply that objectification, utilization of others for one's own purposes (which may or may not coincide with their own ends), and the possibility of exploitation are built into almost all research projects with living human beings. Some distance may well be inevitable, perhaps even biologically ordained by our enclosure within our individual nervous systems, but it is not at this level that feminist research practices can seem self-serving. This occurs, instead, when feminists imagine that merely engaging in the discourse of feminism protects them from the possibility of exploiting other women, while their routine research practices are and continue to be embedded in a situation of material inequality.

Responding to an apparent sense of the inadequacy of conventional research practices, feminist scholars whose work depends on personal interviews—who invite personal disclosures—have attempted to focus on the research process as an occasion for intervention and advocacy. To be sure, there are many occasions for such activism, ranging from consideration of how a research project is initially formulated and who sponsors it, to questions regarding the uses the research will or might eventually serve, the forms in which its results will be disseminated, and the material benefits (such as career-building, status, and royalties) that derive from it. To these problems as well, which emerge in many research situations, feminism has brought its special sensibility—without, however, making as much progress in actuality as in the realm of discourse.

Before going into detail concerning the nature of these dilemmas, let me describe how I became concerned with the ethics of research. My own experience of inequalities between researcher and researched did not occur as a result of theorizing about such encounters. In the early 1980s, as part of a project that eventually became a book, I conducted sixty lengthy personal interviews in Brazil.[5] I interviewed ordinary "invisible" women: domestic servants, factory workers, nuns, housewives, secretaries, prostitutes, entrepreneurs, schoolgirls, landowners, and women from many other walks of life. The women were of diverse ages and races, and many more of them—as is true of all Brazilians—were poor than rich. Perhaps because I was not trained in the social sciences, I had not internalized a conventional research persona. Thus, when I began conducting interviews in Brazil, I was keenly aware of being cast into a special role. I discovered the legitimizing function of "having a project," of appearing with a tape recorder and the magic word "research," which turned what might have seemed to be mere personal curiosity into something else—something official, perhaps imposing. The nearly automatic respect I was granted made me feel enveloped by a kind of protective aura; this was an experience unlike anything I had encountered in my past work as a literary critic.

In this general frame of mind, I was slowly made aware of the questionable nature of the interactions on which my research depended. It was the summer of 1981—that is, it was summer in North American terms, but winter in Brazilian terms. In the city of Recife, in the northeast of Brazil, I met Teresa, a black woman who did laundry and ironing for some white acquaintances of mine. She agreed to talk with me and suggested that we go to her house after her morning's work. From the bus stop at the bottom of a hill, we trudged up a muddy road through the slum where she lived. Teresa was not yet forty-five years old, but appeared to be much older. Only four feet ten inches tall and weighing perhaps eighty pounds, she looked very thin and frail and had almost no teeth. As we approached her dwelling, I saw that a piece of metal wire held shut a low and rickety wooden gate in the makeshift fence that surrounded the shack. Teresa untwisted the wire and invited me in. Paintings and statues of Christ decorated the front room, along with pictures of naked women and soccer stars, put up, she explained, by her adult son, who also lived there. As in many poor neighborhoods in Brazil, there was no indoor toilet, no sewer facilities, but there was running water (which Teresa shared with a few neighbors who had none, and then also shared the bill) and electricity. Despite my repeated attempts to refuse her offer of food, which perhaps offended her, Teresa insisted on giving me something to eat and drink. She went to the refrigerator for a bottle of soda and then brought over a piece of cake— the one remaining piece that was sitting on a plate on top of an otherwise bare counter. I accepted the food, and Teresa sat next to me at the table that occupied most of the front room and watched me eat.

I do not really know how much food there was in Teresa's house on that particular day, but the refrigerator was bare when she opened it, and she herself looked worn out and undernourished. On my return to Brazil two summers later, I learned that she had died suddenly of a heart attack a few months after our meeting.

Thus, long before I began to think about the larger issues of how we use other people in our research, and how inadequate are our usual questions about our purposes or procedures, I was made aware, by that scene in Teresa's house, of the unease of being a well-fed woman briefly crossing paths with an ill-fed and generous poor woman whose life I was doing nothing to improve. Teresa, I should explain, was not by Brazilian standards especially exploited: the people she worked for, whom I knew, were decent employers. On the days that she worked at their house, she at least ate adequately. And she was paid the going rate, about $5 a week for her two days of washing and ironing. In addition to that income, she had a widow's pension of $40 a month. On a total of about $60 a month, then, she supported herself and contributed to the support of her twenty-three-year-old son and occasionally of another relative as well. It was all a very ordinary Brazilian story, the kind that well-fed people usually respond to in terms of individual charity, before turning their attention to other things.

When, some years later, I sat down to write about Teresa, other questions intruded. Did she, on that day, imagine that I would describe her appearance and the poverty of the house? Did she have an inkling that the food she served me might become part of her story, that everything about the episode might in turn be served up to readers far away? How would she have felt about it had she known these things? Would she have recognized herself in my sketch of her? Might she have thought that I have portrayed her weaknesses more than her strengths? Would she have felt betrayed? Used? And do these things matter? She never asked me any questions about what I was planning to do with her words (although I explained my project in a general way), let alone with the other impressions I was taking away from our meeting.

If I had to guess what she felt about my interest in her life, I would say that she was somewhat frightened but also pleased at the attention. I suppose that the prospect of being part of a foreigner's book—a book that she, being illiterate, could never have read even if it had been published in Portuguese—meant something to her. When we left her house, as she accompanied me back to the bus stop at the bottom of the hill, we passed one of her neighbors leaning out of her front window. As soon as we were slightly out of hearing range, Teresa commented that she had asked this neighbor if she, too, would like to talk with me, but the woman had said no. Teresa then smiled at me complicitously and said "gente sem cultura"—people with no breeding. That comment is one of my few clues to what our conversation meant to Teresa and it, of course, is problematic. Did I provide Teresa with a fleeting opportunity to escape her situation by allying herself with a white foreigner? What does such an encounter have to do with the claims of feminism? Does one even have the right to interfere in people's lives in this small way? Is the formal permission—the agreement people lend to the interview situation and the use of their words—an exoneration?

It was difficult to stay within the usual rules of the interviewing game in the face of the very real material inequalities that divided me from many of the women I interviewed. All researchers who work with living persons face problems of this sort, but the researcher who utilizes oral history, especially when foregoing questionnaires and the narrow definitions that are common in topical and thematic oral history, faces particularly intense versions of these more general ethical problems. The reasons for this can be readily understood: when lengthy personal narratives, in particular, are gathered, an intimacy (or the appearance of intimacy) is generated that blurs any neat distinction between "research" and "personal relations." [6] We ask of the people we interview the kind of revelation of their inner life that normally occurs in situations of great familiarity and within the private realm. Yet we invite these revelations to be made in the context of the public sphere, which is where in an obvious sense we situate ourselves when we appear with tape recorders and note pads eager to promote our "projects," projects for which other people are to provide the living matter. The asymmetries of the interaction are marked, furthermore, by the different level of disclosure that our interviewees make (or that we hope they will make) and that we are willing or expected to make. While often shyly curious, interviewees never, in my experience, make a reciprocal exchange a condition of the interview. And researchers are almost always much less frank than they hope their subjects will be. As Arlene Kaplan Daniels has written, "Deception is an ever present part of fieldwork."[7]

The interview situation, furthermore, is often an extremely charged one emotionally. Part of what those interviewed "get" from the process is precisely the undivided attention directed at them by another individual. I was surprised, in Brazil, that virtually everyone I approached was willing, even eager, to talk to me, and by the time I had completed several dozen long interviews I became convinced that not enough people are listening, and that the opportunity to talk about one's life, to reflect on its shapes and patterns, to make sense of it to oneself and to another human being, was an intrinsically valuable experience. But unlike those researchers who believe that this makes the interview a "fair exchange," where each partner receives and gives in equal measure, I continued to be struck by the inequalities inherent in the situation, both materially and psychologically.

To take the latter issue first: without wanting to exaggerate my role in the lives of people I interviewed, I can say that I was troubled by the sense of intense emotional involvement that, in my experience, always occurs at the time of the interview. Does this not make all the more problematic the researcher's inevitable retreat to a separate life in a far-off place? Is ostensibly feminist research still so deeply embedded in the imperialist/anthropological model that this dimension of the interview situation is to be buried while researchers present fascinating portraits of exotic "Others?" Does "contributing to knowledge" justify the utilization of another person for one's own (academic, feminist) purposes? Is the relationship terminated along with the research?

Other feminist scholars, too, have been concerned with these and similar issues. In a frequently cited essay, "Interviewing Women: A Contradiction in Terms," Ann Oakley, the British sociologist, outlined her experience conducting interviews for a project on childbirth.[8] She found that the social science methods she had been taught (which she describes in some detail in her essay) simply did not work. The women Oakley interviewed regularly asked her for advice and information, and traditional social science interview guidelines turned out to be impracticable and often ridiculous in these circumstances. The prevailing methodological models typically urged the researcher to deflect questions, to keep the focus on the informant, and to avoid getting drawn into personal exchanges. But, says Oakley, when less educated pregnant women asked her questions about the mechanics of childbirth, how could she possibly answer with the recommended evasions? When people sought much-needed help by asking Oakley about her own experiences, should she cleverly deflect these questions? Such dilemmas led Oakley to reject the old models, which were dependent upon a clear and hierarchical division that definitively separated researcher and researched.

Accepting instead the insight that the personal is political, feminist researchers such as Oakley have turned their attention above all to their interactions with the subjects of their research. The model of a distanced, controlled, and ostensibly neutral interviewer has, as a result, been replaced with that of sisterhood—an engaged and sympathetic interaction between two individuals united by the fact of gender oppression. Like other researchers making this argument, Oakley believes that the outcome is not merely a better research process but also better research results.

But it is quite possible that in breaking free of the androcentric research model, feminist scholars have risked cutting the ground from under their own work. For in the 1980s a deep questioning unfolded regarding how feminist research is to be conducted. Judith Stacey, for example, in her essay "Can There Be a Feminist Ethnography?," has questioned what has perhaps become the new orthodoxy among feminist scholars engaged in ethnographic research.[9] Stacey's work points to the dangers that arise when feminist researchers are unconsciously seductive toward their research subjects, raising their expectations and inducing dependency. These problems, however, are less likely to occur when an interviewer follows the traditional distanced model. When academics do research with women of races, classes, and cultures different from their own, a common experience is that they are perceived as more powerful than the people they are researching. This no doubt proceeds from the quite accurate appraisal on the part of people interviewed that the researcher has greater access to all sorts of resources—from material goods to local officials. The expectation of positive intervention is thus set up—all the more so when the feminist researcher consciously attempts to erase distance—and too often this expectation is disappointed, leading, as Stacey points out, to feelings of betrayal and injury. This danger has always existed in research situations involving hierarchy as well as personal interaction, but feminists may be more likely to generate this particular problem, for, quite understandably, our research styles have been developed, often in an ad hoc way, in reaction to the discarded positivist model that is seen as impersonal, "masculinist."

The "feminist" research model, in other words, may in its own ways be just as ill-advised. For in a world divided by race, ethnicity, and class, the purported solidarity of female identity is in many ways a fraud—in this case perhaps a fraud perpetrated by feminists with good intentions. Having rejected the objectification of research subjects construed as "Others," the new, ostensibly feminist scenario substitutes the claim of identity, our identity as women, while often straining to disregard ethnic, racial, class, and other distinctions that, in societies built on inequality, unavoidably divide people from one another.

Such a desire to affirm oneness is exemplified in Carole J. Spitzack's essay, "Body Talk: The Politics of Weight Loss and Female Identity." Influenced by Oakley's work on the importance of nonhierarchical interaction as the proper model for women interviewing women, Spitzack spent considerable time talking with each woman in her research sample prior to the actual interview: "I wanted each woman to understand that she was not simply an exploitable information source, but someone I wished to talk *with* about body experience, a person with whom I would choose to spend time outside the context of academic research" (Spitzack's italics).[10] The problem with this honorable intent is its disingenuousness. The appeal to "sisterhood," the failure to recognize difference—even when the research is conducted close to home—leads too easily to mystification. It also raises a further problem: can, and should, we do research only when we would choose to make friends with the people we are interviewing? Is it even honest to suggest that all research subjects are or need to be potential intimates? Is this an improvement on the old model? Or is it a particularly egregious form of manipulation? Spitzack's comment, in its odd parodying of women's traditional nurturing role, reveals the misuse of sentiment as a research tool—a very real danger as feminists attempt to devise alternative practices as if in a vacuum.

In the by now commonplace emphasis on the interview process and the human qualities brought by the feminist researcher to the encounter, we seem to be merely creating a bracketed moment, a moment taken out of the broader context of unequal relations in which our research is typically done. Simply enjoying this moment, and using it to revive our flagging spirits, is not enough. By abstracting the interview from the larger social context of the real world, we are in effect returning to the discarded positivist model (with a slight twist) that situates our research practices outside of reality. But now we have, for a short time, transported our narrators with us.

Facile assumptions about our commonality as women, and celebrations of the intimacy generated by "feminist" research methods, are inadequate responses. Instead, I believe we must question the entire system that seems to allow for no other approach than manipulative distance, on the one hand, and spurious identification, on the other. At the very least, this will keep us from mistakenly assuming that the discourse of feminism itself constitutes a solution to the fact of women's oppression.

I do not, however, think that generic solutions can be found to the dilemmas feminists face in conducting research, nor do I for an instant hold out the hope of devising exact "rules" that will resolve these issues for us. In my view, this is impossible because ethical problems do not arise as absolutes requiring "blind justice." When Anatole France observed that the law in its majestic impartiality forbids both the rich and the poor to sleep under bridges, to beg in the streets, and to steal bread, he reminded us, with bitter humor, that ethical problems emerge in concrete human contexts, contexts that are always specific and always material.[11] And I believe these problems surface with special intensity in research with living persons because many of us sense that ethics is a matter not of abstractly correct behavior, but of relations between people. The personal interview is, therefore, a particularly precise locus for ethical issues to surface—unless, that is, we are busy (as indeed we often are) suppressing our awareness of these issues.

It is in this context that I want to argue for the importance of recognizing the material inequalities that create the conditions for much feminist research. Such a focus points to the fissures between our theory and our practice. The difficulty many of us face in drawing attention to the issue of material inequalities as a key factor in research—even in feminist research—suggests, to my mind, that the desire to transform the world is often weaker than the wish to enjoy it as it is. Less caustically, one might say that perhaps we tend to avoid these problems because they could lead to despair, which makes action impossible. Like the experience of guilt, these are personal emotions, which may deflect attention from the nonpersonal, institutional, and political contours of the problem of material inequality. However powerfully we may experience these problems on an individual basis in concrete research situations, we must not lose sight of the fact that these are not, in fact, personal problems of overly sensitive individuals. They are, rather, genuine ethical dilemmas that the broader society, built on inequalities, strategically induces us to disregard.

When the inequalities between researcher and researched are extreme, all the ethical dilemmas inherent in research with living persons are intensified. Let me outline a model I have developed for thinking about what conventionally goes on when U.S. academics interview third-world people. Collecting personal narratives, when done with professional and publishing goals in mind, is invariably in part an economic matter. The difficulty we have in establishing appropriate practices for such research situations may lie precisely in the odd transformation of familiar economic roles that the process brings about. An individual telling her own story can be construed to be in possession of raw material, material without which the entrepreneurial researcher could not perform the labor of producing a text. In this situation, it is the researcher who owns or has access to the means of production that will transform the spoken words into commodities. This may not be the main function of oral histories, life history studies, or other research projects using "native informants," but it is certainly one of the functions of such texts. Function is, after all, determined in part by one's particular vantage point. To a commercial publisher, the existence of a book as a commodity may be its main function. To a professor, it could be a step toward promotion and salary increases.

This model of provider and extractor is, however, muddied by the fact that the researcher typically plays the role not only of capitalist but also of laborer, which may be one reason for the complacency of many of those who use personal narratives in their work. The constant shifting of roles prevents us from developing a suitable model for understanding, analyzing, and assigning rights and duties in the personal interview situation. From the point of view of the researcher's labor, the life story appears as a mere potentiality waiting to be actualized. What occurs in the preparation of a text utilizing a personal narrative does involve the transformation of "raw material," a transformation accomplished through the researcher's labor of turning spoken words into written ones, editing, translating if necessary, or studying and analyzing the stories or data.[12] One sort of discourse becomes another, and it is the transformer who derives the greatest benefit from the enterprise. Whether construed as capitalist entrepreneur or as laborer, then, the researcher is the person whose time and investment is acknowledged and rewarded. And, as in any asymmetrical exchange, exploitation is always a possibility.

In another essay I have discussed the different moments of oral history work in which ethical problems emerge, moments ranging from the interview itself, through the uses made of personal narratives and the rewards accruing to the interviewer, to post-interview obligations.[13] But it is not enough to address these specifics, for however subtle the guidelines we might develop for appropriate ethical behavior at these different stages, we must not disregard the very facts—and these are material ones—that determine who gets to do research on whom; who has access to research grants, travel funds, the press; whose words, at the most basic level, are granted authority in representing others.

The feminist precept of "returning the research"—presumably to those communities who made it possible—is one attempt to deal with the inequality of the typical exchange between researcher and researched. But even this raises many problems. How is the research returned? To whom, in what form, and to what avail? Again, of the frequent claim that the interview process, as conducted by feminists, is empowering in that it "gives a voice" to those who might otherwise remain silent, one may well ask: is it empowerment or is it appropriation?[14] When is the purported empowerment or affirmation just another psychological surrogate, a "feel good" measure, a means by which researchers console themselves for the real imbalances in power that they know—despite all the talk of sisterhood—exists? What does it mean, furthermore, for researchers to claim the right to validate the experiences of others? And even where empowerment does occur, as indeed it may, is it a justification for the appropriation that occurs along with it? The only projects that avoid these problems are those that are at all stages genuinely in the control of a community, with the community assuming the role of both researched and researcher.[15] But such projects are only a small fraction of the feminist research being conducted in many fields—all of it urgently needed to redress the distortions of generations of androcentric work that constitutes "knowledge."

The researcher's desire to act out feminist commitments, relinquish control, and involve the researched in all stages of the project runs the risk, however, of subtly translating into the researcher's own demand for affirmation and validation. Liz Kennedy, in describing her experiences with an oral history project in the lesbian community in Buffalo, New York, came to question her expectation of other people's intense involvement with the project. She found that often her subjects were not interested in her follow-up communications and failed to respond to them.[16] This reminds us that even in the best of circumstances, we must guard against foisting onto others a demand or a wish for reinforcement in our work and our concerns.[17] Otherwise, researchers may find themselves abdicating their intellectual responsibilities and training, in perpetual pursuit of their subjects' approval. It is in fact exceedingly difficult to strike a balance that neither exploits the researched nor imposes on them our own psychological demands. Which brings us once again to the simple recognition that some measure of "objectification," or separation and distance, is not only inevitable but, indeed, desirable in most research situations.

When I undertook a small survey to determine how other researchers who work with living persons dealt with the ethical problems generated by their work, I discovered that many of them were comfortable with the usual rationales: informants were becoming "part of history"; their stories were being transmitted; they were affirmed and validated in the process; the researcher perhaps (this occurred more rarely) shared royalties, or donated them to a cause reflecting the interests of the researched. It did not take feminist scholars, with our language of "empowerment," to come up with such rationales; these have been around for a long time, and are often quite correct as far as they go. Interestingly, my brief ethical survey also failed to turn up significant gender differences, with the exception that far fewer women replied to my letter than men (14 percent as compared to 43 percent). The replies did, however, suggest that not gender, or feminist commitments, but what I would call more general political commitments or concerns seemed to divide those who were troubled by the ethical problems of their research from those who were not.[18]

The complexity of raising ethical questions about research with living persons can be further illustrated by looking at two types of problems. One of them is intricate and subtle, the other apparently simple and clear. The first has to do with the currently popular notion, mentioned earlier, that telling one's story constitutes "empowerment." In many respects this is of course true. Agnes Hankiss, in an intriguing article called "Ontologies of the Self: On the Mythological Rearranging of

One's Life-History," discusses how, as speakers narrate their life story, they endow certain episodes with a symbolic meaning that in effect turns these episodes into myths. This is a never-ending process, she points out, for an adult must constantly select new models or strategies for life.[19] A similar idea is expressed more simply in an essay by Maria Lugones and Elizabeth Spelman: "Having the opportunity to talk about one's life, to give an account of it, to interpret it, is integral to leading that life rather than being led through it."[20] Some researchers, however, are not content to let this process work by itself; or, rather, because they are very much aware of the subtle ways in which the researcher invariably shapes even the content of an interview, they argue that researchers ought deliberately to attempt to raise the narrator's consciousness. Marjorie Mbilinyi, for example, describes her oral history work in Tanzania in terms that reveal that "consciousness raising"—or political propaganda, as it might seem to others—was an explicit goal of the project. She considers this legitimate and desirable, an articulation of an agenda that is always present but not usually thought through by researchers.[21]

Marie-Françoise Chanfrault-Duchet, on the other hand, rejects the notion that feminist methodology should involve an attempt to transform the speaker's ideas. She refers to this practice as a form of "savage social therapy."[22] I agree. It seems to me, as well, that to treat interviews with other women as opportunities for imposing our own politically correct analyses requires an arrogance incompatible with genuine respect for others. And respect is a minimum condition if we are not to treat others as mere means to our own ends—if we are not, in other words, to reproduce the very practices of domination that we seek to challenge. In addition, to utilize the interview as an occasion for forcing on others our ideas of a proper political awareness, however we understand that, is to betray an implicit trust. Is it likely, after all, that anyone would agree to an interview if we announced beforehand that while we were getting their life story we would be steering the conversation so as to demonstrate to them what, in our view, their political situation was and how their lives should be understood accordingly? But if this is indeed our agenda, not to set it forth at the outset is certainly to disguise our true intentions and to manipulate the person interviewed in a way that should be considered incompatible with feminism. This would be "savage social therapy," indeed.

Consider now another, apparently very minor, type of ethical breach, frequently present in even the simplest research situations utilizing personal interviews. Whether the interaction is brief and one-time or involves long-term participant observation, a common experience of researchers is that they make promises to the people they have interviewed—to send them this or that item, to stay in touch, and so on. But with how many dozens of people can a researcher, however feminist, however sincere, consistently communicate? For how long? I found myself overwhelmed by the prospect of maintaining contact with the sixty women I interviewed in Brazil. On the other hand, on what basis should I have chosen among them? Thus, even with simple matters such as keeping one's word, not to mention the larger issues arising from structural inequalities that the feminist researcher can in no way lessen, problems of power and betrayal expose the fragility of easy assumptions of sisterhood and reciprocity.

In the end, even "feminist" research too easily tends to reproduce the very inequalities and hierarchies it seeks to reveal and to transform. The researcher departs with the data, and the researched stay behind, no better off than before.[23] The common observations that "they" got something out of it too—the opportunity to tell their stories, the entry into history, the recuperation of their own memories, perhaps the chance to exercise some editorial control over the project or even its products, etc.—even when perfectly accurate, do not challenge the inequalities on which the entire process rests. Neither does a sisterly posture of mutual learning and genuine dialogue. For we continue to function in an overdetermined universe in which our respective roles ensure that *other* people are always the subject of *our* research, almost never the reverse.

Is there no alternative, then, to insuperable distance on the one hand, and mystifying chumminess on the other? Are there no choices other than exploitation or patronage? Difference or identification? Faced with this very real dilemma, feminist researchers in today's culture of self-reflexivity often engage in merely rhetorical maneuvers that are rapidly acquiring the status of incantations. A currently popular strategy is that of "situating" oneself by prior announcement: "As a white working-class heterosexual . . . ," or "As a black feminist activist. . . ." Sometimes these tropes sound like apologies; more often they are deployed as badges. Either way, they give off their own aroma of fraud, for the underlying assumption seems to be that by such identification one has paid one's respects to "difference"—owned up to bias, acknowledged privilege, or taken possession of oppression—and is now home free.[24] But this posture has no impact on the fact that "difference" in today's world comes packaged in socially constructed disparities. More than a verbal acknowledgment of personal or group identity is required. Indeed, such rhetoric once again deflects attention from the systemic nature of inequality. Identity politics, with its characteristic focus on oppression rather than exploitation, engages in a subtle maneuver whereby, as Jenny Bourne notes in an incisive essay, the question of "What is to be done has been replaced by who am I."[25]

The self-righteous tone that at times characterizes feminist work may be merely a capitulation to feminist discourse, which, like any other discourse, draws boundaries that define what we see and fail to see, what we accept and contest. Feminism, however, should not be turned into a cudgel used against ourselves or others. Nor should it be a bromide allowing researchers to proceed behind the screen of an uncritical notion of sisterhood. But having raised these issues—a far easier thing to do than resolving them—I do not want to imply that the appropriate response is to abandon the complex research situations in which oral narratives are typically gathered and utilized. It is a mistake to let ourselves be overwhelmed by these problems. The fact that doing research across race, class, and culture is a messy business is no reason to contemplate only difficulties and ourselves struggling with them. As Jenny Bourne says, "*What we do is who we are.*"[26] The world will not get better because we have sensitively apologized for privilege, nor if, from the comfortable heights of the academy, we advertise our identification with the oppressed or compete for distinction as members of this or that oppressed group.

Neither purity nor safety resides in calling one's research "feminist." But no controversy attends the fact that too much ignorance exists in the world to allow us to await perfect research methods before proceeding. Ultimately we have to make up our minds whether our research is worth doing or not, and then determine how to go about it in such ways that it best serves our purported goals.

There is much to be gained from the ongoing discussion of appropriate research methods. But in an unethical world, we cannot do truly ethical research. The problems I have been discussing, in other words, are political, and require for their solution not only transformations in consciousness, but also, and above all, political action. Our individual research efforts thus return us to the world, which can be counted on to puncture any illusions that a "correct" feminism will resolve these matters for us.[27]

NOTES

1. Micaela Di Leonardo, *The Varieties of Ethnic Experience: Kinship, Class, and Gender among California Italian-Americans* (Ithaca: Cornell University Press, 1984), 41, has noted that it is more difficult to interview "up" than "across" or "down," for wealthy and powerful people are likely to be less receptive to scholarly interest in their personal lives. Marcia Greenlee, in a roundtable discussion on "Appropriation or Empowerment: Oral History, Feminist Process, and Ethics," Oral History Association Meeting, Baltimore, Maryland, October 16, 1988, spoke of the consequences of such class distinctions for the interviewer. "You do not have to brief someone of high social status in what their rights are. [They know that] they don't need to talk about certain subjects." With less powerful people, not to mention disempowered ones, however, the researcher's desire to get certain information is often in conflict with ethical behavior that would protect the subject's interests. Greenlee believes that it is crucial to explain to those we interview that they can at any point say "I don't care to comment on that for the record." She also protests against the institutional constraints that often set the researcher's interests in opposition to those of the researched.

2. Gail Webber, "Sisterly Conduct: Do Feminists Need Guidelines for Ethical Behavior with One Another?," *Women's Studies International Forum* 8, 1 (1985): 57.

3. See, for example, Patti Lather, "Feminist Perspectives on Empowering Research Methodologies," *Women's Studies International Forum* 11, 6 (1988): 569–81. Lather's empowering methodologies are greatly undermined by her selection of a homogeneous research environment: a university classroom in the United States.

4. Cited in Israel Shenker, "E. B. White: Notes and Comment by Author," *New York Times*, July 11, 1969, 43.

5. Daphne Patai, *Brazilian Women Speak: Contemporary Life Stories* (New Brunswick: Rutgers University Press, 1988).

6. A different, perhaps traditional, view of this issue is expressed by Jack D. Douglas, in his essay "Living Morality versus Bureaucratic Fiat," in *Deviance and Decency: The Ethics of Research with Human Subjects*, ed. C. B. Klockars and F. W. O'Connor (Beverly Hills: Sage Publications, 1979), 13–33. Douglas writes that the relationships we develop in friendship and in research situations differ only in degree, and that we have fewer social obligations to our research subjects since we tend to be less intimate with them. Carrying on about moral problems in social research, in his view, "may be very satisfying to our feelings of pride," but "it is a great distortion of social realities. The fact is that all human beings are social researchers" (27–29). Cited by Karol R. Ortiz, "Mental Health Consequences of Life History Method," *Ethos* 13, 2 (Summer 1985): 99–120. Such a perspective, of course, does away with any discussion of "ethical" dilemmas, while quietly affirming the inevitability of a particular social "reality."

7. Arlene Kaplan Daniels, "Self-Deception and Self-Discovery in Fieldwork," *Qualitative Sociology* 6, 3 (Fall 1983): 196.
8. Ann Oakley, "Interviewing Women: A Contradiction in Terms," in *Doing Feminist Research,* ed. Helen Roberts (New York: Routledge and Kegan Paul, 1981), 30–61.
9. Judith Stacey, "Can There Be a Feminist Ethnography?," *Women's Studies International Forum* 11, 1 (1988): 21–27, and, in a slightly revised version, in *Women's Words: The Feminist Practice of Oral History,* ed. Sherna Berger Gluck and Daphne Patai (New York: Routledge, 1991), 111–19.
10. Carole J. Spitzack, "Body Talk: The Politics of Weight Loss and Female Identity," in *Women Communicating: Studies of Women's Talk,* ed. Barbara Bate and Anita Taylor (Norwood, N.J.: Ablex Publishing Corp., 1988), 54–55. At times the disclosures made in the course of a lengthy life-history interview exceed the bounds of intimate conversation and resemble instead a confession. For a discussion of the moral aspects of confession that is suggestive for those who elicit life histories, see Sissela Bok, "Confession and Moral Choice," in *Foundations of Ethics,* ed. Leroy S. Rouner (Notre Dame: University of Notre Dame Press, 1983), 133–48, especially 140–45, where Bok discusses authority and vulnerability in the relationship between listener and confessant.
11. Anatole France, *Le Lys rouge* (1894; reprint, Paris: Imprimerie Nationale, 1958).
12. A simple illustration of the conflicts that may emerge between the researcher and the researched is provided by Nell Irvin Painter in her preface to the oral history she did with Hosea Hudson. Painter (viii) describes their disagreement over the book's title and author. Hudson wanted to appear in both, while Painter wanted to be recognized as the author. They finally settled on a compromise and the book was published as *The Narrative of Hosea Hudson: His Life as a Negro Communist in the South* (Cambridge: Harvard University Press, 1979), with Painter listed as author. An extreme case of a researcher's appropriation of the speaker's life is discussed by Paul John Eakin in his foreword to Philippe Lejeune's *On Autobiography,* ed. Paul John Eakin, trans. Katherine Leary (Minneapolis: University of Minnesota Press, 1989), xvii–xix. The case involves Lejeune's changing reactions to Adélaide Blasquez's book *Gaston Lucas, serrurier, chronique de l'anti-héeros* (Paris: Plon, 1976). Initially, Lejeune judged this to be a masterpiece of ethnographic truth-telling, a belief somewhat shaken when he discovered that Blasquez had erased each interview with Lucas after transcribing it. There is, furthermore, the problem of Blasquez's representation, in her book, of her collaboration with Lucas as idyllically egalitarian, a representation that was exploded when Blasquez's publisher invited Lejeune to interview Blasquez for a video. Lejeune suggested that Gaston Lucas, who was still alive, should also be the subject of a video, but Blasquez replied that the living Gaston Lucas had nothing of value to say, for he truly existed only as the character that she, through her art, had created in her book. See also Lejeune's very interesting comments on the relationship between what he

calls "the model" and the "ethnobiographer," in his essay, "The Autobiography of Those Who Do Not Write," in Lejeune, *On Autobiography*, 185–215.

13. Daphne Patai, "Ethical Problems of Personal Narratives, Or, Who Should Eat the Last Piece of Cake?," *International Journal of Oral History* 8, 1 (February 1987): 5–27.

14. This is the formulation used in a roundtable discussion entitled, "Appropriation or Empowerment: Oral History, Feminist Process, and Ethics," organized by Sherna Gluck at the Oral History Association meeting in Baltimore, Maryland, October 16, 1988.

15. See Part IV of Gluck and Patai, *Women's Words* for examples of how "return" and community involvement can, in certain types of action and advocacy research, be built into the project as ongoing features.

16. Elizabeth Kennedy, at the roundtable discussion on "Appropriation or Empowerment: Oral History, Feminist Process, and Ethics," Oral History Association meeting, Baltimore, Maryland, October 16, 1988.

17. These problems are discussed with exceptional forthrightness in Sondra Hale, "Feminist Method, Process, and Self-Criticism: Interviewing Sudanese Woman," in Gluck and Patai, *Women's Words*, 121–36.

18. Patai, "Ethical Problems of Personal Narratives."

19. Agnes Hankiss, "Ontologies of the Self: On the Mythological Rearranging of One's Life-History," in *Biography and Society: The Life History Approach in the Social Sciences*, ed. Daniel Bertaux (Beverly Hills: Sage Publications, 1981), 203–9.

20. Maria C. Lugones and Elizabeth V. Spelman, "Have We Got a Theory for You! Feminist Theory, Cultural Imperialism, and the Demand for 'The Woman's Voice,'" *Women's Studies International Forum* 6, 6 (1983): 593.

21. Marjorie Mbilinyi, comments made at the conference, "Autobiographies, Biographies and Life Histories of Women: Interdisciplinary Perspectives," sponsored by the Center for Advanced Feminist Studies at the University of Minnesota, Minneapolis, May 23–24, 1986. A version of Mbilinyi's conference paper appears as "'I'd Have Been a Man': Politics and the Labor Process in Producing Personal Narratives," in *Interpreting Women's Lives*, ed. Personal Narratives Group (Bloomington: Indiana University Press, 1989), 204–27.

22. Marie-Françoise Chanfrault-Duchet, "Narrative Structures, Social Models, and Symbolic Representation in the Life Story," in Gluck and Patai, *Women's Words*, 77–92.

23. As Calvin Pryluck puts it, "Ultimately we are all outsiders in the lives of others. We can take our gear and go home; they have to continue their lives where they are." In Calvin Pryluck, "Ultimately We Are All Outsiders: The Ethics of Documentary Filmmaking," *Journal of the University Film Association*, 28, 1 (Winter 1976): 22. I am grateful to Professor Mark Jonathan Harris, of the School of Cinema-Television at the University of Southern California, for sending me this article.

24. There are, of course, serious problems of possible bias, of which researchers have increasingly become aware. Marsha Darling, in "The Disinherited as Source: Rural Black Women's Memories," *Michigan Quarterly Review* 26, 1 (Winter 1987): 49, writes of the ways in which our very ideas of what constitutes a legitimate "source" are shaped by methodological, conceptual, and political notions. Claire Robertson has also addressed these issues. See her "In Pursuit of Life Histories: The Problem of Bias," *Frontiers* 7, 2 (1983): 63–69. Despite her sensitive and sensible approach, Robertson herself engages in ethically questionable behavior when, according to her own account, while in Ghana working with an interpreter, she deceived some of her informants about her increasing competence in the Ga language. As she explains: "On occasion, I found it helpful to pretend total ignorance of Ga because the informant was telling Mankah [the interpreter] things that she assumed I would not understand" (64). For our purposes, what is significant about this statement is Robertson's apparent lack of awareness that this behavior raised ethical problems.
25. Jenny Bourne, "Homelands of the Mind: Jewish Feminism and Identity Politics," *Race and Class* 29, 1 (Summer 1987): 3.
26. Ibid., 22 (emphasis in original).
27. Passages and lines of argument utilized in this essay first appeared in my "Ethical Problems of Personal Narratives" (cited above), "Who's Calling Whom Subaltern?," *Women and Language* 11, 2 (Winter 1988): 23–26; and in "U.S. Academics and Third-World Women: Is Ethical Research Possible?," *Women's Studies in Indiana* 15, 1 (November/December 1989): 1–4.

REFERENCES

Bok, Sissela. "Confession and Moral Choice." In Leroy S. Rouner, ed., *Foundations of Ethics,* 133–48. Notre Dame: University of Notre Dame Press, 1983.

Bourne, Jenny. "Homelands of the Mind: Jewish Feminism and Identity Politics." *Race and Class* 29, 1 (Summer 1987): 1–24.

Chanfrault-Duchet, Marie-Françoise. "Narrative Structures, Social Models, and Symbolic Representation in the Life Story." In Gluck and Patai, *Women's Words,* 77–92.

Daniels, Arlene Kaplan. "Self-Deception and Self-Discovery in Fieldwork." *Qualitative Sociology* 6, 3 (Fall 1983): 195–214.

Darling, Marsha Jean. "The Disinherited as Source: Rural Black Women's Memories." *Michigan Quarterly Review* 26, 1 (Winter 1987): 48–63.

Di Leonardo, Micaela. *The Varieties of Ethnic Experience: Kinship, Class, and Gender among California Italian-Americans.* Ithaca: Cornell University Press, 1984.

Douglas, Jack D. "Living Morality versus Bureaucratic Fiat." In C. B. Klockars and F. W. O'Connor, eds., *Deviance and Decency: The Ethics of Research with Human Subjects*, 13–33. Beverly Hills: Sage Publications, 1979.

France, Anatole. *Le Lys rouge*. 1894. Reprint. Paris: Imprimerie Nationale, 1958.

Gluck, Sherna Berger, and Daphne Patai, eds. *Women's Words: The Feminist Practice of Oral History*. New York: Routledge, 1991.

Greenlee, Marcia. "Appropriation or Empowerment: Oral History, Feminist Process, and Ethics." Roundtable discussion at Oral History Association Meeting, Baltimore, Maryland, October 16, 1988.

Hale, Sondra. "Feminist Method, Process, and Self-Criticism: Interviewing Sudanese Women." In Gluck and Patai, *Women's Words*, 121–36.

Hankiss, Agnes. "Ontologies of the Self: On the Mythological Rearranging of One's Life-History." In Daniel Bertaux, ed., *Biography and Society: The Life History Approach in the Social Sciences*, 203–9. Beverly Hills: Sage Publications, 1981.

Kennedy, Elizabeth. "Appropriation or Empowerment: Oral History, Feminist Process, and Ethics." Roundtable discussion at Oral History Association Meeting, Baltimore, Maryland, October 16, 1988.

Lather, Patti. "Feminist Perspectives on Empowering Research Methodologies." *Women's Studies International Forum* 11, 6 (1988): 569–81.

Lejeune, Philippe. *On Autobiography*. Edited by Paul John Eakin. Translated by Katherine Leary. Minneapolis: University of Minnesota Press, 1989.

Lugones, Maria C., and Elizabeth V. Spelman. "Have We Got a Theory for You! Feminist Theory, Cultural Imperialism and the Demand for 'The Woman's Voice.'" *Women's Studies International Forum* 6, 6 (1983): 573–81.

Mbilinyi, Marjorie. Comments made at the conference on "Autobiographies, Biographies and Life Histories of Women: Interdisciplinary Perspectives," sponsored by the Center for Advanced Feminist Studies at the University of Minnesota, Minneapolis, Minnesota, May 23–24, 1986.

Oakley, Ann. "Interviewing Women: A Contradiction in Terms." In Helen Roberts, ed., *Doing Feminist Research*, 30–61. New York: Routledge and Kegan Paul, 1981.

Ortiz, Karol R. "Mental Health Consequences of Life History Method." *Ethos* 13, 2 (Summer 1985): 99–120.

Painter, Nell Irvin. *The Narrative of Hosea Hudson: His Life as a Negro Communist in the South*. Cambridge: Harvard University Press, 1979.

Patai, Daphne. *Brazilian Women Speak: Contemporary Life Stories*. New Brunswick: Rutgers University Press, 1988.

———. "Ethical Problems of Personal Narratives, Or, Who Should Eat the Last Piece of Cake?" *International Journal of Oral History* 8, 1 (February 1987): 5–27.

Pryluck, Calvin. "Ultimately We Are All Outsiders: The Ethics of Documentary Filmmaking." *Journal of the University Film Association* 28, 1 (Winter 1976): 21–29.

Robertson, Claire. "In Pursuit of Life Histories: The Problem of Bias." *Frontiers* 7, 2 (1983): 63–69.

Shenker, Israel. "E. B. White: Notes and Comment by Author." *New York Times,* July 11, 1969, 43.

Spitzack, Carole J. "Body Talk: The Politics of Weight Loss and Female Identity." In Barbara Bate and Anita Taylor, eds., *Women Communicating: Studies of Women's Talk.* Norwood, N.J.: Ablex Publishing Corp., 1988.

Stacey, Judith. "Can There Be a Feminist Ethnography?" In Gluck and Patai, 111–19.

Webber, Gail. "Sisterly Conduct: Do Feminists Need Guidelines for Ethical Behavior with One Another?" *Women's Studies International Forum* 8, 1 (1985): 51–58.

2.

SCOLDING LADY MARY WORTLEY MONTAGU? THE PROBLEMATICS OF SISTERHOOD IN FEMINIST CRITICISM

DEVONEY LOOSER

As with many women writers "found" by second-wave feminisms, Lady Mary Wortley Montagu has been held up as an exemplary model of womanhood. Montagu is frequently taught alongside her eighteenth-century British "sisters," Aphra Behn, Mary Astell, and Mary Woll-stonecraft, all of whom carved significant spaces outside of traditional feminine roles in their lives and writings. Montagu has not lacked a contemporary audience, her letters garnering space in *The Norton Anthology of Literature by Women* as well as *The Norton Anthology of English Literature*. The ways we read Montagu, however, have become increasingly complicated as of late. In recent years Montagu has served as a site of facile co-optation, critical angst, and feminist struggle. The locus of these struggles, I believe, is the applicability of the labels "feminist" and "progressive." Is Montagu a feminist? Is she progressive? Both? Neither? These questions and their resulting conflicts challenge us—not merely to take sides—but to take stock of our critical practices. An overview of Montagu's changing reputations as a "feminist" provides a case study of how women writers have been recuperated and institutionalized and compels us to rethink our feminist authorial models.

It is no revelation that much of second-wave feminist criticism—
including criticism on Montagu—was celebratory to a troubling degree.
In the majority of feminist scholarship produced in the last two decades,
Montagu is congratulated for her gender politics. In 1978, Pat Rogers
described Montagu as "a brave spirit who challenged the male domination of the literary world by writing moving letters and ladylike epis-
tles."[1] Montagu was dubbed "a staunch advocate of feminism" in Dale
Spender's *Women of Ideas* (1982).[2] In 1978, Alice Anderson Hufstader
wrote about Montagu in a chapter titled "The Rebel." For Hufstader,
Montagu "had far more in common with the feminists of today and
yesterday than had her gentler successors. It was to remain her cast-iron
conviction that life is a bad bargain, and that women have the worst of
it."[3] In this body of criticism, praise and appreciation covertly become
the most allowable critical functions—the only functions, in fact, that
are in line with feminist sisterhood.

We might now justifiably ask what it is that we have celebrated and
how we have constituted our sisterhood. In the last five years, this
project has begun in earnest as some feminist criticism on Montagu has
eschewed uncomplicated praise. Recent Montagu scholars, including
Cynthia Lowenthal, Lisa Lowe, and Joseph Lew, have read Montagu's
letters with an eye to Orientalism, as outlined by Edward Said.[4] Said
himself doesn't mention Montagu in *Orientalism* (1978), and considerations of Montagu's Orientalism have only now begun to circulate
widely. Of course, not all recent scholarship on Montagu has moved
away from easy praise. John McVeagh's *English Literature and the
Wider World* (1990) deems Montagu "full of appreciation of the exotic
cultures she encountered."[5] Even the scholarship published on Montagu
and Orientalism leaves us with unanswered questions about the correla-
tion of "progressive" gender politics to those of race, class, and nation.
Especially in regard to Montagu's Turkish Embassy letters, the verdict is
not yet in.

What we know as the Turkish Embassy letters (written from 1716 to
1718 while Montagu's husband was ambassador to Turkey) were origi-
nally published in 1763, a year after Montagu's death. This manuscript,
*Letters of the Right Honorable Lady M. . .y W. . .y M. . .e: written
during her travels in Europe, Asia and Africa*, was read by Montagu's
contemporaries among whom it circulated during her lifetime. In 1724
Montagu's friend Mary Astell wrote a preface to the letters, calling for

their publication and detailing how they should be read and received. Astell argued along with Montagu that these letters contained more true representations of Turkey than had been previously available to readers.

A celebratory tradition of reading Montagu, then, began during her lifetime. Astell's preface is a well-known document, often cited by feminist literary critics for its sisterly sentiments. Astell desired that the world would "see to how much better purpose the Ladys Travel than their Lords, and that Whilst [the world] is surfeited with Male Travels, all in the same Tone and stuft with the same Trifles, a Lady has the skill to strike out a New Path and to embellish a worn-out Subject with a variety of fresh and elegant Entertainment" (CL, 1:467).[6] Specifically calling on Montagu's women readers, Astell hoped that they, at least, would read Montagu with sympathy: "In short, let her own Sex at least do her Justice; Lay aside diabolical Envy and its Brother Malice with all their accursed Company, Sly Whispering, cruel backbiting, spiteful detraction, and the rest of that hideous crew, which I hope are very falsely said to attend the *Tea Table,* being more apt to think they haunt those Public Places where Virtuous Women never come" (CL, 1:467). Astell wanted women to rise above "male" backbiting:

Let the Men malign one another, if they think fit, and strive to pul down Merit when they cannot equal it. Let us be better natur'd than to give way to any unkind or disrespectful thought of so bright an Ornament of our Sex, merely because she has better sense. . . . Rather let us freely own the Superiority of this Sublime Genius as I do in the sincerity of my Soul, pleas'd that a *Woman* Triumphs, and proud to follow in her Train. Let us offer her the *Palm* which is justly her due, and if we pretend to any Laurels, lay them willingly at her Feet. (CL, 1:467)

Astell asks women to band together and join in celebrating the achievements of their "sister," letting only the men criticize each other. Women, the preface suggests, must have only praise for a successful woman. We must therefore join in Montagu's triumph. Or must we? What happens when we do not simply celebrate the "triumphs" of Lady Mary Wortley Montagu, as Astell requests? What is the result when we see Montagu's texts as implicated in the less-than-triumphant? Finally, what happens to the category "women" in such an enterprise? To begin to address these questions, it is necessary to recount the critical frames into which Montagu's texts have been received.

Montagu's Turkish Embassy letters have long been read as among the more sympathetic accounts of eighteenth-century Turkish customs—

and of Turkish women. In eighteenth-century England, Turkish women were frequently pitied for their status as concubines or heathens. In her *Poems on Several Occasions* from 1696, Elizabeth Singer Rowe argues that English women have reason and sense and are undervalued by English men. She uses Turkish women as her foil. Rowe writes of "a plain and an open design to render us meer *Slaves,* perfect Turkish *Wives,* without *Properties,* or *Sense,* or *Souls*"; she asks her readers "whether these are not *notorious* Violations on the *Liberties of Freeborn English Women?*"[7] Rowe bristles at Turkish women's lives but does so primarily to show how unjust it is to exploit English women.

On the other hand, Montagu remarks on parallels between English and Turkish practices in order to claim that both deserve celebration. She likens customs from the two countries by calling them both the "manners of mankind"—a generous claim in an eighteenth-century British context. Montagu's "going native" while in Turkey is well-documented. Montagu often went out veiled, and she delivered her daughter in accordance with local childbearing practices. When she returned to England, Montagu kept her Turkish costumes, and Alexander Pope commissioned Godfrey Kneller to paint her in her Turkish dress in 1720.[8] Continually correcting the excesses of previous travel writers, Montagu insists that Turks are not so vulgar as the English have been led to think. Most pointedly, Montagu's representations of Turkish *women* provide an alternative view. Differing with contemporaries such as Rowe, Montagu does not find Turkish women to be "sinners" without souls. The degree to which this view may be seen as "sympathetic" or "progressive," and the implications of these labels, deserves further investigation.

Montagu's letters have proven interesting to contemporary readers for their descriptions of the differences and the similarities between Turkish and English women's manners. Beauty and disguise—and freedom and confinement—provide the most difficult aspects of these letters. The most famous is perhaps Montagu's visit to the women's bagnios or the Turkish baths, especially because Montagu claims she was the first foreign woman to have gotten inside a Turkish harem and to have spent a good deal of time with Turkish women. On first being observed by these Turkish women, Montagu describes how they interpret her dress and behavior: "I was in my travelling Habit, which is a rideing dress, and certainly appear'd very extraordinary to them, yet there was not one of 'em that shew'd the least surprize or impertinent

Curiosity, but receiv'd me with all the obliging civillity possible. I know no European Court where the Ladys would have behav'd them selves in so polite a manner to a stranger" (CL, 1:313). Later we discover that an "extraordinary" surprise to the Turkish women were Montagu's stays, which they believed were a contraption fitted by her husband to ensure her fidelity. After this cross-cultural misreading on the part of the Turkish women, Montagu's own (mis)interpretations continue.

Montagu reports that in the bath she observed about 200 women, arranged according to status, ladies on couches with slaves behind them. She argues, though, that differences were effaced because the women were "without any distinction of rank by their dress, all being in the state of nature, that is, in plain English, stark naked, without any Beauty or deffect conceal'd, yet there was not the least wanton smile or immodest Gesture amongst 'em. They walked and moved with the same majestic Grace which Milton describes of our General Mother. . . . To tell you the truth, I had wickedness enough to wish secretly that Mr. Gervase could have been there invisible" (CL, 1:313–14). Montagu's wish for a portrait painter is needless. She herself has rendered these "invisible" women visible. She alone claims the right, pointing out that previous European travelers' accounts must not be firsthand ones because it was death for a man to be found in one of these places (CL, 1:315).

In conjunction with making them "visible," Montagu claims that Turkish women are less confined than previously thought. Montagu takes issue with the widespread "myth" that Turkish women were "slaves," seeing freedom where others saw confinement. In one letter she describes Turkish women's dress to her sister, concluding,

I cannot forbear admiring either the exemplary discretion or extreme Stupidity of all the writers that have given accounts of [Turkish women]. Tis very easy to see that they have more Liberty than we have, no Woman of what rank so ever being permitted to go in the streets without 2 muslins, one that covers her face all but her Eyes and another that hides the whole dress of her head and hangs halfe way down her back. . . . You may guess how effectually this disguises them, that there is no distinguishing the great Lady from her Slave, and 'tis impossible for the most jealous Husband to know his Wife when he meets her, and no Man dare either touch or follow a Woman in the Street. (CL, 1:328)

Montagu claims that "This perpetual Masquerade gives them entire Liberty of following their Inclinations without danger of Discovery" (CL, 1:328). Many Turkish women, Montagu claims, have affairs without letting their "gallants" know who they are. Montagu ends this section with her now famous statement: "Upon the Whole, I look upon the Turkish women as the only free people in the Empire" (CL, 1:329). Because of such remarks, Montagu has long been regarded as "progressive" and as escaping (to some degree) the ethnocentricity of many of her contemporaries.

Where others before her saw mere strangeness to be noted and dismissed, Montagu saw value and exoticism. This "native sympathy" is one of the reasons that Montagu has been written about as an advocate for all women. Some contemporary readers have accepted Montagu's protestations of fairness at face value. Robert Halsband led the way for this reading of the letters in 1960 when he argued, "By virtue of their clear-sighted observation, their expansive tolerance, and their candid sympathy for an alien culture, they are Lady Mary's valid credential for a place in the European 'Enlightenment'" (CL, 1:xiv). As recently as 1983, others concurred; Michele Plaisant concluded of Montagu's written sentiments toward the Turks: "Peut-on imaginer plus belle leçon de tolérance?"[9]

Feminist critics have long read these letters as uncomplicated accounts of Montagu's sincerity or philanthropy. About Montagu's trip to Turkey, Hufstader writes:

Here, as in her campaign for women's intellectual integrity, Lady Mary was in advance of her time. . . . In her letters from the East, Lady Mary suspended the sarcasm with which she so expertly satirized Western society. As she approached the Ottoman frontier, she addressed herself without mockery to an unknown culture. . . . It is this tone of sincere inquiry that sets apart her Embassy Letters from her familiarity-breeds-contempt vignettes of London, and makes them more, or less, favored depending upon their readers' tastes.[10]

In this version of literary history (again, from 1978), Montagu, like all great women, is able to step out of her historical context as she is "before her time." Like most good feminists, Montagu has a sense of humor—but only up to a certain political point. Montagu can "get serious" when the situation calls for it.

Even at the time Hufstader and others were making these claims of cross-cultural magnanimity for Montagu, there was disagreement over the extent of the liberty that Montagu wanted to assign to Turkish women. Katharine Rogers wrote that Montagu's statements on Turkish women were mere veilings of her true beliefs and did not see this portion of Montagu's writings as more "sincere." Rogers found it inconceivable that Montagu "meant" what she said in her anecdotes about the veils of Turkish women providing them with more liberty. In *Feminism in Eighteenth-Century England* (1982), Rogers concluded, "Of course [Montagu] must have realized that this was a frivolous proof of liberty and that Turkish women were even more restricted and less valued than English ones. But this was how she made the point that English women were only supposed to be free." [11] As early as 1979, Rogers asserted that Montagu's "insistence on the happy liberty of Mohammedan Turkish women functions as a wicked comment on the Englishman's complacent assumption that England was 'the paradise of wives'; but it is upsetting to note that she defined woman's liberty in terms of spending money and carrying on adulterous affairs with impunity. She had radical ideas about women, but evidently felt the need to camouflage them." [12] For Rogers, Montagu's "feminism is typically veiled in apology or flippancy" and though "Montagu prided herself on being a properly conducted aristocrat and a tough-minded rationalist . . . she ruthlessly suppressed feminist feelings that seemed to conflict with these ideals." [13] The Turkish Embassy letters, then, are not truer but more deceptive accounts of Montagu's views on women, according to this dissenting view.

Whether seen as "actually" representative of Montagu's feminism or as subversive attempts to hide her "true" beliefs, all of these second-wave feminist versions of the Turkish Embassy letters have, in varying degrees, followed the pleas of Mary Astell. Montagu is only praised for her beliefs and writings, and where she is not praised, she is assigned "understandable" intentions to explain why her writings might be classified to the contrary. Even Rogers, who has problems accepting Montagu's statements at face value, used her critical efforts to "save" Montagu and to put her squarely within the "requirements" of contemporary feminism.

Must Montagu must be held up as a politically progressive figure at all costs? As I mentioned earlier, the criticism linking Montagu to Orientalism has changed the focus of feminist readings in the 1990s from quests for heroic feminism to suggestions of implicit racism. Lowenthal's 1990 article, "The Veil of Romance: Lady Mary's Embassy Letters," argued that Montagu used European aesthetic models of romance and courtly love that only allowed her to see Turkey through her own cultural mirror—an Orientalist gesture. Although Montagu's letters may seem at first glance to offer a "sisterly" attitude toward Turkish women, this sisterhood is only with upper-class women and only at the expense of alternately aestheticizing or Westernizing their attributes, Lowenthal argued.

This groundbreaking article was followed by Lisa Lowe's *Critical Terrains: French and British Orientalisms* (1991) and Joseph Lew's "Lady Mary's Portable Seraglio" (1991). Both scholars view Orientalism in Montagu's texts as one of several competing discourses within her letters and her social milieu. These arguments are distinctive in that they simultaneously exonerate Montagu from and implicate her in Orientalist practices. Lowe finds a dual tendency in Montagu's letters, which she calls a rhetoric of identification and a rhetoric of differentiation with Turkish women. The rhetoric of identification is "an emergent feminist discourse" that speaks of common experiences among women of different societies; the rhetoric of differentiation follows in the tradition of Orientalism that Said has outlined—one of "othering."[14] Joseph Lew, like Lowe, sees a portion of Montagu's writings as "progressive"—as escaping Orientalism because Montagu sometimes speaks in a "women's discourse." This women's discourse is a language that knows no cultural boundaries—is said, in fact, to be its own culture and language.

The strength of Lowe's, Lew's, and others' work in this vein is its assertion that Montagu's "Orientalist logic and statements often exist in a climate of challenge and contestation."[15] There is, in other words, no monolithic discourse of "Orientalism" but rather many degrees of adherence and deviation. What we have "gained" through these readings of racial and class politics is an appreciation of the complexity of dominant and marginal Orientalist practices. What we have sometimes lost, however, is the complexity of *gender* in relation to these practices.

Strangely, in the recent reviews of this scholarship on Montagu and Orientalism, the difficulties involved in dealing simultaneously with gender, ethnicity, class, and colonialism are frequently *not* the issues taken up. In fact, in some responses to the criticism about Montagu's "Orientalism," what is offered is a defense of Montagu herself—usually in the name of historical veracity. Isobel Grundy's review of Lowe's *Critical Terrains* (1993) faults that book primarily for its historical inaccuracies, but Grundy's critiques are ultimately more far-reaching. Grundy believes that Lowe has "undeclared baggage: an expectation or a hope that Montagu will conform to twentieth-century feminist, democratic, multicultural positions."[16] Grundy complains that Montagu is "implicitly blamed" when she allows "identity by class to override identity by gender."[17] This seems to suggest that we should give Montagu a critical break and read her on eighteenth-century terms. But long before Lowe, feminists read Montagu through contemporary interpretive models. It is equally problematic to claim that dubbing Montagu anything other than a "feminist heroine" is to have "undeclared baggage." Why is keeping her within the confines of "great woman author" equal to "traveling light"?

Grundy's views are not anomalous. In 1992 Susan Groag Bell used tropes similar to Grundy's to rescue Montagu. Bell takes issue with the charge of "Orientalism" because "Lady Mary Wortley Montagu, in common with both men and women of her time, took her situation as an aristocrat for granted." [18] Bell believes that "to scold Lady Mary for not objecting to the Turkish lady lying naked on her cushioned marble bench among the two hundred in the women's bath—and having her own naked servant standing behind her in 1717—is to misunderstand the mentality of the eighteenth century. It is as anachronistic as it would be to expect every medieval peasant to have a private bedroom and bath ensuite." [19] Responses like Bell's and Grundy's miss the critical point of Orientalisms, and ultimately, of many historically attuned feminisms. Bell suggests that critical tactics involving "scolding" imply that Montagu herself needed to correct her behavior. To make these demands of Montagu would, I agree, be anachronistic as well as pointless. Who could expect Montagu to "rise above" her class, her gender, her race, and her historical moment to some "transcendent truth" about life for all times and places?

The critical "scolding" I would rather do is directed toward those who would only praise "feminist" authors for being role models and heroines. Any emphasis on reading Montagu's texts through her own eyes and intentions, through Mary Astell's, or through some hopelessly universalizing eighteenth-century mentality, is therefore problematic. To hold up Montagu as a feminist model of strength and independence—without concomitantly holding her up as a model of how women are implicated in Orientalist and elitist practices *against other women*—is to repeat the eighteenth-century context as appropriate for our own. Bell, for one, does just that. She ironically suggests that if we had only adhered to Lady Mary's "feminist" ways, we might not even need a women's movement today. Bell claims, "Perhaps we should rather have wished that the middle class accepted Lady Mary Wortley Montagu's aristocratic family values of women's independence within marriage. Had this happened instead of the domestic middle-class values that raged through the Victorian period—the need for what Juliet Mitchell called *The Longest Revolution,* i.e., the women's revolution, might also have been obviated."[20] This kind of critical practice—claiming halcyon lost origins—makes it difficult to read Montagu with anything but feminist nostalgia.

How else might we read? Those who implicate Montagu in Orientalisms often exonerate her by suggesting that she was doing her best with the cultural and linguistic tools she was given; she was stating something so new that it precluded her ability to reach anything but hostile audiences. But even if we grant her this, to what extent should we use a word like "sympathetic" or "progressive" to describe Montagu's texts? To whom is she "progressive" or, rather, whom does her "progressiveness" serve or not serve? Assumed "political progressiveness" in Montagu's letters, as well as in the twentieth-century literary-critical work that attends to her letters, creates problems that must be reconsidered.

Feminist models for women's authorship have sometimes assumed a progressive woman masquerading in one of three guises: (1) repression (Rogers's version—a veiling of true beliefs in the woman's writings), (2) suppression (women as historically silenced and unauthorized to write, though we have now unearthed some of these secreted documents), or (3) oppression (women's history and authorship as rare to nonexistent). Early British women writers may then be seen as overcoming the "patriarchal powers" to be able to liberate themselves—to partially undo their shackles. It is often tacitly overlooked—and sometimes downplayed—that these women's texts not only challenge dominations but themselves repress, suppress, or oppress other marginalized groups. Attempting to sort out the contradictions of race, class, and gender at work in Montagu's letters, however, points up the dangers in unqualifiedly dubbing any one of the categories—or any one author—"politically progressive." To do so will involve glossing over "othering" in different categories.

Strangely, this "glossing over" is true of the scholarship that explicitly deals with Montagu's own "othering" as well. As this criticism has shown, Montagu's views on veiling practices provide examples of the limited kind of "sympathy" and "sisterhood" her texts offer. Nonwestern understandings of the veil illustrate the necessity of investigating Montagu's "perpetual masquerade" views, as Lew argues:

In the novelistic tradition, women (the Clarissas, Emily St. Auberts, Catherine Morlands, and Evelinas) enter the sexual arena as prey when they leave the shelter of the Father's House. But in the Muslim East . . . the superficial similarity of the immurement of females performs a precisely opposite function: it protects men. This opposite function indicates an alternative view of female sexuality. . . . The double veils (murlins) . . . are designed to protect men from the women's contagious sexuality.[21]

This distinction is important for its recognition that masquerade need not translate into freedom in all historical and cultural contexts. Lew was not, of course, the first to make these arguments about Turkish veiling. He points to the work of Lila Abu-Lughod and Fatima Mernissi, to which also might be added the work of Leila Ahmed, Nikki Keddie and Beth Baron, and Judy Mabro, among others. Strangely, however, Lew uses this information about the complexity of veiling practices to reassert their subversiveness. For Lew, Montagu does in fact recognize the intricacies of these cultural interpretations of veiling. He reasserts with her the veil's subversive potential.

To "credit" Montagu with stepping out of her own cultural lens and seeing both the oppressive and the subversive potentials of veiling for Turkish women may grant Montagu too much. Lowe, too, implicitly gives Montagu undue credit when she calls Orientalism a "male tradition."[22] We must question whether women somehow subvert "the Orientalist tradition" by virtue of their sex. Isn't it possible that women writers are as implicated in Orientalisms as their male counterparts? "Sympathy" for "other" women does not *necessarily* steer Montagu clear—even partially—of biases. She grafts her own cultural wishes and expectations onto the lives of Turkish women. If we move away from the "feminist/not a feminist" or "progressive/not progressive" dichotomy in regard to Montagu, are we left with a critical vacuum? Rather than working to castigate or exonerate Montagu more thoroughly, a turn to generic, historical, and disciplinary questions—to difficult matters of historicizing—may prove a way to deal with these either/or feminist options.

An investigation of Montagu's positionings of texts, authors, and masquerade is one way to proceed. Montagu's status is as an all-knowing onlooker or ethnographer, and in her gaze, Turkish women become *objets d'art*—or as Lowenthal puts it, "bodyscapes" situated in a timeless present.[23] Perhaps rather than seeing Turkish women as situated in a timeless present, though, one might posit that Montagu presents them as part of a timeless *past*. In the course of her letters, Montagu herself is inserted into history: she is the "first" to see a Turkish harem. The Turkish women are drawn as if in a landscape—like characters on a Keatsian urn. In claiming herself as the first to "make visible" the

Turkish women in all of their naked and noble splendor, Montagu puts herself in "history" and dehistoricizes her subjects.

Returning to the difficult issues of Montagu and veiling, similar problems of "history" can be explored. Terry Castle's *Masquerade and Civilization: The Carnivalesque in Eighteenth-Century English Culture and Fiction* may provide a helpful historicizing corrective. Although recent critical writings on Montagu cite Castle, none seem to take seriously her points about English masquerade, politics, and history in regard to Montagu's *Letters*. Castle herself strangely misconstrues Montagu's discussion of masquerade, claiming: "Mary Wortley Montagu, always a devotee of disguise and masquerade, wrote of the congeniality of the Mediterranean carnival season, and the freedom it offered, particularly for women." [24] Castle's mysterious creation of a "Mediterranean carnival season" is itself an unfortunately Orientalist appropriation of veiling practices. Despite these questionable conclusions, Castle's work remains important in other respects.

Issues of ahistoricity and gendered Orientalisms are brought to the fore in Castle's discussion of masquerade. Castle concludes that masquerade was seen as a hybrid form of English and non-Englishness that intermixed all classes.[25] Unescorted English women were allowed at masquerades as in no other spaces, and the mask was seen as allowing these women to speak more freely.[26] All of these claims make Montagu's interpretation of veiling that much more clear. Masquerade was seen *in England* as a classless, freeing, and, finally, a foreign practice: "Masquerades were persistently associated with diabolical foreign influence, imported corruption, the dangerous breach of national boundaries, contamination from without." [27] Montagu identifies in Turkey a similar classlessness (belied by her other statements about rank) and a high level of freedom for women. In valorizing masquerade, Montagu essentially takes those things for which masquerade had been denounced in England, naturalizes them in a foreign context, and argues for their being right and good.

The points that may be left out in such a discussion, however, are the political and historical dimensions Castle outlines. She notes: "The frequent refrain in Horace Walpole's correspondence—that 'balls and masquerades supply the place of politics' and 'histories of masquerades' take up 'people's thoughts full as much' as national events—suggest something of the masquerade's intrusive force." [28] It may be tempting to read back on this scene a kind of postmodern malaise—a version of vapid celebrity "news" ignoring the "real issues." Castle's other remarks make this a difficult conclusion to reach. In discussing newspaper accounts of masquerades, Castle writes that the surrealistic prominence of these accounts jars the modern reader; masquerades are "juxtaposed quite unself-consciously to reports of troop movements, Parliamentary sessions, and other more somber public doings."[29] For Castle, this reinforces that on some level the masquerade was news as much as any other public occasion. She notes, "Indeed, an odd blurring sometimes takes place in the eighteenth century between the masquerade and politics: they absorb similar kinds of public attention."[30] The masquerade, therefore, *is* "history" and *is* "politics."

In her appropriations of Turkish veiling practices, Montagu is not fashioning a "bilingual women's discourse," nor is she merely making aesthetic objects of Turkish women within a literary model. Her use of the masquerade trope in her *Letters* inserts her fully into mainstream histories and politics. She cannot be said to simply "rebel" or "progress" in this sense. Furthermore, Castle argues that the masquerade evokes a world of *temps perdu:* "It tends to elude all but the most nostalgic and distorting forms of recuperation."[31] To take this one step further, if the "masquerade" itself was a kind of "history" or a kind of "politics," it is both more "political" and more "historical" than we recognize it to be today—as well as more "timeless" in its own eighteenth-century British context. By positing masquerade as strictly a women's realm in Turkey, Montagu may effectively politicize and historicize some women in England through an attempt to bring them front and center in the public sphere. She cannot carry out the same project for Turkish women, however. Montagu, political and historical figure, self-fashioned English woman/native/other, becomes the only "appropriate" apex of these contradictions. She rescues herself and places herself prominently within masquerade, news, politics, history, letters ("literature"), and (remembering Astell) women. Just as surely, she erases the historicity and cultural specificity of her intended female Turkish subjects.

What is most ironic is that the negation and erasure I am describing is what today's feminist appropriations of Montagu, seeking to categorize her as a feminist heroine, repeat. At the moment when masquerade was tottering between "history," "politics," and *"temps perdu,"* Montagu's firm alignment of masquerade with women eventually backfires by serving only to distance them further from historical events. Not incidentally, this distancing culminates in the Victorian notion of women as outside of history.[32] It also culminates in the scholarship of those like Lew who see women as connected eternally, linguistically, and cross-culturally through a "women's discourse." Neither version offers a clearly emancipatory "end," despite their contrary intentions. We must consider the possibility of our own "emancipatory," celebratory feminisms backfiring. To be sure, when Montagu is first and foremost—or even mostly—a heroine in our feminist scholarship, we are prevented from scolding her for what she could not "control." However, through this practice, we are also implicated in a prioritizing of "harms" that puts women—in this case, white aristocratic European women—above the fray of other conflicts and discourses.

If discourses of gender, like those of Orientalism, exist in a climate of challenge and contestation, how are we to map out the "common oppressions" and "solidarity" among women on which Astell and some contemporary feminists insist? Wouldn't we also be "glossing over the pain of some women," as Lowenthal puts it in regard to Montagu? How might we have gendered "solidarity" without grafting our respective cultural wishes and expectations onto the lives of "other" women? Reading Montagu, I think, gives the lie to Orientalism as a "male tradition." It also gives the lie to a "women's discourse" that crosses centuries or national boundaries. The force of these "lies" must be in theorizing and putting into critical practice ways that will no longer "answer" for feminist scholarship.

In Astell's preface, "solidarity" implies unconditional praise. This is not a forgotten strategy. The sense remains in some feminist circles that you are either with us or against us. "With us" means primarily lauding the female/feminist writers of history, as well as recent feminist critics; "against us" means critiquing historical female subjects or criticizing other feminists' work. Some feminists believe that a deconstruction of the category "women" threatens feminist politics—that this theoretical project can't truly be called "feminist." To question the category "women," however, is not to do away with feminist politics or practices—or to be more precise, with talking about gender and its demarcations, limitations, or harms. Does seeing the category "women" as a construction—as something that does not always require solidarity in advance—have to be a threat? Or does seeing "women at odds" also provide a possibility? As Judith Butler has argued, "To deconstruct the subject of feminism is not, then, to censure its usage, but, on the contrary, to release the term into a future of multiple significations, to emancipate it from the maternal or racialist ontologies to which it has been restricted, and to give it play as a site where unanticipated meanings might come to bear."[33] Preconceiving a unity of "women," then, is not automatically an act of resistance against dominant discourses.

Through the last several decades of constructing a "women's literary tradition" or a "women's history"—particularly through celebrating women on the basis of their gender politics—we have created much work on which to draw as we continue to assess our earlier critical models. The majority of what has been called "gynocriticism" or "herstory" dealt well with issues of gender, just as it elided questions of ethnicity, class, or nation. Although feminist scholarship has come a good distance from this earlier work, much of our scholarship continues implicitly or explicitly in this tradition. This is the case when we invoke labels such as "subversive" and "progressive," or when we "uncomplicate" gender to make points about race, class, and nation. Romanticizing "sisterhood" has had critical benefits, to be sure, but it has also had critical costs. This matter deserves, not just our scolding, but a more difficult task: our scrutiny. The feminist protection of—veiling of—the category of "women" is not inherently liberatory. As with Montagu's texts, such a veiling prevents making visible harms that are in collusion with or contradicting those of gender. Montagu's "sisterhood" is not inherently global. Rather than scolding or exonerating her (or any of our predecessors), we might instead move toward more complex tasks of shifting, local theorizing, and examining complicity as thoroughly as we do resistance.[34]

NOTES

1. Pat Rogers, ed., *The Eighteenth Century: The Context of English Literature* (New York: Holmes and Meier, 1978), 29.
2. Dale Spender, *Women of Ideas: And What Men Have Done to Them* (London: Pandora, 1982), 68–69.
3. Alice Anderson Hufstader, *Sisters of the Quill* (New York: Dodd, Mead, 1978), 7.
4. Edward Said, *Orientalism* (New York: Random House, 1978). See also Said's "Orientalism Reconsidered," in *Literature, Politics and Theory: Papers From the Essex Conference 1976–84*, ed. Francis Barker et al. (London: Methuen, 1986), 210–29.
5. John McVeagh, ed., *English Literature and the Wider World. Volume 1: All Before Them: 1660–1780* (London: Ashfield, 1990), 8.

6. Robert Halsband, ed., *The Complete Letters of Lady Mary Wortley Montagu* (3 vols.) (Oxford: Clarendon, 1965). Quotations are cited in the text as CL.
7. Quoted in Vivien Jones, ed., *Women in the Eighteenth Century: Constructions of Femininity* (New York: Routledge, 1990), 144–45.
8. Robert Halsband, *The Life of Lady Mary Wortley Montagu* (New York: Oxford University Press, 1960), 88, 98–99.
9. Michele Plaisant, "Les Lettres Turques de Lady Mary Wortley Montagu," *Bulletin de la Sociétés d'Etudes Anglo-Américaines des XVII et XVIII Siècles* 16 (1983): 72.
10. Hufstader, *Sisters*, 33, 40.
11. Katharine M. Rogers, *Feminism in Eighteenth-Century England* (Urbana: University of Illinois Press, 1982), 94.
12. Katharine M. Rogers, *Before Their Time: Six Women Writers of the Eighteenth Century* (New York: Frederick Ungar, 1979), x.
13. Rogers, *Feminism*, 93.
14. Lisa Lowe, *Critical Terrains: French and British Orientalisms* (Ithaca: Cornell University Press, 1991), 32.
15. Ibid., 51.
16. Grundy, Isobel, Review of *Critical Terrains: French and British Orientalisms*, by Lisa Lowe, *Eighteenth-Century Studies* 26, 3 (1993): 486.
17. Ibid., 486.
18. Susan Groag Bell, "Comment: Letters as Literature in Eighteenth-Century France and England," Western Association of Women Historians Conference, San Marino, Calif., Huntington Library, 30 May 1992.
19. Ibid.
20. Ibid.
21. Joseph W. Lew, "Lady Mary's Portable Seraglio," *Eighteenth-Century Studies* 24 (1991): 449–50.
22. Lowe, *Critical*, 47.
23. Cynthia Lowenthal, "The Veil of Romance: Lady Mary's Embassy Letters," *Eighteenth-Century Life* 14 (1990): 73–74.
24. Terry Castle, *Masquerade and Civilization* (Stanford: Stanford University Press, 1986), 14.
25. Ibid., 24, 28, 33.
26. Ibid., 32, 34.
27. Ibid., 7.
28. Ibid., 3.
29. Ibid.
30. Ibid.
31. Ibid., 7.
32. On the Victorian separation of "women" and "history," see Christina Crosby, *The Ends of History: Victorians and "The Woman Question"* (New York: Routledge, 1991).
33. Judith Butler, "Contingent Foundations: Feminism and the Question of 'Postmodernism,'" *Praxis International* 11 (1991): 160.

34. For an interesting article on romanticizing resistance and complicating feminist diagnostics of power, see Lila Abu-Lughod, "The Romance of Resistance: Tracing Transformations of Power through Bedouin Women," *American Ethnologist* 17 (1990): 41–55.

REFERENCES

Abu-Lughod, Lila. "A Community of Secrets: The Separate World of Bedouin Women." *Signs* 10 (1985): 637–57.
———. "The Romance of Resistance: Tracing Transformations of Power through Bedouin Women," *American Ethnologist* 17 (1990): 41–55.
Ahmed, Leila. *Women and Gender in Islam.* New Haven: Yale University Press, 1992.
Bell, Susan Groag. "Letters as Literature in Eighteenth-Century France and England." Comment presented at the annual meeting of the Western Association of Women Historians Conference at the Huntington Library, San Marino, California, 30 May 1992.
Butler, Judith. "Contingent Foundations: Feminism and the Question of 'Postmodernism.'" *Praxis International* 11 (1991): 150–65.
Castle, Terry. *Masquerade and Civilization: The Carnivalesque in Eighteenth-Century English Culture and Fiction.* Stanford: Stanford University Press, 1986.
Crosby, Christina. *The Ends of History: Victorians and "The Woman Question."* New York: Routledge, 1991.
Grundy, Isobel. Review of *Critical Terrains: French and British Orientalisms,* by Lisa Lowe. *Eighteenth-Century Studies* 26, 3 (1993): 484–87.
Halsband, Robert, ed. *The Complete Letters of Lady Mary Wortley Montagu.* 3 vols. Oxford: Clarendon, 1965.
———. *The Life of Lady Mary Wortley Montagu.* New York: Oxford University Press, 1960.
Hufstader, Alice Anderson. *Sisters of the Quill.* New York: Dodd, Mead, 1978.
Jones, Vivien, ed. *Women in the Eighteenth Century: Constructions of Femininity.* New York: Routledge, 1990.
Keddie, Nikki R., and Beth Baron, eds. *Women in Middle Eastern History.* New Haven: Yale University Press, 1991.
Lew, Joseph W. "Lady Mary's Portable Seraglio." *Eighteenth Century Studies* 24 (1991): 432–50.
Lowe, Lisa. *Critical Terrains: French and British Orientalisms.* Ithaca: Cornell University Press, 1991.
Lowenthal, Cynthia. "The Veil of Romance: Lady Mary's Embassy Letters." *Eighteenth Century Life* 14 (1990): 66–82.
Mabro, Judy, ed. *Veiled Half-Truths: Western Travellers' Perceptions of Middle Eastern Women.* London: I. B. Tauris, 1991.
McVeagh, John, ed. *English Literature and the Wider World. Volume 1: All Before Them: 1660–1780.* London: Ashfield, 1990.

Mernissi, Fatima. *Beyond the Veil*. London: Al Saqi Books, 1985.

Plaisant, Michele. "Les Lettres Turques de Lady Mary Wortley Montagu." *Bulletin de la Sociétés d'Etudes Anglo-Américaines des XVII et XVIII Siècles* 16 (1983): 53–75.

Rogers, Katharine M. *Before Their Time: Six Women Writers of the Eighteenth Century*. New York: Frederick Ungar, 1979.

———. *Feminism in Eighteenth-Century England*. Urban: University of Illinois Press, 1982.

Rogers, Pat, ed. *The Eighteenth Century: The Context of English Literature*. New York: Holmes and Meier, 1978.

Said, Edward. *Orientalism*. New York: Random House, 1978.

———. "Orientalism Reconsidered." In *Literature, Politics and Theory: Papers From the Essex Conference 1976–84*, edited by Francis Barker et al., 210–29. London: Methuen, 1986.

Spender, Dale. *Women of Ideas: And What Men Have Done to Them*. London: Pandora, 1982.

3.

LOUISA SUSANNA McCORD:
SPOKESWOMAN OF THE MASTER CLASS
IN ANTEBELLUM SOUTH CAROLINA

MANISHA SINHA

In recent years, the importance of gender as an indispensable category of historical analysis has been acknowledged by many scholars.[1] However, practitioners in the relatively new field of women's history are still faced with the dual task of illuminating the female past and developing theoretical frameworks conducive for its study. Two of the major paradigms used by historians of American women, the framework of "oppression" and the idea of a separate female community and culture, posit an artificial homogeneity in women's historical experience based on their biological and social identity as women. As Nancy Hewitt has pointed out, "The notion of a single women's community rooted in common oppression denies the social and material realities of class and [racial] caste in America." And, as Joan Kelly argues, the theory of a separate female culture and values overlooks the fact that "woman's place is not a separate sphere or domain of existence but a position within social existence generally."[2]

Such challenges to conventional approaches to American women's history have emanated from scholars sensitive to issues of class, race, and inequality, mainly historians of working class women and black women.[3] While rejecting the Victorian notion of separate spheres and the cult of domesticity, which undergirded much of the early work on nineteenth-century northern, middle-class women,[4] these historians have also generally and correctly implied that their subjects were victims of greater oppression than bourgeois, white women. This scholarship, combined with some pathbreaking monographs on the woman's rights movement and women's political activism, has presented a dominant picture of women in American history as "victims" and "heroines."[5]

The search for a "usable feminist past" and the reigning trends in American women's history have led some historians to extend the focus on women as victims and rebels to an unlikely group of women— southern white slaveholding women. Such interpretive frameworks, Elizabeth Fox-Genovese argues and demonstrates convincingly in her work, are untenable for a majority of slave-owning women in the Old South. Indeed, as this study of one such woman will illustrate, southern, white, slaveholding women were far more likely to be found in the ranks of the "oppressors" than the "oppressed."[6]

Louisa Susanna McCord (née Cheves), the most prolific and intense female polemicist to emerge from the South Carolina slaveholding aristocracy, was an exceptional woman by any standard. Born in 1810, her adult life spanned the turbulent years of the sectional conflict and Civil War. Daughter of Langdon Cheves, a wealthy rice planter and a leading state politician, she probably imbibed the proslavery views and precocious political separatism of the Carolina gentry fairly early in life. Cheves's political and emotional influence on his adoring daughter cannot be overstated. Louisa McCord was educated not only in the art of letters and language but also in the prerogatives and worldview of her class.

A woman whose essays and literary productions testify to "native abilities of high order," she never played the stereotypical role of a flirtatious southern belle. Unlike many other women of her class, she married at a fairly late age. In 1840, Louisa Cheves wed David James McCord, who had been an advocate of nullification, or state veto of federal tariff laws. It was David McCord's second marriage; he died in 1855, leaving Louisa to raise their three children. Ironically, Louisa's father had sided with the antinullification party. But Langdon Cheves had criticized the idea of nullification not so much as a unionist but as a southern nationalist. Marriage to a former nullifier, no doubt, bolstered

Louisa's commitment to the sacred cows of Carolina politics: free trade, proslavery, and southern separatism. As Sally Baxter Hampton, a northern visitor who would marry into one of Carolina's richest planter families, wrote, "The Chives [sic] and McCord family is as much a stronghold of the slavery party as the Adams faction is of the Abolitionists. Mrs. McCord is hotly engaged in the strife and almost all her feeling and intellect seem to be expended on that one topic, and she and her husband warmly espouse the cause in every paper and periodical to which they can get admission." [7]

Clearly, Louisa McCord's intellectual mindset and passion for politics set her apart from most women of her class, who rarely stepped out of the confines of home and hearth. Even those planter women who displayed an interest in politics acted mainly as private advisors and confidantes to their husbands.[8] McCord was exceptional not because of her virulently proslavery and southern nationalist views, which she shared with many other Carolinian slave-owning women. Indeed, as Fox-Genovese contends, southern slaveholding women were far from being proto-abolitionists and proto-feminists, as some historians would have us believe. A few may have complained about particular injustices, which they faced as individuals, but their class-based allegiance to slave society was unquestionable.

Instead, it was McCord's assumption of a public persona, as a defender of southern slavery, which distinguishes her from most members of her sex in antebellum South Carolina. While McCord's proslavery views may have been representative of her class, her literary career as a polemicist for the slave South set her apart from most men and women in her society. In this sense, she acted far more like generations of Carolinian slaveholding men and planter-politicians, who had established a reputation for themselves in the country for their ideological defense of human bondage and political extremism.[9]

Furthermore, McCord's vindication of so-called natural inequality and social hierarchy, which marked her proslavery profferings, led her to openly denounce the fledgling woman's rights movement. Like most proslavery ideologues, she correctly discerned the philosophical and political connections between woman's rights and the antislavery movement in antebellum America. She thus penned some of the most powerful critiques of the women's movement in print and embraced the role of an anti-woman's rights—or to use an anachronistic term, an anti-feminist—crusader. By doing so, McCord was philosophically and logically consistent to the conservative, hierarchical values of proslavery ideology but practically inconsistent. Her life and literary career reveal the obvious contradiction embodied by most conservative women, who assume a public role in defending women's allegedly natural and divinely ordained position in society as wives and mothers.

Until recently, McCord's relatively impressive array of proslavery and anti-feminist productions have been neglected by most historians of women. Far greater attention has been lavished on Mary Boykin Chesnut, the famous Carolinian diarist whose occasional asides at slavery and women's lot has made her a more attractive object of historical scrutiny. However, even as scholars are re-evaluating hasty appraisals of Chesnut as an incipient abolitionist cum feminist, a thorough examination of McCord's theoretical defense of racial slavery and female inequality is much needed. Not only would such an analysis demonstrate slaveholding women's political commitment to slave society, but it would also call into question "essentialist" and "trans-historical" views of women.[10] For, paradoxically, by evoking a female experience transcending class and racial boundaries as an interpretive framework to understand all women's history, some scholars rest their arguments on the same kind of biological determinism that their opponents subscribe to.

Besides a play and a book of poems, Louisa McCord published more than half a dozen essays in the *Southern Quarterly Review, Southern Literary Messenger,* and *De Bow's Review,* the preeminent vehicles of proslavery and southern nationalist thought in the 1840s and 1850s. Her first forays into the world of print, however, were not so much on behalf of slavery as of free trade. In 1848, Louisa McCord, as "Mrs. D. J. McCord," published a translation of Frederic Bastiat's indictment of protectionism with suitable introductory exhortations by her nullifier husband and Dr. Francis Lieber, the German political scientist at South Carolina College. This is quite understandable when one considers that Carolina's slaveholding elite nearly provoked disunion in 1832 by their opposition to the tariff or protective duties. The political and ideological legacy of nullification in South Carolina was a strange stew of free trade, states' rights, proslavery, and southern nationalist thought. Moreover, a free and unburdened trade with their biggest markets in England and Europe was always in southern planters' immediate economic interest.[11]

However, McCord's admiration for the principles of free trade and political economists like Bastiat also arose from another source. According to her, the principles of bourgeois economy alone could check "the wild dream of 'fraternity' and socialism" invading the Atlantic world. In a later review, in which she effectively dissected the rather confused work of Henry Carey, an American protectionist, she even went so far as to brand protectionism as "socialism." Antislavery in the United States, she and some southern proslavery ideologues pointed out, was merely another species of socialism. She wrote, "In our own country, we see too plainly at every turn the insidious effects of this fearful fallacy. Free soilers, barn-burners, anti-renters, abolitionists stare us in the face at every turn, and frightful to the thinking mind is the anarchy which must follow could they have their way." Socialism, McCord claimed, would reduce all to "one level of starvation and beggary" because it was based on the false premise that capital was "inimical to labor." The people, she concluded, must be taught the truths of political economy before they succumb to the "hydra of communism" and the tyranny of democracy. The "masses" must be taught "to think rightly. *Popularize* (allow us the word) popularize political economy."

McCord enlisted the principles of liberal political economy, *"laissez faire, laissez passer,"* in her fight against abolitionism, democracy, "vague" ideas of equality, anarchism, socialism and universal individual rights, not the least bothered by ideological contradictions. In fact, many Carolinian slaveholders defended free trade and the "right to property" with an ardency that would have put their bourgeois adherents to shame. Langdon Cheves would echo his daughter's condemnation of Proudhon's "terrible declaration" that all property was robbery in his famous address to the southern convention at Nashville in 1850. Carolinian planter-politicians like James Henry Hammond would call upon northern capitalists to keep in check the radical democratic and antislavery elements in their society that threatened not only slavery but the security of all property. Oddly enough, or perhaps not so oddly, McCord used the principles of liberal political economy to defend southern slave society and its conservative, antidemocratic, and hierarchical values.[12]

At the same time, McCord remained devoted enough to a slavery-based economy to spurn Carey's call to develop manufacturing in the South. Like many other southern slaveholders and planters, she seems to have assumed that slavery and industry were incompatible. She noted pungently that asking the slave South to develop cotton manufacturing would be similar to asking New Englanders to grow cotton. And like the "Cotton is King" proponents, she was dismissive of Carey's observation that the southern states' position as supplier of raw cotton for the world market put them in a dependent, colonial relationship with their buyers, particularly with England. It would be English society, she argued, that would perish in "a blaze of revolution" if the slave South ceased to supply it with cotton. In fact, using the principles of free trade and the theory of comparative advantages, she argued that it was natural and in the slave South's best interests to grow rather than manufacture cotton.[13]

McCord's direct justification of human bondage revealed even more strongly her championship of the southern social order. In her first systematic defense of the South's "peculiar institution," she departed from the proslavery mainstream by resting her case on scientific racism or on the theory of the diverse origins of different "races." Influential Carolinian divines like John Bachman and James Henley Thornwell had rejected polygenesis as going against the Adamic unity of man stated in the Bible. This hardly meant that proslavery clergymen and theologians were immune to the lures of racism. For example, Reverend John B. Adger, the Carolinian Presbyterian minister, argued that while black people were of "Adam's race," they were of an "inferior variety." McCord, however, also argued against a "literal" and "dogmatic" reading of the Bible, the mainstay of proslavery Christian theology, and supported polygenetic theory. Casting latter-day scientific racists in the image of Galileo, she invoked the classical fight between religious superstition and scientific progress. And like Galileo, she argued that the Bible could be interpreted in the light of modern "scientific" discovery, which was nothing more than a revelation of the true nature of God's works. Scientific racism or a belief in the multiple origins of man would thus not lead to atheism but enlightened piety.

Even more importantly for McCord, knowledge of the diversity of races would promote the cause of the slave South in the rest of the world and vanquish its critics. Naturalists and scientists would be able to prove the rightfulness of racial slavery by grounding it in scientific inquiry. As she wrote,

Could the civilized world be convinced that all the races do *not* have the same abilities, enjoy the same powers, or show the same natural dispositions, and are not, therefore, entitled to the same position in human society; could the subject be fairly brought before the white man, and investigated as a great philosophic question deserves to be investigated, we verily believe, so well is the negro fitted for his position, that the philanthropist of every nation would arm in defence of our institutions, and presumptuous ignorance which seeks to force out *God's* law, in order to displace it by some "Icarie" of its own invention, would be hooted from the position which it now so impudently assumes.

The world would then know the slaveholders' "truth," that the "white man" was made for "liberty" and the "negro" for slavery. She claimed that the lot of black slaves was better than that of the "white slaves" or the white working class in free society, as the former were "naturally" suited to their position in society. "The negro," she wrote, "by *his nature*, has crouched contented, in the lowest barbarism." "White slavery," she concluded typically, was therefore a greater "evil" than "negro slavery."

McCord's verbal violence knew no bounds when it came to denigrating the idea of black equality. She claimed that if the "negro" was an "inferior man," then the antislavery movement was a "hideous deformity of vice, and gibbering out of its horrible obscenities of 'socialism' and 'communism,' drags upon its track a shouting mob, who, in their ravings for 'negro abolition' and 'universal equality,' trample under foot at once God's law and man's law." She wrote that "Satan . . . comes now in the likeness of an 'all men are born free and equal' advocate." Expounding at tedious length on black people's alleged "anatomical inferiority," she compared their divinely and naturally ordained position as slaves with the position God had assigned to "asses." Thus, "negroism," like "donkeyism," would mean the end of the "white man" and civilization. "Messrs. Sambo, Cuffee and Co.," she maintained, were incapable of civilization, hastily adding that the Egyptians were not "negroes." She repeated fantastical and crude myths and exaggerations about African societies to buttress her point. After abolition, black people would apparently regress to "hopeless barbarism" and their "brutish extincts" would wreak havoc on their erstwhile white masters. The world would then witness the fruits of "Congo civilization! Hottentot civilization! Haytien [sic] civilization!!"

Ironically, the "brutality" most apparent here is personified in McCord's own words and thoughts. Most historians and biographers using contemporary testimony of visitors to Lang Syne, the McCord plantation, and of McCord's daughter, have argued that she was a benevolent and thoughtful slaveholder. However, the extreme racialism that suffuses her works makes one wonder how benevolent this plantation mistress was to even those black men and women who labored for her in their "proper" position. At least one northern visitor was convinced that despite the McCords' apparently exemplary performance of the "duties" of slaveownership, one of their slaves silently prayed for freedom. On emancipation, like many ex-slaveholders, Louisa McCord would have nothing but bitter words for her former slaves.

But McCord's virulent racism did not lead her to espouse a racially based white egalitarianism. A loyal advocate of the slaveholding planter class and well schooled in South Carolina's profoundly antidemocratic political structure and culture, she was no believer in "herrenvolk democracy" or in "Mr. Jefferson's humbug flourish" of universal equality and liberty. In a manner strikingly similar to that of Carolinian male proslavery ideologues, she dismissed the "mischievous fallacy contained in six unlucky words" of the Declaration of Independence. "No man is born free, and no two human beings, perhaps, were ever born equal," she noted. The Declaration, she wrote, was clearly meant for only "white men," but "the assumed position of equality even in the limited sense which we adopt is plainly a false one. There is no such thing as equality possible or desirable among the masses of society." In another place, she severely castigated the author of the famous 1850 "Brutus" pamphlet, which called upon the nonslaveholders of the state to rebel against the rule of slaveholders and planters as a "bold and impudent effort to rouse the poorer classes against the rich." "Perfect freedom," she insisted, "could be found only in a condition of perfect isolation." She clarified: "In the various grades of society . . . there are great differences of rights, and consequently great differences in degrees of freedom. . . . All have their rights, according to the class which they belong." McCord's espousal of a rigid racial hierarchy was thus an integral part of her overall commitment to the general principles of inequality and social subordination.

If McCord's championship of scientific racism was relatively unusual in the slave South, her advocacy of black inferiority was riddled with the same contradictions that plagued many proslavery southerners. On the one hand, she claimed that "negro emancipation" would lead to the extermination of that race by the superior master race of whites. Hence, slavery supposedly protected black people from the dire fate of native Americans. In a strange argument, which challenged her own contention that black slaves did not possess the ability to conceive of liberty, she claimed that the free black population in the northern states would have died out if it had not been replenished by fugitive slaves from the south. On the other hand, she argued, pointing to the example of Haiti, that abolition would lead to "negro rule" that would destroy "white civilization." In this instance, she claimed that "negro emancipation is the emancipation of brute force." If not enslaved, the so-called "inferior race" could end white progress and even existence. At one point, she concluded without being aware of any contradiction: "Abolition is the extinction of the one or the other."[14]

Louisa McCord's vigorous defense of human bondage soon involved her in the sectional war of words and ideas in pre–Civil War America. In 1852, Harriet Beecher Stowe published *Uncle Tom's Cabin,* which not only became one of the all-time best-sellers in American publishing history but also single-handedly inspired a slew of proslavery works. William Gilmore Simms, Carolinian novelist and editor of the *Southern Quarterly Review,* thought it would be "poetic justice" to have a southern woman review Stowe's book. Unlike many southern women who produced vapid literary rebuttals to *Uncle Tom's Cabin,* McCord wrote what one might call in modern parlance a "hatchet job" on the novel. While most southern critics of Stowe were quick to point out particular fallacies in her work, it was clear from the tone of their reviews that her depiction of the inherent inhumanity of the southern slave system had hit home. One Carolinian reviewer, Edward Pringle, complained that Stowe had judged slavery simply from its abuses. McCord admitted that the "abominable woman's abominable book" was "as malicious and gross an abolitionist production (though I confess a cunning one) as ever disgraced the press." In fact, she confessed "most painful it is to us to comment upon a work of this kind." Appalled by the abolitionist "vulgarity" and "libels" of the book, she wrote a shrill review that belied some of her own most telling criticisms.

McCord effectively refuted certain depictions in the book, thus damaging Stowe's credibility and questioning her knowledge of southern slavery. She dwelt at length at the fact that southern characters in the book spoke "Yankee" English or that a slave trader is able to dictate his terms to a planter. Moreover, she vigorously challenged Stowe's implication that most benevolent slaveholding men and women secretly abhorred slavery. McCord was at her best when she cannily noted that despite Stowe's sympathy for black people, most of the "persecuted individuals" in her novel were portrayed "as whites, of slightly negro descent, not negroes." Stowe herself, she argued, betrayed the strong "instinct" of race, as the real tragic figure in her book was the mulatto. Most of Stowe's stories, she alleged, were garnered from the border slave state of Kentucky, where abolitionist interference had introduced peculiarities in the peculiar institution. Happily inverting Stowe's argument, she contended that abolitionists rather than slaveholders were responsible for all the abuses within slavery.

But the same excessiveness that marked McCord's earlier proslavery essays soon led her down a slippery slope. Thus, she wrote that the only implausible story missing from *Uncle Tom's Cabin* was that of slaveholders "fattening negro babies for the use of the soup-pot." And failing to pursue the romantic racialism in Stowe's book, she launched into a racist diatribe of her own. Stowe, she charged, was an advocate of racial "amalgamation," and she resented her portrayal of "woolly-headed and yellow-skinned," elegantly attired "mulatto" women, who were shown to possess more ladylike qualities than southern white women. Most of all, she lashed out at Stowe's statement that "the negro is intellectually the white man's equal." And in a somewhat ridiculous aside meant to support her claim that black people had never built a "civilization," she claimed that Uncle Tom could not look like the Bishop of Carthage, as not all "men of color" are "negroes." Black people, she reiterated monotonously, lacked intellect and had never built a "civilization."[15]

Stowe's emergence as the literary heroine of the Atlantic world especially rankled McCord. Not only had Stowe acquired the kind of celebrity that had eluded her, but her novel, by dramatically appealing to sentiment and emotion, had swept aside McCord's own "learned" and "scientific" discourses on racial slavery. "It is sad to see the world gulled by the fictions of a Mrs. Stowe," she bemoaned. All, especially the "negrophilists," seemed to follow, she exclaimed exasperatedly, the tune of "Mrs. Stowe and Uncle Tom! Mrs. Stowe and Uncle Tom! Mrs. Stowe and Uncle Tom! ding, ding, dong." She hopefully predicted that "Uncle Tomism" would run its course and Stowe would be dislodged from her "position of a heroine and prophetess." Instead of weeping over the fate of Uncle Toms, McCord advised abolitionists to look to the condition of the laboring poor in free societies. Disputing their accusations of the brutality of slavery, she contended that the slaveholder was the real "protector" of the slaves as he was guided by law, custom, interest, and humanity. But she once again managed to undermine her own argument by a rather fanciful comparison of the punishment meted out to slaves and whites: "The negro gets his whipping, goes home to warm himself by his fire, and perhaps laugh in his sleeve at '*Massa*,' who thinks, 'dat kind o'lashin ebber hut nigga,' while the white man bears the double infliction of imprisonment and stripes." [16]

The appearance of Stowe's book also seemed to confirm McCord's suspicions on the connection between antislavery and the women's movement. She wrote, "The woman's rights theory is putting ladies into their husband's pantaloons; and Mrs. Stowe's theory would lead them, Heaven knows where! All spirit of joking leaves us as we look shudderingly forward to *her* results. Amalgamation is evidently no bugbear to this lady." The abolition movement was composed only of "old ladies" and "negro men." Indeed, she surmised that it was not the least surprising that advocates of "equal rights without distinction of sex or colour" were one and the same people. The "amiable Sojourner," she pointed out, "can come under either wing of the improvement squad." But in the South, "a strong *corps de reserve* of sober, quiet women, who, satisfied to find our duties at home, (not for want of thought, but because thought teaches us that therein lies woman's highest task, and the fulfillment of her noblest mission,) can nevertheless start up with true feeling of womanhood in defence of right and property, hearth and home." Southern "Christian" women were hence not only not enamored by the cry for female rights but were ready to do battle with their hoydenish northern sisters to protect slavery.

McCord had, in fact, long opposed the nascent women's movement as another symptom of the dangerous contagion of "universal equality." In her review of the proceedings of the woman's rights movement at Worcester, she sneeringly called, "Follow close, ladies. The door of privilege is open pretty wide for the admission of Cuffee. Should *he* get in, surely *you* might follow. . . . Mounted on Cuffee's shoulders, in rides the lady!" According to McCord, just as God and nature had assigned a place for black people, they had done so for women. Sex and color, she proclaimed, were "immutable creations," distinctions given by the Almighty himself. Thus, she wrote, "God, who has made every creature to its place, has, perhaps, not given to woman the most enviable position in his creation, but a most clearly defined position he *has* given her. Let her object, then, be to raise herself *in* that position. *Out* of it, there is only failure and degradation." To ask for the right to vote was to step outside that divinely ordained place.

Southern defenders of slavery needed to look no further than to Aristotle to expound on the "natural" position of women and slaves in the household. Thomas R. Dew, the proslavery Virginian professor, was willing to go further. While expounding at length on the differences between the sexes, he was ready to admit that such differences may be the product of education and the environment. But McCord evoked woman's nature and "true woman's love" to support her argument in a manner that would have outdone the most sickly Victorian sentimentalist. Women should fulfill their "destiny" and "*cherish*" their "*mission.*" "Woman's sphere is higher, purer, nobler," she intoned. Woman was designed to be man's helpmate and not his rival, a "perfected woman, not the counterfeit man." For when it comes to a physical showdown, she warned, women would surely become "the inevitable victim of brutal strength." While admitting that the "weaker" sex suffered many injustices, she argued that their true redemption lay in fulfilling their womanly duties in accordance with their divinely appointed nature.

Like most proslavery ideologues, McCord decried the "petticoated despisers of their sex" and "unsexed" creatures who in her view were not only aping men but degrading their exalted roles as "mother, wife and sister." Women's righters were thus overthrowing "the true cause of womanhood" and were mere seekers of "notoriety." Her denunciation of women activists, whether in the cause of slavery or women's rights, fitted right in with the way in which they had been lampooned in proslavery discourse. Most male defenders of slavery clearly thought that these "Amazonian" women did not deserve any brand of southern chivalry. In fact, Simms had reached a new low in his 1837 review of Harriet Martineau's work in which he referred to her as an "unsexed spinster" and ridiculed her deafness. A poem entitled "The Response," written most probably by McCord, referring perhaps to Martineau, attributed her critique of slavery to the fact that she had failed to lure any southern man into marriage.

While fierce remorse assails with poisoned fangs,
The heart thy pen has doomed to endless pangs.
Unhappy fair one! did disappoint then,
Attend thy visit to our Southern men?
. . . .
Oh cruel country!—Oh ungrateful men!
To come a maid, and maid return again.

. . . .
Betrayed, forsaken, unwedded and forlorn,
What wonder if the vials of her wrath,
Bedew with henbane her retreating path

Despite her own long spinsterhood, McCord chose to draw upon a stereotypical picture of a bitter spinster who vented her frustrations by uttering calumnies against southern slave society.

McCord seemed to be virtually unaware of the fact that her own public persona as a defender of southern slave society contradicted her theories on women's proper place. She, however, did make it a point to state that while women were physically inferior to men, in intellect they were their equals. Female intellect was different rather than below that of a man, she wrote.[17] McCord's vigorous championship of slavery gained her a place and reputation in the southern literary and publishing world, which was denied to most southern women. Indeed, her proslavery and antifeminist credentials and her social station overcame any objections that some may have entertained about her stepping out of woman's sphere.

In her writings and her personal life, Louisa McCord solved the contradictions of her position to her own satisfaction. Thanks to an indulgent father, she had received an exemplary education and was even allowed to follow her brothers' mathematics lessons after displaying an interest in the subject. Clearly, in intelligence and education she towered above not only most women but also many men. After having attained her "womanly" position as wife and mother, she had embarked on a fairly well received writing career in the South. McCord was lucky to possess not only the privileges of her birth and class, but also to have men in her life who encouraged her literary aspirations. While her father read her callow efforts at poetry, her husband, author of legal reports and several essays and coeditor of a multivolume anthology of the state's laws, had her poems secretly published, launching her literary career.

Whatever may have been Louisa McCord's accomplishments as wife, mother, and plantation mistress, she was most notable as a spokeswoman for the slaveholding class. David and Louisa McCord shared a study with their tables on opposite ends, where they wrote and published together. Their marriage was perhaps all that she could have wished for. Although Louisa's daughter remembered her with great admiration, her most affectionate memories were of her "maums," the slave women who had performed many of their mistress's maternal "duties." McCord's writing and health languished after the deaths of her husband and father. During the Civil War, she devoted all her efforts and possessions to the ill-fated Confederacy, losing her adored son on the altar of the slave nation. She would die in 1879, commemorating the vanished world of slaveholders and their abortive effort to gain independence.[18]

An assessment of McCord's writing makes it clear that she excelled as a polemical and sectional warrior for the slave South rather than as a poet and author. Her book of poems, *My Dreams,* dedicated to her father, is marked by its unrelieved pallid and mundane sentimentality. McCord herself was rather embarrassed by its publication. Her second literary effort, a play entitled *Caius Gracchus: A Tragedy in Five Acts,* dedicated to her son, was better received. But most commentators have examined the play as evidence of McCord's classical and "Doric" mind-set and have identified her with the wise Cornelia, one of its characters, instead of praising its brilliance. Indeed, in form and style it seems to follow Shakespeare's *Julius Caesar* and lacks originality. Ironically, the drama's chief protagonist is a champion of democracy, but it ends with enough evocative scenes of slave fidelity to appeal to any proslavery ideologue.[19]

The fact that McCord excelled at writing political pieces rather than the supposedly more feminine persuasion of literature has led some scholars, beginning with Simms, to attribute a "masculine" side to her. Most recently, Carmel Chapline has argued that she was the "epitome" and "antithesis" of a southern lady, seeing "herself as male and female, depending on which sphere she occupied at any time." However, such interpretations merely reproduce uncritically the notion of separate spheres. We have no reason to believe that McCord saw herself as anything but a woman, albeit an exceptional woman of a certain class and position. While she had little patience with certain gender conventions, especially as far as she herself was concerned, her championship of female subordination was at least as vigorous as her espousal of slavery. As Fox-Genovese argues, "Her theory of gender relations proved inseparable from her theories of class and race relations."

Not only did McCord uphold the hierarchical nature of all social relations in slave society with a fearful ardency, but she made an individual exception for herself in assuming a public role as a champion of the slave south. Even her daughters were deemed unworthy of too much "school training" and educated informally as befitted women. After decrying female activists who took to the stump, she made a public speech before a crowd serenading her on South Carolina's secession. Indeed, the state's most prominent planter-politicians were serenaded in this fashion on disunion. By 1860, Louisa McCord had managed to carve for herself the role of a leading defender in her state of the slave South, for which she was publicly hailed. Slavery, as many historians have argued, stifled the women's movement in the South, but it certainly led to the path of recognition for McCord.

McCord's career illustrates that as long as women were willing to support their allegedly divinely ordained position in society, they could transcend it as individuals. Ironically, McCord's "accomplishments" as a woman were fundamentally anti-women. Her defense of the oppressive hierarchies of slave society were also theoretically contradictory: she invoked modern ideas of liberal political economy, scientific racism, and womanhood to defend the essentially conservative and hierarchical world of slaveholders. Furthermore, McCord's life and work reveal that women's historical agency has not always been "progressive" and that women as a group are not always found on the right side.[20] As far as Louisa McCord was concerned, the advantages of her class and "race" far outweighed the disabilities of her sex. And she knew it.

NOTES

1. See, for example, Joan Wallach Scott, *Gender and the Politics of History* (New York, 1988); Berenice A. Carroll, *Liberating Women's History: Theoretical and Critical Essays* (Urbana, 1976), espec. Parts I and IV; and Nancy F. Cott and Elizabeth Pleck, eds., *A Heritage of Her Own: Toward a New Social History of American Women* (New York, 1979). For some synthetic overviews, see Carl N. Degler, *At Odds: Women and the Family in America from the Revolution to the Present* (New York, 1980); Mabel E. Deutrich and Virginia C. Purdy, eds., *Clio Was a Woman: Studies in the History of American Women* (Washington, 1980); William H. Chafe, *The American Woman: Her Changing Social, Economic, and Political Roles, 1920–1970* (New York, 1972).

2. Nancy Hewitt, "Beyond the Search for Sisterhood: American Women's History in the 1980s," *Social History* 10 (October 1985): 300; Joan Kelly, "The Doubled Vision of Feminist Theory: A Postscript to the 'Women's Power' Conference," *Feminist Studies* (Spring 1979): 221. Also see Susan Levine, "Labors in the Field: Reviewing Women's Cultural History," *Radical History Review* 35 (April 1986): 56; Elizabeth Fox-Genovese, "Gender,

Class, and Power: Some Theoretical Considerations," *The History Teacher* 15 (February 1982): 255–76 and "Placing Women's History in History," *New Left Review* 133 (May/June 1982): 5–29; Ellen C. DuBois et al., "Politics and Culture in Women's History: A Symposium," *Feminist Studies* 6 (Spring 1980): 26–84.

3. See, for example, Alice Kessler-Harris, *Out to Work: A History of Wage-Earning Women in the United States* (New York, 1982); Thomas Dublin, *Women at Work: The Transformation of Work and Community in Lowell, Massachusetts, 1826–1880* (New York, 1979); Christine Stansell, *City of Women: Sex and Class in New York, 1789–1860* (New York, 1986); Dolores E. Janiewski, *Sisterhood Denied: Race, Gender and Class in a New South Community* (Philadelphia, 1985); Deborah Gray White, *Ar'n't I a Woman? Female Slaves in the Plantation South* (New York, 1985); Jacqueline Jones, *Labor of Love, Labor of Sorrow: Black Women, Work, and the Family from Slavery to the Present* (New York, 1985). Also see Angela Y. Davis, *Women, Race and Class* (New York, 1981); bell hooks, *Ain't I a Woman: Black Women and Feminism* (Boston, 1981).

4. Nancy F. Cott, *The Bonds of Womanhood: "Woman's Sphere" in New England, 1780–1835* (New Haven, 1977); Barbara Welter, "The Cult of True Womanhood: 1800–1860," *American Quarterly* 18 (Summer 1966): 151–74; Carroll Smith-Rosenberg, "The Female World of Love and Ritual: Relations between Women in Nineteenth-Century America," *Signs* 1 (Autumn 1975): 1–29; Katheryn Kish Sklar, *Catherine Beecher: A Study in American Domesticity* (New Haven, 1973); Ann Douglas, *The Feminization of American Culture* (New York, 1977); Mary P. Ryan, *Cradle of the Middle Class: The Family in Oneida County, New York, 1790–1865* (Cambridge, Eng., 1981). Also see Caroll Smith-Rosenberg, *Disorderly Conduct: Visions of Gender in Victorian America* (New York, 1985); Sheila M. Rothman, *Woman's Proper Place: A History of Changing Ideals and Practices, 1870 to the Present* (New York, 1978).

5. See Ellen C. DuBois, *Feminism and Suffrage: The Emergence of an Independent Women's Movement in America, 1848–1860* (New York, 1979); Eleanor Flexner, *Century of Struggle: The Women's Rights Movement in the United States* (Cambridge, Mass., 1975); Keith Melder, *The Beginnings of Sisterhood: The Woman's Rights Movement in the United States, 1800–1840* (New York, 1977); Dorothy Sterling, *Ahead of Her Time: Abby Kelley and the Politics of Antislavery* (New York, 1991); Charles Capper, *Margaret Fuller: An American Romantic Life* (New York, 1992); Dublin, *Women at Work*; Meredith Tax, *The Rising of the Women: Feminist Solidarity and Class Conflict, 1880–1917* (New York, 1980); Aileen S. Kraditor, *The Ideas of the Woman Suffrage Movement, 1890–1920* (New York, 1965); Linda Gordon, *Woman's Body, Woman's Right: A Social History of Birth Control in America* (New York, 1976); Ellen Chesler, *Woman of Valor: Margaret Sanger and the Birth Control Movement in America* (New York, 1992). Also see Linda Gordon, "What's New in Women's History,"

in Teresa de Lauretis, ed., *Feminist Studies, Critical Studies* (Bloomington, Ind., 1986), 21–30, and Elizabeth Fox-Genovese, "The Personal Is not Political Enough," *Marxist Perspectives* 2 (Winter 1979/80): 94–113.

6. Anne Firor Scott, *The Southern Lady From Pedestal to Politics, 1830–1930* (Chicago, 1970); Catherine Clinton, *The Plantation Mistress: Woman's World in the Old South* (New York, 1982); Suzanne Lebsock, *The Free Women of Petersburg: Status and Culture in a Southern Town, 1784–1860* (New York, 1984). Also see Sudie Sides Duncan, "Southern Women and Slavery, Part One," *History Today* 20 (January 1970): 54–60; Margaret Ripley Wolfe, "The Southern Lady: Long Suffering Counterpart of the Good Ole' Boy," *Journal of Popular Culture* II (Summer 1977): 18–27; Jean Friedman, "Women's History and the Revision of Southern History"; and Anne Firor Scott, "Historians Construct the Southern Woman," in Joanne V. Hawks and Sheila L. Skemp, eds., *Sex, Race, and the Role of Women in the South* (Jackson, Miss., 1983), 3–12, 95–110; Elizabeth Fox-Genovese, *Within the Plantation Household: Black and White Women of the Old South* (Chapel Hill, 1988) and *Feminism without Illusions: A Critique of Individualism* (Chapel Hill, 1991), chap. 6; Eugene D. Genovese, "Toward a Kinder and Gentler America: The Southern Lady in the Greening of the Politics of the Old South," in Carol Bleser, ed., *In Joy and Sorrow: Women, Family, Marriage in the Victorian South, 1830–1900* (New York, 1991), 125–35. For a recent work on southern women's history that emphasizes regional distinctiveness and the "community" identity of southern women, see Jean E. Friedman, *The Enclosed Garden: Women and Community in the Evangelical South, 1830–1900* (Chapel Hill, 1985); for a pioneering work on southern women, see Julia Cherry Spruill, *Women's Life and Work in the Southern Colonies* (Chapel Hill, 1938); on the possibilities and limitations of a southern biracial "sisterhood," see Minrose C. Gwin, *Black and White Women of the Old South: The Peculiar Sisterhood in American Literature* (Knoxville, 1985); Catherine Clinton, "'Southern Dishonor': Flesh, Blood, Race, and Bondage," in Bleser, *In Joy and Sorrow*, 52–68, and "Caught in the Web of the Big House: Women and Slavery," in Walter J. Fraser, Jr., et al., eds., *The Web of Southern Relations: Women, Family, and Education* (Athens, Ga., 1985), 19–34.

7. Mary Forrest, *Women of the South: Distinguished in Literature* (New York, 1866), 480–82; James Wood Davidson, *The Living Writers of the South* (New York, 1869), 351–60; Fox-Genovese, *Within the Plantation Household*, chap. 5; Margaret Farrand Thorpe, *Female Persuasion: Six Strong-Minded Women* (New Haven, 1949), 179–214. For details on Louisa McCord's life, see Jessie Melville Fraser, "Louisa C. McCord," M.A. thesis, University of South Carolina, 1919; Carmel E. Chapline, "'A Tragedy in Five Acts': The Life of Louisa S. McCord, 1810–1879," M.A. thesis, The Citadel and The University of Charleston, 1992. On Langdon Cheves and the Cheves family, see Archie Vernon Huff, Jr., *Langdon Cheves of South Carolina* (Columbia, S.C., 1977); Susan Bennett, "The Cheves Family of South Carolina," *South Carolina Historical and Genealogical Magazine*

(SCHGM) 35 (July/October 1934): 79–95, 130–52; [Langdon Cheves], *Occasional Reviews No. I and II* (Charleston, 1832); *Speech of the Honorable Langdon Cheves, Delivered before the Delegates of the Nashville Convention* . . . (Columbia, 1850); Langdon Cheves to David McCord, August 15, 1831, Langdon Cheves Papers, South Caroliniana Library, University of South Carolina. On David McCord, see Susan Smythe Bennett, "The McCords of McCord's Ferry, South Carolina," *SCHGM* 34 (October 1933): 177–93; *Speech of Mr. McCord at a Meeting of the Inhabitants in the Town Hall of Columbia* . . . (Columbia, 1827); Ann Fripp Hampton, ed., *A Divided Heart: Letters of Sally Baxter Hampton, 1853–1862* (Spartanburg, S.C., 1980), 21–23.

8. Many Carolinian slaveholding women shared their husband's political concerns and to a certain extent, their relationships embodied the ideal of companionate marriages. See, for example, William Elliot to his wife, November 24, 29, December 6, 10, 14, 1828, December 1, 9, 1831, September 1, 1851, Elliot-Gonzales Papers, Southern Historical Collection, University of North Carolina; Robert F. W. Allston to his wife, Adele, December 16, 1849, May 24, September 22, 1850, Robert F. W. Allston Papers, South Carolina Historical Society; Elizabeth Perry to Benjamin Perry, November 22, December 13, 1840, December 1, 8, 1844, November 30, 1845, November 30, December 3, 5, 14, 17, 1850, November 27, December 5, 1851, December 14, 1852, Benjamin Perry to Elizabeth Perry, December 16, 1859, April 17, 29, 1860, Benjamin F. Perry Papers, South Caroliniana Library, University of South Carolina; Rebecca Rutledge to Lt. Edward Rutledge, September 6, October 5, 10, November 19, December 18, 1832, January 7, 30, March 9, 1833, Rutledge Family Papers, South Caroliniana Library, University of South Carolina; Laurence Keitt to Sue Sparks Keitt, July 11, 1851, [1855], June 6, 1855, May 10, June 8, 1856, Sue Sparks Keitt to her father, Sunday 26 [1860], Sue Sparks Keitt to A. D. Banks, March 1, 1860, Lawrence Massillon Keitt Papers, Perkins Library, Duke University; Elmer Don Herd, Jr., "Sue Sparks Keitt to a Northern Friend, March 4, 1861," *South Carolina Historical Magazine* 62 (1961): 82–87. Also see Carol Bleser, "The Perrys of Greenville: A Nineteenth-Century Marriage," in Fraser et al., *The Web of Southern Relations*, 72–89.

9. Fox-Genovese, *Within the Plantation Household*. On Carolinian slaveholders' pioneering role in the formulation of proslavery ideology and their cutting edge position in the secession movement, see my "The Counter-Revolution of Slavery: Class, Politics and Ideology in Antebellum South Carolina," Ph.D. diss., Columbia University, 1994.

10. An obvious exception is of course Fox-Genovese, *Within the Plantation Household*, chap. 5; also see chaps. 1 and 7. On Mary Chesnut, see C. Vann Woodward, ed., *Mary Chesnut's Civil War* (New Haven, 1981); Elisabeth Muhlenfeld, *Mary Boykin Chesnut: A Biography* (Baton Rouge, 1981); Drew Gilpin Faust, "In Search of the Real Mary Chesnut," *Reviews in American History* 10 (March 1982): 54–59.

11. Frederic Bastiat, *Sophisms of the Protective Policy*, trans. (from the 2d

French edition). Mrs. D. J. McCord of South Carolina with an Introductory
Letter by Dr. Francis Lieber (New York, 1848). On the nullification crisis,
see William W. Freehling, *Prelude to Civil War: The Nullification Controversy in South Carolina, 1816–1836* (New York, 1965); and my "Counter-
Revolution of Slavery," chaps. 1 and 2.

12. L. S. M. [Louisa Susanna McCord], "Justice and Fraternity," *Southern
Quarterly Review (SQR)* 15 (July 1849): 356–74; idem, "The Right to
Labor," *SQR* 16 (October 1849): 138–60; idem, "Negro and White Slav-
ery—Wherein Do They Differ?" *SQR* 20 (July 1851): 119–20; idem,
"Carey on the Slave Trade," *SQR* 25 (January 1854): 115–53. For a
slightly different view, see Fox-Genovese, *Within the Plantation Household*,
281–82; *Speech of the Honorable Langdon Cheves, Delivered before the
Delegates of the Nashville Convention*; *Speech of Mr. J. A. Woodward, of
South Carolina* (Washington, 1848); *Congressional Globe*, 35th Congress,
1st Session, 68–71. For a classic study of liberal political economy, see
C. B. MacPherson, *The Political Theory of Possessive Individualism: Hob-
bes to Locke* (Oxford, Eng., 1962); on the south as a distinct slave society,
see Eugene D. Genovese, *The Political Economy of Slavery: Studies in the
Economy and Society of the Slave South* (New York, 1965); Eugene D.
Genovese and Elizabeth Fox-Genovese, *The Fruits of Merchant Capital:
Slavery and Bourgeois Property in the Rise and Expansion of Capitalism*
(New York, 1983), chap. 2.

13. L. S. M., "Carey on the Slave Trade," 122–34, 141–52; idem, "British
Philanthropy and American Slavery," *De Bow's Review (DBR)* 14 (March
1853): 277. For the "Cotton is King" argument, see Hammond's speech in
the *Congressional Globe* cited above and E. N. Elliot, ed., *Cotton Is King
and Pro-Slavery Arguments* (Augusta, Ga., 1860): 271–336; for the relationship between slavery and industry, see Genovese, *The Political Economy
of Slavery*, part 3; Fred Bateman and Thomas Weiss, *A Deplorable Scarcity:
The Failure of Industrialization in the Slave Economy* (Chapel Hill, 1981);
Robert S. Starobin, *Industrial Slavery in the South* (New York, 1970).

14. L. S. M., "Diversity of the Races; Its Bearing upon Negro Slavery," *SQR*
(April 1851): 392–419; idem, "Negro and White Slavery—Wherein Do
They Differ?," 118–32; idem, "Negro Mania," *DBR* 12 (May 1852): 507–
24; idem, "Justice and Fraternity," 373–74; idem, "Carey on the Slave
Trade," 162–67; idem, "Charity Which Does Not Begin at Home," *South-
ern Literary Messenger (SLM)* 19 (April 1853): 195; John Bachman, *The
Doctrine of Unity of the Human Race Examined on the Principles of
Science* (Charleston, 1850); John B. Adger, *Christian Mission and African
Colonization* (Columbia, 1857), 18; Stillman Drake, ed., *Discoveries and
Opinions of Galileo* (Garden City, N.Y., 1957), 175–216. Also see William
Stanton, *The Leopard's Spots: Scientific Attitudes toward Race in America,
1815–1859* (Chicago, 1960); Eugene D. Genovese, *"Slavery Ordained of
God": The Southern Slaveholders' View of Biblical History and Modern
Politics* (Gettysburg, Penn., 1985); H. Shelton Smith, *In His Image, But
. . . : Racism in Southern Religion, 1780–1910* (Durham, 1972), chaps. 1–

3; Thomas Virgil Peterson, *Ham and Japheth: The Mythic World of Whites in the Antebellum South* (Metuchen, N.J., 1978). On McCord as a plantation mistress, see Fraser, "Louisa C. McCord," 9–11; Chapline, "A Tragedy in Five Acts," 29–32, 53–67, 160–61, and, on her religious beliefs, 74–77; Thorpe, *Female Persuasion*, 198; Fox-Genovese, *Within the Plantation Household*, 274–76; Dr. E. D. Worthington to David Ross McCord, 1894, "Sketch of Mrs. David J. McCord, by the Hon. William Porcher Miles, Mayor of Charleston, Member of the Confederate Congress, and President of the South Carolina College, 1880," McCord Family Papers. See the idyllic picture of slavery in "Recollections of Louisa Rebecca Hayne McCord," South Caroliniana Library, University of South Carolina.

15. [Edward J. Pringle], *Slavery in the Southern States by a Carolinian* (Cambridge, Mass., 1852), 10–13, 31–32, 47–51; "Stowe's Key to Uncle Tom's Cabin," *SQR* 24 (July 1853): 214–54; Jeanette Reid Tandy, "Pro-Slavery Propaganda in American Fiction of the Fifties," *Southern Atlantic Quarterly* 21 (1922): 41–50; Thorpe, *Female Persuasion*, 205; McCord is quoted in Chapline, "A Tragedy in Five Acts," 94; L. S. M., "Uncle Tom's Cabin," *SQR* 23 (January 1853): 81–120.

16. L. S. M., "Charity Which Does Not Begin at Home," 208; idem, "British Philanthropy and American Slavery," 258–80; idem, "Carey and the Slave Trade," 153–81.

17. L. S. M., "Uncle Tom's Cabin," 90; idem, "Carey on the Slave Trade," 153–69; idem, "British Philanthropy and American Slavery," 279; idem, "Charity Which Does Not Begin at Home," 198; idem, "Enfranchisement of Woman," *SQR* (April 1852): 322–41; idem, "Woman and Her Needs," *DBR* 13 (1852): 267–91; Ernest Barker, ed., *The Politics of Aristotle* (New York, 1958), 8–38; Thomas R. Dew, "Dissertation on the Characteristic Differences between the Sexes," Nos. 2 and 3, *SLM* 1 (July-August 1835): 621–32, 672–91; William Gilmore Simms, "The Morals of Slavery," in *The Pro-Slavery Argument: As Maintained by the Most Distinguished Writers of the Southern States* (Charleston, 1852), 175–285; *The Response* (Charleston, 1848), David James and Louisa Susanna McCord Collection, South Caroliniana Library, University of South Carolina. The poem refers to a northern woman and Martineau was an Englishwoman. But its contents seem to indicate that she was McCord's intended target.

18. Fraser, "Louisa C. McCord"; Chapline, "A Tragedy in Five Acts"; "Recollections of Louisa Rebecca Hayne McCord," and "Sketch of Mrs. McCord by Miss I. D. Martin," McCord Family Papers, South Caroliniana Library, University of South Carolina. On the revolutionary republican ideal of educated motherhood and southern women's education, see Mary Beth Norton, *Liberty's Daughters: The Revolutionary Experience of American Woman, 1750–1800* (Boston, 1980); Linda K. Kerber, *Women of the Republic: Intellect and Ideology in Revolutionary America* (Chapel Hill, 1980); Catherine Clinton, "Equally Their Due: The Education of the Planter Daughter in the Early Republic," *Journal of the Early Republic* 2 (April 1982): 39–60; Steven M. Stowe, "The Not-So-Cloistered Academy: Elite

Women's Education and Family Feeling in the Old South," in Fraser et al., *The Web of Southern Relations*, 90–106. On southern women and the Civil War, see George C. Rable, *Civil Wars*; H. E. Sterkx, *Partners in Rebellion: Alabama Women in the Civil War* (Rutherford, N.J., 1970); Drew Gilpin Faust, *Southern Stories: Slaveholders in Peace and War* (Columbia, Mo., 1992), 113–40, 174–92.

19. "Sketch of Mrs. David J. McCord, by the Hon. William Porcher Miles," McCord Family Papers, South Caroliniana Library, University of South Carolina; Louisa S. McCord, *My Dreams* (Philadelphia, 1848); idem, *Caius Gracchus: A Tragedy in Five Acts* (New York, 1851); Davidson, *The Living Writers of the South*, 351–60; Thorpe, *Female Persuasion*, 186, 194–200.

20. Chapline, "A Tragedy in Five Acts," ii–iv, 93, 96–97, 164–66; "Recollections of Louisa Rebecca Hayne McCord," 23–24; Fox-Genovese, *Within the Plantation Household*, 281; Hewitt, "Beyond the Search for Sisterhood," 315–16.

REFERENCES

Adger, John B. *Christian Mission and African Colonization.* Columbia, 1857.

Bachman, John. *The Doctrine of Unity of the Human Race Examined on the Principles of Science.* Charleston, 1850.

Barker, Ernest, ed. *The Politics of Aristotle.* New York, 1958.

Bastiat, Frederic. *Sophisms of the Protective Policy.* Translated from the 2d French ed. by Mrs. D. J. McCord of South Carolina with an Introductory Letter by Dr. Francis Lieber. New York, 1848.

Bateman, Fred, and Weiss, Thomas. *A Deplorable Scarcity: The Failure of Industrialization in the Slave Economy.* Chapel Hill, 1981.

Bennett, Susan. "The Cheves Family of South Carolina." *South Carolina Historical and Genealogical Magazine* 35 (July/October 1934): 79–95, 130–52.

———. "The McCords of McCord's Ferry, South Carolina." *South Carolina Historical and Genealogical Magazine* 34 (October 1933): 177–93.

Bleser, Carol, ed. *In Joy and Sorrow: Women, Family, Marriage in the Victorian South, 1830–1900.* New York, 1991.

Capper, Charles. *Margaret Fuller: An American Romantic Life.* New York, 1992.

Carroll, Berenice A. *Liberating Women's History: Theoretical and Critical Essays.* Urbana, Ill., 1976.

Chafe, William H. *The American Woman: Her Changing Social, Economic, and Political Roles, 1920–1970.* New York, 1972.

Chapline, Carmel E. "'A Tragedy in Five Acts': The Life of Louisa S. McCord, 1810–1879." M.A. Thesis, The Citadel and The University of Charleston, 1992.

Chesler, Ellen. *Woman of Valor: Margaret Sanger and the Birth Control Movement in America.* New York, 1992.

[Cheves, Langdon]. *Occasional Reviews Nos. 1 and 2.* Charleston, 1832.

————. *Speech of the Honorable Langdon Cheves, Delivered before the Delegates of Nashville.* Columbia, 1985.

Clinton, Catherine. "Equally Their Due: The Education of the Planter Daughter in the Early Republic." *Journal of the Early Republic* 2 (April 1982): 39–60.

————. *The Plantation Mistress: Woman's World in the Old South.* New York, 1982.

Clinton, Catherine, and Nina Silber, eds. *Divided House: Gender and the Civil War.* New York, 1993.

Congressional Globe, 35th Congress, 1st Session, 68–71.

Cott, Nancy F. *The Bonds of Womanhood: "Woman's Sphere" in New England, 1780–1835.* New Haven, 1977.

Cott, Nancy F., and Elizabeth Pleck, eds. *A Heritage of Her Own: Toward a New Social History of American Women.* New York, 1976.

Davidson, James Wood. *The Living Writers of the South.* New York, 1869.

Davis, Angela Y. *Women, Race and Class.* New York, 1981.

Degler, Carl N. *At Odds: Women and the Family in America from the Revolution to the Present.* New York, 1980.

Deutrich, Mable E., and Virginia C. Purdy. *Clio Was a Woman: Studies in the History of American Women.* Washington, 1980.

Dew, Thomas R. "Dissertation on the Characteristic Differences between the Sexes." *Southern Literary Messenger* 1 (July-August 1835): 621–32, 672–91.

Douglas, Ann. *The Feminization of American Culture.* New York, 1977.

Drake, Stillman, ed. *Discoveries and Opinions of Galileo.* Garden City, N.Y., 1957.

Dublin, Thomas. *Women at Work: The Transformation of Work and Community in Lowell, Massachusetts, 1826–1880.* New York, 1979.

DuBois, Ellen C. *Feminism and Suffrage: The Emergence of an Independent Women's Movement in America, 1848–1860.* New York, 1979.

DuBois, Ellen C., et al. "Politics and Culture in Women's History: A Symposium." *Feminist Studies* 6 (Spring 1980): 26–84.

Duncan, Sudie Sides. "Southern Women and Slavery, Part One." *History Today* 20 (January 1970): 54–60.

Elliot, E. N., ed. *Cotton Is King and Pro-Slavery Arguments.* Augusta, Ga., 1860.

Faust, Drew Gilpin. *Southern Stories: Slaveholders in Peace and War.* Columbia, Mo., 1992.

Flexner, Eleanor. *Century of Struggle: The Women's Rights Movement in the United States.* Cambridge, Mass., 1975.

Forrest, Mary. *Women of the South Distinguished in Literature.* New York, 1866.

Fox-Genovese, Elizabeth. *Feminism without Illusions: A Critique of Individualism.* Chapel Hill, 1991.

————. "Gender, Class, and Power: Some Theoretical Considerations." *The History Teacher* 15 (February 1982): 255–76.

————. "The Personal Is Not Political Enough." *Marxist Perspectives* 2 (Winter 1979/80): 94–113.

————. "Placing Women's History in History." *New Left Review* 133 (May/June 1982): 5–29.

————. *Within the Plantation Household: Black and White Women of the Old South.* Chapel Hill, 1988.

Fraser, Jessie Melville. "Louisa C. McCord." M.A. Thesis, University of South Carolina, 1919.

Fraser, Walter J., Jr., et al., eds. *The Web of Southern Relations: Women, Family and Education.* Athens, Ga., 1985.

Freehling, William W. *Prelude to Civil War: The Nullification Controversy in South Carolina, 1816–1836.* New York, 1965.

Friedman, Jean. *The Enclosed Garden: Women and Community in the Evangelical South, 1830–1900.* Chapel Hill, 1985.

Genovese, Eugene D. *The Political Economy of Slavery: Studies in the Economy and Society of the Slave South.* New York, 1965.

————. *"Slavery Ordained of God": The Southern Slaveholders' View of Biblical History and Modern Politics.* Gettysburg, Penn., 1985.

Genovese, Eugene D., and Elizabeth Fox-Genovese. *The Fruits of Merchant Capital: Slavery in the Rise and Expansion of Capitalism.* New York, 1983.

Gordon, Linda. *Woman's Body, Woman's Right: A Social History of Birth Control in America.* New York, 1976.

Gwin, Minrose C. *Black and White Women of the Old South: The Peculiar Sisterhood in American Literature.* Knoxville, 1985.

Hampton, Ann Fripp, ed. *A Divided Heart: Letters of Sally Baxter Hampton, 1853–1862.* Spartanburg, S.C., 1980.

Hawks, Joanne V., and Sheila L. Skemp, eds. *Sex, Race, and the Role of Women in the South.* Jackson, Miss., 1983.

Herd, Elmer Don, Jr. "Sue Sparks Keitt to a Northern Friend, March 4, 1861." *South Carolina Historical Magazine* 62 (1961): 82–87.

Hewitt, Nancy. "Beyond the Search for Sisterhood: American Women's History in the 1980s." *Social History* 10 (October 1985): 300–321.

hooks, bell. *Ain't I a Woman: Black Women and Feminism.* Boston, 1981.

Huff, Archie Vernon, Jr. *Langdon Cheves of South Carolina.* Columbia, S.C., 1977.

Janiewski, Dolores E. *Sisterhood Denied: Race, Gender and Class in a New South Community.* Philadelphia, 1985.

Jenkins, William Sumner. *Pro-Slavery Thought in the Old South.* Reprint. Gloucester, Mass., 1960.

Jones, Jacqueline. *Labor of Love, Labor of Sorrow: Black Women, Work, and the Family from Slavery to the Present.* New York, 1985.

Kelly, Joan. "The Doubled Vision of Feminist Theory: A Postscript to the 'Women's Power' Conference." *Feminist Studies* (Spring 1979): 216–27.

Kerber, Linda K. *Women of the Republic: Intellect and Ideology in Revolutionary America.* Chapel Hill, 1980.

Kessler-Harris, Alice. *Out to Work: A History of Wage-Earning Women in the United States.* New York, 1982.

Kraditor, Aileen S. *The Ideas of the Woman Suffrage Movement, 1890–1920.* New York, 1965.
Lauretis, Teresa de, ed. *Feminist Studies, Critical Studies.* Bloomington, Ind., 1986.
Lebsock, Suzanne. *The Free Women of Petersburg: Status and Culture in a Southern Town, 1784–1860.* New York, 1984.
Levine, Susan. "Labors in the Field: Reviewing Women's Cultural History." *Radical History Review* 35 (April 1986): 49–56.
MacPherson, C. B. *The Political Theory of Possessive Individualism: Hobbes to Locke.* Oxford, Eng., 1962.
[McCord, David J.] *Speech of Mr. McCord at a Meeting of the Inhabitants in the Town Hall of Columbia.* Columbia, S.C., 1827.
[McCord, Louisa S.] L. S. M. "British Philanthropy and American Slavery." *De Bow's Review* 14 (March 1853): 258–80.
——. *Caius Gracchus: A Tragedy in Five Acts.* New York, 1851.
——. "Carey on the Slave Trade." *Southern Quarterly Review* 25 (January 1854): 115–53.
——. "Charity Which Does Not Begin at Home." *Southern Literary Messenger* 19 (April 1853): 193–208.
——. "Diversity of the Races; Its Bearing upon Negro Slavery." *Southern Quarterly Review* (April 1851): 392–419.
——. "Enfranchisement of Woman." *Southern Quarterly Review* 21 (April 1852): 322–41.
——. "Justice and Fraternity." *Southern Quarterly Review* 15 (July 1849): 356–74.
——. *My Dreams.* Philadelphia, 1848.
——. "Negro Mania." *De Bow's Review* 12 (May 1852): 507–24.
——. "Negro and White Slavery—Wherein Do They Differ?" *Southern Quarterly Review* 20 (July 1851): 118–32.
——. *The Response.* Charleston, 1848.
——. "The Right to Labor." *Southern Quarterly Review* 16 (October 1849): 138–60.
——. "Uncle Tom's Cabin." *Southern Quarterly Review* 23 (January 1853): 81–120.
——. "Woman and Her Needs." *De Bow's Review* 13 (September 1852): 267–91.
Melder, Keith. *The Beginnings of Sisterhood: The Women's Rights Movement in the United States, 1800–1840.* New York, 1977.
Muhlenfield, Elisabeth. *Mary Boykin Chesnut: A Biography.* Baton Rouge, 1981.
Norton, Mary Beth. *Liberty's Daughters: The Revolutionary Experience of American Woman, 1750–1800.* Boston, 1980.
Peterson, Thomas Virgil. *Ham and Japheth: The Mythic World of Whites in the Antebellum South.* Metuchen, N.J., 1978.
[Pringle, Edward]. *Slavery in the Southern States by a Carolinian.* Cambridge, Mass.,1852.

The Pro-Slavery Argument; As Maintained by the Most Distinguished Writers of the Southern States. Charleston, 1852.

Rable, George C. *Civil Wars: Women and the Crisis of Southern Nationalism.* Urbana, 1989.

"Recollections of Louisa Rebecca Hayne McCord." South Caroliniana Library, University of South Carolina.

Rothman, Sheila M. *Woman's Proper Place: A History of Changing Ideals and Practices, 1870 to the Present.* New York, 1978.

Ryan, Mary P. *Cradle of the Middle Class: The Family in Oneida County, New York, 1790–1865.* Cambridge, Eng., 1981.

Scott, Anne Firor. *The Southern Lady: From Pedestal to Politics, 1830–1930.* Chicago, 1970.

Scott, Joan Wallach. *Gender and the Politics of History.* New York, 1988.

Sinha, Manisha. "The Counter-Revolution of Slavery: Class, Politics and Ideology in Antebellum South Carolina." Ph.D. diss., Columbia University, 1994.

Sklar, Kathryn Kish. *Catherine Beecher: A Study in American Domesticity.* New Haven, 1973.

Smith, H. Shelton. *In His Image, But . . . : Racism in Southern Religion, 1780–1910.* Durham, N.C., 1972.

Smith-Rosenberg, Carroll. "The Female World of Love and Ritual: Relations between Women in Nineteenth Century America." *Signs* 1 (Autumn 1975): 1–29.

———. *Disorderly Conduct: Visions of Gender in Victorian America.* New York, 1985.

Spruill, Julia Cherry. *Women's Life and Work in the Southern Colonies.* Chapel Hill, 1938.

Stansell, Christine. *City of Women: Sex and Class in New York, 1789–1860.* New York, 1986.

Stanton, William. *The Leopard's Spots: Scientific Attitudes toward Race in America, 1815–1859.* Chicago, 1960.

Starobin, Robert S. *Industrial Slavery in the South.* New York, 1970.

Sterkx, H. E. *Partners in Rebellion: Alabama Women in the Civil War.* Rutherford, N.J., 1970.

Sterling, Dorothy. *Ahead of Her Times: Abby Kelley and the Politics of Antislavery.* New York, 1991.

"Stowe's Key to Uncle Tom's Cabin." *Southern Quarterly Review* 24 (July 1853): 215–54.

Tandy, Jeanette Reid. "Pro-Slavery Propaganda in American Fiction of the Fifties." *South Atlantic Quarterly* 21 (1922): 41–50.

Tax, Meredith. *The Rising of the Women: Feminist Solidarity and Class Conflict, 1880–1917.* New York, 1980.

Thorpe, Margaret Farrand. *Female Persuasion: Six Strong-Minded Women.* New Haven, 1949.

Welter, Barbara. "The Cult of True Womanhood, 1800–1860." *American Quarterly* 18 (Summer 1966): 151–74.

White, Deborah Gray. *Ar'n't I a Woman? Female Slave in the Plantation South.* New York, 1985.

Wiley, Bell Irvin. *Confederate Women.* Westport, Conn., 1975.

Wolfe, Margaret Ripley. "The Southern Lady: Long Suffering Counterpart of the Good Ole' Boy." *Journal of Popular Culture* II (Summer 1977): 18–27.

Woodward, C. Vann, ed. *Mary Chesnut's Civil War.* New Haven, 1981.

Woodward, C. Vann, and Elisabeth Muhlenfeld. *The Private Mary Chesnut: The Unpublished Civil War Diaries.* New York, 1984.

[Woodward, J. A.] *Speech of Mr. J. A. Woodward, of South Carolina.* Washington, 1848.

MANUSCRIPT COLLECTIONS

Allston, Robert F. W. Papers. South Carolina Historical Society, Charleston.

Cheves, Langdon. Papers. South Caroliniana Library, University of South Carolina, Columbia.

Elliot-Gonzales Papers. Southern Historical Collection, University of North Carolina, Chapel Hill.

Keitt, Lawrence Massillon. Papers. Perkins Library, Duke University, Durham, N.C.

McCord Family. Papers. South Caroliniana Library, University of South Carolina, Columbia.

Perry, Benjamin F. Papers. South Caroliniana Library, University of South Carolina, Columbia.

Rutledge Family. Papers. South Caroliniana Library, University of South Carolina, Columbia.

4.

WOMANISM REVISITED: WOMEN AND THE (AB)USE OF POWER IN *THE COLOR PURPLE*

TUZYLINE JITA ALLAN

The sisterhood that is necessary for the making of feminist revolution can be achieved only when all women disengage themselves from the hostility, jealousy, and competition with one another that has kept us vulnerable, weak, and unable to envision new realities.

—bell hooks, *Ain't I a Woman*

In this country, lesbianism is a poverty—as is being brown, as is being a woman, as is being just plain poor. The danger lies in ranking the oppressions. *The danger lies in failing to acknowledge the specificity of the oppression.* . . . Without an emotional heartfelt grappling with the source of our own oppression, without naming the enemy within ourselves and outside of us, no authentic, non-hierarchical connection among oppressed groups can take place.

—Cherríe Moraga, "La Güera"

The woman-centered universe of *The Color Purple* is often cited as the definitive womanist feature of Alice Walker's Pulitzer-Prize-winning novel. Critics have pointed to the text's inscription of an unoppressive, nonhierarchical model of power relations, as indicative of the author's unimpeachable pro-woman stance.[1] Black women in the novel, for example, are seen as bearers of what Michael Awkward calls "(comm)u-

nity," a collective sense of "expressive power" informed by a "supportive" sisterhood (Awkward 1989). Awkward does not use the term
"womanist" to describe this communal ideal, but he provides an accurate chart of its development through a power-sharing women's cooperative that subverts male dominance. The creative flowering of Celie,
Mary Agnes, and Shug Avery, he argues, comprises the richest portion
of a harvest produced by the politics of nondomination initiated by the
women in the novel.

While Walker's recreation of the dynamics of power in *The Color
Purple* clearly focuses on women's solidarist attitudes, the radical nature
of her womanist imaginary is overlooked by attempts to locate women
in the novel outside the sphere of destructive power play. "Womanist"
behavior, in addition to being woman-identified, is first and foremost
"audacious," "willful," and probing.[2] In *The Color Purple* it takes the
form of an investigative interest in the exercise of power, not only by
men against women but also fundamentally by women against each
other. The novel's exploration of intra-female oppression based on race
and class, like its account of black male misogyny, is part of a womanist
strategy to challenge both traditional and nontraditional power structures that block human liberation.

Walker's introduction in 1982 of this complex model of power relations coincided with a fledgling, albeit rapidly growing, feminist discourse engaged in sculpting an identity from gender opposition. Consequently, feminist critique of *The Color Purple* has focused on male
hegemonic dominance and has generally ignored oppressive power relations among women. In the wake of current feminist rethinking of the
dynamics of power, an examination of the novel's offensive against
abusive assertions of power by women is likely to yield useful insights
into the subversive performance of womanism. Jana Sawicki's (1991: 8)
advocacy of "a radically pluralist feminism" imbued with Foucauldian
insights on power formation suggests a readiness by some feminist critics
to resketch the contours of domination and move them beyond their
current deterministic gender boundaries into the orbit of intrasexual relations.[3]

Walker's running critique of the internecine nature of women's relationships is documented in her collection of womanist essays, *In Search
of Our Mothers' Gardens*. She is an early and harsh commentator on
the colonizing economy of white feminist discourse, particularly the
exclusion of black women from critical and theoretical reconfigurations

of womanhood. Like Audre Lorde, she also rips at a bloated black female anti-self that feeds on colorism, homophobia, and careerism.[4] In other words, through womanist agency Walker has long recognized the need for feminism to reconstruct, if not destabilize, the oppressive subject in order to account for nonmasculinist circuits of power use, such as localized forms of female self-sabotage. An astute observer of the damaging authority concentrated within partriarchal centers of power, she is equally attentive to the self-wounding ways the female fringe shows strains of male domination. *The Color Purple* pivots around this dual concern, although the climate of opinion has unduly favored the novel's proscription against the tyranny of female violation by men. My essay is therefore prompted by the desire to reexamine the unequal distribution of power in the novel with a view to broaching the vexing issue of woman-abusive women.

First, however, I need to elaborate Walker's view of patriarchal power, lest her critique of same-sex oppression be misread as an act of blaming the victim. In *The Color Purple* patriarchy is conceived both as a micro- and macro-force. The former is black and localized, a discretionary power that runs amok until its assault on black women is repelled by the aggressive assertion of female subjecthood. This micropower and its eventual defeat have borne sufficient scrutiny to forego further discussion here. The latter—white, systemic, and implacable—communicates the terrible reality of institutionalized power. Its capacity to destroy the racial, sexual, and cultural other is infinite. Walker's acute awareness of this fact underscores the difference between her thinking about power and Foucault's. The Foucauldian injunction to "eschew the model of the Leviathan in the study of power" (Foucault 1980: 102) embodies, as Sawicki aptly notes, a "self-refusal [that] may be an appropriate practice for a privileged white male intellectual as Foucault, [but] . . . is less obviously strategic for feminists and other disempowered groups" (1991: 106).

Walker has no illusions about the omnipotence and ubiquity of the dominant class. In *The Color Purple,* for example, she recognizes in the brutal force that subdues Sofia on behalf of a small-town mayor in America a historical contiguity with the imperialistic plunder of an African village thousands of miles away. And in *Meridian* she leaves no doubt that there is a mismatch between ruler and ruled, no matter how resistant the latter may be. Louvinie's act of self-recovery, for instance, stirs the wrath of the powerful and her de-tongueing completes her objectification as slave. Similarly, Meridian's stubborn will all but guarantees her destruction. Her emaciated body is proof of the high cost of rebellion.

For Walker, then, there is a pinnacle position of power, delineated in her work as white patriarchy, against which resistance is both necessary and tenuous—necessary because of what Roy Boyne describes as the dominant group's "desire for the death of the other" (1990: 143) and tenuous because of what she sees as the collaborative promise held by local regimes of power. In *The Color Purple,* white patriarchal power is pushed down to the level of an undercurrent (albeit a strong one) to allow micro-patterns of domination to emerge and display their own vicious intensity. This viciousness by itself can be destructive, but Walker detects a greater problem in the way it helps to maintain the dominant power structure. To enlist an example, the two rape acts in the novel are yoked together as much by violence as by the image of the black woman as sexual object, and since the image originates in white patriarchy, Pa's rape of Celie lends tacit but strong support to the (white) sheriff's violation of Mary Agnes.

The novel's disclosure of female self-abuse and complicity in patriarchy may be less provocative than its portrait of black sexism, but the purpose is the same: to petition for an understanding of and end to the irrepressible desire to dominate. The overwhelming evidence of female solidarity in the novel is an outcome achieved at the cost of some embarrassing revelations concerning the reality of women's relationships, the most disturbing of which points to a sisterhood in peril, buffeted by racial and class divisions, as well as sexual competition. Sofia's humiliation and deathly beating, for example, offer an instructive paradigm of the power gap between black and white women and of the latter's willingness to use this fact to their advantage.

The paternalistic gaze the Mayor's wife fixes on Sofia at first registers a stereotype: the black woman as breeder, her strong-toothed children as "[c]ute as buttons" (86). Her "going on over colored" (86) may very well have culminated in coin-giving to the other woman's children, like Flannery O'Connor's race-crazed heroine in "Everything That Rises Must Converge,"[5] had her gaze not shifted onto the prize-fighter's car and Sofia's wristwatch. These status symbols furnish her with a different view of Sofia, one that suddenly threatens her class privilege and provokes jealousy and, consequently, a cutting-down-to-size reaction: "Would you like to work for me, be my maid?" (86). The lesson in humiliation also serves to confirm Sofia's racial inferiority. It is a painful reminder that neither shared gender nor economic success can make Sofia an equal of the white woman she is forced to call, in the vocabulary of subordination, "Miz Millie."

Reduced to virtual slavery, Sofia, however, continues to outshine her mistress, as one of Nettie's letters to Celie makes clear: "I don't know if you have ever seen the mayor's wife. She looks like a wet cat. And there was her maid looking like the very last person in the world you'd expect to see waiting on anybody, and in particular not on anybody that looked like that" (123). Nettie's depoliticized narrative of difference reverses the order of otherness, relocating it not within the confines of race but in that intangible entity known as personality. Miz Millie's self-defeating demeanor, however, bespeaks less of a natural state of docility than her own colonization within the gender system. However, crippled by her gender, Miz Millie is simultaneously enabled by her race and class, a fact that conspires against sisterly connection between herself and her maid.

During her costly initiation into same-sex politics, Sofia discovers that Miz Millie's privileged social status is fully protected from the racial "other" under white patriarchy. The crushing blow she is dealt as punishment for her intransigence is aimed both at her body and spirit. It is a culturally endorsed act, one that is intended to bring defiant blacks to heel, and Miz Millie's complicity extends beyond her role as provoker and silent spectator. Intimidated from the very beginning by Sofia's fecund appearance, she tries to de-sex her. "They won't let me see my children. They won't let me see no mens" (101), Sofia laments. Finally, in a rare moment of recognition of their shared vulnerability in patriarchy—when her husband buys her a car because "colored . . . have cars" (100) but will not stoop to teach her how to drive—Miz Millie turns to Sofia for mutual comfort: driving lessons in exchange for a day's family visit. Sofia ends up the loser in this deal, her full day of family reunion shrunk to fifteen minutes. "White folks is a miracle of affliction" is how she sums up the experience (103), replicating her mistress's habit of defining the other in strictly racial terms.

Eleanor Jane's avowed affection for Sofia undercuts her mother's cooperation in the oppression of the servant woman. To her Sofia is more a surrogate mother than a maid, a poignant reversal of Miss Millie's de-sexing tactics. Walker's displacement of Miss Millie as mother does not only have a basis in historical fact—the black slave woman as primary nurturer of white children—it also textually has the effect of evening the parental score between mistress and maid. When Sofia finally returns to her children, Eleanor Jane, in a gesture tantamount to a renunciation of her racist parents, opts for Sofia's expansive and inclusive family.

This is no display of false emotion by Eleanor Jane, but rather a real act of self-salvation made possible by Sofia's hard-hitting honesty. Sofia disabuses Eleanor Jane of the naive and racist assumption that oppressed blacks have a constitutional fondness for their white oppressors, an assumption that underwrites her attempt to draw from Sofia a confession of love for her son, Reynolds Stanley Earl. A quiet authoritarianism belies Eleanor Jane's polite tag questions, turning what could have been a friendly rapport into a coercive interrogation:

> Ain't Little Reynolds sweet? say Miss Eleanor Jane, to Sofia. Daddy just love him, she say. Love having a grandchild name for him and look so much like him, too. . . .
> And so smart, say Eleanor Jane. Daddy say he never saw a smarter baby. . . .
> Don't you think he sweet? she ast again.
> He sure fat, say Sofia. . . .
> But he sweet, too, say Eleanor Jane. And he smart. . . .
> Ain't he the smartest baby you ever saw? she ast Sofia.
> He got a nice size head on him, say Sofia. You know some peoples place a lot of weight on head size. . . .
> Just a sweet, smart, cute, *innocent* little baby boy, say Miss Eleanor Jane. Don't you just love him? she ast Sofia point blank. (232)

Sofia correctly reads this mind-bending inquiry as an arrogant attempt to dismiss her own feelings of hurt and humiliation built up during twelve years of servitude in the Mayor's household. Her response, therefore, is also "point blank": "No ma'am . . . I do not love Reynolds Stanley Earl. . . . That's what you been trying to find out ever since he was born. And now you know" (233). Stunned by this bald-faced honesty, Eleanor Jane retreats into the racial underbrush of her thinking, accusing Sofia of being an "unnatural" exception to the colored-women-love-white-children rule. Sofia, in turn, seizes the opportunity to shatter the myth of the black mammy, whose overlove for the white child indelibly inscribes her self-hatred. "I love children," she replies. "But all the colored women that say they love yours is lying. They don't love Reynolds Stanley any more than I do. . . . Some colored people so scared of whitefolks they claim to love the cotton gin" (233). By conflating Reynolds Stanley, oppressor-to-be, and the cotton gin, that notorious symbol of black oppression and exploitation, Sofia hopes to uncover the benign imperialism undergirding Eleanor Jane's love game. Refusing to play on an uneven field of racial love, Sofia forces her young mistress to adopt an alternative practice of affective reciprocity. Later, as an active caretaker of Henrietta, Sofia's sick daughter, and a dedicated employee of her former maid, Eleanor Jane demonstrates her willingness to open up the field to allow for equal participation.

Womanist exploration of the dynamics of female self-oppression in *The Color Purple* extends beyond racial and class boundaries into the less traveled region of black women's interpersonal relationships where Walker sees a lure of domination that is equally strong. The idea of black women as agents of their own oppression is yet to take hold within black feminist discourse in light of the more urgent need to address the corrosive impact of race and gender oppression on black female identity. In fact, the effort to recuperate this identity has created a tendency to valorize black women's relationships. According to Gloria Naylor, for example, "Black women have always had each other when we had very little else" (Naylor and Morrison 1985: 578). The sentiment is echoed in Mary Helen Washington's analysis of black women's literary tradition: "Women talk to other women in this tradition and their friendships with other women—mothers, sisters, grandmothers, friends, lovers—are vital to their growth and well-being" (1987: xxi). And, although the following statement by Gloria I. Joseph refers specifically to black mother/daughter relationships, it represents the thinking among black women about their sense of communality: "The interpersonal problems and conflicts are transcended to accommodate the cooperative effort needed to solve the common problems they face as black women in today's America" (1981: 94). This wish for transcendence often produces what Walker, admitting her own complicity in the matter, refers to as "a deep reluctance to criticize other black women" (1983: 322).

Some black women, however, share Audre Lorde's counterimpulse "to confront and wade through the racist constructs underlying our deprivation of each other" (1984: 64). Lorde sees black women's relationships as troublingly paradoxical: "unmentionably clear and immeasurably dangerous" (1984: 157), the former instinct stemming from shared suffering and the latter produced by racist and sexist conditioning. In her aptly titled essay, "Eye to Eye," she cuts through the surface romanticism of these relationships and uncovers a deep reservoir of "harshness that exists so often within the least encounter between black women, the judgment and the sizing up, that cruel refusal to connect" (1984: 159).

Her avowed reluctance notwithstanding, Walker too has noted with anguish the self-cancelling modes of relation between black women, ranging from skin color intolerance to an exacting pro-black-male loyalty.[6] She recalls a painful experience during a 1973 symposium on black women when her effort to rally her educated, well-heeled audience around the increasing suicide rate among black women was met with a strong antifeminist reaction. Walker writes: "I will never forget my sense of horror and betrayal when one of the panelists said to me (and to the rest of that august body of women gathered there): 'The responsibility of the black woman is to support the black man; *whatever* he does'" (1983: 317). For Walker, this public testimony against black womanhood, rooted in black Nationalist gender ideology of the 1960s, is a reliable gauge of black woman's disloyalty to each other, clearly "a dangerous state of affairs that has its logical end in self-destructive behavior" (1983: 318).

In *The Color Purple,* the author traces the patterns of such behavior within the intimate sphere of black women's relationships. If race and class are the levers of power for Miss Millie and Eleanor Jane, sexual competition underpins the oppressive acts of the black female characters. Shug Avery's admonition that "you have to git men off your eyeball, before you can see anything a'tall" (179) serves as an ironic reminder of the myriad ways this fundamental feminist tenet is breached by black women in the text. A good place to start is with Shug's own infractions of the principle she so cogently articulates. Critics have generally praised Shug for her liberated sexual ethic, practiced with the éclat of a *femme fatale,* and in the process have overlooked the way in which her actions serve the interest of patriarchy. Little has been said about Shug's near-pathological heterosexist complex and even less about how it crystallizes around the oppression of other women. She admits, for example, to feeding her sexual appetite for Albert at the emotional expense of two already exploited women—Annie Julia and Celie. Her confessed treatment of the former shows her to be more than a home-wrecker. Like a man, Shug enjoys the thrill of female conquest: "I went to school with Annie Julia. . . . She was pretty, mean, Black as anything, and skin just as smooth, Big black eyes look like moons. And sweet, too. Hell . . . I liked her myself. Why I hurt her so? I used to keep Albert away from home for a week at the time. She'd come and beg him for money to buy groceries for the children" (116–17).

This confession is being made to Celie, who has also been stung by the acrimony Shug reserves for her replacements in Albert's home. First dismissed as ugly, Celie too will come to be seen as "sweet," then coveted (and possessed) and later "hurt" by being cast aside for Shug's new male interests—Grady and Germaine. The few teardrops that accompany her confession are thrown into ironic perspective by the unapologetically egocentric conclusion: "I never really wanted Albert for a husband. But just to choose me . . . cause nature had already done it" (117). On display here is a self-possession that has scored points with feminist critics who have not been able to detect its androcentric quality. Celie too is enamored of Shug, but she rightly interprets the text of Shug's self-imagining as male-inspired. Her verdict, rendered at another occasion when Shug compliments Sofia on "look[ing] like a good time" is that "Shug talk and act sometime like a man" (82).

Shug's willful cultivation of male behavior accords with, on the one hand, her nonvictim status (the only woman in the novel thus privileged) and the oppressive aspect of her self-identity, on the other. In her critique of what she considers to be the novel's endorsement of heterosexuality, bell hooks makes the interesting point that Shug's "name suggests that she has the power to generate excitement without the ability to provide substantive nourishment" (Gates 1990: 457). Put another way, Shug is trapped within a tantalizing male sexual economy that thrives on victimization rather than emotional fulfillment. Her proto-victim is Celie, whom she soothes out of Albert's punishing grip, resexualizes through lesbianism, and abandons for young, virile men. As the novel concludes, Albert asks Celie if she dislikes him because he is male. Feeling sufficiently rehabilitated, she throws a jab at her former oppressor: "Take they pants off . . . and men look like frogs to me. No matter how you kiss 'em . . . frogs is what they stay" (224). This revised ending to a famous fairy tale unwittingly implicates Shug, who also is incapable of complete surrender to the transformative power of Celie's love. Homophobia, unlike race and class, does not serve as an active agent of oppression in the novel. Yet Walker suggests through Shug's sexual titillation of and retreat from Celie the exploitative potential inherent in lesbian relationships.

In a conversation with Toni Morrison, Gloria Naylor includes in her comments on the death of Sula and Nel's friendship, in Morrison's celebrated novel *Sula,* a statement about sexual competition between black women: "We do share our men. We may not like it very much, but there is a silent consensus about that and it really hasn't torn us apart as women" (1985: 578). If the truth of this remark is debatable in real life, in *The Color Purple* it is argued even more vigorously. Walker agrees with Celie that "wherever there's a man, there's trouble" (186), but she also thinks that the truism masks women's collaboration in this trouble-making. She aims, therefore, to force recognition of the debilitating conflicts between women that complicate the vision of female bonding.

A case in point is the emotional fallout that contaminates the burgeoning friendship between Corrine and Nettie. At first glance, this relationship contrasts sharply with the one that exists between Miz Millie and Sofia. For one, Nettie is not forced into Corrine's employ and she certainly does not suffer the brutal act of disempowerment visited on Sofia. Moreover, Nettie's employment status—she is a governess, not a maid—puts her on a near-equal social footing with Corrine. Nettie may lack her employers' distinguished, middle-class background and its attendant racial uplift ideology, but she is sufficiently educated, adventurous, and race-conscious to feel comfortable in their philanthropic circles. A narrow social gap thus separates Corrine and Nettie to allow for mutual respect, the key ingredient missing in the mistress/servant arrangement between Miz Millie and Sofia.

Respect, however, fails to translate into real friendship. Beneath the surface of Christian fellowship, sexual jealousy of the unvenial sort smolders and eventually erupts in bitter confrontation. While this flash point occurs outside the militarized racial zone of Miz Millie's battle with Sofia, it burns with equal emotional intensity. Corrine invokes the power of her identification as married woman to perform a drastic reduction of her single "sister's" self-image which, though less ebullient than Sofia's, is just as strongly defined. Recasting Nettie as a usurper armed with fecund youth, Corrine unleashes a stunning accusation that chokes off the flow of amiable feeling between herself and Nettie and reveals her own entrapment within patriarchal ideology.

Corrine succumbs to what Adrienne Rich describes as "the pressures on women to validate themselves in maternity" (1986: ix). Her irrepressible desire to mother (reflected in her career choice), her body's inability to reproduce, and her stern faith in the marriage contract all together yield a poisonous mix of paranoia and self-loathing intended for Nettie's consumption and ultimately consuming Corrine herself. This emotional contagion is administered to Nettie in two shocking doses. The first takes the form of a gory ritual of divestiture. Corrine seeks to dispel the Olinka women's and her own suspicions about Nettie's likely maternal link to Adam and Olivia by dispossessing her "rival." Nettie is stripped of not only Corrine's clothes but, more importantly, the close bond that has existed between her adopted family and herself. She is told to replace the intimacy of first-name-based greeting with the religious formality of "brother and sister" in her transactions with the missionary couple and to disavow the children's term of endearment ("Mama Nettie"). This expulsion from the shareable confines of family combines with Nettie's already outsider status within Olinka society to effect her double erasure.

Having pared down her sexual "rival" to a debilitating otherness, Corrine still feels unvindicated. Her next despotic act subjects Nettie's body to a perverse reading for signs of culpability: the indelible inscription of maternity on the female known as "stretch marks." The evidence would more than justify Nettie's humiliation. It would be, from Corrine's married and missionary perspectives, grounds for the moral condemnation of an unmarried mother. It is not coincidental that Corrine's righteous indignation over her "betrayal" is unevenly distributed along gender lines, with the scales weighed against Nettie in a case in which both she and Samuel stand accused. Except for a mild (though, for the Christian Corrine, significant) Bible-sworn oath, Samuel tellingly escapes the vitriol unleased by Corrine's seizures of jealousy. Within patriarchal ideology, he is exonerated from the "sin" of the unmarried mother, a fact Corrine chooses to affirm rather than challenge.

Indeed, as revealed in the death-bed confession, Corrine perpetrates a terrible injustice against Nettie. The eruption of her unconscious brings up an important piece of repressed history: she had once intuitively yet accurately identified Celie as her children's biological parent. With this act of retrieval, Corrine comes to terms with her oppression of the wrong woman and her own debilitating sense of sexual inferiority. The self-exorcism fails to save her life, but it clears the way for a peaceful death and for her victim to move beyond sexual stereotype and fully fashion her own identity.

The novel's configuration of intra-female oppression thus includes a troubled stretch of acts performed by women like Corrine who would no doubt be misdiagnosed as power-prone but who at the same time heed the castration appeal underpinning female relationships. Celie and her betrayal of Sofia offer another glimpse at this type of performance. The quintessential victim-turned-subject, Celie appropriately signals the status of power relations in the novel. Her eventual entry into confident selfhood is aided in large measure by her ability to intuit the subtext on the cross-gender lines of power that encompass at once virulent acts by "Pa" and Albert and milder but no less hurtful intra-female antagonisms. Two performances at the beginning of Celie's confessional epistle frame the subtext: her rape by the man she thinks is her father and the legacy of "cuss[es]" (meaning both insults and curses) bequeathed her by her dying and suspecting "mama" (12). While the former has been accurately identified within feminist discourse as an act of female disempowerment, the latter, patently oppressive both in intent and gesture, has yet to be recognized as such. Celie's cursed maternal inheritance, like Corrine's despoliation of Nettie, belongs to the troubling reality of women's complicity in patriarchy.

Celie's early awakening to the fact of female self-abuse serves as an allegory for the text's strategy of re-imaging gender-based power relations. Having counseled Harpo on how to tame Sofia ("Beat her"), she watches in amazement as the latter is transformed into an instrument of brutal power in the ensuing battle:

Harpo and Sofia. They fighting like two mens. Every piece of furniture they got is turned over. Every plate look like it broke. . . . They fight. He try to slap her. What he do that for? She reach down and grab a piece of stove wood and whack him cross the eyes. He punch her in the stomach, she double over groaning but come up with both hands lock right under his privates. He roll on the floor. He grab her dress tail and pull. She stand there in her slip. She never blink a eye. He jump up to put a hammer lock under his chin, she throw him over her back. He *bam* up gainst the stove. (44)

One could correctly argue that the image of female superpotency drawn here is consistent with the womanist idea of audacious womanhood. Sofia pointedly enacts a self-enabling ethos deemed necessary to deform patriarchy. Her appropriation of masculine violence sets off the novel's offensive against male oppression. Like the verbal whipping Albert later receives from Celie, Harpo's shameful beating relieves him of the ideological burden of masculinity, leading to the eventual release of his repressed humanity.

The episode, however, articulates, though obliquely, another gender position with respect to power. Through force of metaphor, Sofia's *man*handling of Harpo—they fight "like two mens"—breaks for a moment the illusion of justified self-defense to suggest an undifferentiated sexual economy of power. In other words, in this cockfight, Sofia is no less mean-spirited or ferocious than Harpo, nor is she any less avid for conquest. Rather, she unleashes a predatory nature unspoiled by the learned behavior traditionally separating women from power. To Celie, the picture is more terrifying than liberating. Recalling the self-serving act that triggered the fight—getting Harpo to beat up Sofia perhaps to satisfy her own strongly felt but unfulfillable desire to do so—she realizes that Sofia is not an anomaly, that women, too, are enforcers of domination.

This insight is epiphanic. It marks the turning point in Celie's engagement with the dynamics of power: from insipid victim (and, in the lone instance cited above, victimizer) to moral agent. Henceforth, she is able to critique with admirable discernment the display of personal antagonisms in the novel. Epiphanies, however, are not psychologically cost-free and Celie's exacts a toll on her psyche:

> For over a month I have trouble sleeping. I stay up late as I can before Mr. _____ start complaining bout the price of kerosene, then I soak myself in a warm bath with milk and epsom salts, then sprinkle little witch hazel on my pillow and curtain out all the moonlight. Sometimes I git a few hours sleep. Then just when it look like it ought to be gitting good, I wakes up. . . .
> What it is? I ast myself.
> A little voice say, Something you done wrong. Somebody spirit you sin against. Maybe.
> Way late one night it come to me. Sofia. I sin against Sofia spirit. (45)

We have no problem accepting Celie's use of Christian love to explain the wages of "sin," given her impeccable biblical credentials. Her narrative of insomnia, however, would seem more plausible if it were located in the interstice between guilt and fear. The former emotion, an outcome of her natural virtue, is self-punishment for her fall from moral magnanimity to juvenile jealousy, from the person who "never struck a living thing" (47) to a backstabber. It is anxiety over an unspecified threat to her robust sense of good.

By contrast to this private trial by guilt, Celie's fear embodies the author's attempt to anchor her liberationist ethic in the heroine's unconscious. Endowed with the greatest possibility for imaginative growth, Celie is the ideal site to input the text's radical content of female friction. The fight between Sofia and Harpo ("two mens," according to Celie) initiates the process by "outing" destructive female power. Sofia's display of lethal might captures for Celie the deadly potential of repressed female desire for dominance. In addition, it serves as a frightful reminder of the anti-Sofia feelings she had projected onto Harpo, turning him, in effect, into a surrogate oppressor. Seeing her own capacity for domination reflected in Sofia's show of brute force, Celie is traumatized into recognizing her deep-seated aversion to hubristic power.

Cathartic self-reproach (guilt) and fear thus combine to induce Celie's epiphany and consequently a transformative textual activity demanding constant vigilance. Celie repositions herself conspicuously and confidently to index the text's genealogies of power, both affiliative and antagonistic. As the novel's guiding consciousness, she stimulates the difference between these modes of power by deftly evoking the latter's menace and the former's restorative promise. Two episodes, considered in tandem, illustrate Celie's achieved maturity in reading the subtextual dynamics of female power relations. In the first she locates Squeak's prickly encounter with Sofia's implacable fighting hand within female socialization, suggesting that the senseless sexual jealousy that blinds Squeak to the physical disparity between herself and Sofia originates in and abets patriarchal ideology:

> Who dis woman, say Squeak, in this little teenouncy voice.
> You know who she is, say Harpo.
> Squeak turn to Sofia. Say, You better leave him alone.
> Sofia say, Fine with me. She turn round to leave.
> Harpo grab her by the arm. Say, You don't have to go no where. Hell, this your house.
> Squeak say, What you mean, Dis her house? She walk out on you. Walk away from the house. It over now, she say to Sofia.
> Sofia say, Fine with me. Try to pull away from Harpo grip. He hold her tight.
> Listen Squeak, say Harpo, Can't a man dance with his own wife?
> Squeak say, Not if he my man he can't. You hear that, bitch, she say to Sofia.
> Sofia gitting a little tired of Squeak, I can tell by her ears. They sort of push back. But she say again, sorta end of argument like, Hey, fine with me.
> Squeak slap her up cross the head.
> What she do that for. Sofia don't even deal in little ladyish things such as slaps. She ball up her fist, draw back, and knock two of Squeak's side teef out. Squeak hit the floor. One toof hanging on her lip, the other one upside my cold drink glass. (83)

This scene poignantly demonstrates the socialized attitudes that inform intra-female hatreds. Squeak's behavior is flagrantly male-identified and needs, in Celie's view, the kind of purging Sofia is eminently qualified to administer. Indeed Squeak, like Harpo, awakens from her beating into a state of consciousness inhabited by new strains of mental attitude—from her confident reclamation of voice and name (Mary Agnes) to optimal support of a counter-power culture.

Celie draws attention to the novel's emerging dispensation in the second episode, which projects, in addition to her own growing perspicacity and Squeak's new demeanor, signs of movement within the power paradigm, away from combativeness toward cooperation. Squeak both spearheads and absorbs the shocks of this reconstructive enterprise. For example, cooperating in a group effort to manumit the vanquished Sofia, she submits to a ritual of racial cross-dressing fraught with danger:

> Us dress Squeak like she a white woman, only her clothes patch. She got on a starch and iron dress, high heel shoes with scuffs, and a old hat somebody give Shug. Us give her a old pocketbook look like a quilt and a little black bible. Us wash her hair and git all the grease out, then I put it up in two plaits that cross over her head. Us bathe her so clean she smell like a good clean floor.
>
> What I'm gon say? she ast.
>
> Say you living with Sofia husband and her husband say Sofia not being punish enough. Say she laugh at the fool she make of the guards. Say she gitting along just fine where she at. Happy even, long as she don't have to be no white woman maid.
>
> Gracious God, say Squeak, how I'm gonna tune up my mouth to say all that? (92)

Squeak's objectification ends in rape. Her "passing" counts for little in a sexual regime that suppresses both black and white women via rape. Squeak may have, however, auditioned for her life, as well as the life of the group, given the panache with which she sets out to liberate herself and to help consolidate group solidarity. Conspicuously absent from her relationship with Grady, Shug's husband, is the animus she hurled at Sofia in a jealous reaction to Harpo's continued interest in his ex-wife. Guided by the new idea of reciprocity, she succeeds in integrating self and other, even when the latter is a formidable sexual rival, like Shug. As Squeak metamorphoses into Mary Agnes, she drops the restrictive habit of sexual competition for the capacious ties of community. It is a narrative opportunity accorded most of the female characters in the novel. Their painful acceptance stands testimony to the author's quest for unoppressive systems of human exchange.

My reading of women as instruments of power in a text that is said to fetishize female victimization underlines the credibility of the womanist probe of interlocking oppressive systems. Part of *The Color Purple*'s agenda and strategy is to demark the boundaries of hostilities within the colonized space of race, gender, and class and to delineate the "specificity" of overlapping economies of power, as suggested in this essay's second epigraph. Like Moraga and hooks, Walker is cynical of the feminist practice of forcing the discourse of oppression into a masculine pigeonhole, calling instead for a multivarious perspective to account for the ubiquity of domination. Hence in a novel awash in hegemonic masculine dominance, Walker evokes the specter of a predatory femininity as a stinging reminder of the inexorable logic of power. The female characters—black and white—collude in patriarchy in wrenching ways, but there is also an uneasy sense (most evident in the battles royal starring Sofia) of an inherently destructive female power.

This thornier issue is neither developed nor resolved in the novel, its open-endedness intended perhaps to invite debate. But the very fact that we get to glimpse it, coupled with the picture of specific female complicities in patriarchy, attests to the radical potential of the womanist ethic.

NOTES

1. See, e.g., Bernard Bell, *The African American Novel and Its Tradition* (Amherst: University of Massachusetts Press, 1987), 242–65; Christine Froula, "The Daughter's Seduction: Sexual Violence and Literary History," in *Feminist Theory in Practice and Process*, ed. M. R. Malson, J. F. O'Barr, S. Westphal-Wihl and M. Wyer (Chicago: University of Chicago Press, 1989), 155–62.
2. The full definition of "womanist" appears in Alice Walker's *In Search of Our Mothers' Gardens* (New York: Harcourt Brace Jovanovich, 1983), xi–xii.
3. See, e.g., Judith Butler, *Gender Trouble: Feminism and the Subversion of Identity* (New York: Routledge, 1990); Irene Diamond and Lee Quinby, eds., *Feminism and Foucault: Reflections on Resistance* (Boston: Northeastern University Press, 1988); Laura E. Donaldson, *Decolonizing Feminisms: Race, Gender, and Empire-Building* (Chapel Hill: University of North Carolina Press, 1992); Marianne Hirsch and Evelyn Fox Keller, eds., *Conflicts in Feminism* (New York: Routledge, 1990).
4. See Walker's "One Child of One's Own," "Looking to the Side, and Back," "Breaking the Chains and Encouraging Life," and "If the Present Looks Like the Past, What Does the Future Look Like?," in *In Search of our Mothers'*

Gardens; also Audre Lorde, *Sister Outsider: Essays and Speeches* (Freedom, Calif.: Crossing Press, 1984), 145–75.
5. See Flannery O'Connor, *The Complete Stories* (New York: Farrar, Straus and Giroux, 1986), 405–20.
6. See Walker's essay, "If the Present Looks Like the Past, What Does the Future Look Like?," in *In Search of Our Mothers' Gardens.*

REFERENCES

Awkward, Michael. *Inspiriting Influences: Tradition, Revision, and Afro-American Women's Novels.* New York: Columbia University Press, 1989.
Bell, Bernard. *The African American Novel and Its Tradition.* Amherst: University of Massachusetts Press, 1987.
Boyne, Roy. *Foucault and Derrida: The Other Side of Reason.* London: Unwin Hyman, 1990.
Butler, Judith. *Gender Trouble: Feminism and the Subversion of Identity.* New York: Routledge, 1990.
Diamond, Irene, and Lee Quinby, eds. *Feminism and Foucault: Reflections on Resistance.* Boston: Northeastern University Press, 1988.
Donaldson, Laura E. *Decolonizing Feminisms: Race, Gender, and Empire-building.* Chapel Hill: University of North Carolina Press, 1992.
Foucault, Michel. *Power/Knowledge: Selected Interviews and Other Writings, 1972–1977.* Edited by C. Gordon. Translated by C. Gordon, L. Marshall, J. Mepham, and K. Soper. New York: Pantheon Books, 1980.
Froula, Christine. "The Daughter's Seduction: Sexual Violence and Literary History." In *Feminist Theory in Practice and Process,* ed. M. R. Malson, J. F. O'Barr, S. Westphal-Wihl and M. Wyer, 139–62. Chicago: University of Chicago Press, 1989.
Gates, Henry Louis, Jr., ed. *Reading Black, Reading Feminist: A Critical Anthology.* New York: Meridian/Penguin, 1990.
Hirsch, Marianne, and Evelyn Fox Keller, eds. *Conflicts in Feminism.* New York: Routledge, 1990.
hooks, bell. *Ain't I a Woman.* Boston: South End Press, 1986.
Joseph, Gloria I., and Jill Lewis. *Common Differences: Conflicts in Black and White Feminist Perspectives.* Boston: South End Press, 1986.
Lorde, Audre. *Sister Outsider: Essays and Speeches.* Freedom, Calif.: Crossing Press, 1984.
Moraga, Cherríe, and Gloria Anzaldúa, eds. *This Bridge Called My Back: Writings by Radical Women of Color.* New York: Kitchen Table, 1983.
Naylor, Gloria, and Toni Morrison. "A Conversation." *Southern Review* 21 (Summer 1985): 567–93.
O'Connor, Flannery. *The Complete Stories.* New York: Farrar, Straus and Giroux, 1986.
Rich, Adrienne. *Of Woman Born: Motherhood as Experience and Institution.* New York: W. W. Norton, 1986.

Sawicki, Jana. *Disciplining Foucault: Feminism, Power, and the Body.* New York: Routledge, 1991.

Walker, Alice. *The Color Purple.* New York: Washington Square Press / Simon and Schuster, 1983.

————. *In Search of Our Mothers' Gardens.* New York: Harcourt Brace Jovanovich, 1983.

————. *Meridian.* New York: Harcourt Brace Jovanovich, 1976.

Washington, Mary Helen. *Invented Lives: Narratives of Black Women, 1860–1960.* New York: Anchor Press/Doubleday, 1987.

5.

MIXED BLOOD WOMEN: THE DYNAMIC OF WOMEN'S RELATIONS IN THE NOVELS OF LOUISE ERDRICH AND LESLIE SILKO

JENNIFER SHADDOCK

I will tell you something about stories,
   [he said]
They aren't just entertainment
Don't be fooled.
They are all we have, you see,
   all we have to fight off
     illness and death.
         —Leslie Silko, *Ceremony*

Women, perhaps more than any other oppressed group, have internalized the cultural narratives that legitimize our oppression. Flattered by and covetous of male attention, willing to align ourselves with male power even at the cost of our own freedom and integrity, too often silent and passive in the face of our own victimization, and, worse, frequently complicitous in the more socially pervasive forms of misogyny, women enact on a day-to-day basis the plot of a deeply embedded sexist narrative. Historically unable, in Simone de Beauvoir's words, to "authentically assume a subjective attitude," to interpolate ourselves as a continuously sustained, if also diverse "we," women continue to be defined by the very patriarchal narratives of woman as object/other that divide us from one another and from ourselves.[1]

Two contemporary women novelists writing on Native American survival within an Anglo-dominated United States explore the personal and cultural devastation caused by the internalization of an oppressive ideological narrative. Both Louise Erdrich's *Tracks*(1988)[2] and Leslie Marmon Silko's *Ceremony*(1977)[3] are interested, not in Anglo oppression itself, but rather in the active engagement by Indians in narratives that implicitly construct the Anglo as subject and the Indian as object, and the self-destructive factionalism that this inevitably causes within the Native American community. Their work is significant for feminist theories of oppression in that it posits strategies of resistance through language, specifically through story, and, in the process, retheorizes oppression itself.

For many native cultures, language is much more than a vehicle through which reality is translated; for these cultures, language creates reality. Acoma Pueblo poet Simon Ortiz, who considers language to be "a way of life," expounds upon this concept: "[Through language] we create knowledge. Our language is the way we create the world. . . . Consciousness comes about through language. Life—language. Language is life, then."[4] Silko writes in a similar vein: "You don't have anything / if you don't have the stories" (2). She asserts that it is "more effective to write a story . . . than to rant and rave" against oppression, explaining that "for me the most effective political statement I could make is through my art work. I believe in subversion rather than straight-out confrontation. I believe in the sands of time, so to speak. Especially in America, when you confront the so-called mainstream, it's very inefficient, and in every way possible destroys you and disarms you."[5] Because of the power that Silko invests in language, her novel *Ceremony* is not merely a creation story, but rather the very agent of creation. She begins her novel:

> Thought-Woman, the spider,
> named things and
> as she named them
> they appeared.
>
> She is sitting in her room
> thinking of a story now

I'm telling you the story
she is thinking.

(1)

This brief, yet powerful, poem asserts creation's inherence in story, and thus implies not only Thought-Woman's but also Silko's role as creator.

The idea that language has the power to create rather than simply reflect reality has been a preoccupying theme not only of Native American thought but also of twentieth-century Western European semiotic and narrative studies. In the last twenty years, Western feminists, in particular, have recognized language both as a foundational structure for the oppression of women and, consequently, as one of the most powerful sites for transformation. In fact, Nancy Armstrong argues in *Desire and Domestic Fiction* that, through language and specifically the novel, nineteenth-century women were active agents in constructing a model of domesticity that relegated vast arenas of cultural life to the control of middle-class women.

And yet women too frequently deny the narrative power we do wield. As Armstrong claims, self-empowered academic feminists have failed "to acknowledge the fact that our voice has exercised no little political force." [6] What *Tracks* and *Ceremony* demonstrate is what can be gained politically when we explicitly acknowledge the power of our own oral and written narratives to both express the realities of our oppression and, *at the same time,* to remythologize woman's cultural identity in terms of an empowered and recalcitrant subjectivity.

Within a dualistic linguistic system, which simultaneously enables and limits reality, subjectivity itself becomes one among many contested linguistic sites: Who, for example, is interpolated as subject (or enabled), and who is relegated to the position of object (or limited)? The urgent political questions implied here are who controls language, and how can narrative function to create a recalcitrant subjectivity for oppressed people in the face of hostile narratives that deny such subjectivity. For Erdrich and Silko, who both work from the premise that language is transformative rather than merely mimetic, oppression is palpable and threatening—it has meaning—to the extent that the contested culture abdicates its own narrative subjectivity by self-destructively engaging in the narratives of its oppressors.

In *Tracks,* two narrators, the young mixed-blood Pauline and the grandfatherly Nanapush, vie for creative authority, foregrounding language as the site of cultural survival. Both invoke their rhetorical skills to control the representation of Fleur Pillager, whom Nanapush honors as "the funnel of our history" (178) and Pauline fears as the wife of Misshepeshu, water monster and devil. As James Stripes observes about these dueling narratives, "Depending on who you listen to, Fleur is a culture hero or a pawn of the Devil, the last member of an important family or a stubborn hold-out, living in the past." [7]

Through her own narrative construction, however, Pauline progressively reveals herself as ever more masochistic in her identification with Anglo culture—and so ultimately sabotages her narrative credibility.[8] Her persecution of Fleur Pillager, the repository of Native American culture and Pauline's own surrogate mother, personifies the historical destruction of Native American culture and Pauline's own surrogate mother, personifies the historical destruction of Native American culture by a rapacious Anglo ideology, or what Silko identifies in *Ceremony* as "the witchery." The witchery, an annihilating force working through Anglo dominance, is so greedy and voracious that it is destined not only to eradicate Native American culture but also, finally, to consume its own means of sustenance, Anglo culture.

The sixty-two-year-old Nanapush, who has seen the annihilation of virtually his entire people, challenges Pauline and the witchery through the story. Early in the novel, Nanapush relates how, after going "half windigo" from grief at the loss of his entire family to illness, he revives himself through narration, talking incessantly to his first visitor in months: "I kept Father Damien listening all night, his green eyes round, his thin face straining to understand, his odd brown hair in curls and clipped knots. Occasionally, he took in air, as if to add observations of his own, but I pushed him under with my words" (7). Nanapush's narrative in *Tracks* is an endeavor to push Pauline's narrative perspective under with his words. In a sustained dramatic monologue, punctuated only by Pauline's version of events, Nanapush informs Lulu, Fleur's daughter, of her estranged mother's history, attempting to reconcile the girl to her mother in spite of Pauline's destructive efforts. In so doing, he hopes to ensure the continuity of the Pillagers and, more generally, of the tribal community.[9]

Pauline's persecution of Fleur, the metaphoric site of traditional Native American culture within the novel, begins before the two women even meet. In essence it begins with Pauline's choice to reject her native heritage and identify fully with her mother, "who showed her half-white" (14). She convinces her father to send her south to the white town, ignoring his warnings that "you'll fade out there." She consents to speak English only, and she refuses to bead like other Indian women, desiring instead to learn lace-making from the nuns. "I was made for better," she tells her father. She perceives identification with the Indians as death: "I saw that to hang back was to perish. I saw through the eyes of the world outside of us" (14).

The self-denial of Pauline's choice to live within the narrative of Anglo culture is apparent in her increasing commitment to the Catholic Church, for Pauline's efforts toward self-preservation through the Church ironically result in her own self-destruction. Since the order will not admit Indian girls, Pauline explicitly denies her Indian blood, creating a fictitious story about her background in order to be accepted. In so doing, she commits her final psychological separation from her native community: "'The Indians,' I said now, 'them.' Never *neenawind* or us'" (138). She has a vision of God in which "He said that I was not whom I had supposed. I was an orphan and my parents had died in grace, and also, despite my deceptive features, I was not one speck of Indian but wholly white" (137).

Not only does Pauline deny her own heritage when she becomes a novice but, by embracing the narrative perspective of Christianity, she also threatens through the Anglo witchery she embraces to devalue and destroy the integrity of the entire tribal culture. Even before she joins the Church, she had already figuratively aligned herself with the destruction of the native community by moving in with Bernadette Morrissey and her brother Napoleon, who were "well-off people, mixed-bloods who profited from acquiring allotments that many old Chippewa did not know how to keep" (63). In fact, the Morrisseys later contribute directly to the loss of Fleur's land. More literally, Pauline inherits from Bernadette the tribal role of easing Indian souls into death. She becomes Bernadette's helper in washing and laying out the dead. She is maligned as "death's bony whore" (86), and indeed she "passed death on" among the Indians (69), viewing it as a Christian sacrament: "I alone, watching, filled with breath, knew death as a form of grace" (68).

Throughout the novel, both narrators associate Pauline with death and Fleur with life. Although Fleur almost drowns three times in Lake Matchimanito at the hands of the water monster, Misshepeshu, each time she miraculously lives, becoming an increasingly awesome symbol of survival: "as always Fleur lived" (13). Pauline, on the other hand, is "good at easing souls into death but bad at breathing them to life, afraid of life in fact, afraid of birth, and afraid of Fleur Pillager" (57).

Pauline's self-destructive identification with Catholicism's salvation narrative—a narrative that, in the novel's terms, offers salvation in exchange for Indian acceptance of Anglo racism and dominion—eventually takes the form of full-fledged martyrdom. In her quest to destroy the Indian devil, Pauline enacts Silko's concept of the self-consumptive witchery, for not only does she plan to "save" the Indians by eradicating their "pagan" culture, but she herself, as part Indian, must logically fade out in the process. She says of her alliance with Christ, "He gave me the mission to name and baptize, to gather souls. Only I must give myself away in return, I must dissolve" (141). For Pauline, who describes herself as a "shadow," who perceives herself as "not wanted" and "invisible," and who relates that even a dog "never smelled me or noticed me above Fleur's smoky skin" (22), her self-dissolution is an all-too-natural consequence of a self-image corroded by internalized racism.

In essence, Pauline disdains her mixed-blood heritage: "I was cleft down the middle by my sin" (195). Feeling she must choose between her two backgrounds, she struggles to deny her Indian identity, seeing it as the "new devil," an enemy with "copper scales"—the lake monster, Misshepeshu (195). The "true," "blue-eyed" God must destroy this Indian devil. "I must hate one, the other adore," she claims of her two "masters" (193). "Armored and armed," Pauline prepares to fight for her "lamblike and meek" God in an attempt to achieve a complete identity. "If I did not forsake Jesus in His extremity, then He would have no other choice but to make me whole" (195). Pauline sees only the Anglo way to salvation; she effects the witchery by annihilating her native identity. Like a molting snake renewing itself, Pauline "shed a skin. . . . Every few days I shed another, yet another. . . . Fraction by fraction I increased in the Lord's eyes. New flesh grew upon my hands, smooth and pink as a baby's only tighter, with no give to it, a stiff and shrunken fabric" (195–96). By repudiating her tribal life, Pauline prepares the way for her final sacrifice for Christ: "I was pledged to a task, and when it was accomplished I would have no further use, or quarter, for this lost tribe of Israel" (196). In her mission to annihilate the Indian devil in the name of salvation, Pauline begins to embody a mummylike mockery of the renewal of life.

Pauline's concerted effort to challenge and destroy Fleur through her narrative is her most audacious threat to native culture. Fleur represents traditional Chippewa life and the power of the feminine in its connection to nature, birth, and the survival of the people. Both narrators, Pauline and Nanapush, invest Fleur with fearful powers. For Pauline these powers are awesome, but unnatural and perverse. After Fleur recuperates from an illness that kills her entire family, Pauline describes what she perceives as Fleur's transformation into a witch:

Alone out there, she went haywire, out of control. She messed with evil, laughed at the old women's advice and dressed like a man. She got herself into some half-forgotten medicine, studied ways we shouldn't talk about. Some say she kept the finger of a child in her pocket and a powder of unborn rabbits in a leather tongue so she could see at night, and went out, hunting, not even in her own body. We know for sure because the next morning, in the snow or dust, we followed the tracks of her bare feet and saw where they changed, where the claws sprang out, the pad broadened and pressed into the dirt. By night we heard her chuffing cough, the bear cough. By day her silence and the wide grin she threw to bring down our guard made us frightened. (12)

Despite her need to diminish Fleur, Pauline's narrative invests Fleur with extraordinary shapeshifting powers. In addition to describing Fleur as a bear, she frequently attributes wolf-like characteristics to Fleur, depicting her smile as "steady and hungry, teeth glinting" (88), "the white wolf grin a Pillager turns on its victims" (19). In a crucial establishing scene, Pauline watches as Fleur is raped, describing Fleur in her struggle as a powerful sow snorting at and trampling her adversaries. She suggests that Fleur embodies the horrifying storm that snouts out, sowlike, her rapists and demands a terrible retribution.

Even Nanapush, a more reliable narrator than Pauline, speaks of Fleur's ample powers, although for him they represent Fleur's connection to awesome, but natural, forces of life and harmony. He relates how she is feared, known to kill men who get too close to her or her land (9), to disturb the spirits of the dead, and to control the deadly lake monster. Through Nanapush we hear how Fleur transformed herself into a doe to seduce the hunter Eli toward her woodland camp. Fleur is depicted, moreover, by both Nanapush and Pauline as a medicine woman who possesses a powerful knowledge of herbal remedies and an inexplicable ability to control nature, tending a garden that "flourished madly, almost in defiance" (218). Fleur is rooted to the earth, appearing to Pauline as "great and dark as a fixed tree" (158) and to Nanapush as "a rain-dark young tree" (200). Identified as closely with plants and animals as with humans, Fleur seems an extension of the natural world.

Pauline's self-destructive rejection of Fleur's feminine power fuels an obsessive guilt over her betrayal. Her narrative becomes as much a confession as a polemic on Fleur. Pauline relates that during Fleur's rape she watched, almost gloating, as Fleur was attacked by three white men. Ironically, Fleur has been the only person to treat Pauline with kindness in the white town: "I was lifted, soothed, cradled in a woman's arms and rocked so quiet that I kept my eyes shut" (20). Yet when Fleur needs help during the attack, Pauline deters the young Russell from defending her and admits later that she "should have gone to Fleur, saved her" (26). Instead, afterwards, Pauline locks the three men in a meat locker where they freeze to death.

Both fearing and loving the powerful Fleur, Pauline punishes those who threaten her, herself included. The rape is the first in a series of passive/aggressive acts of destruction and atonement that lead Pauline deeper and deeper into a perverse martyrdom and mortification. Her disruption of Nanapush's cure for the spiritually ailing Fleur is a later, more self-abusive example of this violent and self-punishing cycle. During the cure, Pauline, "so like a scavenger, a bird that lands only for its purpose" (189), lays her eyes with their "still look" upon Fleur. She watches as Nanapush plunges his arms, protected by an herbal paste, into a boiling stew kettle. In an effort to compete with Nanapush and "prove Christ's ways" more powerful than his, Pauline

prayed loudly in Catholic Latin, then plunged her hands, unprepared by the crushed roots and marrows of plants, into the boiling water. She lowered them farther, and kept them there. Her eyes rolled back into her skull and the skin around her cheeks stretched so tight and thin it nearly split. If she opened her mouth, I thought, pure steam might blast into the air. Moments passed. Then she shrieked, jumped. She clawed straight through the flimsy tent walls, scattering the willow poles, collapsing the blankets and skins around us all. Then she ran, by the light of her scalded arms, and followed the dark path back to town. (190)

Pauline's mortifying act, obstructing Fleur's spiritual healing and at the same time guiltily atoning for this betrayal, horribly exemplifies the self-consuming masochism at the heart of her calling.

Pauline's work to weaken Fleur, ostensibly to save the Chippewa from themselves, is necessarily tangled in her own narrative self-abuse.

Christ's love, she says, is "a hook sunk deep into our flesh, a question mark that pulls with every breath" (205). She makes a set of underwear from potato sacks that chafe, reminding her of Christ's sacrifice; she breaks the crusts of ice off buckets of water with her bare hands until they bleed; she refuses to urinate except at dawn and dusk, relishing her discomfort; and she tells a story that annihilates the life-affirming Fleur. Pauline's rejection of Fleur is the essence of a life spent in self-destruction, a search for status "beyond hindrance or reach" (198).

How can Fleur survive such virulent attacks? How can one woman withstand such an obsessive hatred, a hatred inspired by the pervasive narrative constructions of an increasingly dominant Anglo culture? We can look to both *Tracks* and *Ceremony* for an answer that pertains directly to contemporary academic feminists who struggle to articulate cultural paths of resistance to the internalization by women of dominant patriarchal narratives. Both novels reveal that the reality of oppression is determined not by its intention but by its ultimate effectiveness in objectifying and thus subordinating native identities. The Anglo witchery has, in the past, proved its annihilating force through the disease, starvation, alcoholism, and economic and spiritual malaise brought onto the Native American cultures by Anglo intervention. Yet both *Tracks* and *Ceremony* explore how twentieth-century Indians often willingly succumb to the lure of material wealth and power—transmitted through narrative—that the Anglo lifestyle seems to offer, sabotaging themselves in the process and denying their own cultural power. As we will see, both authors assert that to resist the seductive yet lethal lure of this witchery, the participants must enact their own story, must not be provoked into engaging with and thus tacitly accepting the terms of their oppressors' narrative reality—even in self-defense.

Ceremony's mixed-blood (Mexican and Indian) protagonist Tayo explicitly uses story to heal himself and his people from the divisive wounds produced by their ancestor's neglect of the mother corn altar in favor of the magic of the witchery, embodied in the novel as Anglo cultural mythologies (46–49). In the course of the novel, by entering into the traditional Laguna origin myth and concluding its story, Tayo reshapes and energizes the myth, thus aligning himself with the creative force of woman (represented by the storyteller and original creator, Spider-woman). Tayo revitalizes what appears to be an obsolete and therefore powerless tribal myth, creating from it a revised yet contiguous story that depends upon both the feminization of masculine culture and the interconnectedness of racial cultures as the primary means to Laguna balance and harmony.[10]

Six years before, Tayo had been seduced by an Anglo army recruiter's narrative of opportunity for all Americans in the U.S. military during World War II. He abandons his Uncle Josiah and the ranch, enlisting in what he later realizes is a white man's war. After the war, Tayo returns home to the reservation psychically and spiritually wounded and alienated from himself and his heritage. He attributes the long drought on the reservation to his willful participation in this massively destructive war and, in particular, to the moment he had cursed the incessant rain that had thwarted his attempts to save his wounded cousin Rocky's life (14).

Tayo ultimately resists the witchery's fatalistic pull by enacting the empowering, self-defining ceremonial story. This story remythologizes the sacred origin myth that runs parallel to Tayo's story throughout the novel. As part of Old Betonie's healing ceremony to make Tayo spiritually whole, Tayo must revise the clan story by participating in it and thus reinvesting it with significance. Old Betonie explains to Tayo that "things which don't shift and grow are dead things. They are things the witchery people want. Witchery works to scare people, to make them fear growth. But it has always been necessary, and more than ever now, it is. Otherwise we won't make it. We won't survive. That's what the witchery is counting on: that we will cling to the ceremonies the way they were, and then their power will triumph, and the people will be no more" (126).

In order to change the clan story, Tayo must move into the story—he must sit within the sand-painting ceremonial cycle of self-articulation. Tayo must invigorate the old myth with meaning by literally choosing life over death in twentieth-century terms: He must search out and reclaim his family's lost mixed-breed cattle, thus making good on his past obligation to his uncle and symbolically asserting pride in his own mixed-blood heritage; he must embrace the feminine principle of life, nurturance, and continuity, represented by the love expressed between himself and the powerful mountain spirit Ts'eh; and he must come to understand time and space not in Western European linear terms but rather "as it always was: no boundaries, only transitions through all distances and time" (246).

Through Tayo's healing process, the enactment of a ritualized story of self-definition, the witchery of the white people becomes "hollow and lifeless," powerless to hurt him (204).

They unraveled
the dead skin
Coyote threw
on him.

They cut it up
bundle by bundle.

Every evil
which entangled him
was cut
to pieces.

(258)

By the end of the novel, the Laguna myth refers not to an anachronistic, objectified people, a people divided among themselves by Anglo colonialism, but to a vital culture breathing new life in its unification against the witchery. Tayo has recuperated a mythic sense of achronological time, allowing the past, present, and future to exist without boundary: "Josiah was driving the wagon, old Grandma was holding him, and Rocky whispered 'my brother.' They were taking him home" (254). Through entering the story and revising it, Tayo has brought on the healing rain—"as far as he could see, the land was green again" (234).

What Tayo and Fleur hold in common is their focus on enacting ritual and thus constructing, in the face of opposition, a recalcitrant subjectivity. Both Fleur and Tayo, if they are to survive, must not be distracted, lulled, or antagonized into engaging with Anglo witchery—represented in *Tracks* by Pauline's manipulations and in *Ceremony* by Indian war veteran Emo's violent challenge to Tayo. Each must act instead only to complete their own story.

Tayo barely survives the witchery's lethal pull. Nearing the end of the ceremonial story, Tayo watches from afar as Emo flays his buddy Harley alive. Conflating Emo's aggression with the persecution of Native Americans and with vast human suffering, "Tayo could not endure it any longer. He was certain his own sanity would be destroyed if he did not stop them and all the suffering and dying they caused—the people incinerated and exploded, and little children asleep on streets outside Gallup bars. He was not strong enough to stand by and watch any more.

He would rather die himself" (252). Tayo realizes, however, that in thinking this way he is dangerously close to fulfilling the story according to the witchery's plan. He has only "to complete this night, to keep the story out of the reach of the destroyers for a few more hours, and their witchery would turn, upon itself, upon them" (247). If he kills Emo, Tayo will be "another victim, a drunk Indian war veteran settling an old feud" (253), a bitter reminder to his people of one they could not save.

Instead, waiting out Emo, "the destroyer," Tayo completes the transition; his story, a story that merges Japanese and Laguna voices, Josiah's voice and Rocky's voice, is told: "The ear for the story and the eye for the pattern were theirs; the feeling was theirs: we came out of the land and we are hers" (255). The whirling darkness of the witchery has come back upon itself. In a drily humorous conclusion, Emos is exiled from the reservation, and leaves for California, the locus of Anglo self-consumption.

Fleur, too, withstands the witchery, although Pauline's narrative seeks to convince us that she has defeated Fleur. In Pauline's story, Pauline conquers the lake monster, source of Fleur's strength, by strangling him with her rosary.

I believe that the monster was tamed that night, sent to the bottom of the lake and chained there by my deed. For it is said that a surveyor's crew arrived at the turnoff to Matchimanito [Fleur's land] in a rattling truck, and set to measuring. Surely that was the work of Christ's hand. I see farther, anticipate more than I've heard. The land will be sold and divided. Fleur's cabin will tumble into the ground and be covered by leaves. The place will be haunted I suppose, but no one will have ears sharp enough to hear the Pillagers' low voices, or the vision clear enough to see their still shadows. The trembling old fools with their conjuring tricks will die off and the young, like Lulu and Nector, return from the government schools blinded and deafened. (205)

In Pauline's narrative version, the lake monster's destruction has weakened Fleur, allowing for Anglo intervention at the heart of the Native American community (a "measuring" of the land), and ultimately Fleur's demise. The site of Fleur's dominion will be deforested and parceled out, and even her memory will be obliterated among her people as the old traditionalist Chippewa die and the young are assimilated into Anglo culture through government schools.

In Nanapush's narrative version, however (and he has the last word in the novel), Fleur survives. She lives on despite Pauline's violent attempt to gain a "whole" identity, to heal the schism inside her, by destroying one racial identity in favor of another. Like Tayo, Fleur is intensely focused on enacting her own story, on living her own narrative reality, barely heeding others' constraints upon her. Early in the novel, when Eli stumbles upon Fleur's woodland camp, for example, and taps her on the shoulder as she concentrates upon skinning a deer, Fleur

> never noticed him. . . . She never even twitched. He walked around her, watched the knife cut, trespassed into her line of vision.
>
> At last she saw him, he said, but then scorned him as though he were nothing.
>
> "Little fly." She straightened her back, the knife loose and casual in her hand. "Quit buzzing." (43)

Fleur is similarly oblivious when Pauline disrupts her healing ceremony. "Fleur's eyes closed, she leaned into the folded robes behind her. Her breath was shallow and her attention was directed within, so she did not witness Pauline's dreadful proof" (190). Fleur's inner directedness demands that others accept her defining terms.

Fleur's determined refusal to accept Pauline's adversarial narrative perspective forces Pauline's "witchery" to turn back on itself. Like the self-consumptive Anglo society, Pauline becomes increasingly masochistic, and finally, in Erdrich's *Love Medicine,* she is confined in a convent specifically for troubled nuns. Fleur, on the other hand, leaves a vital, if erratic, trail, which Nanapush the storyteller "tracks," re-creates, to persuade Fleur's daughter, Lulu, of the value of her mother's love. Fleur, although exiled from her land and alienated from her daughter, survives, living deep in "the tough bush" (210). She has become more wild than in her wayward youth, more powerfully ephemeral than her shaman cousin, Moses. Uprooted from the responsibilities and privileges of the material world, now a landless nomad, Fleur is a spare and mobile symbol of Native American endurance and power in the face of long persecution.

When Fleur and Tayo refuse to engage with their oppressors, "the destroyers" are powerless to affect them and exist virtually without meaning for these redemptive characters. Neither *Tracks* nor *Ceremony,* however, promotes a Buddhist-like vision of the transcendence of pain and suffering through passivity and self-reflection, nor do they endorse passive resistance in the face of oppression. Rather, Fleur survives Pauline's betrayals and Tayo resists the witchery through a self-conscious engagement in and reconstruction of the old ways, the myths and stories of their past. Both novels foreground storytelling as the foundation of these myths of cultural empowerment. Stories are potent rituals that reveal and re-create history and, concomitantly, provide imaginative signposts for the future. They are the "tracks" enabling a coherent identity within a contested culture, the literal ground for forgiveness, inspiration, and cultural reawakening, the "ceremony" of constant becoming.

What do these novels suggest for academic feminists in our struggle against women's internalization of the very patriarchal values that oppress them? *Tracks* and *Ceremony* speak to the power of language to determine women's realities. Consequently, they raise a question about the ultimate benefit to women of selectively focusing critical energy on the oppression of women, on women's persecutors and their systems of persecution—or even on women's oppression of other women—without a simultaneous acknowledgment of the sources for women's empowerment.

I am concerned, like Nancy Armstrong and, most recently and provocatively, Katie Roiphe, how "the rhetoric of victimization" has worked by and about women. Not only, as Armstrong notes, do powerful academic women "insist on the powerlessness of women," [11] but, as Roiphe points out, rape-crisis feminists, in their efforts to end the sexual victimization of women, "produce endless images of women as victims." [12] Roiphe suggests that these images generate their own myths of the innocent child-woman, intellectually and emotionally vulnerable to persuasive male coercions. These images, Roiphe argues, deny women "the basic competence, free will and strength of character" that men are assumed to possess.

While Roiphe's position seems at times extreme and strained, I too have grown increasingly alarmed by the pervasive and largely unchallenged claims by young students in my women's studies courses that women have absolutely no choices, no power, and no means of empowerment in issues ranging from hospital-coerced cesarean birth to sexist advertising and domestic abuse. Why do these young university women perceive power as a naturally monolithic force that only men can manipulate? With the exponential growth in the seventies and eighties of academic departments, conferences, and publications organized around the subjection of women, have feminist theorists unknowingly reinstitutionalized the very narratives that have constrained women? Are women, in embattled attempts to expose the vast workings of patriarchal oppression, actually reifying the "woman as victim" trope?

Tracks and *Ceremony* suggest that academic feminists cannot afford to ignore the agency of language in creating cultural history *as we speak.* We need to develop in our own narratives a sustained dialogic voice, a voice that asserts women's power even as we expose the systems of our disempowerment. In all of our various "stories" of woman and her oppressions, feminists must self-consciously create through oral and written images recalcitrant women subjects that, like Fleur and the feminized Tayo, can survive beyond the realization of their oppression. Feminist voices must provide a younger generation of women hope that despite immense suffering and very real constraints on choice, women nonetheless can collectively and individually tell our own stories and create an enduring subjectivity in the process. *Tracks* and *Ceremony* demonstrate, moreover, that we need more of the remythologizing of a Toni Morrison, an Adrienne Rich, an Audre Lorde, more of the utopian visions of an Ursula LeGuin and a Helene Cixous, more of the revisionist autobiography of Maxine Hong Kingston—more, much more, of the connective tracks between and across various cultures of women. These narrative tracks will enable women to minimize the rhetoric of victimization in favor of a more effective and long-lasting source of regeneration—women's oral histories, women's storytelling, women's myths, women's language.

NOTES

1. Simone de Beauvoir, *The Second Sex* (New York: Vintage Books, 1952), xxii.
2. Louise Erdrich, *Tracks* (New York: Harper and Row, 1988). All subsequent page references are to this edition.
3. Leslie Marmon Silko, *Ceremony* (New York: Penguin Books, 1977). All subsequent page references are to this edition.
4. Laura Coltelli, *Winged Words: American Indian Writers Speak* (Lincoln: University of Nebraska Press, 1990), 107–8.
5. Ibid., 147–48.
6. Nancy Armstrong, *Desire and Domestic Fiction: A Political History of the Novel* (Oxford: Oxford University Press, 1987), 255.
7. James D. Stripes, "The Problem(s) of (Anishinaabe) History in the Fiction of Louise Erdrich: Voices and Contexts." *Wicazo Sa Review* 7 (1991): 29.
8. In contrast to Pauline's character, contemporary Native American literature frequently invokes the half-breed as the symbol of reconciliation and resolution for Indians living within an Anglo-dominated country.
9. Nanapush's name is, not coincidentally, closely related to the Midwestern

Algonkian Ojibwa name for the trickster Great Hare, Nanabush, who acts both as a lighthearted anarchic force and, at the same time, as a deliverer of his people from danger, a provider, and ultimately a creator.

10. For a reading of *Ceremony* as "all about the feminization of a male," see Paula Gunn Allen's brief comments about the novel in her interview with Laura Coltelli in *Winged Words* and her chapter on *Ceremony*, "The Feminine Landscape of Leslie Marmon Silko's *Ceremony*," in *The Sacred Hoop: Recovering the Feminine in American Indian Traditions* (Boston: Beacon Press, 1986).

11. Armstrong, *Desire*, 255.

12. Katie Roiphe, "Date Rape's Other Victim," *New York Times Magazine*, 13 June 1993, 26.

REFERENCES

Armstrong, Nancy. *Desire and Domestic Fiction: A Political History of the Novel*. Oxford: Oxford University Press, 1987.

de Beauvoir, Simone. *The Second Sex*. New York: Vintage Books, 1952.

Coltelli, Laura. *Winged Words: American Indian Writers Speak*. Lincoln: University of Nebraska Press, 1990.

Erdrich, Louise. *Tracks*. New York: Harper and Row, 1988.

Roiphe, Katie. "Date Rape's Other Victim." *New York Times Magazine*, 13 June 1993, 26.

Silko, Leslie Marmon. *Ceremony*. New York: Penguin Books, 1977.

Stripes, James D. "The Problem(s) of (Anishinaabe) History in the Fiction of Louise Erdrich: Voices and Contexts." *Wicazo Sa Review* 7 (1991):26–33.

II.

BONDS OF MOTHERHOOD

6.

MOTHERS AND SISTERS: THE FAMILY
ROMANCE OF ANTISLAVERY
WOMEN WRITERS

JENNIFER FLEISCHNER

Give my love to all the family, both black and white.
—Elizabeth Keckley, 1838

Part of the work facing antebellum antislavery women writers in the
U.S.—both black and white—was to enlist the sympathies of white
women on behalf of enslaved African-American women. This was complicated, and critical, in a culture structured in part by the absolute dualism between "black" slavery and "white" freedom and by racialist notions of biological difference.[1] Nor was a belief in inherent racial
differences limited to racist proslavery ideologues, who naturalized the
enslavement of Africans by enshrining notions of the moral and physical
superiority of whites over blacks. Identity as being in part a condition of
biological inheritance was the premise of proslavery and antislavery writers, most notably during the 1840s and 1850s. Harriet Beecher Stowe, for
instance, whose spectacularly popular *Uncle Tom's Cabin, or, Life
among the Lowly* (1852) launched a powerful assault on the institution
of slavery, also promoted racialist and colonialist views. Though for
Stowe, racial differences could be ameliorated by Christianizing Africa,

the superiority of the Anglo-Saxon over the African evidenced her romantic racialism: "The Saxon, born of ages of cultivation, command, education, physical and moral eminence; the Afric, born of ages of oppression, submission, ignorance, toil, and vice!" (267).[2] The combination of abolitionist fervor and racialist splitting was by no means uncommon, and colonization (sending freed slaves back to Africa) was one mechanism for dealing with the tensions between the two.

But biology also provided grounds for an argument for sameness. For despite laws against miscegenation, frequent interracial sexual relations (most often between white masters and slave women) produced children whose biological inheritance (contrasted with their *legal* inheritance of a slave status from the slave mother) was mixed, making it possible to assert racial crossings.[3] In an 1831 tract, Mrs. W. Maria Stewart, considered to be the earliest black feminist, cites racial mixing as one reason "our souls are fired with the same love of liberty and independence with which your [white American men's] souls are fired. We will tell you that too much of your blood flows in our veins, and too much of your color in our skins, for us not to possess your spirits" (19–20). Stewart inverts racialist justifications for social and political inequality into a threat against those white men who have most benefitted from such rationalizations. The institution justified primarily by notions of racial difference created a population whose very being undermined its own most vital assumption.

It is within the context of the paradoxical tensions generated by the belief in fundamental racial differences that antislavery women writers attempt to affirm the belief in an interracial sisterhood and draw analogies between their own disenfranchisement and the oppression of slave women. Given the lure of romantic racialism, it is perhaps inevitable that white feminist antislavery writers would shape the figure of the suffering mulatto slave woman according to the contours of the romance genre. Hawthorne complained that American life did not provide the material for the imagination, making romance, which gave a "latitude" to the mind, the appropriate form for an American fiction. In contrast, Lydia Maria Child, an abolitionist and feminist who would edit Harriet Jacobs's *Incidents in the Life of a Slave Girl,* saw in the "materials" of quadroons' lives the stuff of romance. "Reader, do you complain I have written fiction?" she asks at the end of her 1842 publication of the story "The Quadroons." "Believe me, scenes like this are no infrequent occurrence at the South. The world does not afford such materials for tragic romance, as the history of the Quadroons" (taken from *Liberty Bell,* 141). In this paragraph, omitted when the story was republished four years later in a collection entitled *Fact and Fiction,* Child collapses fiction, history, and romance. Consequently, she legitimates northern women's authority to be historians of the South by locating slavery's wrongs in the history of its wrongs against womankind, for which the quadroons become a synedoche. Worthy of high romance, these women are doomed to endure the moral pain of fallen women, or the physical and psychological torments (imprisonment, beatings, threats, rape) of enslaved serving women; they are textual versions of Pamela, who, despite her servitude, has the "soul of a princess." The quadroons' mixed blood implied their racial superiority over other enslaved women; their "highly cultivated" mind and manner proved the ease with which they might be assimilated to the cultural norms of northern society.[4] But these tragic heroines who "are fated to suffer social ostracism or slavery for the sins of her white father or male relatives" are more than "merely white ingenues in blackface" (Elfenbein 1989, 2, 5).

As processed through such sentimental forms as, for example, the "tragic romance," the slave woman of mixed racial heritage was a symbol enabling negotiation between sameness and difference, an intermediary area of potential intersubjectivity between self and other. Imagining the history of the quadroons as "tragic romance" provided white antislavery women writers with a way to manage cultural anxieties emanating from the dissonance between two contradictory principles of belief: the principle of racial difference and the principle of universal womanhood (gender identification). This contradiction was energized at the point at which the facts of slavery most directly came into conflict with the cultural insistence on female virtue and the cult of motherhood. Accordingly, one psychic project of the antislavery romance was to manage the fear of difference and neutralize the threat to the integrity of white womanhood implied by sameness. This could be done by idealizing difference and transforming it into a mode of identification.

The paradigm of feminine suffering, as it established an empathic bond between white female readers and their enslaved "counterparts" and affirmed the slave woman's "womanhood," was a way to sustain a relation between white and black women able to accommodate the paradox of two predominating antebellum romances: racialism and the cult of womanhood. In particular, narrative reinforcement of the slave woman's *mute* suffering helped allay cultural anxieties about the propriety of overidentification. As Franny Nudelman has argued, the narrative codes of sentimental forms employed by white women writers necessitated the separation of the slave woman from her audience (whose sexual degradation excludes her from the domestic culture of her audience), and is structured by the fact that she is typically object, not subject, of sentimental discourse. Indeed, the tradition in which they wrote, though it required empathy and an identification with sexual vulnerability, was maintained by distance. Sentimental forms emphasized difference by stressing the slave woman's subordination and vulnerability in contrast to her sympathizing "sister's." Moreover, they provided an outlet for northern moral outrage (a disavowal of identification with southern oppression of blacks). Ultimately, then, the tradition of women's antislavery writing transformed fearful sympathy (based on symmetry between white women and black women) into tearful pity (based on a reassuring asymmetry between white and black women).

The efficacy of romance to enact fantasies of identification and difference in order to satisfy instinctual impulses as well as to maintain the integrity of a self-image has its analogue in the family romances described by Freud, in which the invention of a new family for the self serves to alleviate the internal pressures thought to spring from oedipal wishes and fears.[5] In antislavery romances, the circularity of fantasy and reality suggests the volatile presence of the return of the repressed: romance becomes gothic when the trope of antislavery family romances merges with the reality of familial relations, when fantasies of incestuous, miscegenetic affairs are embodied in the bodies of quadroons. Calling upon the trope of family relations (mothers, daughters, sisters) to familiarize enslaved African-American women for their northern audiences, sentimental narrators tend to turn away from the implications for identity of literal familial relations; but invoking the metaphor and exposing the primal scenes of interracial mixing, these works are charged with the anxieties that activate the family romance.

Child's tale, "The Quadroons," demonstrates a narrative's successful management of the anxieties of familial (sexual) relations between black and white, successful in that it suggests identification but maintains difference. The narrator uses conventional descriptions to establish the inherent differences between her "pretty rivals," the quadroon, Rosalie (whom the white antihero, Edward, truly loves), and the white Charlotte (whom he marries out of political ambition, abandoning Rosalie and their daughter, Xarifa). The narrative invokes romantic codes of dark and fair, a logic of opposition familiar to readers of Sir Walter Scott (to whom, interestingly, Child refers in her 1833 preface to *Appeal in Favor of the Class of Americans Called Africans*). The narrative uses the reader's mastery over the signs of the form as a mechanism for mastery over the emotional unruliness of sexual betrayal and rivalry. The opposition between heroines is naturalized and idealized, rendered timeless and unchanging: the quadroon has "raven hair," is "graceful as an antelope, and beautiful as the evening star," while "her complexion as rich and glowing as an autumnal leaf" is contrasted with her rival's "blush-rose-buds" (62, 65).

Significantly, for the narrative's political purposes, attention to the women's personal rivalry is deflected into a more socially and politically conscious critique of the arbitrary and unjust "edicts of society," thus emphasizing the women's mutual vulnerability to "man's perfidy." This is a tale of "sisterhood": "I promised thee a sister tale, / Of man's perfidious cruelty:," reads the epigraph, quoted from Coleridge. "Come then and hear what cruel wrong / Befell the dark Ladie." Inviting the reader's sympathy for a "sister tale" for "the dark Ladie," the narrative constructs a reader who is white, and whose story, though it differs in degree from her "sister's," does not necessarily differ in kind (62, 61). Reinforcing identification, this sister tale is also a mother's tale. Rosalie is implicitly compared to the moon who gazes upon Edward, a "mild, but sorrowful ... Madonna [who] seems to gaze on her worshipping children, bowed down with consciousness of sin" (67). Earlier, as Rosalie contemplates her beautiful daughter, whose fate she fears will follow her own, there is "in the tenderness of the mother's eye ... an in-dwelling sadness" (64). In this vision of sorrowful maternalism, motherhood is used to reinforce the notion of transcendent womanhood, a sisterhood of "in-dwelling sadness," internalized, immobilized in the figure of a socially outcast, already dying woman.[6]

Elsewhere, describing the daughter of Rosalie and her white "husband," Edward, the narrator suggests distance from the "other" in temporal, developmental terms: the "melting, mezzotinto outline" in Xarifa's dark eye "remains the last vestige of African ancestry, and that gives that plaintive expression, so often observed, and so appropriate to that docile and injured race" (63). Suddenly an aesthetic appreciated by a white eye, the "mezzotinto outline" in the dark eye evidences the displacement of black by white as an aspect of historical development.

Xarifa's African lineage is exoticized as an ancient, dying trace just visible in its evolution toward whiteness. Thus, paradoxically, the transitional figure serves to split off black from white even further: on the "other side" of Xarifa (from Charlotte, or the narrator) is the "excellent old negress" whom the guilty father hires to "take charge of the cottage" and care for the soon motherless Xarifa (71). This slave woman's absolute difference is implicit in her pervasive blackness and total silence. It is her radical "otherness" that threatens the narrative regulation of sameness, sustained in the figure of the maternal quadroon. If Rosalie is an etherealized Madonna, who watches over her white male child/husband, and is in fact a slave, this woman is nature herself, nurse to Xarifa (the "fair" marked by an "X"), and free, if only to be hired.[7] Rosalie, then, is part of the white, symbolic order, within the oedipal father's law; the "old negress," mentioned in the story just this once, indicates a preoedipal realm, prior to language, potentially disruptive, potentially beyond control. Only in Xarifa, in the end, are the two mothers brought "face-to-face," but then simply to show the dangers to self-integration such a juncture creates. Xarifa is depicted as a "raving maniac" in a double image evocative of an internal conflict between desire and self-denial: "That pure temple was desecrated . . . and that beautiful head fractured against the wall in the frenzy of despair" (76).

This final image contains a counternarrative to the "tragic romance" of suffering dark women that "The Quadroons" puts forth. That *all* women are (at least potential) victims of men is the *culturally acceptable* basis of identification between the women, according as it does with the ideal of female passivity. Despite its final scene, this is the value endorsed by "The Quadroons," where the quadroon's desire to protect her rival's feelings ensures that she will never tell, and the white woman's "inexpressive" eye and "reluctance" to interfere with her husband's seemingly benevolent care of his quadroon daughter effectively mutes her as well (65, 70, 72). But in Child's ironically titled "Slavery's Pleasant Homes: A Faithful Sketch," a variant of the "tragic romance," a covert, unacceptable basis for identification between women emerges. For it allows a scene of violence between women that, though it is quickly repressed, nonetheless opens up the possibilities of a secret alliance based not on passivity and recognition of mutual suffering, but rather on the capacity for aggression against one another, and then, ultimately, against men.

"Slavery's Pleasant Homes," published in *The Liberty Bell* in 1843, is an emotionally volatile tale in which the family romance, charged by incestuous relations and intense sibling rivalry, is repeatedly disrupted by outbursts of aggression. What makes this story particularly intriguing is the ambiguous "color" status of the dark heroine, Rosa. She is encoded in every way as a tragic quadroon, yet never explicitly labelled in any way. That she is desired by three differently racially marked men—white, mulatto, and quadroon—contributes to the narrative ambiguity. More precisely, the narrative's careful description of her body and blush links fluctuating skin color with sexual desire: "Rosa, a young girl, elegantly formed, and beautiful as a dark velvet carnation. The blush, so easily excited, shone through the transparent brown of her smooth cheek, like claret through a bottle in the sunshine" (148).

Racial slippage is one element in the narrative impulse toward disintegration. The other is the narrative obsession with splitting and doubling. This is a story about sibling rivalries gone amok, without the controlling presence of maternal or paternal authorities, self-enclosed and simmering, a family of brothers and sisters that acts out the unconscious fantasies said to underlie the family romance. Marion, Frederic Dalcho's bride, is Rosa's foster-sister (they were both nursed by Rosa's mother) and her mistress. Suggestive of a Kleinian split ("good" breast/"bad" breast), the foster-sisters' attitudes toward one another, and the narrator's attitude toward each of them, switches frequently between aggression and benevolence, the latter perhaps a defense against a more primary aggression and the fear of retaliation.[8] Marion's pleasure in her possession is indicated by the fact that she "loved to decorate her with jewels" (149). Saying "You shall wear my jewels whenever you ask for them," Marion gives permission to Rosa to desire, but draws clear limitations around this with her ownership. Yet if Rosa is Marion's doll, so Marion is the narrator's, who calls her a "pretty waxen plaything" (148).

Narrative anxiety (indicated by splitting and reactive shifts) intensifies when sisterhood gives way to sexual rivalry. Frederic's quadroon brother and slave, George, falls in love with Rosa, and when Marion asks her husband to allow them to marry, Frederic's interest in Rosa warms. Soon, one night, Marion awakes to find her husband missing. Hearing voices in Rosa's room, "the painful truth flashed upon her. Poor young wife, what a bitter hour was that!" (152). Allied by sisterhood, reinforced by their mutual betrayal, Marion and Rosa are inevitably (for the romance form) pitted against one another as rivals. Their only remaining encounters highlight the tensions of identification and separation by

being represented in modes suggestive of the presence of the unconscious—during a violent outburst and during a dream. In such states,
barriers against unconscious impulses are dropped. Until the betrayal,
object-splitting between Rosa and Marion has served to manage passion
by keeping it separated from the woman with the means to enact it
(that is, the passionate slave woman is imagined as passive; the fragile,
impassive white woman is given an outlet for rage, at least socially
downward, if not up against her husband). But this defense against
destructive impulses gives way when Marion, provoked perhaps by
Rosa's reactive, exaggerated obedience (to assuage, for one thing, her
sense of guilt), gives Rosa a blow. Thus Marion's clear, but relatively
benign, expressions of domination early in the story are no longer contained and open out into physical assault.

In the morning, Rosa came to dress her, as usual, but avoided looking in her
face, and kept her eyes fixed on the ground. As she *knelt* to tie the satin shoe,
Marion spoke angrily of her awkwardness, and gave her a blow. It was the first
time she had ever struck her; for they really loved each other. The beautiful slave
looked up with an expression of surprise, which was answered by a strange,
wild stare. Rosa fell at her feet, and sobbed out, "Oh, mistress, I am not to
blame. Indeed, indeed, I am very wretched." Marion's fierce glance melted into
tears. "Poor child," said she, "I ought not to have struck you; but, oh, Rosa, I
am wretched, too." The foster-sisters embraced each other, and wept long and
bitterly; but neither sought any further to learn the other's secrets. (152–53)

Marion violates cultural injunctions against female force in two
stages: verbal abuse escalates to physical abuse.[9] Her aggressive outburst
is contained (repressed) rapidly, though, by a quick reversion to maternal concern ("Poor child"), then to identification as a sister who also
suffers. Calling the two "foster-sisters," the narrator seems to assert
reparation and puts back in order the familiar. But, as "foster-sisters"
also implies, their relation has developed as a history of displacements:
Marion's displacement of Rosa at her mother's breast finds an answer in
Rosa's displacement of Marion in bed. It is hinted, too, that Marion is
self-alienated in her moment of violence, and alienated from narrator
and reader, as well. Narrative empathy ("Poor young wife!") and narrative alignment with Marion's perspective (Rosa's eyes are directed downward) are withdrawn in the moment when Rosa "looked up with an
expression of surprise," and Marion mutely "answers" with "a strange,
wild stare." Rosa initiates the look, positioning the "mute" Marion as
the "other," a shift reinforced by the description of Marion's stare

("wild," "strange") in terms conventionally applied to the "other." Thus the "strange, wild stare" that looks back at her foster-sister's look is an expression of the double, the uncanny experience of unconsciously recognizing oneself in the form of another. The return of an early form of rage that has been rejected as unacceptable and, over time, repressed, the double's presence suggests that what Rosa sees ("with an expression of surprise") is the return of her own anger that has been split off and projected onto the "other."[10] And so Marion's blow, by inversion, is also a manifestation of Rosa's aggression against a white foster-sister kneeling at her feet.

If this is so, then the narrator's insistence on the slave girl's excessive passivity is founded partially on fear of the slave girl's anger and aggression against white women. That this rage is not so easily buried is conveyed in Rosa's haunting of Marion's dreams after Rosa's death (brought on by Frederic's sadistic flogging of Rosa when she is pregnant, the result of rape). "The memory of her foster-sister mingled darkly with all her dreams. Was that a shriek she heard? It was fearfully shrill in the night-silence! Half sleeping and half waking, she called wildly, 'Rosa! Rosa!'" (157). Rousing herself, Marion learns that her husband was just discovered dead, "a dagger through his heart," murdered, it turns out, by his brother (George) in vengeful fury (157). In the world of the dream, the inner (unconscious) world and the outer world intermingle, and the prohibitions (internalized as conscience, or a value, such as self-denial) against the rage and aggressive impulses of both women find their final discharge in Frederic's murder.

Despite the fetishization of suffering, the defenses meant to bind feminine aggression (idealization and splitting) find expression nonetheless. For indeed, by another inversion, the narrative insistence on the slave girl's passivity is a way to allay the anxieties raised by Marion's role in and the narrative's powerful fascination with the violence that surrounds Rosa. If dreams are also wishes (as Freud claimed), then Marion, who dreams her husband's death (she hears him shriek), awakes to find her dream come true. When she thinks of Rosa in the trauma of awakening, Marion may be seeking disavowal of her own thoughts by conjuring up the image of her split-off, projected, negative self. Horror occurs when real events correspond to unacceptable fantasies, when repressed thoughts seem to have caused real events; and dissociation is one refuge for the mind.

Child's use of the tragic romance, with its emphasis on passivity, purity, and pain as positive values, seems meant to repress the fantasies of sexual violence and uncontrollable rage that are triggered by the terrors of a totalizing identification or an unrelieved difference. Such are the primary childhood anxieties caused by fears of engulfing merger with the maternal object or fears of loss of the object. Interestingly, motherlessness, as represented in "Slavery's Pleasant Homes" and at the end of "The Quadroons," not only exposes the daughters to sexual dangers, but also provides a space—with the mothers out of the way— for the outlet of the daughters' own impulses and desires. In this way, Child resists structuring the relations between her white audience and the slave girl in terms of the relation of mother to child. She does posit a sisterhood, fraught with the conflicts and tensions of that relation. Stowe, on the other hand (as I will suggest), reproduces a relation of domination in the maternal discourse with which she constructs her view of an interracial bond.

It is motherhood as the quintessence of female suffering that underwrites Stowe's narrative position in *Uncle Tom's Cabin* and forges the link she endeavors to create between reader and slave woman. Accordingly, the narrator addresses the white "mothers of America" (472), calling upon both their motherly feelings for the "daughters of an injured race" and their empathy for the sufferings of slave mothers. Slavery dismembers families, slave and free, and it remains for America's mothers to put an end to the institution that disrupts motherhood and destroys homes. The quadroon Eliza's "desperate leap" across the icy Ohio River, bearing her son in her arms, "impossible to anything but madness and despair" (72), conveys the power of a mother's love to save her children. Maternal affection structures the narrator's relation to her reader, whom she guides, like a mother leading her children, through scene after scene of pathos and pain, educating the reader in, quite simply, how to feel. She instructs her reader in the process of identification, most notably, for example, in the Quaker Ruth Stedman's response to Eliza and her son, who have found sustenance and safety in the ample warmth of Rachel Halliday's kitchen. Ruth explains why she can empathize immediately with Eliza: "If I didn't love John and the baby, I should not know how to feel for her" (153). The phenomenology of reading another's situation empathically entails such identifications based on shared emotional experiences.

Throughout the novel, the mother that the narrative evokes is the good preoedipal mother, associated with ample food, warmth, comfort, security, order, continuity, and bodily and emotional presence. Rachel's kitchen is "large, roomy, neatly painted . . . , its yellow floor glossy and smooth, and without a particle of dust; a neat, well-blacked cooking-stove; rows of shining tin, suggestive of unmentionable good things to the appetite" (148). Seated in her rocking chair by Eliza's side, Rachel promises eternal connection and, by metonymy, a lap (chair) in which to sit: "For twenty years or more, nothing but loving words, and gentle moralities, and motherly loving kindness, had come from that chair;—headaches and heartaches innumerable had been cured there,—difficulties spiritual and temporal solved there,—all by one good, loving woman, God bless her!" (148–50). As George, Eliza's fugitive husband, recognizes after he arrives, Rachel's house is a "home," a heaven as domesticity, radiating outward from a mother in her kitchen serving up communion with griddle-cakes: "Rachel never looked so truly and benignly happy as at the head of her table. There was so much motherliness and fullheartedness even in the way she passed a plate of cakes or poured a cup of coffee, that it seemed to put a spirit into the food and drink she offered" (156). Goodness is repeatedly associated in the preoedipal terms of a body that supplies the other's (the child's) needs, identical at this early stage with its pleasures, as with the little mother "Eva, who carried a large satchel, which she had been filling with apples, nuts, candy, ribbons, laces, and toys of every description, during her whole homeward journey" to distribute among her family's slaves (182).

The novel strengthens its argument that the (preoedipal) mother might heal the deformation of humanity that slavery causes in the negative example of Marie St. Clare. Marie's cruelty to her slaves is related to her more primary failing as a mother, suggested in her self-involvement, instability, hypocrisy, coldness, selfishness, and artificiality, all negations of motherhood, illustrated in one brief image: there she "stood, gorgeously dressed, on the veranda, on Sunday morning, clasping a diamond bracelet on her slender wrist" (198). Taking instead of giving, clasping not a child to her heart, but a hard-chiselled stone to her pulse, Marie, unlike Ruth or Rachel, does not love *any* others: "I don't feel a particle of sympathy for such cases [Prue, the distraught, grieving slave mother who was whipped to death]. If they'd behave themselves it would not happen" (253).

The narrative splitting between "good" mother and "bad" mother, however, works to check the aggressive impulses of the narrative's mothering against her "children"—the slaves over whom she bends with

concern. That "true womanhood" not entail passion, erotic or destructive, is essential to the narrative's defensive posture. Of Cassy, Simon
Legree's quadroon slave, it is said that "despair hardened womanhood
within her, and waked the fires of fiercer passions, [and] she had become
in a measure his mistress, and he alternately tyrannized over her and
dreaded her" (428). Cassy exemplifies a motherhood active in her outrage against those who violate her. However, the tendency of the narrative is to link activity to destruction and passivity to a higher love.
Motherhood that destroys in the name of love, when Cassy murders her
infant son, momentarily upsets the splitting that sustains the narrative's
overt maternal vision. Implicit in motherhood is domination, and especially powerful is the infant's mother, a fact culturally obscured by
sentimentalizations of mother and babe. Having lost control of two
older children to slavery, Cassy determines, "I would never again let a
child live to grow up!" (392). Though, perhaps, inviting ambivalent
responses, the violence in Cassy's past is contained, quarantined from
the narrator's maternal attitude. The narrator distances herself from
Cassy's "wild, passionate utterances" by constructing this portion of her
history as an interpolated tale, told by Cassy herself to Tom. Or, more
to the point, this history is Cassy's criminal confession, a necessary
beginning in her moral recovery. That this narrative line culminates with
Cassy's recovery of her long-lost son and daughter implies that had
Cassy not killed her son, he too might have been recovered from slavery.

Yet despite this narrative separation, the maternal imago idealized by
the narrative is also a mother who will not let her "child grow up." The
maternal affection expressed toward the slave girl depends upon the
slave's infantilization—specifically, upon her powerlessness in relation
to the white mother.

When she [Eliza] awoke [in Rachel's house], she found herself snugly tucked up
on the bed, with a blanket over her, and little Ruth rubbing her hands with
camphor. She opened her eyes in a state of dreamy, delicious languor, such as
one has who has long been bearing a heavy load, and now feels it gone, and
would rest. The tension of the nerves, which had never ceased a moment since
the first hour of her flight, had given way, and a strange feeling of security and
rest came upon her; and, as she lay, with her large, dark eyes open, she followed,
as in a quiet dream, the motions of those about her. She saw the door open into
the other room; saw the supper-table, with its snowy cloth; heard the dreamy
murmur of the singing tea-kettle; saw Ruth tripping backward and forward with
plates of cake and saucers. . . . She saw the ample, motherly form of Rachel, as
she ever and anon came to the bedside, and smoothed and arranged something

about the bedclothes, and gave a tuck here and there, by way of expressing her good will; and was conscious of a kind of sunshine beaming down upon her from her large, clear, brown eyes. . . . There were low murmurs of talk, gentle tinkling of teaspoons, and musical clatter of cups and saucers, and all mingled in a delightful dream of rest. (154–55)

Swaddled in the bed, watching passively the movements of those over her, registering dreamily sensations of sight, smell, sound, and touch in a series of appearances and disappearances not causally or temporally related, Eliza is that preoedipal mother's infant, before murmurs, tinkling, and clatter rearrange themselves as sounds distinguishable from one another and oneself, a level of consciousness, reinforced in the vagueness ("something about the bedclothes") and uninflected ("She saw . . . saw . . . saw. . . . She saw. . . .") quality of her comprehension. And when she awakes from a dream of "a beautiful country," in which she sees her "son playing" and hears her "husband's footsteps," and finds her weeping husband beside her, his double appearance, first in her dream, then out of her dream, suggests the child's sense of omnipotence in her own thoughts, an illusion derived from a feeling of merger with the mother. The good-enough mother who anticipates her child's wishes and produces them fosters this illusion of omnipotence, then disperses it. After the Quaker mothers produce the husband, the narrative intones, "It was no dream" (155).[11]

Thus, the maternal domination of Eliza disenfranchises her from equality with the white mothers. She is implicitly denied the social and political power of white women in the novel when, in "The Freeman's Defence," George exclaims, "O, Eliza, if these people only knew what a blessing it is for a man to feel that his wife and child belong to *him!*"[12]

Invitations to readerly identification with the suffering quadroon mothers are ultimately rearranged as relations of white maternal domination. The narrative maternalism that characterizes *Uncle Tom's Cabin*, fixed in the preoedipal, depends on the image of the dependent slave whose identity (racial and spiritual) is conceived of as moving toward merger with the more powerful (all-powerful) white mother. So Tom (a model of passivity) is imagined as "now entirely merged with the Divine," and passing into a state of "cheerfulness . . . alertness . . . and quietness which no insult or injury could ruffle" (419). Such an image of Mother, insusceptible to the kind of destabilizing oedipal rivalries at work in Child's two stories, suppresses difference, or more precisely, difference from *her*. In this family romance, all the "mothers of

America" are "white," the free white fathers are "anti-patriarchal," and
the enslaved black fathers are noble and brave. As for the slave mother,
she recovers familial bonds when she crosses over the Ohio River to the
safety of the white mother's domain. In antebellum North or South,
home is the place where when you get there a white woman rules. The
incorporation of the (m)other by the Mother characterizes the narrative
representation of its own composition. In "Concluding Remarks," the
narrator explains that her narrative incorporates the stories of those on
whose behalf she speaks: "The separate incidents that compose the
narrative are, to a very great extent, authentic, occurring, many of them,
either under her own observation or that of her personal friends"
(467).[13]

As linguistic outlets for the negotiation of sameness and difference,
these antislavery narratives evidence some of the conflicts inherent in the
effort to create an interracial sisterhood within the context of romantic
racialism. Moreover, the issues of identity raised by these narratives
point to the need for a more complex understanding of the ways in
which individual and collective identity are conceived and represented in
these texts. Critical emphasis on the group (whether linked by a cause,
such as antislavery, or gender, or race) has tended to deflect attention
from the individual natures of people's encounters with the world and
their self-conceptions. So, too, Stowe's dominating presence within critical accounts of the tradition of sentimental antislavery literature has
obscured our view of Child. Child's radical difference from Stowe, her
ability to imagine a sisterhood that can tolerate inversions of power
relations, offers an alternative view of interracial relations among
women. Significantly, her tales penetrate more acceptable ideas about
womanhood and sisterhood to the level of antisisterly rage and potential
for violence that racism makes inevitable. Finally, though I have worked
to show that the promises of sisterhood under slavery were simply
another family romance, it warrants saying emphatically that the efforts
of these women to construct a sisterhood mobilized a political force that
did change their worlds.

NOTES

I wish to thank Christopher Bongie, Dagmar Herzog, and Mary K. Jaeger
for reading a very rough draft of this essay and for their wonderful suggestions. I also owe thanks to Richard M. Hunt, Jay Maclean, and the Harvard

University Mellon Faculty Fellowship program for providing me with a forum for presenting my work. This essay is part of a larger project, *Mastering Slavery: Trauma, Writing, and Identity in Women's Slave Narratives.*

1. For a discussion of the implications of this dualism for slavery in the American South, see Oakes, *Slavery and Freedom,* chap. 1.

2. George M. Frederickson describes romantic racialism as "The American 'ethnologic' self-image, whether described as Anglican, Anglo-Saxon, Celtic-Anglo-Saxon, or simply Caucasian, [which] was formulated and popularized at the very time when the slavery controversy focused interest on the Negro character" (100).

3. In 1850, census takers counted 246,000 mulatto slaves out of a total slave population of 3.2 million; again, in 1860, census takers identified 411,000 mulatto slaves out of a total slave population of 3.9 million. But as John Hope Franklin and Alfred A. Moss, Jr. caution, these numbers may be inaccurate, since census takers counted only as mulattoes those who *appeared* to be of mixed parentage.

4. For a brief discussion of the assumption of "mulatto superiority" and its persistence after slavery, see C. W. Harper, "Black Aristocrats: Domestic Servants on the Antebellum Plantation."

5. See Freud, "Family Romances" (1908).

6. Anna Shannon Elfenbein sees reproduction of the quadroon mother's fate in the daughter's tale as being characteristic of their racially overdetermined fate: "Unlike Hester, her fate was often to reproduce her own tragedy. . . . She could not prevent her daughters from suffering as she had suffered" (3). Indeed, unlike Pamela, no amount of resistance or self-assertion could lead to her socially and legally sanctioned marriage to the lord of the manor.

7. This play on and in Xarifa's name was pointed out to me by Christopher Bongie.

8. In "Infantile Anxiety-Situations Reflected in a Work of Art and in the Creative Impulse," Klein explains the alternation between destructive impulses and reactive tendencies as arising out of the anxiety produced by the girl's aggressive impulses toward her mother and her fear that her mother, in turn, wishes to destroy her.

9. Despite the evidence of slave narratives that white southern mistresses often verbally and physically abused their slaves themselves, proslavery ideology insisted on the physical frailty, delicacy, and passivity of women for its own purposes. According to Fox-Genovese, such a view of white southern womanhood implicitly distanced her from her dark African slaves and justified her need for servants. It also turned white male aggression and domination into a positive value, necessary to protect the southern lady against "unruly" men, white or black. See Fox-Genovese, chap. 4, "Gender Conventions."

10. See Freud, "The 'Uncanny'" (1919).

11. For D. W. Winnicott, illusion belongs to an early stage in development during which the mother, adapting to her infant's needs, fosters the infant's illusion that what the infant creates in thought really exists. Accordingly,

disillusionment, effected when the child recognizes the mother as something outside itself, is necessary for development. The intermediary area of illusion, accepted as belonging both to internal and external (shared) perceptions, finds adult expression in, for one thing, art. See Winnicott, "Transitional Objects and Transitional Phenomena" in *Playing and Reality.*

12. The implications of this passage were first pointed out to me by Judith Fetterley.

13. Stowe's narrative tendency toward incorporation is illustrated in her encounter with the slave narrator Harriet Jacobs. In 1853, Jacobs learned that Mrs. Stowe wanted to use the "extraordinary event" of Jacobs's seven years of hiding in a crawlspace in her *A Key to Uncle Tom's Cabin.* Jacobs responded with "such a spirit of rivalry" (as she wrote to her confidante, Amy Post) that "I hardly know where to begin. . . . For I wished it [her narrative] to be a history of my life entirely by itself which would do more good and it needed no romance" (Jacobs 1987, 235).

REFERENCES

Child, Lydia Maria. *Fact and Fiction: A Recollection of Stories.* New York: C. S. Francis and Co., 1846.

———. "Slavery's Pleasant Homes" in *The Liberty Bell* by Friends of Boston, 147–60. Boston: Anti-Slavery Fair, 1843.

Elfenbein, Anna Shannon. *Women on the Color Line: Evolving Stereotypes and the Writings of George Washington Cable, Grace King, Kate Chopin.* Charlottesville: University of Virginia Press, 1989.

Fisher, Philip. *Hard Facts: Setting and Form in the American Novel.* New York: Oxford University Press, 1987.

Fox-Genovese, Elizabeth. *Within the Plantation Household: Black and White Women of the Old South.* Chapel Hill: The University of North Carolina Press, 1988.

Franklin, John Hope, and Alfred A. Moss, Jr. *From Slavery to Freedom: A History of Negro Americans.* 6th ed. New York: McGraw-Hill, 1988.

Frederickson, George M. *The Black Image in the White Mind: The Debate on Afro-American Character and Destiny, 1817–1914.* New York: Harper and Row, 1971.

Freud, Sigmund. "Family Romances" (1908). In *The Standard Edition of the Complete Works of Sigmund Freud,* 9: 235–44. Translated and edited by James Strachey. London: Hogarth Press, 1961.

———. "The 'Uncanny'" (1919). In *The Standard Edition of the Complete Works of Sigmund Freud,* 18: 219–52. Translated and edited by James Strachey. London: Hogarth Press, 1961.

Harper, C. W. "Black Aristocrats: Domestic Servants on the Antebellum Plantation." *Phylon* 46 (1985): 123–35.

Jacobs, Harriet A. *Incidents in the Life of a Slave Girl: Written by Herself.* Edited by Jean Fagan Yellin. Cambridge: Harvard University Press, 1987.

Klein, Melanie. "Infantile Anxiety Situations Reflected in a Work of Art and in the Creative Impulse" (1929). In *Love, Guilt and Reparation and Other Works, 1921–1945*, 210–18. New York: Dell Publishing Co.

Nudelman, Franny. "Harriet Jacobs and the Sentimental Politics of Suffering." *ELH* 59 (1992): 939–64.

Oakes, James. *Slavery and Freedom: An Interpretation of the Old South*. New York: Vintage, 1990.

Stewart, Maria W. "Productions of Mrs. Maria Stewart." In *Spiritual Narratives*, 1–84. Edited by Sue E. Houchins. New York: Oxford University Press, 1988.

Stowe, Harriet Beecher. *Uncle Tom's Cabin, or, Life among the Lowly*. 1852. Reprint. New York: New American Library, 1981.

Winnicott, D. W. *Playing and Reality*. 1971. Reprint. London: Routledge, 1991.

7.

TRUE CRIMES OF MOTHERHOOD: MOTHER-DAUGHTER INCEST, MULTIPLE PERSONALITY DISORDER, AND THE TRUE CRIME NOVEL

ROSARIA CHAMPAGNE

PATIENT: Mother, I am frightened.
CHARCOT: Note the emotional outburst. If we let things go unabated we will soon return to the epileptoid behavior. . . . (The patient cries again: "Oh! Mother.")
CHARCOT: Again, note these screams. You could say it is a lot of noise over nothing.

(Charcot the Clinician 104–5)

Feminism has historically relied on the mother-daughter bond as a non-contested category for women's connection and social activism (Chodorow; Friday). And yet, with the genre of women's true crime fiction, mother-daughter abuse shows up in every narrative gap. There are two formula plots for this genre: in the first, a white upper-middle-class woman murders her daughters; her neighbors and tennis pals are shocked; her husband didn't see it coming. (These narratives flourish in white middle-class women's magazines, such as *Redbook* and *Woman's Day*). The second model, typified by Flora Rheta Schreiber's *Sybil*, centers the mother-daughter relationship around incest, not murder.

Important elements of plot and politics distinguish this model: the featured presence of abusive mothers; lesbianism in the bodies of women already sanctioned as heterosexual; the production of a multiple daughter, whose unproblematized discourse of confession, disclosure, and confrontation fails to reconstruct the individual (that is, humanism cannot restore the multiple to a single consciousness); and the replacement of the incestuous mother with the mother-therapist. It is this therapist-mother role that, I will argue, inscribes the misogyny that sustains mother-daughter abuse by setting up the crazy mother who "makes" a crazy daughter and then pits the crazy mother against the mother-therapist, who emerges at the narrative's close as the good and more deserving mother.

Discussions about incest and its aftereffects almost always configure a father (or father figure) perpetrator, and a daughter (or surrogate) victim/survivor. While it is absolutely true that men commit sexual abuse more often than women, women can also function as perpetrators of incest. By privileging the father-daughter incest paradigm, we successfully inscribe the "sentimental romance" of heterosexuality (Zwinger) and cannot account for one of the signal aftereffects of incest—multiple personality disorder (MPD). MPD, only recognized by the American Psychiatric Association as an aftereffect of incest since 1980 (DSM-III, 269–72; Howland, 299), frustrates the father-daughter incest paradigm because, at least as represented in women's true crime novels, mothers cause MPD. But, I will argue, "mothers" recast as mother-therapists also "cure" MPD by recapitulating a desperately felt belief in the healing power of motherhood.

In this essay, I will use Flora Rheta Schreiber's *Sybil* and Joan Frances Casey's *The Flock: The Autobiography of a Multiple Personality* to show how mother-daughter abuse, the open secret of women's true crime novels, troubles the nostalgic relationship between women that feminism often desperately assumes. I will focus this essay not only on the individual mothers and daughters brought to light by these novels, but also on the role of motherhood and daughterhood. Both novels show that abusive mothers assume power through the social role of motherhood. Importantly, this same social role facilitates the feminist therapists, who function as surrogate mothers, with the power to heal. Indeed, daughters who suffer from MPD find wholeness only when they shift loyalty from the evil mother to the good one, a shift often accomplished with bribes and solicitations from the mother-therapist.[1]

These mother-therapists are indeed better mothers than the sadistic mothers that precede them, but their cure comes with a price: entrapment, always, in some mother's narrative. That is, by naturalizing and idealizing the role of motherhood and its usefulness in feminist therapy, the MPD daughter is merely reinscribed in another mother's narrative— i.e., one that is not her own. Even with sanity, good daughterhood is a dead-end street.

In *Sybil,* the story of Sybil Isabel Dorsett, who was sexually, physically, and verbally abused by her mother, Hattie Dorsett, from infancy, and her relationship with the "real"[2] Dr. Cornelia B. Wilbur (who still serves as a leading spokesperson about MPD), is narrated by Sybil herself, who, amnesiac and unaware of her sixteen other personalities, knows and feels shame because she "loses time." Vicky, Sybil's memory trace[3] who emerges when she is twelve but knows the history of the body from the age of two, works with Dr. Wilbur as a co-analysand. The Peggys— Peggy Lou and Peggy Ann—interrupt Sybil's life and therapy to express rage and anger directed at Hattie Dorset. The other twelve personalities appear and confront Dr. Wilbur throughout Sybil's eight years of therapy, and some even try at various times to "murder" Sybil.

In therapy with Dr. Wilbur, Sybil consistently replays themes that point to child abuse—secrecy, isolation, entrapment. While the aftereffects are ever-present—the most evident of which is her severe MPD— the events themselves (ritualized incest, medical abuse, verbal abuse) are "lost" in the pre-mirror stage talk and not transferable into a comprehensible narrative for the conscious, adult Sybil. While the Peggys know that Hattie sexually abused Sybil, Sybil does not. And while Vicky knows the tale of Sybil's sad plight, she believes she is an entirely separate person from Sybil. Interestingly, even though Hattie's abuse was sadistic, ritualized, and consistent, Sybil does not remember it. She only recalls that Hattie was "at once overprotective and unsympathetic" (37). When one of Sybil's alters "returns" her body to her, leaving Sybil to explain her amnesia to her boss, the police, or to a member of the medical community, she repeats in rote: "I am an only child and my parents are very good to me" (42).

Hattie perpetrated incest by tying Sybil in a bondage ritual with dish towels, penetrating her with kitchen utensils, and inducing ejaculation with unnecessary enemas. She then enforced silence and repression by "erasing" the event, by veiling it with her role as mother. Hattie reportedly said, "Now don't you dare tell anybody anything about this. If you do, I won't have to punish you. God's wrath will do it for me!" (209). (Importantly, the narrator, Flora Schreiber, writes from the psychiatrist's perspective; and so Sybil's story is really Cornelia Wilbur's story, just as Freud's case studies of his famous hysterics are his, not theirs.) The Peggys "talk" this trauma because they don't think Hattie Dorset is their mother; in fact, the fifteen other personalities that take over Sybil's body claim to have no mother at all (306). Thus, the alters capably read Hattie as perpetrator only because they refuse to read her as mother. For Sybil, the role and title of "mother" veils all abuse: "Sybil invested the perpetrator of the tortures with immunity from blame. The buttonhook was at fault, or the enema tip, or the other instruments of torture. The perpetrator, however, by virtue of being her mother, whom one had not only to obey but also to love and honor, was not to blame" (222). This mother-daughter abuse is more psychologically dangerous than father-daughter abuse precisely because her stereotyped social role overdetermines how her behavior will be read.[4]

In addition to the social role that protected Hattie's abuse from discovery was her own self-projected image—as an advocate of children's rights, of all things: "Hattie Dorsett enunciated solemn strictures about exemplary child care. Never hit a child, Hattie Dorsett preached, when it is possible to avoid it, and under no circumstances hit a child on the face or head" (223). This projected image successfully prohibits Sybil from taking seriously her therapy with Dr. Wilbur until after Hattie's death. Hattie sabotages Sybil's first relationship with Dr. Wilbur by intentionally not giving Sybil a phone message that Dr. Wilbur had to cancel an appointment. Sybil feels stood up and abandoned, as Hattie had hoped, and Hattie caps the moment with another injunction for mother-love: "Dr. Wilbur didn't really care for you. . . . She tells you one thing now. But when she gets you where she wants you, she'll tell you altogether different things. And remember young lady, she'll turn on you if you tell her you don't love your own mother" (46). The only reason Sybil has the strength and desire to return to Dr. Wilbur after Hattie's death is because Sybil buffers Hattie's warning with Hattie's fundamentalist Christianity and its proscriptions against psychiatric help. (Hattie warned Sybil that Dr. Wilbur would "make [her] crazy . . . and then . . . put [her] in an institution because that's the way doctors make money" [46].)

Sybil, like all abused children, was told never to tell. For this reason, she is "scared about words" (298), and also, for this reason, she perfected a skill that afforded her nonverbal communication. For Sybil, the only terrain untouched by her mother's abuse and prohibition was drawing. When trapped, Sybil colors her way out of and into amnesia. For example, when the evangelical pastor of her family's Omaha church, hoping to involve her in church activities, asks Sybil to help him scare Satan away by painting his sermons, Sybil agrees. Because the words of the evangelical preacher scare her (Vicky tells Dr. Wilbur that, in church and in their appointments, Sybil was "scared about words" [298]), Sybil illustrates the sermons from a "scaffold nine feet above [the preacher] at an easel covered with drawing paper and spanning the entire width of the church" (299). Often during these sermons, Sybil would illustrate and "split"[5] into one of her alters. This "strategy of discourse," drawing and splitting, allows Sybil to negotiate between unnamed events and their potential meanings.[6] We see here that MPD actually helps Sybil to cope. But MPD, in its plethora of visual figures and many-voiced talk, is, ultimately, antinarrative. That is, it constitutes an endless return to the site of the mother's domination, but by reading the mother's social role over her behavior, it fails to recognize the mother as perpetrator. For Sybil, all that is left are feelings and words disconnected from agents or actors.

Psychoanalysis figures victims of MPD as almost always physically, sexually, and psychologically abused before the age of two, before the Lacanian mirror stage, the moment when the child becomes enraptured with its separateness from its mother. While the mirror stage functions as "the origin of the origin" (Roof, 93), for the multiple daughter, this origin is nebulous. Thus Anna O's famous "talking cure" cannot aid the victim of MPD because the multiple daughter cannot retrace trauma done in the presymbolic with discourse.[7] So even though the "drug of choice for multiples seems to be talk—the kind of talk that permits each of the separate traumas to be identified and relived" (Howland, 300), the talk produced by a multiple is abject[8] and therefore the trauma cannot be easily abreacted. Thus, MPD discourse (presymbolic), not (narrative) name, is talk whose signifier does not reflect its signified.

Self-help theory, as represented by Ellen Bass and Laura Davis in *The Courage to Heal: A Guide for Women Survivors of Child Sexual Abuse* (referred to by the False Memory Foundation, a family-values organization in the business of discrediting incest survivors and their therapists,[9] as the "Bible" of the incest industry and its favorite "cult" text), describes MPD as a condition produced by early childhood sexual and physical abuse that "splits" the core personality into "alters" or "multiples" who function as distinct, complex personalities and who may or may not be aware of each other (423–24). These personalities are both adaptive and defensive, using the only means available to the disempowered—manipulation of the psyche. That trauma literally shatters the child is made evident by Judith Herman, who writes that "traumatic events violate the autonomy of the person at the level of basic bodily integrity. The body is invaded, injured, defiled" (Herman, *Trauma and Recovery*, 52–53). And it is for this reason that "the traumatic event thus destroys the belief that one can *be oneself* in relation to others" (53; Herman's italics). MPD is dissociation to the extreme; triggered by shame and self-loathing, it represents the release of the rage that victims/survivors embody. Those children who were tortured at a very young, preverbal age, and who have nowhere else to turn, turn inward. Dr. Wilbur adds psychological abuse ("demeaning, denigrating, or ridiculing infants and children" [4]) to the list of MPD-producing traumas. And Margaret Smith features MPD in her recent book, *Ritual Abuse,* stating that the entrapment of ritual abuse almost always results in MPD.

Because of his failure to offer escape, Willard Dorsett, Sybil's father, also serves as an accomplice to Hattie's crime. Importantly, though, he also participated in a bedtime ritual that is sometimes defined as incest. Until the age of nine, Sybil slept in a crib in her parent's bedroom and, three times a week, was forced to watch them have sex. In a list of abusive practices headed by the descriptor, "How Can I Know If I Was a Victim of Childhood Sexual Abuse," Bass and Davis include "made to watch sexual acts or look at sexual parts" (21) as an example. Schreiber writes: "Three or four nights a week, year in and year out, parental intercourse took place within her hearing and vision. And not infrequently, the erect penis was easily visible in the half-light" (185). Importantly, neither the narrator nor the psychiatrist nor the patient blames Willard Dorsett for this display. Instead, Vicky tells Dr. Wilbur that "Hattie Dorsett actually wanted her daughter to look" (186), and the doctor concurs.

Indeed, Willard is not ever made to take responsibility for his behavior, and this reader is left wondering if this omission is not an extension of male privilege—in this case the privilege of freedom from the responsibility for proper parenting. This is made especially clear in the confrontation that Dr. Wilbur has with Willard Dorsett. Dr. Wilbur commands

Willard to meet her in her office (in spite of his poor health, advanced age, and difficulty traveling) under the pretense of needing more "hard evidence" to legitimate and authorize the experiences of child abuse revealed by Sybil's alters. In a chapter called "Confrontation and Verification," Dr. Wilbur stages a showdown that successfully emasculates Willard Dorsett, making clear to the reader who really wields the power of the phallus. After Dr. Wilbur feeds Willard memories from the past, his large stature seems to shrink. Like a mollusk, Willard Dorsett had always stayed within his shell, insulated in the private sea of his own concerns. He has been resolute in pursuing a path of conformity, refusing to look in any other direction. Now the mollusk, out of the sea, was steaming in hot water, its shell cracking (271). And just in case the drama of Dr. Wilbur's emasculation of Willard Dorsett is not readily apparent, the narrator tells us: "It was a pivotal moment, the kind that the classic Greek dramatists describe as a peripety—the moment in which the action of a drama assumes a quick catastrophic new turn, a reversal" (273). Importantly, Willard is only held accountable for facilitating Hattie's abuse through his absence. Finally, when Dr. Wilbur repeatedly asks Willard why he allowed Hattie to raise Sybil, even when "this schizophrenic mother came very close to killing her child" (274), Willard is reduced to repeating himself like a traumatized child: "It's a mother's place to raise a child" (274), he chants.

Enforced voyeurism also shows up again in Sybil's life, when Sybil watches her mother sexually abuse the small children Hattie babysat for on Sundays (204) and witnesses Hattie masturbating the adolescent, but "lower crust," lesbians at the beach (205). And medical records indicate forms of more recognizable child abuse: "The dislocated shoulder, the fractured larynx, the burned hand, the bead in the nose, [nearly suffocating in] the wheat crib, the black eyes, the swollen lips" (221). Through this "training," Sybil developed other aftereffects associated with incest: eating disorders (42), time and memory lapses (47, 57) that eventually convert into MPD (96, 98, 99, 207), the acting out of particular scenes (Peggy Lou, who breaks glass in an effort to escape Hattie's kitchen [66]; "the blonde" who hurls herself against walls and glass doors trying to escape traumatic blows to the body [432]); the deep shame regarding her body and her inability to stay present (70, 151); the inability to feel anger because, even after her death, Hattie won't allow it (72, 75); the unexplained neurological disorders (165); the transference of fear from the perpetrator to the objects of abuse (222); and the fear of intimacy and people (341). Also evident was Sybil's repressed rage at the teachers who never ask, the grandparents who live above the kitchen and never hear, the family physician who knows but never tells, the father who pretends never to notice, and the religion that declares, to quote the title of Alice Miller's excellent book, "Thou shalt not be aware" of parental abuse.

With the whole culture behind her, the abusive mother is entirely unreadable; she becomes visible only when we read her through her daughter's aftereffects, such as MPD.

In *The Flock: The Autobiography of a Multiple Personality,* Joan Casey, the personality recuperated by therapist Lynn Wilson, experiences a childhood similar to Sybil's. Lynn, a social worker at a university clinic, expresses anxiety over her lack of medical credentials and consults Cornelia Wilbur, leaning on Dr. Wilbur to guide her through the process of Joan's therapy and integration. The narrative of *The Flock* is held together by this intertextual therapy-driven matriarchy: Cornelia Wilbur "mothers" Lynn Wilson, who "mothers" Joan Casey; Joan reads *Sybil* with an obsession, feels Sybil is an older sister, and encourages Joan to model Dr. Wilbur's therapy/parenting approach. (Dr. Wilbur denies that she ever used a "parenting" approach, and insists that the narrator, Flora Schreiber, embellished this role for the purpose of creating a good story.) Joan has twenty-four personalities, differing in age, gender, and sexual orientation. The personalities of Jo (withdrawn, academic, unfeminine), Renee (fun, sexual, personable), Missy (a needy six-year old), Iris (a lesbian), Joan Frances (suicidal over unrequited mother-worship), Rusty (an illiterate, misogynist boy), and Josie (a two-year-old who hurls herself into walls and through glass and, by so doing, constantly relives and performs her mother's physical abuse) function as primary storytellers in Joan Casey's life. Secrets abound in *The Flock.* Just as Sybil "quickly . . . reassured herself that what she didn't dare tell had not been told" because "she realized she would never be able to tell" (43), so too Jo tells Lynn, "It's like I'm carrying around this huge secret that I'm never supposed to tell. But since I don't remember just what I'm supposed to keep secret, [I'm afraid] I'll tell it by mistake" (30).

In *The Flock,* Joan's father was an incest perpetrator. Long before Missy tells Lynn that Joan was raped by her father and Josie replays the scene in Lynn's office (and breaks two of Lynn's ribs in the process), Joan's mother, Nancy, pooh-poohs her daughter's weakness, telling her,

"Look at me. You don't see me running to a therapist with every little crisis. My stepfather abused me—you've seen the scars on my back from the beatings—and I came through it without a therapist" (24). Indeed, Joan Frances replays her mother's words in her therapist's office: "Joan Frances admitted no blankness, no multiplicity, but provided only vague statements about the ideal childhood her mother claimed she had" (56). And while Jo has no early childhood memories of her mother and none of Missy's memories of rape, she does remember "happy" early childhood times with her father—playing driver of his car—until his erection intrudes: "Daddy's hardness under her buttocks and the hard steering wheel in her hands were equally part of the experience" (77). In spite of father-daughter incest, Lynn (and eventually Joan) believes that her mother's physical brutality followed by emotional coldness before the age of two caused Joan's MPD. The alter Josie remembers this brutality and "desires" the repetition compulsion of blacking out by beating her head and body on the wall or floor: "One day when [Mother] screamed in rage at her two-year-old daughter, Josie found herself propelled against a wall. Josie, created in that instinctual certainty that she was about to die, remembered her terror and then a wonderful blackness that brought peace" (79). So even though the father assumes the role of incest perpetrator in *The Flock*, it is the preverbal mother-daughter abuse that splits Joan into a multiple.

Joan embodies the abuse of the incestuous parent with the concomitant neglect and betrayal of the other parent. Unlike Sybil, who has no access to her alters when they talk with Dr. Wilbur, Joan hears the therapy sessions with Lynn, but does not have access to the behaviors of the alters when they take over the body. And so Joan watches Josie relive a rape scene, and then turns to Lynn and her husband Gordon (who becomes a co-therapist of "the flock," the term Joan uses to describe herself), saying: "Josie was raped by her father" (157). Rusty, who hates women and is sure he will grow a penis in time to escape the body, emerges when Ray, Joan's father, initiates father-daughter camping trips (172). Rusty can't read because part of this incest ritual includes the "woods game" (173), a chase of entrapment when Ray writes his lust for his daughter in the sand with his urine, which he then forces his daughter, who transmogrifies into the illiterate Rusty, to read (173). The frustration Rusty feels for his inability to perform the task of reading overshadows the body's fear of incest. Importantly, Rusty is raped by words he cannot read, as is evident in his repetition compulsion during therapy with Gordon (whom he calls "Dad"): "The words . . . they're everywhere, Dad. The words, Dad. They're gonna cut me. They're gonna kill me" (260). Screaming castration anxiety, Rusty turns into Josie, and Gordon watches as Joan relives the feeling of being "cut" open with Ray's penis, the instrument of the words in the sand.

Joan manifests aftereffects that don't make sense to her because the MPD-producing trauma predates the mirror stage, the organizing moment of narrative. But even though Nancy does not perpetrate incest against her daughter as Hattie does, it is her abuse that "splits" Joan because Joan feels she cannot afford escape—either physical or emotional—from her mother.

The narrator and the therapist in both *Sybil* and *The Flock* collude against the crazy biological mothers; in the course of therapy, they become surrogate mothers. This is a dangerous move, since all mothers function as potentially abusive mothers when mother-love and mother-abuse define mothering on any terms as something that daughters literally, painfully, need. Furthermore, because mother-daughter abuse often extends "normal" mother-daughter intrusions (such as excessive medicalization), mother-love is simultaneously lethal and necessary. Thus this alliance of narrator and therapist against the abusive mother in the "battle for the daughter" misreads the role of the therapist in recovery. Narrative positioning aligns the narrator (and audience) with the female therapists who assume the role of good mothers, castigate the abusive mothers as bad mothers, and retain the role of motherhood as an unproblematic one. This collusion breaks with a fundamental distance necessary, according to Judith Herman, for the empowerment of women in therapy. According to Herman (in chapter 7 of *Trauma and Recovery*), a feminist therapist should promise to bear witness, work in solidarity with the survivor, empower the survivor by making her responsible for her decisions and for her truth-telling. But once the feminist-therapist asks for emotional support from the survivor in the form of devotion and mother-love, a dangerous boundary has been transgressed, a line Lynn Wilson has clearly crossed.

This transgression occurs because of the transference and countertransference in therapy (processes whereby unconscious wishes and needs are swapped between client and therapist) and because, isolated, Lynn as therapist-mother starts to undergo a secondary victimization, taking on Joan's pain, isolation, and secrecy. The problem begins because Lynn feels isolated in her place of work. She makes it clear that her supervisor does not "believe" in MPD and that she is then unable to include him in the diagnostic process. Lynn writes: "The lack of support I feel among my colleagues makes me unwilling to talk with them about this case. . . . I have been taking my own uncertainty and excitement home" (29). Lynn here manifests a particularly dangerous countertransference; she imagines herself indispensable, the all-loving mother who alone knows what Joan needs and stands with her multiple patient against the world. This countertransference makes Lynn take on the role of rescuer when Joan needs to learn how to help herself. Judith Herman refers to just such a therapist-patient relationship when she describes a therapist who

come[s] to feel that she is the only one who really understands the patient, and she may become arrogant and adversarial with skeptical colleagues. As she feels increasingly isolated and helpless, the temptations of either grandiose action or flight become irresistible. Sooner or later she will indeed make serious errors. It cannot be reiterated too often: *no one can face trauma alone.* If a therapist finds herself isolated in her professional practice, she should discontinue working with traumatized patients until she has secured an adequate support system. (*Trauma and Recovery*, 152–53; Herman's italics)

Perhaps because *The Flock* is narrated through the journals that Lynn Wilson and Joan Casey kept throughout their six years of work together, no "error" of the kind Herman points to is disclosed. But the narrative ends abruptly with Lynn and Gordon's untimely death in a boating accident. With no (narrative) time to "process" this abandonment, *The Flock* concludes with Joan energized and alienated in her unresolved grief over her loss of the entire symbolic parental unit. This reader knows a crash and possible relapse will follow, but *The Flock* ends before such a crash occurs. Our last glimpse of Joan captures her with her husband, her son, and her tenure-track job, none of which inspires great confidence on my part.

The mother-therapist role becomes solidified when the abusive mothers, jealous of the therapists, participate in the therapist-patient relationship with their own transference. When Sybil's and Joan's mothers try to sabotage their daughters' relationships with their therapist, Dr. Wilbur and Lynn Wilson transmogrify into overly protective and threatened mothers themselves. This also functions as a kind of transference, where the crazy mothers' desire to own their daughters is projected onto the therapists themselves, who unwittingly become the characters they oppose. It is here that the therapists threaten to become "phallic mothers," as the fantasy of the phallic mother is to be everything for the child. While Dr. Wilbur shows more restraint, Lynn Wilson becomes energized and excited by her role as a surrogate mother for Joan, as is evident when she speculates in her journal:

Gordon's and my success so far is beyond my wildest dreams. We are not only providing what the various personalities need at various times; we are also modeling good parenting and a healthy marriage for all of them. Jo and Missy both watch me carefully to see how I'll respond to their enjoyment of Gordon. Unlike her mother, I'm not envious of the relationship they have. In some respects, the mother role is not a new transition, just one newly recognized. I've known for two years of cuddling Missy and the other very young personalities that I was providing healthy maternal love. Although Renee would never accept hearing this, I mother her as well, using what I learned when my own daughters were teenagers. Like any wise mother of a teenager, I allow Renee to depend on my counsel without ever drawing attention to the fact of her dependency. Mothering Jo is a joy, if for no other reason than her beginning to realize that, even within her own limited personality, she is a lovely young woman whom I am proud to call my daughter. (166)

By becoming a mother again, Lynn can avoid her mid-life slump.[10] Lynn steps into the role of motherhood without recognizing that this same social role aided and abetted Joan's trauma. Playing out the good daughter role she knows so well, Joan accepts these new parents, referring to Lynn and Gordon as her "therapist-parents" (207). Lynn thinks of the post-integration Joan with the same "marvel [she] felt in seeing [her] first grandchild" (288). And while Cornelia Wilbur is maternal in her own way, in her "exorcism" of Hattie Dorsett she also positions herself as the protective mother-replacement: " 'I'm helping you to grow up,' the doctor would [say]. 'You're getting better, and you're going to be able to use all your talents.' The incantation, the exorcising of Hattie Dorsett, would proceed: 'Your mother taught you not to believe in yourself. I'm going to help you do so'" (358). And here we see the ultimate danger, the feminist therapist who colludes with the patriarchal idealization of motherhood: pitting women against each other in a duel that allows the good mother to assume the very same role that constituted the evil mother and that fed her sadism. Indeed, it is the role of motherhood that conceals and therefore conditions this abuse.

By not confronting the category of motherhood and only identifying the individuals that occupy social spaces as the agents of transgression, both texts assume as neutral and natural that Hattie and Nancy were simply evil anomalies of motherhood. When Joan attempts a confrontation with her mother, through Joan's selected omission we see how she still feels trapped by her mother's expectations that she will not "remember" her mother's abuse. After telling Nancy that Ray molested and raped her, and then "steeling [herself] for [Nancy's] angry denial" (293), Joan is amazed when her mother says: "it makes sense" and "I didn't know" and "your father always had sexual problems" (293–94). Importantly, Joan doesn't ask Nancy to take responsibility for her abusive behavior. Both Dr. Wilbur and Joan advance misdirected confrontations that serve to protect the mother-roles that the mother-therapists have now assumed. It should be recalled that when Dr. Wilbur confronts Willard, Sybil isn't even in the room to hear and see herself vindicated. In Joan's case, she doesn't confront Nancy with the issue that she has spent most of her therapy dollars addressing—the physical and verbal abuse Nancy hurled at her daughter, beginning at her birth when Joan was not the boy her mother wanted, and continuing throughout Joan's adulthood until Lynn "saves" her.

These misdirected confrontations echo the problems raised by replacing the evil mothers with the good mother-therapists. Confronting the role of motherhood threatens to destroy the power of the mother-daughter relationship that Joan and Sybil have with their therapists. Thus Joan and Sybil both become their therapists' "more-than-daughters," [11] their narratives tying together incestuously. Mothers may die, but daughters may never be autonomous, self-generating women. Importantly, these feminist therapists do not question the role of motherhood because it threatens their place vis-à-vis their new daughters. Indeed, the signal aftereffect of mother-daughter incest after MPD is the very symbiotic dynamic that sets up the potential abuse: the utter impossibility of maintaining separate boundaries between mother and daughter. Bass and Davis quote one survivor of mother-daughter incest on this point: "For a while I didn't know where my mother left off and I began. I thought she had a psychic hold on me. I was convinced she knew every thought I had. It was like she was in my body, and she was evil. I felt I was possessed, that I was going to be taken over. I've had a real fear that if I look at all that stuff that I don't like about myself, it will be my mother inside of me" (97).

Women's true crime novels that feature MPD daughters also feature a war of the mothers; the Gothic element of this war is made manifest when daughters never connect the abuser with the social role that commands that abuse.

Because heterosexism foundationalizes the theories that describe cultural practices,[12] mother-daughter abuse still cannot be narrated. Father-daughter incest is almost always portrayed as an act of sexual seduction and therefore "normalized" as an obvious extension of heterosexual practice; but abusive mothers are doubly veiled, first by the power they wield and second by a culture blinded by the stereotype of mother-love. Yet although women's true crime novels offer a cultural repository for this unnarrativizable power, they do not expose the abusive mother per se; they reveil her as evil in comparison to the nurturant feminist psychotherapist who emerges at the novel's end as the good mother. What gets lost in this war of the mothers is the voices of the multiple daughters, who always speak from some mother's abyss. In both the genre of women's true crime and the discourse of the contemporary feminist recovery movement, evil mothers assume the position of an individual's problem, not a social one. Because MPD offers an important entrance into subject construction (Hurley and O'Regan), feminist theory would do well to position daughters outside the mother's script and to read the potential abusive power inherent in the role of motherhood, instead of concealing this power in the romanticized social stereotype that refuses to name the open secret of mother-daughter bond(age).

NOTES

For their generous readings and helpful suggestions on various drafts, I thank Susan Edmunds, Teresa Goddu, Debra Moddelmog, Judith Roof, Joy Rouse, and the editors of *Feminist Nightmares*.

1. For example, Sybil's therapist, Dr. Wilbur, finds her estranged patient walking the streets at night. (Of course, one wonders why a psychiatrist trails after her patients after office hours!) She wraps her patient in her own mink coat and promises that once Sybil finds wholeness she can have a sleeve from it (370).

2. Importantly, Cornelia Wilbur (the psychiatrist) and Flora Schreiber (the narrator) are two of only a handful of "characters" in true crime novels who use real names. In the genre of true crime fiction, real names are reserved only for the guilty.

3. The "memory trace" is the alter who knows the history of all the other alters. She carries the memory, pain, and triumph of the others, and when

social demands require that the victim produce memory and history, this alter often cues in.

4. As Jane Gallop puts it, "The phallic mother is more dangerous because less obviously phallic. If the phallus 'can only play its role when veiled (Lacan),' then the phallic mother is more phallic precisely by being less obvious" (118).

5. Bass and Davis define "splitting" as a common dissociative aftereffect of sexual abuse. They write: "In its milder form, you live exclusively on the mental level, in your thoughts, and aren't fully present. At its most extreme, you literally leave your body" (209).

6. Kristeva shows how this allows "the subject to articulate abrupt passages between the real, the imaginary and the symbolic" (Kristeva, 218). Sybil, when splitting, talks in the pre-Symbolic real, and inscribes truth in what Kristeva calls "hysterical discourse": "In hysterical discourse, truth, when not weighed down by the symptom, often assumes the obsessive, unsayable and emotionally charged weft of visual representation. Floating in isolation, this vision of an unnamed real rejects all nomination and any possible narrative" (227).

7. See Breuer and Freud, *Studies in Hysteria,* Case Study 1, "Fraulein Anna O.," and Diane Hunter's brilliant essay, "Hysteria, Psychoanalysis, and Feminism: The Case of Anna O."

8. The abject is "neither subject nor object . . . [it] makes clear the impossible and untenable identity of each. . . . The abject is an impossible object, still part of the subject: an object the subject tries to expel but which is uneliminable. . . . These ingested/expelled objects are neither part of the body nor separate from it. . . . The abject is undecidably both inside and outside (like the skin of milk); dead and alive (like the corpse); autonomous and engulfing (like infection). It signals the precarious grasp the subject has over its identity and bodily boundaries, the ever-present possibility of sliding back into the corporeal abyss out of which it was formed" (Wright, 197–98).

9. The False Memory Foundation is located at 3401 Market Street, Suite 130, Philadelphia, Pennsylvania, 19104; 1–800–568–8882. They are a 3,000–plus member organization that began in March, 1992. Neither the organization nor the syndrome has been formally recognized by the American Psychological Association.

10. In the prologue, Lynn writes: "When I first met Joan, on a snowy day in 1981, I was approaching a transition in my life. My daughter Lisa, youngest of five, was finishing her final year at home. For the first time in thirty years, I would have no children with me. For the first time in our seventeen years of marriage, my second husband, Gordon, and I would be alone together" (1).

11. This may be a stretch, but in Mary Shelley's early fiction, especially her incest narratives *Mathilda* (1819) and *Frankenstein* (1818), incest assumes the place of "normal" familial extensions, not obviously marked transgressions. This phrase of Mary Shelley's, "more-than-daughter," is a symptom-

atic repetition revealing, I believe, the particular pain that occurs when abuse is normalized and naturalized by social practice. I use this phrase here because the transgression from therapist to surrogate mother is, ultimately, a transgression of incest.

12. See, for example, a most intriguing side comment by Nancy Chodorow in *The Reproduction of Mothering:* "Mother-daughter incest may be the most 'socially regressive' in the sense of a basic threat to species survival, since a mother and son can at least produce a child. But the threat of mother-daughter incestuous and exclusive involvement has been met by a girl's entry into the oedipus situation and her change of genital erotic object" (132). Not only does the daughter become responsible for the incest potential of the phallic mother here, but, we are told, if she plays her heterosexually determining cards right, then she need not fret about mother-invasion at all.

REFERENCES

American Psychiatric Association, Diagnostic and Statistical Manual of Mental Disorders, 3d ed. (DSM-III). Washington, D.C.: American Psychiatric Association Press, 1980.

Bass, Ellen, and Laura Davis. *The Courage to Heal: A Guide for Women Survivors of Child Sexual Abuse.* New York: Harper and Row, 1988.

Bijkerk, Inie, and Kathy Evert. *When You're Ready: A Woman's Healing from Childhood Physical and Sexual Abuse by Her Mother.* Rockville, Md.: Launch Press, 1987.

Breuer, Josef, and Sigmund Freud. *Studies in Hysteria.* In *The Standard Edition of the Complete Psychological Works of Sigmund Freud,* vol. 2. Translated by James Strachey. London: Hogarth Press, 1955.

Casey, Joan Frances, and Lynn Wilson. *The Flock: The Autobiography of a Multiple Personality.* New York: Fawcett, 1991.

Chodorow, Nancy. *The Reproduction of Mothering: Psychoanalysis and the Sociology of Gender.* Berkeley: University of California Press, 1978.

Foucault, Michel. *The History of Sexuality. Volume 1: An Introduction.* Translated by Robert Hurley. New York: Vintage Press, 1987.

Friday, Nancy. *My Mother/My Self: The Daughter's Search for Identity.* New York: Delacorte, 1977.

Gallop, Jane. *The Daughter's Seduction: Feminism and Psychoanalysis.* Ithaca: Cornell University Press, 1981.

Hacking, Ian. "Making Up People." In *Forms of Desire: Sexual Orientation and the Social Constructionist Controversy,* edited by Edward Stein, 69–89. New York: Routledge, 1992.

———. "Two Souls in One Body." *Critical Inquiry* 17.4 (1991): 838–67.

Herman, Judith Lewis. "Backtalk: The Abuses of Memory." *Mother Jones,* March/April 1993, 3–4.

———. *Father-Daughter Incest.* Cambridge: Harvard University Press, 1981.

————. *Trauma and Recovery: The Aftermath of Violence.* New York: Basic Books, 1992.

Howland, Frances, M.D. "Afterword." In Casey and Wilson, 299–303.

Hunter, Diane. "Hysteria, Psychoanalysis, and Feminism: The Case of Anna O." In *The (M)other Tongue: Essays in Psychoanalytic Interpretation,* eds. Shirley Nelson Garner, Claire Kahane, and Madelon Sprengnether, 89–115. Ithaca: Cornell University Press, 1985.

Hurley, Thomas J. III, and Brenden O'Regan. "Multiple Personality—Mirrors of a New Model of Mind?" *Investigations: Institute of Noetic Sciences* 1 (3/4).

Kristeva, Julia. "The True-Real." Translated by Sean Hand. *The Kristeva Reader,* ed. Toril Moi, 216–37. New York: Basil Blackwell, 1986.

Lacan, Jacques. *Ecrits: A Selection.* Translated by Alan Sheridan. New York: Norton, 1977.

————. *Feminine Sexuality: Jacques Lacan and the "ecole freudienne."* Edited by Juliet Mitchell and Jacqueline Rose. Translated by Jacqueline Rose. London: Macmillan, 1982.

————. *The Four Fundamental Concepts of Psycho-Analysis.* Edited by Jacques-Alain Miller. Translated by Alan Sheridan. New York: Norton, 1981.

Laplanche, Jean, and J.-B. Pontalis. "Fantasy and the Origins of Sexuality." *International Journal of Psycho-Analysis* 49 (1968): 1–18.

————. *The Language of Psycho-Analysis.* Translated by Donald Nicholson-Smith. New York: Norton, 1973.

Miller, Alice. *Thou Shalt Not Be Aware: Society's Betrayal of the Child.* Translated by Hildegarde and Hunter Hannum. New York: Meridian, 1984.

Roof, Judith. *A Lure of Knowledge: Lesbian Sexuality and Theory.* New York: Columbia University Press, 1991.

Schreiber, Flora Rheta. *Sybil.* New York: Warner Books, 1973.

Smith, Margaret. *Ritual Abuse.* New York: Harper-Collins, 1993.

Wilbur, Cornelia B., M.D. "Multiple Personality and Child Abuse: An Overview." *Psychiatric Clinics of North America* 7.1 (1984): 3–7.

Wright, Elizabeth, ed. *Feminism and Psychoanalysis: A Critical Dictionary.* New York: Basil Blackwell, 1992.

Zwinger, Lynda. *Daughters, Fathers, and the Novel: The Sentimental Romance of Heterosexuality.* Madison: University of Wisconsin Press, 1991.

8.

EQUALITY, OPPRESSION, AND ABORTION: WOMEN WHO OPPOSE ABORTION RIGHTS IN THE NAME OF FEMINISM

LINDA C. McCLAIN

The ability of women to participate equally in the economic and social life of the nation has been facilitated by their ability to control their reproductive lives.
— *Planned Parenthood v. Casey*, 112 S.Ct. 2791, 2809 (1992)
(citing Petchesky 1990)

A State's restrictions of a woman's right to terminate her pregnancy also implicate constitutional guarantees of gender equality. . . . By restricting the right to terminate pregnancies, the State conscripts women's bodies into its service, forcing women to continue their pregnancies, suffer the pains of childbirth, and in most instances, provide years of maternal care. . . . Th[e] assumption—that women can simply be forced to accept the "natural" status and incidents of motherhood—appears to rest upon a conception of women's role that has triggered the protection of the Equal Protection Clause.
— *Casey*, 112 S.Ct. at 2846–47 (Blackmun, J.) (citations omitted)

FFLA ["Feminists for Life of America"] opposes abortion as an oppression of women and as discrimination against unborn children.
— Feminists for Life of America Bylaws

OVERVIEW

There are vigorous debates among feminist theorists who share a commitment to securing reproductive freedom and keeping abortion legal concerning the best "feminist" justification of abortion rights, the most persuasive rhetoric, and the proper relationship among law, theory, and women's actual experiences.[1] Despite their differences, these feminist theorists most likely would concur that the right to choose abortion is a "core issue of women's equality and liberty" (Law 1984: 1028). But some women who identify themselves as feminists claim that, to be true to feminist principles, one should oppose legal abortion. They argue not only that legal abortion is against the best interests of women and a reflection of women's inequality, but also that it is a violent and unacceptable killing of vulnerable, helpless human life, a violence incompatible with feminist principles. A central tenet of the "pro-life" (or "anti-choice") feminists[2] studied here is that restricting legal abortion will force society to eliminate the constraints now, in their view, leading women to choose abortion.

To note that *women* are at odds over abortion is not a novel observation, nor is it controversial to point out the prominence of women in advocacy for and against keeping abortion legal (Luker 1984; Ginsburg 1989). I shall look at the more provocative claims by a small but increasingly visible and vocal organization, Feminists for Life of America ("FFLA"), which imply that *feminists* are at odds over a commitment to legal abortion.[3] This essay examines a cluster of claims made by FFLA and other "pro-life" feminists and raises a number of questions about how such a group links its position on abortion to historical and contemporary feminism and situates itself as part of an asserted conflict among feminists.

This essay also explores the striking mirroring, or inversion, of the language of sex equality and oppression in arguments supporting a right to abortion, on the one hand, and those opposing legal abortion, on the other hand. Two parallels are particularly notable: (1) claims that abortion is legally available to facilitate irresponsible, predatory sexual behavior by men and that abortion is violence against women; and (2) claims that women are driven to abortion because of societal failure to accommodate pregnant women and mothers. Despite these parallels, such arguments diverge on the ultimate question of state regulation of women's reproductive decisions.

Finally, this essay raises a number of questions about how to assess the claims made by "pro-life" feminism. The questions go to issues of substance, method, strategy, and rhetoric. In conclusion, I ask whether the parallels in rhetoric about abortion among pro-choice and "pro-life" feminists point to any genuine common ground.

ABORTION AS "A BADGE AND INCIDENT OF THE OPPRESSION OF WOMEN"

Bray v. Alexandria Women's Health Clinic

In *Bray v. Alexandria Women's Health Clinic*, 113 S. Ct. 753 (1993), the Supreme Court considered the question of whether Operation Rescue members, who engaged in blockades of abortion clinics at which abortions (among other medical services) were provided, had been properly enjoined under a Reconstruction-era federal civil rights law. The National Organization for Women (NOW) and other organizations argued that Operation Rescue's activities constituted a conspiracy to deprive women who sought to enter the clinics of the equal protection of the laws. Although FFLA's bylaws indicate that it takes "no position on rescues" (FFLA Bylaws),[4] FFLA together with other organizations filed an *amicus curiae* ("friend of the court") brief in support of Operation Rescue (FFLA 1991). FFLA offered its brief as relevant to the issue of whether the motivation of the protestors was animus toward women, which was required to justify enjoining the blockades under the statute. Indeed, Operation Rescue's brief made women's opposition to legal abortion and participation in "rescues" a core element of its denial of any animus toward women (1991). FFLA stated that its brief was "largely devoted" to presenting the Supreme Court with contemporaneous "evidence" that nineteenth-century feminist condemnation of abortion was based not on animus against women, but upon a conviction that abortion was "the oppression of women as well as the killing of children" (1, 10). In addition, it argued that the assumption that "true" feminists today were of only one opinion on abortion could not withstand "empirical validation" (1). FFLA claimed that contemporary feminist theory is "divided on whether abortion is essential to the emancipation of women, or, as the early feminists believed, a badge and incident of the oppression of women" (3).

Mentioning the work of contemporary feminist legal theorists Robin West and Catharine MacKinnon, FFLA claimed: "A contrast is sometimes drawn in feminist theory between 'cultural' feminists, who emphasize the importance of women in the creation and nurturing of human life, and 'radical' feminists, who identify this very role as the source of oppression of women" (29). As applied to pregnancy and abortion, FFLA argued (invoking both *Roe v. Wade,* 410 U.S. 113 [1973], and West 1988): "Feminism presupposes that a pregnant woman 'is not isolated in her privacy,' . . . and that her connection to the unborn child has a profound effect upon her life, that of her child, and society at large" (1). On one side of the alleged divide, FFLA placed NOW and the other organizations opposing Operation Rescue in *Bray,* attributing to them the viewpoint that "abortion on demand" is "an indispensable component of equality and autonomy for women; and that opposition to abortion is the absolute equivalent of sex discrimination" (5). On the other side, argued FFLA, are other feminists and the "majority of American women," who supposedly reject abortion as an "authentic" gender discrimination issue, unlike "women's rights to equal pay and promotion opportunities and freedom from sexual harassment in employment," and who reject the "underlying assumption that equal protection under the Fourteenth Amendment requires unlimited abortion on demand" (6–7).

The Supreme Court reversed the lower court's holding that Operation Rescue violated the federal civil rights statute. In his opinion for the Court, Justice Scalia pointed to the presence of women in abortion protests as a fact supporting his conclusion:

Whatever one thinks of abortion, it cannot be denied that there are common and respectable reasons for opposing it, other than hatred of or condescension toward (or indeed any view at all concerning) women as a class—as is evident from the fact that men and women are on both sides of the issue, just as men and women are on both sides of petitioners' unlawful demonstrations. (*Bray,* 113 S.Ct. at 760)

Three members of the Court disagreed with Justice Scalia, both as to the motivation of the protesters and the significance of the presence of women among them. Justice O'Connor (joined by Justice Blackmun) observed in dissent that the issue before the Court was not Operation Rescue's opposition to abortion, which petitioners were free to express in a number of ways (*Bray,* 113 S. Ct. at 802). Rather, petitioners impermissibly chose "to target women seeking abortions and to prevent them from exercising their equal rights under law" (*Bray,* 113 S.Ct. at 802). Further, "the victims of petitioners' [unlawful] actions are linked by their ability to become pregnant and by their ability to terminate their pregnancies, characteristics unique to the class of women" (*Bray,* 113 S.Ct. at 802).

Justice Stevens, also in dissent, disagreed with Justice Scalia that paternalism could not underlie Operation Rescue's activities. He instead found sex-based discrimination: "It is . . . obvious that petitioners' conduct was motivated 'at least in part' by the invidious belief that individual women are not capable of deciding whether to terminate a pregnancy, or that they should not be allowed to act on such a decision." He concluded: "Petitioners' conduct is designed to deny *every* woman the opportunity to exercise a constitutional right that *only* women possess" (*Bray,* 113 S.Ct. at 788).

FFLA's denial that abortion rights play a proper role in women's equality, contrasted with Justice Stevens's observations concerning the sex discrimination present in the outright denial of choice to women, is an apt point of departure for a fuller consideration of how women could invoke feminism and equality to justify eliminating women's legal rights.

Feminists for Life of America: Opposing Abortion as "An Oppression of Women and as Discrimination against Unborn Children"

"It is tragic that the National Organization for Women feels that the rights of women depend on the death of children," says Rachel MacNair, president of Feminists for Life of America. "True feminism teaches us to respect the bodies of both women and children—not to regard their rights as being in conflict. Only a society which is accustomed to inflicting injustices on pregnant women could regard inflicting death on their children as an everyday matter." (FFLA 1992a)

Analyses of women and women's organizations who actively oppose legal abortion often conclude that "right to life" activists reject the idea of sex equality with respect to women's and men's rights and responsibilities. Such women believe that men and women are not similarly situated and do and should have different gender roles (Luker 1984: 159–60, 165; Williams 1991: 1586–88), and, indeed, trace their individual and organizational activism to their opposition to the Equal Rights Amendment and disagreement with feminism (Cuniberti 1985). Kristin Luker's study, *Abortion and the Politics of Motherhood,* is a standard citation for the proposition that such women view both contraception and abortion as threats to their social and gender roles as housewives and caretakers and as symptomatic of an increasingly undervalued realm of maternal and feminine nurture (1984). They also believe that abortion encourages the sexual exploitation of women by men as well as male irresponsibility. "Equality" has most relevance for such women with respect to the equal protection they believe is due to prenatal life, which they equate with persons (Luker 1984: 144–46).

While FFLA similarly sounds themes of male irresponsibility and the equality of prenatal life, it overtly identifies itself, and its positions on abortion and a range of other issues affecting women, as feminist and claims a general commitment to women's equality (Graham 1992; Sweet 1985).[5] FFLA's claims revolve around a cluster of core tenets: (1) the early feminists properly condemned abortion as violence against women and unborn children caused by male domination and irresponsibility; (2) consistency with feminist principles and achievement of full equality for women requires condemnation of abortion, a violent act against helpless human life; (3) real equality for women results from society recognizing and meeting pregnant women's and mothers' needs, not giving women abortion rights as a "quick fix"; and (4) eliminating legal abortion will force society to accommodate women's needs and "eliminate the crisis, not the child."

In assessing FFLA's opposition to legal abortion, one must separate out two different bases for its argument: (1) that abortion is bad for women; and (2) that a fetus is a person deserving of constitutional equal protection and, hence, abortion is killing children. FFLA condemns abortion as "an oppression of women and as discrimination against unborn children" (FFLA Bylaws) and uses the slogan, "pro-woman, pro-life," postulating a harmony between the two propositions.[6] But the second proposition, more than the first, appears to be the driving force behind FFLA's opposition. First, it supplies much of the content as to why abortion is bad for women (it requires them to kill their "children" to achieve equality). Second, while a conviction that abortion is bad for women would not necessarily lead to opposition to legal abortion, a genuine conviction that abortion is unjustified killing of children almost certainly would.

"What Did Our Feminist Foremothers Think about Abortion?"

FFLA poses the question, "What did our feminist foremothers think about abortion?" (FFLA Handbook, 26–27).[7] Without distinguishing the context of early feminist opposition to abortion, FFLA prominently features vivid quotations from such feminists as Elizabeth Cady Stanton linking abortion to "the masculine element everywhere overpowering the feminine" and leading to the "suffering and murder of helpless children" (FFLA 1991: 22). Thus, in forming the Susan B. Anthony List (announced as a "pro-life" counter to pro-choice funding organizations for female political candidates, Emily's List and WISH List), FFLA recounted Anthony's "scathing" condemnation of abortion as "violence against both mother and child, caused by male control over female lives" (FFLA 1992b). Such quotations are among the bases for FFLA's claims about "true" feminism and their challenge to NOW, which they claim does not speak for them or for many other women on the abortion issue (Mathewes-Green 1991).[8]

The early feminists, FFLA argues, condemned abortion as "child murder" and diagnosed it as resulting from women's lack of power (FFLA Handbook 26). In its *amicus curiae* brief in *Bray*, FFLA argued that the early feminists viewed abortion as a consequence of the oppression of women by men and that their reasons for condemning abortion are still relevant today (1991: 6, 11–20). Women turned to abortion to resolve a "crisis" pregnancy caused by coercive and sexually irresponsible men, as well as "the lack of economic and social support for pregnant women, abandoned by the fathers of their children" (19).

The twin themes of exploitative men and an unaccommodating society recur in contemporary "pro-life" feminist rhetoric. Now, as then, it is argued, abortion serves men's interests by separating sexuality from reproductive responsibility and allows society to avoid meeting the needs of pregnant women and mothers. As one FFLA member observes, "How quickly 'woman's right to choose' comes to serve 'man's right to use'" (Sweet 1985: 185). Now, as then, feminists should promote nonviolent solutions: empowering women in their sexual relationships with men and enabling women to have children (Stafford 1991). While the nineteenth-century feminists whom FFLA invokes sought to empower women through "voluntary motherhood" and the right otherwise to abstain from sex,[9] FFLA calls for a model of feminist, "fertility-aware sexuality" that includes a right to use safe, nonabortofacient contraception and for eliminating rape and violence against women (Sweet 1985: 183–92; FFLA Bylaws). FFLA's model of sexuality, thus, requires acceptance by women and men of responsibility for the possible procreative consequences of sexual activity, namely, the responsibility of parenthood (or childbearing followed by adoption).

Feminist Principles and Equality: Linking the Fate of Women and "Unborn Children"

As stated in its brief in *Bray,* FFLA asserts that there is a "division in feminist theory over whether 'women can [ ] ever achieve the fulfillment of feminist goals in a society permissive toward abortion'" (1991: 28 [quoting Callahan 1986: 232]). FFLA draws upon Sidney Callahan, a member of FFLA and an author who is one of the most prominent opponents of legal abortion identified with a "pro-life feminist" stance (1986). The claim is that a true feminist vision of justice will include "protection for the unborn child" since women create, nurture, and value life. Callahan places nonviolence and protecting the more vulnerable and powerless at the core of such a stance. In her view, feminists should side with women over men, and with prenatal life in a conflict between women and prenatal life (1986; Callahan and Callahan 1984: 296–97). Callahan argues that there is a "pro-life feminism" emergent in recent years reflecting such commitments, which often include pacifism (MacNeil-Lehrer News Hour 1989).

FFLA literature echoes Callahan's themes and resorts to frequent analogies between prenatal life and the historical treatment of women and slaves. Drawing analogies between prenatal life and categories of persons previously deprived of human rights and expressing a "concern with the social and cultural devaluation of dependent people" are predominant themes across the "right to life" movement (Ginsburg 1989: 9). How, in the view of "pro-life" feminists, are arguments using such analogies *feminist* arguments against abortion? Callahan suggests "pro-life" feminists take the view that "all the arguments asserting the value of women's development in the face of male power and hostility to feminine equality can be made on behalf of the fetus"—a parallelism making it imperative that women identify with the fetus, not the male aggressor (Callahan and Callahan 1984: 296). Thus, "pro-life" feminists argue that just as women's fates have often depended on whether they are "wanted" or "unwanted" by men, the fate of prenatal life should not depend on whether it is "wanted" or "unwanted" by, or has value in the eyes of, persons with power (pregnant women or society)—and here, prominent examples are FFLA's rejection of abortion in cases of fetal birth defects and poverty (Callahan and Callahan 1984: 156–57; Sweet 1985: 128–30). "Pro-life" feminists further contend that a core tenet of feminism is a commitment to human rights and equality, especially for the vulnerable and dependent, and that women's equality should not be achieved at the expense of "unborn children" (Callahan and Callahan 1984; Sweet 1985). They assert that women's rights are not served by treating "unborn children" as "disposable property" (here invoking Elizabeth Cady Stanton) and reject abortion as a "macho, oppressive kind of control" (FFLA Handbook 15).

Such premises about the equality of all human life appear to undergird FFLA's stated commitment to making abortion illegal, except when a pregnant woman's life is at risk (Donohoe 1993; FFLA Handbook 13–15). FFLA supports what it calls the "Inclusive Equal Rights Amendment," a combination of the Equal Rights Amendment (which it supports as long as it is "pro-life or abortion neutral") and the Human Life Amendment, which would treat prenatal life from the moment of conception as constitutionally protected persons (FFLA Bylaws; NPR 1992). FFLA writings offer differing interpretations as to the consequences of the HLA for the legality of abortion, whether complete prohibition or a scheme of individual state regulation as in the days prior to *Roe* (Sweet 1985: 35–39). As an interim strategy, it favors regulating abortion and has filed "friend of the court" briefs in support of the restrictions upheld in *Webster v. Reproductive Health Services,* 492 U.S. 490 (1989), and the informed consent provisions upheld in *Casey,* restrictions FFLA calls women's "right to know" laws (FFLA 1992c). Support for such interim measures further illustrates the determinative role played by FFLA's conviction about the status of prenatal life, since FFLA argues that many women who get abortions report later that they were not told the truth about fetal development by those in the "lucrative, unregulated abortion industry" and lament that "'if only I had known that my baby was alive, what my baby looked like, I would never have chosen abortion'" (FFLA 1989; FFLA 1992c).[10]

Abortion as Oppression of Women: Beyond Abortion Rights to Real Equality for Women

"Actually, being pro-choice only helps to oppress women. True feminists work for the right to be equal citizens, to be women with children who place emphasis on family leave, day care, and equal pay. By turning to abortion, women cower from the responsibility of fighting society's prejudice against women with children." (Rizzoni 1992)

The notion that legal abortion is a cop-out, a "quick fix," and an acquiescence to a sexist society recurs in FFLA's rhetoric.[11] Women are "oppressed" by legal abortion when they resort to it due to an inhospitable society. Women are oppressed further by the harmful physical and psychological effects of abortion, which FFLA believes are greatly underreported (FFLA 1989; FFLA 1992c). The existence of legal abortion thus permits society to ignore women's reproductive needs.

This argument builds on a claim that the female body, with its natural physical process of pregnancy, is forced through abortion to conform to a male norm. (At the same time, if a "male norm" means engaging in sex without reproductive consequences, FFLA's support for contraception suggests at least a partial acceptance of such a norm.) Thus, one FFLA member claims: "[Abortion is sexist because] it forces women to kill their unborn children in order to succeed in a man's world. . . . [Abortion] allows men to avoid sexual responsibility and employers to discriminate" (Vrazo 1992). Consider this striking formulation: "We work for a world where women are empowered and don't need to surgically alter their bodies through an abortion in order to fit into a man's world. We want to elect feminists who will work to eliminate human problems, not human beings" (Malo, quoted in "In Session" 1993).

The claims about male norms and real equality oddly echo pro-choice feminist legal theorists' work on the issue of pregnancy discrimination in the workplace and challenges to the male worker without childbearing or childrearing responsibilities as the norm (Finley 1986; Williams 1991). Indeed, "pro-life" feminists concur that women who attempt to be both mothers and workers face a range of unequal burdens and pay an unacceptable price; hence they demand that society address the costs of motherhood (Sweet 1985: 35–39). Offering abortion as a solution to pregnancy, the argument goes, accepts the male, nonpregnant body as the norm, encourages a picture of pregnancy as a disease and burden, and permits society to treat pregnant women and mothers as second-class citizens (Callahan 1986; FFLA Handbook 16). Instead, pro-life feminists seek a "society which bends to women's biological identity" and accepts women's nurturing power, instead of forcing women to alter their identity through abortion (Sweet 1985: 4).

"Eliminate the Crisis, Not the Child"

Finally, FFLA claims that eliminating legal abortion rights will force society to solve the problems posed by "crisis" or "problem" pregnancies. Thus, in support of the Human Life Amendment, FFLA testified:

> Abortion on demand has done nothing and will do nothing to change the inferior status of women. In reality, it is a reactionary solution to a problem pregnancy, for it reinforces the status quo, encouraging society not to change the conditions which force women into abortion. . . . It is our greatest hope that passage of the Hatch human life amendment will *force all of us* to work together to create a society which recognizes that fertility control is the joint responsibility of women and men and affirms that authentic reproductive freedom will only be possible in a world where women and men accept equally the responsibility for child nurturing and rearing and where there is respect for all human life. (FFLA 1981: 1157–58 [emphasis added])

This claim by FFLA is sometimes accompanied by the assertion that they will not have accomplished their goal merely by making abortion illegal; rather, they must eliminate the need for, and change attitudes about, abortion so that it becomes "unthinkable," like cannibalism (National Public Radio 1992). FFLA appears to take seriously the claim that circumstances constrain pregnant women. A recurring refrain is to "eliminate the crisis, not the child" (Mathewes-Green 1992). In doing so, FFLA members reject the term "convenience abortion" (often employed by opponents of legal abortion) as insensitive to women and speak of the "burdens" of pregnancy, which are even greater when it is "unplanned and unwanted" (FFLA Handbook 5; Mathewes-Green 1991: 28).[12]

Hence, FFLA claims that its agenda includes not merely legal but also social change, including calls for child support enforcement efforts, for policies by government or employers enabling families to care for children and dependents (such as flex-time, part-time work, day care, and maternity and paternity leaves), and for recognition of full-time child rearing as a full-time career choice (FFLA Bylaws; Sweet 1985; Callahan and Callahan 1984). Recent campaigns by the National Women's Coalition for Life, in whose formation FFLA played a prominent role, express the impulse to "go right to the heart of the issue and find out what it would have taken for aborted women to carry their babies to term, and then come up with a model program of assistance" (Morse 1992).[13]

Commenting on such a recent campaign, the "Real Choices" project, FFLA Vice President Frederica Mathewes-Green observed: "Whether abortion [is] legal or not, we can find ways to reduce those numbers and give women better choices. . . . [T]he abortion issue has shattered the unity we ought to have as women, seeking solutions for women" (Frolik 1993).

Taking the rhetoric of FFLA at face value, many of FFLA's positions described above strikingly mirror or invert prominent themes in the writing of some pro-choice feminist legal theorists on the abortion issue, parallels to which I now turn.

MIRRORS AND INVERSIONS: FFLA AND PRO-CHOICE FEMINIST THEORISTS

FFLA's *amicus curiae* brief in *Bray* purported to locate a debate among "cultural" and "radical" feminists over the compatibility of legal abortion with feminist goals as well as the link between women's equality and the right to choose abortion. Indeed, Sidney Callahan's invocation of cultural feminism to make a "case for a pro-life feminism," and FFLA's citation of Callahan, imply that "cultural feminism" opposes legal abortion and FFLA simply mirrors that stance. However, the "cultural" and "radical" feminists West categorizes generally do not divide on whether abortion should be legal. Indeed, the most common contemporary source inspiring cultural or "relational" feminism among feminist legal theorists, the work of Carol Gilligan, expressly articulated an ethic of care and responsibility in the context of studying women's decisions to *have* abortions (Gilligan 1982: 64–105). A number of feminist theorists advocate invoking notions of care, responsibility, and relational thinking to support women's right to choose (Goldstein 1988; West 1990; Colker 1992), although some critics view such a justification as unpersuasive, contradictory, and problematic (on this point sometimes noting the prominent use of language of responsibility, care, and obligation in FFLA's opposition to legal abortion) (Karlan and Ortiz 1993).

So the "cultural"/"radical" feminist division does not account for the division FFLA claims exists on the abortion issue. Interestingly, "radical" feminist analysis of equality and abortion reveals striking points of convergence with FFLA's rhetoric and assumptions, although there are critical points of divergence. I will explore two common themes in

FFLA's stance and certain strands of feminist legal theory: (1) women are driven to, and permitted to get, abortions (a violent, undesirable procedure) because of gender inequality; and (2) women have no real choice but to get abortions because of societal failure to accommodate pregnant women and mothers.

Abortion and Male Domination: "Getting Laid Was at Stake"

Feminist legal theorist Catharine MacKinnon's diagnosis of the existence of abortion as necessitated by women's inequality vis-à-vis men and society's discriminatory treatment of pregnant women and mothers offers a striking illustration of convergence with FFLA's equality arguments opposing legal abortion (MacKinnon 1987; MacKinnon 1991). Her analysis takes as the point of departure the unequal conditions under which women become pregnant. Because women do not control the conditions underlying sexual reproduction and sexual intercourse with men, sex inequality creates the conditions making abortion necessary: men's domination of women and appropriation of their bodies and women's passivity, a condition of feeling that they cannot use birth control or insist upon avoiding pregnancy, or even want to do so (1987: 95). Moreover, the legal recognition of women's abortion rights resulted from and serves men's interest in sexual access to women and in freedom from the inconvenient consequences of sexual intercourse: children (1991: 1300). As MacKinnon puts it, quoting Andrea Dworkin: "Getting laid was at stake" (1987: 99).

MacKinnon realizes that her diagnosis of the relationship between legal abortion and men's interests is echoed in anti-abortion argumentation (as are her references to *Playboy*'s funding of abortion rights [Sweet 1985: 158]). Indeed, in support of her systemic claim that abortions are legally permitted to secure women's sexual availability for use by men, she offers as "documentation" the following "pungent juxtaposition":

> Juli Loesch, a self-styled "pro-life feminist" associated with Operation Rescue [she is also a member of FFLA], says, "the idea [of abortion] is that a man can use a woman, vacuum her out, and she's ready to be used again[.]" A NOW chapter advises feminists involved with anti-choice men to "control his access to your body. . . . 'Just say no' to more sex." . . . Pro-choice and anti-choice women meet on common ground. (MacKinnon 1991: 1300 [citations omitted])

Also resonant with the rhetoric of FFLA and other groups opposed to legal abortion are MacKinnon's claims that abortion is an undesirable procedure and that it testifies to the magnitude of women's oppression: "Sex doesn't look a whole lot like freedom when it appears normatively less costly for women to risk an undesired, often painful, traumatic, dangerous, sometimes illegal, and potentially life-threatening procedure than to protect themselves in advance" (MacKinnon 1987: 95). MacKinnon also quotes Adrienne Rich's description of abortion as "violence necessitated by rapism" (MacKinnon 1987: 93).[14] Such a view mirrors FFLA's and such groups as Women Exploited by Abortion's ("WEBA") characterization of abortion as violence against both women and prenatal life and of the physical and psychological harms to women claimed to be caused by abortion.

Abortion and the Absence of Choice: Women Who Would Be Mothers

MacKinnon also makes recourse to the imagery of motherhood to describe women who have abortions, further reinforcing the picture of pregnant women forced by sex inequality to act against their own wishes. Positing a "unity in oppression" of woman and fetus, and observing that women tend to put the welfare of the fetus above their own, she states:

Many women have abortions as a desperate act of love for their unborn children. Many women conceive in battering relationships; subjecting a child to a violent father is more than they can bear. . . . Some women conceive in part to cement a relationship which dissolves or becomes violent when the man discovers the conception. . . . Many abortions occur because the woman needs to try to give herself a life. But many also occur because the woman faces the fact that she cannot give this child a life. Women's impotence to make this not so may make the decision tragic, but it is nonetheless one of absolute realism and deep responsibility as a mother. (MacKinnon 1991: 1313)

Here, MacKinnon invokes women's thwarted inclinations toward motherhood in defense of women's right to choose. Opponents of legal abortion, by contrast, claim that we should key in on how to redress "women's impotence to make this not so."

Although the emphasis on abortion as "a desperate act of love" by a responsible mother is a new theme in MacKinnon's work on abortion, other feminist legal theorists seeking to make accurate and persuasive arguments about abortion similarly invoke the theme of constraints on women who would be mothers. Such defenses of abortion rights stress that women are "forced" to choose abortion and in effect have no "choice" for a number of circumstantial reasons, including work/family conflict (Williams 1991), and that they face irreconcilable responsibilities (West 1990). (Here it is useful to recall Justice Blackmun's partially dissenting opinion in *Casey*, quoted at the opening of this paper, that restrictive abortion laws conscript women into the "'natural' status and incident of motherhood" and that the assumption of such status as "natural" for women results from a certain traditional conception of women's role, held in other Supreme Court cases to deny equal protection of the laws [112 S. Ct. at 2846–47 (citations omitted)].) Far from rejecting views of women's proper role, such defenses appear to enlist a certain naturalness of motherhood as well as a pregnant woman's inclination toward continuing a pregnancy in order to indict society for the need to resort to abortion, thus reassuring those who are uneasy about abortion that women care about the value of life, are making moral decisions, and would be mothers if they could (Petchesky 1990; Williams 1991). Some feminists have cautioned that the constrained circumstances argument will not fit all abortion decisions (and may have risks for that reason [Petchesky 1990: 388–92]; McClain 1992b: 164–74).

The theme of constrained motherhood, taken at face value, resonates to some degree with the diagnostic and remedial approaches of "pro-life" feminists. But these appeals by pro-choice feminists to circumstances constraining choice may be understood as raising two distinct arguments for legal abortion, one rooted in sex equality and the other in autonomy: (1) under conditions of sex inequality, women must have the legal right to choose whether to terminate a pregnancy, since forced motherhood is another form of such inequality; and (2) because each woman faces different circumstances, women are the proper decision makers about the outcome of their pregnancies.

Whether or not contingent social arrangements, namely, sex inequality, should play a central (or dispositive) part in defending reproductive freedom is itself a lively question among pro-choice feminists (Petchesky 1990: 388–401), but contingent arguments are often accompanied by a vision of a world in which the need for abortion would whither away. Thus, MacKinnon predicts that the complete elimination of sex inequality (which would include female sexual empowerment and equal female and male responsibility for childcare) would so radically reduce the need for abortion and transform the "politics of abortion" as to make the problem "virtually unrecognizable" (1991: 1326–27). This contingent argument defends an existing right while putting forth an impressive list of unequal social and political conditions targeted for change.

FFLA, in contrast, rejects social contingency as a justification for abortion, and differs in demanding that the "escape hatch" of abortion, which it claims prevents society from addressing inequality, be closed immediately. A more academic version of FFLA's slogan, "eliminate the crisis, not the child," may be seen in the assertion by historian Elizabeth Fox-Genovese (who has lectured on abortion under FFLA's sponsorship) that feminists have conflated pregnancy and childrearing, and that the difficulty and sacrifice of childrearing is not a moral and political justification of abortion. She instead argues that abortion shows the need for collective principles and responsibility for the support and education of children (Fox-Genovese 1991: 81–86; Hyman 1991).

Perhaps FFLA's sharpest, and most troubling, divergence from pro-choice equality defenses of abortion is its apparent insistence upon making abortion illegal as the lever for forcing society to eliminate all the constraints on pregnant women, a strategy calling into question the meaning of its stated commitment to women's full citizenship and equality. FFLA's apparent willingness to protect fetuses despite the resultant burdens and suffering imposed on women who need or desire abortions may illustrate Callahan's assertion that "pro-life" feminists take the part of fetuses instead of women in a case of conflict between the two. Thus, FFLA's stated premise about the value of prenatal life and its rejection of the relevance of whether or not particular pregnant women regard a fetus as "wanted" or "unwanted" logically requires that, even if society fails at mitigating the costs of motherhood and eliminating the crises pregnant women face, women be precluded from choosing abortion. Moreover, as FFLA's rejection of a rape or incest exception for abortion illustrates, their opposition to abortion holds even if women lack power over and do not consent to their sexual activity. Indeed, here "pro-life" feminists admit that it is unjust to force a woman who has been raped to carry a pregnancy to term (hence their call to eliminate rape), yet claim that it is a greater injustice to kill the "child, who is innocent and blameless" (Callahan and Callahan 1984: 163–64; Sweet 1985: 175–77).

In contrast, pro-choice equality arguments insist upon abortion rights in the face of pervasive sex inequality while also outlining what is needed to move to a world of equality and true reproductive freedom. I suspect that pro-choice feminists who speak of constraining circumstances would still defend a woman's right to choose abortion even if a particular woman was not, in fact, desperate, literally "forced" to do so by sex inequality, since one possible subtext of such arguments is respect for women's assessment of their circumstances and responsibility. Although some sex equality theorists argue that abortion rights are contingent upon current conditions of sex inequality, at least some argue that even in a world without sex inequality, concerns of women's bodily integrity, autonomy, and individual freedom might, if not certainly would, still support a right to choose abortion (Petchesky 1990: 392–401; MacKinnon 1991: 1327). And, contrary to FFLA, some theorists would argue that, even accepting the premise that fetuses are persons, sex inequality justifies abortion.

Perhaps one account of the difference between these two strategic positions is that pro-choice feminists stressing contingency view abortion as a "necessary evil" given a world where women now need or desire abortion (a defense other pro-choice feminists question [Petchesky 1990: 388–401]), while "pro-life" feminists view banning abortion as a necessary evil to get to a better, nonviolent world (Callahan and Callahan 1984: 321–22).[15] These and other differences between pro-choice and "pro-life" feminists raise questions not only of the import and purpose of rhetoric, but also of the substantive content of feminism, of feminist method, and how to understand "pro-life" feminist claims.

FEMINISTS AT ODDS

Is it possible to speak about a feminism that is opposed to legal abortion? Do, or should, pro-choice feminists take seriously the question: "Can a woman be both a feminist and anti-choice on abortion?" (McDonnell 1984). How should those engaged in feminist inquiry assess women's claims to take a feminist stance against abortion rights in the name of a "different view of what is good for women" (Callahan 1986)?

Pro-choice feminists often state, in media sound bites, that a "pro-life" feminist position is "pseudo feminism," an oxymoron, a contradiction in terms, irrelevant, and on the fringe (Gallagher 1987; Brotman 1989). However, the news media, for whom imagined intrafeminist strife and censorship make lively reading, appear to accept FFLA's self-description as "pro-life feminist," indeed, as rebels or leftists in the abortion battle (Gallagher 1987; Brotman 1989; Hentoff 1992a; Hentoff 1992b; National Public Radio 1992; Voell 1993).[16] Moreover, "pro-life feminism," particularly the writing of Sidney Callahan, receives attention in some academic literature about the abortion issue, including the work of some pro-choice feminists (Callahan and Callahan 1984; Ginsburg 1989; Colker 1992; McConnell 1991; Mensch and Freeman 1993). Finally, despite its small numbers, FFLA presents itself to the courts, the public, and the media as an alternative feminism, indeed, as the true heirs of historical feminism, and this self-presentation in turn feeds the claim that not merely women but indeed feminists are at odds on the difficult and divisive abortion issue (McConnell 1991).[17] All of these reasons, as well as the rhetorical parallels noted above, suggest that it may be appropriate and prudent to examine and address FFLA's claims about feminism and abortion.

There are many questions concerning authenticity, women's experience, and criteria for assessing experience. One starting point is to ask what is at the root of such women's "pro-life" (or anti-choice) commitment (McDonnell 1984; Callahan and Callahan 1984). Is the rhetoric of FFLA and other feminists who oppose legal abortion merely tactical appropriation and shrewd inversion of the feminist pro-choice argument? Is it utilizing the rhetoric of feminist discourse to support profoundly antifeminist agendas with serious consequences for women? Women who identify themselves both as feminist and as "pro-life" claim their opposition to abortion stems from feminist principles. Given that a tenet of feminist method is listening to women's voices and taking their experiences seriously, how should feminists respond to personal narratives of "pro-life" feminists about why they espouse the views held by FFLA, why opposition to abortion is feminist, and about the frustration they feel at being shut off from other feminists and mutual engagement in feminist work because of their position on legal abortion (Sweet 1985: 27–78; Voell 1993)?

Is there common ground on working to eliminate unwanted pregnancies (Ginsburg 1989: 222–26), or are the divergent conclusions about legal regulation of abortion an unbridgeable gap between pro-choice feminists and women who identify as "pro-life" feminists? It is hard to imagine pro-choice feminists objecting to the goal of eliminating the need for abortion by addressing a range of social problems to eliminate sex inequality, both in light of the rhetoric of the feminist legal theorists examined above, and the fact that fighting for a society in which reproduction and nurture do not disqualify women from political and economic life, and in which social institutions accommodate the reproductive needs of women and men, is a central goal of feminism. Perhaps pro-choice feminists' rejection of the possibility of a "pro-life" feminist position has to do with FFLA's ultimate position on legal abortion and the incomprehensibility of invoking feminism, which seems inextricably associated with freeing women from subordinating restrictions upon their lives, in order to justify legal regulation removing from all women decision-making authority about the role that reproduction will play in their lives.

In assessing the substance of FFLA's position, one question is the interpretation of the legacy of earlier feminists' condemnation of abortion, a condemnation FFLA claims is still relevant today. Feminist scholars generally explain why nineteenth-century feminists opposed birth control and abortion, and why twentieth-century feminists do not by focusing on the context of the former's opposition: the earlier feminists viewed abortion as dangerous and often fatal and they feared that the availability of contraception and abortion would weaken women's position within marriage and deny them economic and other protection (Gordon 1982).[18] FFLA, like others opposed to legal abortion, insists that concern for the status and value of prenatal life played a critical role (FFLA 1991; FFLA Handbook 12; McConnell 1991).

Another issue is assessing FFLA's core tenet that real equality for women entails accepting the equation of prenatal life with children and FFLA's frequent deployment of analogies between the destruction of a fetus through abortion and the historical treatment of women and slaves and the legacy of the Holocaust. Although FFLA members appear to find such analogies persuasive, for pro-choice feminists and many other supporters of legal abortion, such analogies, particularly the equation of prenatal life with children, are unpersuasive, if not deeply offensive (Law 1992). And some pro-choice feminists draw from the historical subordination and reproductive exploitation of women in marriage and slavery a strong moral argument for the critical importance of women's right to bodily integrity and choice (Harrison 1987: 26; Davis 1993: 357–75, 393–94). Moreover, some feminists argue that to treat prenatal life as a child not only ignores the role women play in creating life, but reflects convictions that pregnant women should have no choice about playing such a role (Olsen 1989; Siegel 1992).

Moreover, FFLA's stance assumes that every woman would (or should) continue a pregnancy if she properly understood the nature of prenatal life and if society were more amenable to pregnant women's needs. FFLA's rhetoric about women's "biological identity" and abortion as an alteration of the female body (rather than, for example, pregnancy) expresses a naturalistic and unvarying picture of how all women do or should experience pregnancy and the prospect of motherhood. (Arguably, some of the pro-choice feminist theorists examined above use a kind of naturalism to defend abortion rights.) There is no contemplation that a pregnant woman would not—or rather, there is an assumption that she certainly should—view childbirth as the appropriate outcome of pregnancy, once women fight against and eliminate constraints, prejudices, and the model of the "man's world." Here, FFLA would seem to overlook feminism's commitment to listening to women's voices and crediting women's experience and instead rely upon a view about women's proper, natural role. Ruth Colker, a pro-choice feminist who attempts to show respect for "pro-life" positions, concludes that FFLA has a reductive, "essentialist" view of women's experiences of pregnancy and motherhood (1992). Not all women report the experiences that FFLA claims some women have with abortion; indeed, while grief and ambivalence may be present for some (but not all) women, such women generally do not say they regret the decision. Rather, women regret the circumstances leading to the decision (Petchesky 1990).

Additionally, FFLA defines as feminist a commitment to protecting the weak, helpless, dependent, and vulnerable. Is FFLA advocating translating to the realm of law a general principle of protection of, and responsibility to, the vulnerable, and if so, what are its implications? Unless pregnant women are to be the only persons held as a legal matter to this principle, consistency and sex equality might require both a range of social policies (welfare rights, better support for children) and the imposition of legal duties on parents and other persons inconsistent with current notions of bodily integrity and autonomy (e.g., sacrificial behavior and organ donation). In contrast, sex equality theorists argue that precisely the absence of such general legal obligations to be "good samaritans" or engage in sacrificial conduct requires that pregnant women not be singled out for such service.

The abortion issue implicates both individual personal convictions about the morality of abortion and convictions about the proper legal status of abortion, yet personal opposition to abortion (whether on moral, religious, or other grounds) need not translate into an insistence that the criminal law prohibit abortion for all women. Indeed, one tenet of our constitutional order reflected in the abortion cases (as expressed in such notions as liberty, privacy, and freedom of conscience) is that citizens may differ on the most serious issues of conscience and yet agree that the state shall not impose one citizen's view upon others (McClain 1992b; Dworkin 1993). Thus, feminists personally uncomfortable with abortion may nonetheless conclude that each woman should choose for herself (Phelps 1992), or feminists might explore the morality of abortion in particular circumstances. But FFLA and other "pro-life" feminists reject the right to choose abortion as properly within women's constitutional liberty: as they frame the issue, if abortion is violent and a taking of life, privacy has nothing to do with it (FFLA Handbook 19). For those like FFLA who rely on analogies between abortion and murder, personal opposition to abortion must translate into law lest society be asked to tolerate denial of rights and equality to an entire category of persons in the name of freedom of conscience. Thus, FFLA's rejection of a position of personal opposition and government noninterference depends upon convictions about prenatal life, convictions neither universally shared nor reflected in current constitutional law, and not merely about the good of women.

Finally, is it plausible to think that outlawing abortion will force society to solve the problems of sexism and better accommodate mothers and pregnant women? And is FFLA really willing to pursue a strategy they acknowledge will impose suffering on women? Some FFLA members themselves appear to disavow such a position, either rejecting the coercion of pregnant women or acknowledging the need for a "compromise" or "transition period" of some availability of legal abortion until an "ideal solution" is attainable (Sweet 1985: 186–87; Callahan and Callahan 1984: 327). Yet they also insist that the continued availability of legal abortion as an easy way out removes the pressure to solve the real problems leading to abortion.

Why does FFLA assume that a commitment to women's right to legal abortion precludes a commitment to social supports making it possible for women to have children? Why do they assume, contrary to pro-choice feminists, that a reproductive health agenda cannot be pursued simultaneously with defending a right to choose? FFLA's own claimed commitment to furthering social change even while abortion is legal seems to belie that assumption.

Is there, then, common ground between pro-choice and "pro-life" feminists? In recent years, many scholars committed to some form of legal abortion rights have explored compromise and common ground and asked if we can have more public dialogue and debate about abortion, or if the issue will remain a "clash of absolutes" (Tribe 1990; Colker 1992; Mensch and Freeman 1993). An examination of the rhetoric of "pro-life" or "anti-choice" feminism suggests that, on the ultimate question of whether women should have a legal right to choose, compromise may be both "inevitable and impossible" (Law 1992). In the current environment, in which legal abortion is always subject to attack, the most uncompromising rhetoric about autonomy, liberty of conscience, and a right to make one's own decisions may be more protective of women's reproductive freedom than the rhetoric of constraint and circumstance.

But one possible lesson of pro-choice and "pro-life" feminist rhetoric may be that there is common ground on reducing unwanted pregnancy and making it possible for women to be both mothers and equal citizens participating in economic and social life. Here, mutual accusations abound. FFLA and other "pro-life feminists" assert that they have a commitment to helping pregnant women address difficult circumstances without recourse to abortion and charge that the feminist focus on abortion has diverted attention from many crucial women's issues (Graham 1992; Karkabi 1992). At the same time, some pro-choice feminist leaders sharply dispute that the agenda of FFLA and other "pro-life" feminists actually extends beyond "anti-abortion work" to "creating the social support systems for women who want to choose to have a child" (Patricia Ireland, quoted in Brotman 1989). FFLA's charge of diversion capitalizes on the frustration expressed by women's groups, including some pro-choice feminists, that the constant battles to defend abortion rights obscure feminist struggle on other issues of vital concern to women (Manegold 1992). But the earliest calls for abortion rights demanded a reproductive freedom entailing an array of social and economic supports, and contemporary pro-choice feminists increasingly seek to situate abortion within a broader context of reproductive health (Pine and Law 1992). Moreover, pro-choice organizations currently sound themes of abortion as merely one part of reproductive health and responsibility, a last resort. Indeed, a softer version of FFLA's abortion opposition might resemble a stance of simultaneously supporting a legal right while looking forward to a time when abortions (as both President Clinton and the First Lady put it) are "safe, legal, and rare."

A desire to reduce the need for abortion appears to be the likeliest candidate for common ground, as is evident in the recent formation by some activists on both sides of a "common ground for life and choice" coalition (Chandler 1993). Similarly, a two-fold focus on helping women to avoid sexual activity they do not want and use contraception, and to continue pregnancies circumstances render unwanted, might unify both groups. However, probing pro-choice and "pro-life" interpretations of a feminist ethic of sexuality and of reproductive responsibility would likely reveal not only some common ground, but considerable divergence (Callahan and Callahan 1984; Sweet 1985; Petchesky 1990; MacKinnon 1991).[19] If persons engaged in efforts to find "common ground" actually can work together for purposes of such endeavors or on other issues affecting women's well-being, notwithstanding each side's ultimate position on legal abortion, perhaps women need not be wholly at odds.

NOTES

I would like to thank James Fleming, Tracy Higgins, Daniel Ortiz, and Laura Stein for helpful comments on earlier drafts. Thanks also to Jennifer Bush and Cathy DiFiglia for valuable research assistance. I presented an earlier version of this paper at the Feminism and Legal Theory Workshop, "Revisiting Equality," April 2–3, 1993, Columbia University School of Law.

1. For example, many feminist theorists argue that sex equality (as intimated in *Planned Parenthood v. Casey*, 112 S.Ct. 2791 [1992], rather than privacy (as held in *Roe v. Wade*, 410 U.S. 113 [1973], is the better constitutional basis for abortion rights (Law 1984; MacKinnon 1991). The recent confirmation hearings for Justice Ruth Bader Ginsburg, who has published a sex-equality defense of abortion, implicated that debate (1985; Greenhouse 1993). An illustrative list of other debates includes whether the use of liberal legal language about rights, autonomy, and privacy is atomistic and fails to capture women's physical and moral experience (as contrasted with a model of responsibility and connection) (Gilligan 1982; West 1990; McClain 1992a; Karlan and Ortiz 1993), whether the rhetoric of choice obscures the importance of economic and social support of women's reproductive health needs and the constraining circumstances of actual women's decisions (Petchesky 1990; Roberts 1991; Williams 1991), and whether the most "feminist," persuasive argument in favor of legal abortion should include notions of respect for prenatal life and a pregnant woman's obligations to a fetus (Colker 1992; Burns 1990).

2. Choice of terminology is hotly contested among groups supporting and opposing legal abortion, since the way issues are framed may influence their reception. There are good reasons to resist using the label "pro-life" to describe persons or groups who oppose legal abortion, since that label suggests persons who support legal abortion are "anti-life" and suggests the

only possible way to support life is to oppose legal abortion. I would prefer to refer to them as "anti-choice," to stress their position that no woman should be able to choose legal abortion. At the same time, FFLA considers the label "anti-choice" pejorative, analogous to calling pro-choice people "pro-killing." Since I am attempting to offer a fair depiction of their views, I generally refer to "pro-life" feminism in quotations to capture their own self-description.

3. FFLA's membership has been reported to be between 4,000 to 5,000 members (National Public Radio 1992; Donohoe 1993). Media accounts report that FFLA originated in the early 1970s, when certain women reportedly had to leave NOW because they were vocal about their opposition to legal abortion (National Public Radio 1992; Gallagher 1987). I have found one contemporaneous story in which NOW's newly elected president, Karen DeCrow, commented concerning NOW members identified with Feminists for Life, opposed to abortion but not contraception: "You can be a NOW member and be against abortion if you don't speak on behalf of NOW, but I don't think you can be a feminist and be against the right of a woman to choose abortion" (Johnston 1974).

4. Some individual members of FFLA, such as Sidney Callahan, publicly criticize Operation Rescue as reactionary, while others, like Juli Loesch, have participated in rescues. FFLA issued statements condemning the shootings of Dr. David Gunn and Dr. George Tiller, physicians who performed abortions (FFLA 1993).

5. For example, FFLA has publicly indicated support for the Family and Medical Leave Act and the Violence against Women Act. Moreover, its bylaws include this striking echo of feminist critiques of privacy: "Domestic violence has been justified by the idea that a 'man's home is his castle' and we reject as an outrage this private violence, by either gender, whether it is used for pressure for abortion or for any reason." A review of its bylaws, which indicates positions on a range of issues in addition to abortion, indicates its opposition to abuse of children (but for them, this includes disposing of prenatal life as "property"), to all forms of sexual harassment and sexual abuse, to punitive measures (rather than drug treatment) for pregnant women who abuse drugs, to unnecessary hysterectomies and mastectomies, and to legally sanctioned (enforceable) contracts for surrogacy. Recently, FFLA, as did NOW, publicly opposed fiscal incentives for voluntary Norplant use by women receiving welfare payments (Rees 1991). Affirmatively, it calls for inclusion of health care problems specific to women in governmental and private medical research.

6. FFLA's stationery bears this logo. The assumption of harmony is also evident in a recent full-page advertisement in the *New York Times,* July 14, 1992, entitled "A New American Compact: Caring about Women, Caring for the Unborn," and signed by two officers of FFLA and several prominent individuals and organizations. The "Compact" echoes many of FFLA's assertions about inequality and abortion and calls for "the most protective laws possible on behalf of the unborn."

7. FFLA uses this slogan in advertisements it has run in various magazines.

8. While other organizations of women, particularly the conservative group Concerned Women of America, similarly dispute NOW's representation of them, in FFLA's case the backdrop is its genesis in the isolation and expulsion of "pro-life" NOW members.

9. On the "voluntary motherhood" movement and its empowering as well as problematic aspects, see Ginsburg (1989), Gordon (1982), and Siegel (1992).

10. FFLA filed its *amicus curiae* brief in Webster with Women Exploited By Abortion ("WEBA"). A collection of testimonials by a few hundred WEBA members is gathered in Reardon (1987). The pervasive theme in the book is of women exploited by "abortionists" and unreliable, uncaring male partners, and most of the women deeply regretted their decisions. FFLA frequently and uncritically relies on Reardon's book for its claims about the harms of abortion.

11. This type of claim is not unique to FFLA among groups opposed to legal abortion. The founder of WEBA, Nancyjo Mann, makes a similar claim, labeling "the abortion mentality" as "sexism incarnate" and abortion as an easy way out (Reardon 1987: xi–xii).

12. Mathewes-Green says that the crisis is often due to the absence of a loving, faithful man. The author also recommends adoption over motherhood as a general solution in cases of unmarried women, and seemingly advocates the heroism of women who give birth to and give up children (Mathewes-Green 1991: 30). Peggy Noonan similarly invokes the language of altruism and heroic generosity in support of adoption ("She's Come for an Abortion" [1992]).

13. A similar interviewing project undertaken by Mary Cunningham Agee after her own miscarriage (and a curiosity about women's abortion experiences) led her to form the Nurturing Network (Lienert 1993). Agee espouses no view on whether or not abortion should be legal, and the Network serves as a referral service for working women and a college-counseling center for students with unplanned pregnancies.

14. Feminist scholar Rosalind Petchesky powerfully challenges MacKinnon's view (like that of Rich before her) of abortion as "violence against women" as both "disturbing and problematic" (Petchesky 1984).

15. For an illuminating exploration of these and other differences, based on a set of exchanges about the abortion issue but predating many of the "pro-life" and "pro-choice" sources examined in this essay, see Callahan and Callahan (1984: 285–330).

16. In particular, journalist and author Nat Hentoff, who describes himself as a "Jewish, atheist, civil libertarian, left-wing pro-lifer," writes about FFLA as allies, "other heretics," whom he finds "bold, witty, crisply intelligent" and has charged feminists and leftists with stereotyping "pro-lifers" (Hentoff 1992a; Hentoff 1992b).

17. It is difficult to assess with any certainty what impact such presentation has on the climate of opinion. For example, in 1992, contemporaneous with the

march on Washington for reproductive freedom sponsored by NOW, FFLA announced the founding of the National Women's Coalition for Life, a coalition of a number of organizations opposed to legal abortion (FFLA 1992a). Later in the year, invoking the theme of the "year of the woman," FFLA announced the formation of the Susan B. Anthony List, as noted above. Media reports echoed FFLA's public statements about these events as designed to remedy a flaw in the "year of the woman" by adding a "pro-life" perspective (FFLA 1992b; Richardson 1992). Another way in which FFLA's claims about feminism and abortion enter the public realm is through opinion pieces and letters to the editor. For example, a recent "viewpoint" article in a Dallas newspaper by a woman described as a writer and member of FFLA challenged the omission from a recent film on Elizabeth Cady Stanton and women's rights of Stanton's condemnation of abortion (Bruner 1993).

18. Of course, the legacy of feminist struggle also includes the feminist birth control movement associated with Margaret Sanger in the early twentieth century, also sounding themes of women's need to control their own bodies (Petchesky 1990: 89–96).

19. In the space here I can only suggest a few examples. On convergence, the text suggests a common theme of male exploitation and that abortion may allow for male irresponsibility. On divergence, for Sidney Callahan and other "pro-life" feminists, a feminist sexual ethic requires viewing sexual activity and procreation as a unity, and properly confined to persons prepared to serve as parents, while pro-choice feminists call for the development of a female sexuality free from the fear of unwanted pregnancy and motherhood and not limited solely to heterosexual, procreative sex. They would probably similarly differ as to the centrality to women's identity of the experiences of pregnancy and motherhood.

REFERENCES

Brotman, Barbara (1989). "Feminists, But Abortion Opponents, Too." *Chicago Tribune* (November 12).

Bruner, Bureeda (1993). "Early Feminists and Abortion." *Dallas Morning News* (June 10): 23A.

Burns, Sarah E. (1990). "Notes from the Field: A Reply to Professor Colker." *Harvard Women's Law Journal* 13: 189–206.

Callahan, Sidney (1986). "Abortion and the Sexual Agenda." *Commonweal* (April 25): 232–38.

Callahan, Sidney, and Daniel Callahan, eds. (1984). *Abortion: Understanding Differences*. New York: Plenum Press.

Chandler, Kurt (1993). "Abortion Talks Are Calm Eye of the Storm: Some Activists Looking for Common Ground." *Star Tribune* (August 2): 1B.

Colker, Ruth (1992). *Abortion and Dialogue*. Bloomington: Indiana University Press.

Cuniberti, Betty (1985). "Other Voices Crying Out against the Feminists." *Los Angeles Times* (October 2): 5–1.

Davis, Peggy Cooper (1993). "Neglected Stories and the Lawfulness of Roe v. Wade." *Harvard Civil Rights–Civil Liberties Law Review* 28: 299–394.

Donohoe, Cathryn (1993). "Pregnant Pause: The Pro-Life Movement Plots a New Strategy for the Clinton Years." *Washington Times* (February 23): E1.

Dworkin, Ronald (1993). *Life's Dominion.* New York: Alfred A. Knopf.

Feminists for Life of America (undated). Bylaws and Resolutions.

—— (undated). Sound Advice for All Pro-life Activists and Candidates Who Wish to Include a Concern for Women's Rights in Their Pro-life Advocacy (Debate Handbook). Feminists for Life of America, Kansas City, Missouri.

—— (1981). Statement of Paulette Joyer, Feminists for Life of America, Hearings before the Subcommittee on the Constitution of the Committee on the Judiciary, Constitutional Amendments Relating to Abortion, Vol. 1, 1157–58 (December 7 and 16).

—— (1989). Brief of Feminists for Life of America et al. as *Amici Curiae* in Support of Appellants in *Webster v. Reproductive Health Services.*

—— (1991). Brief of Feminists for Life of America et al. as *Amici Curiae* in Support of Petitioners in *Bray v. Alexandria Women's Health Clinic.*

—— (1992a). "Feminists for Life Hold Events to Protest Pro-Abortion March." PR Newswire (March 31).

—— (1992b). "Flaw in 'Year of the Woman' is Remedied—Susan B. Anthony List Founded." PR Newswire (November 9).

—— (1992c). Brief of Feminists for Life of America et al. as *Amici Curiae* in Support of Respondents and Cross Petitioners in *Planned Parenthood v. Casey*

—— (1993). Press Release (August 20).

Finley, Lucinda M. (1986). "Transcending Equality Theory." *Columbia Law Review* 86: 1118–82.

Fox-Genovese, Elizabeth (1991). *Feminism without Illusions.* Chapel Hill: University of North Carolina Press.

Frolik, Joe (1993). "Anti-Abortion Groups Try New Plan." *Cleveland Plain Dealer* (September 8): 1C.

Gallagher, Maggie (1987). "The New Pro-Life Rebels: Feminists for Life of America." *National Review* (February 27): 37.

Gilligan, Carol (1982). *In a Different Voice.* Cambridge: Harvard University Press.

Ginsburg, Faye D. (1989). *Contested Lives.* Berkeley: University of California Press.

Ginsburg, Ruth Bader (1985). "Some Thoughts on Autonomy and Equality in Relation to *Roe v. Wade.*" *North Carolina Law Review* 63: 375–86.

Goldstein, Robert D. (1988). *Mother-Love and Abortion.* Berkeley: University of California Press.

Gordon, Linda (1982). "Why Nineteenth-Century Feminists Did Not Support

'Birth Control' and Twentieth-Century Feminists Do: Feminism, Reproduction, and the Family." In Barrie Thorne and Marilyn Yalom, eds., *Rethinking the Family.* New York: Longman.

Graham, Renee (1992). "Enough Is Enough, They Say." *Boston Globe* (April 29): 43.

Greenhouse, Linda (1993). "On Privacy and Equality." *New York Times* (June 16): A1.

Harrison, Beverly Wildung (1987). "Our Right to Choose." In Barbara Hilkert Andolsen, et al., eds., *Women's Consciousness, Women's Conscience.* San Francisco: Harper and Row.

Hentoff, Nat (1992a). "Stereotyping Pro-Lifers." *Washington Post* (May 16): A25.

——— (1992b). "Pro-Choice Bigotry and Censorship." *Sacramento Bee* (November 29).

Hyman, Jennifer (1991). "Seeking a New Kind of Feminism." *Gannett News Service* (November 22).

"In Session: Notes on the Legislature" (1993). *Austin American-Statesman* (February 16): B3.

Johnston, Laurie (1974). "NOW Elects Syracuse Lawyer as Head." *New York Times* (May 28): 29.

Karkabi, Barbara (1992). "Speaking Out: Anti-Abortion Leader Urges Compassion, Social Engagement." *Houston Chronicle* (December 13): 3.

Karlan, Pamela S., and Daniel R. Ortiz (1993). "In a Diffident Voice: Relational Feminism, Abortion Rights, and the Feminist Legal Agenda." *Northwestern University Law Review* 87: 858–96.

Law, Sylvia A. (1984). "Rethinking Sex and the Constitution." *University of Pennsylvania Law Review* 132: 955–1040.

——— (1992). "Abortion Compromise—Inevitable and Impossible." *University of Illinois Law Review* 1992: 921–41.

Lienert, Anita Pyzik (1993). "A Spiritual Life Helps Bendix Cause Celebre Pursue Mission." *Chicago Tribune* (February 28): 11.

Luker, Kristin (1984). *Abortion and the Politics of Motherhood.* Berkeley: University of California Press.

McClain, Linda C. (1992a). "'Atomistic Man' Revisited: Liberalism, Connection, and Feminist Jurisprudence." *Southern California Law Review* 65: 1171–1264.

——— (1992b). "The Poverty of Privacy?" *Columbia Journal of Gender and Law* 3: 119–74.

McConnell, Michael W. (1991). "How Not to Promote Serious Deliberation about Abortion." (Review of Laurence H. Tribe, *Abortion: The Clash of Absolutes. University of Chicago Law Review* 58: 1181–1202.

McDonnell, Kathleen (1984). *Not an Easy Choice.* Boston: South End Press.

MacKinnon, Catharine A. (1987). *Feminism Unmodified.* Cambridge: Harvard University Press.

——— (1991). "Reflections on Sex Equality under Law." *Yale Law Journal* 100: 1281–1328.

Manegold, Catherine S. (1992). "The Battle over Choice Obscures Other Vital Concerns of Women." *New York Times* (August 2): 4–1.

Mathewes-Green, Frederica (1991). "Unplanned Parenthood: Easing the Pain of Crisis Pregnancy." *Heritage Foundation Policy Review* (Summer): 28.

——— (1992). "Marchers Don't Speak for Many Women." *USA Today* (April 8): 13A.

Mensch, Elizabeth, and Alan Freeman (1993). *The Politics of Virtue: Is Abortion Debatable?* Durham: Duke University Press.

Morse, Anne (1992). "For Some Candidates, 'Year of the Woman' Is Ironic Term." *Cleveland Plain Dealer* (November 20): 7B.

National Public Radio *Morning Edition* (1992). "'Feminists for Life': Leftists against Abortion." Transcript (August 7).

Olsen, Frances (1989). "Unraveling Compromise." *Harvard Law Review* 103: 105–35.

Operation Rescue (1991). Brief for Petitioners in *Bray v. Alexandria Women's Health Clinic.*

Petchesky, Rosalind (1984). "Abortion as 'Violence against Women': A Feminist Critique." *Radical America* 18: 64–68.

——— (1990). *Abortion and Woman's Choice* (rev. ed.). Boston: Northeastern University Press.

Phelps, Teresa Godwin (1992). "The Sound of Silence Breaking: Catholic Women, Abortion, and the Law." *Tennessee Law Review* 59: 547–69.

Pine, Rachel N., and Sylvia A. Law (1992). "Envisioning a Future for Reproductive Liberty." *Harvard Civil Rights–Civil Liberties Law Review* 27: 407–63.

Reardon, David C. (1987). *Aborted Women: Silent No More.* Chicago: Loyola University Press.

Rees, Matthew (1991). "Shot in the Arm: The Use and Abuse of Norplant." *New Republic* (December 9): 16.

Richardson, Valerie (1992). "Feminist Launches PAC for Pro-Lifers: Sees Lopsided 'Year of the Woman.'" *Washington Times* (November 7): A1.

Rizzoni, Dawn M. (1992). "When Women Pull the Lever." *Washington Times* (August 30): B5.

Roberts, Dorothy (1991). "Punishing Drug Addicts Who Have Babies: Women of Color, Equality, and the Right of Privacy." *Harvard Law Review* 104: 1419–82.

"She's Come for an Abortion. What Do You Say?" (1992). *Harper's* (November): 43–54.

Siegel, Reva (1992). "Reasoning from the Body: A Historical Perspective on Abortion Regulation and Questions of Equal Protection." *Stanford Law Review* 44: 261–381.

Stafford, Margaret (1991). "Feminist Group Marches to Its Own Drum." *Los Angeles Times* (February 10): E12.

Sweet, Gail Grenier, ed. (1985). *Pro-Life Feminism: Different Voices.* Toronto: Life Cycle Books.

Tribe, Laurence H. (1990). *Abortion: The Clash of Absolutes.* New York: W. W. Norton.

Voell, Paula (1993). "The Other Side of the Fence." *Buffalo News* (August 17): 1.

Vrazo, Fawn (1992). "A Group Aimed at Those Feminists Who Are against Abortion Rights." *Philadelphia Inquirer* (July 23): B3.

West, Robin (1988). "Jurisprudence and Gender." *University of Chicago Law Review* 55: 1.

────── "Foreword: Taking Freedom Seriously." *Harvard Law Review* 104: 43–106.

Williams, Joan (1991). "Gender Wars: Selfless Women in the Republic of Choice." *New York University Law Review* 66: 1559–1634.

9.

THE POLITICS OF SURROGACY NARRATIVES: NOTES TOWARD A RESEARCH PROJECT

E. ANN KAPLAN

SURROGACY NARRATIVES

In their narratives, surrogate mothers often announce their motive for becoming such mothers as a sisterly desire to help infertile women. Yet, in practice, surrogacy becomes the terrain for incredible, even unprecedented, hostility and violence between women. It is this discrepancy between sisterly motives and unsisterly practice that I want to explore here. Since narratives are always discursively formed, my ultimate aim is to understand what discourses produce the women's stories narrated in popular journals: What audiences do they address? What effect does the context of their publication have on the form of the stories? What economic, political, and other social factors enter in? Here, I limit myself mainly to laying bare some of the common structures to women's stories, and some of the repeated themes, as they illuminate the paradox between sisterly motives and unsisterly practice. A survey of stories in magazines is followed by analysis of a television movie and a feminist video.

Sisterly motives abound in popular narratives about surrogacy,[1] and there is a surprising uniformity in the basics of the story, even in the language used. Surrogate mothers discuss their pleasure in giving birth for another woman; they express sympathy for infertile women—wanting to give the gift of a child (Kane 1988: 20–22; Whitehead 1989: 7; Markoutsas 1981: 71–72). Some discuss having been fulfilled in having their own children, and wanting other couples to share the same joy. "I felt I was made for having babies," is one formulation. For example, Mary Beth Whitehead represents herself as a woman devoted to being a mother and wanting nothing else in life than bearing and nurturing children. "Being a mother was always how I defined myself," she says. "Surrogacy was a way for me to help someone less fortunate" (Whitehead 1988: 89). In this story, surrogate mothering is represented as "a positive, multi-vocal symbol, pointing to previous barrenness and promised fertility" (Deegan 1987: 93). The baby born of a surrogate is seen as both of the flesh and of the law—a member, by contract and law, in a gift relationship (Turner 1969), rather than baby selling on a shameful market, as in some narratives noted below. It is seen as a special celebration of birth itself.

Surrogacy, unlike many other reproductive technologies, is an old technology, and does not actually require medical sophistication. This may be part of its appeal: the historical and biblical precedent of Abraham, Sarah, and Sarah's handmaiden, Hagar, is sometimes quoted (e.g., Lacayo and Svoboda 1986: 36; Neff 1987: 14; Butzel 1987: 7), especially in stories dealing with women who give birth to a sister's baby. Actual sisters acting as surrogates and adoptive mothers is, significantly, often the most positive context for surrogacy in these narratives. Accompanying one such story are images of the sisters hugging, kissing, and crying (King and Fein 1986: 34). The surrogacy in this case is seen as a "family project" (ibid.: 35). When the sister miscarries, it is a trauma. The family accepts the loss within the framework of "God never meant me to have a child" (ibid.: 36). One sister conceptualizes her surrogacy as "I loaned my sister my body for her baby to grow in—I was merely babysitting for nine months" (ibid.: 38). The baby is called "my little passenger." In a similar story, the sisterly surrogacy is seen as paying back the sister for all her love and support (Mills 1985: 20–22).

In this story, the stress is on surrogacy being a community and family process, not in the hands of expert services and professionals: all members involved in the process meet and eat ritual foods, even if only coffee and cake, so as to set the tone for celebratory aspects. In some cases, the artificial insemination is done with a turkey baster, to signify links with Thanksgiving rituals. These narrators represent insemination as another festive occasion, part of the "family album" series of festivities like Christmas, grandma's birthday, and the Fourth of July.

In another narrative, it is literally Thanksgiving Day, and the surrogate mother gives birth alone in the delivery room before the father and adoptive mother arrive (Richards 1989: 22). The event is presented as happy, not sad; the surrogate mother content, grateful. In another case, the woman has been a surrogate mother four times and is yearning to be pregnant again. Her own story follows, as if to explain her situation: at sixteen, she got pregnant, married, and had two children; when her husband joined a motorcycle gang, she gave the children up for adoption. In this narrative, the woman has shown her ability to give up her children and is thus supposedly a good surrogate. Bearing other people's children makes up for the loss of her own.

In yet one more story, the surrogate mother is quoted as saying: "I'll never find a cure for cancer, but I'll always know I've done something important" (Gupta and Feldinger 1989: 141). A surrogate husband, a rare voice in these narratives and about whom I would like to know a lot more, says: "I rationalized that it was a medical experiment." ZIFT surrogacy (zygote intra-fallopian tube transfer), in which the surrogate has no genetic claim to the surrogate mother, is said in the same story to be made possible by God and thus acceptable. In the more complex and still more unusual situation of gamete intra-fallopian transfer (GIFT), one woman is described as gloating over her twelve eggs. "She [the recipient] and I were cycling at the same time—it's like being in a war together" (a telling metaphor that evidences the construction of comradeship between the women involved). The woman undergoing the transfer is quoted: "I almost didn't care if I had a baby—I just wanted to know what having life inside would feel like."

My second set of popular narratives—those I call "negative"—reveal antitechnology sentiments and dwell on the "unsisterly practices" I noted above. Surrogate mothers whose experiences turned negative adopt narratives circulating elsewhere in North American culture (often originating in religious or right wing contexts). One set of negative surrogacy concepts labels it "baby-selling on a shameful market." Other negative surrogacy narratives often conjure up Orwell's *1984* to indicate the negative response. Surrogate reproduction is seen as cold and sterile because it is separated from love and family life (Neff 1987: 14–15; Murphy 1984). "Babies born from frozen embryos will be cold the rest of their lives." Typical headlines for these stories are "Brave New Babies" or "Tales from the Baby Factory." "Baby Farming" is conjured up, especially in relation to third-world women, and the figure of the surrogate mom as human incubator predominates (e.g., Clapp 1987: 14–15; Murphy 1984).

The language of these stories involves a negative judgment on "womb rental fees," and financial arrangements are now highlighted. Mary Beth Whitehead's $10,000 contract is quoted. Indeed, Whitehead's 1989 book gathers together negative motifs in earlier stories and sets the stage for more to come: "I have learned," she says, "that the rental of a woman's body for the sale of the child she bears is wrong. It violates the core of what a woman is" (Whitehead 1989: xiv–xv). The practice is often labeled "commercial trading in flesh," and articles assert that governments should outlaw surrogacy and the use of fetuses for medical purposes. If surrogacy is regularized, a class of breeder women would be created (Clapp 1989; Murphy 1985)—such as Margaret Atwood envisaged in *The Handmaid's Tale* (Kaplan 1992)—women valued both for their biological fertility and the unnatural ability to reject their own flesh and blood. Articles here suggest that childless couples could abandon technological alternatives to give love to troubled young people, adopt "unadoptable" children of mixed race, or those who are older, disabled, or deeply disadvantaged (see diverse perspectives in Montgomery 1988).

Quite often religious figures are quoted decrying surrogacy: for instance, Richard A. McCormick, S.J., said, "The practice is morally unjustifiable, because a third party is introduced into the marriage of two who have become one flesh" (Markoutsas 1981: 72). "Procreation should not be divorced from the context of marital intimacy by involving a third party," a priest is quoted as saying. Yet another priest said to an adoptive surrogacy mother: "Your children have not sinned, but you have. You've used Michael's sperm in another woman's body" (Markoutsas 1981: 74)—despite the biblical precedent regarding Sarah and Hagar noted above. This precedent is viewed by religious spokesmen against surrogacy as the medieval church's tolerance of concubinage to regulate the transmission of property, but is considered inapplicable today (Neff 1987: 14).

Unsisterly practices emerge in different narratives or later on in the same narratives, at the point where sisterliness changes to "women at odds." The drama of "women at odds" in the cases where surrogates do not want to keep to the adoption contract dominates the negative surrogacy stories. Such drama was spelled out graphically in Elizabeth Kane's book, *Birth Mother* (1989). Kane makes a vivid plea against surrogate motherhood on the grounds of the birth mother's inevitable biological bonding with the baby that a surrogate carries.

Following Kane and popularized psychological studies, stories in commercial magazines assume automatic bonding of mother and child. Writers stress the wrenching separation of the couple ("Elizabeth" 1983) and dwell on negative psychological results (Grogan 1989: 36–41). Surrogacy is discussed as symbolic adultery, and the jealous competition between surrogate and adoptive mothers is emphasized. Authors lament effects of the process on other children in either family, along with the awesome psychological implications of signing a contract to give a child away.

A case is often made for the surrogate child as different from the adopted child, whose mother wanted it but could not keep it. In surrogacy, the mother goes into the birth process intending to give the child up. Stories highlight how, indeed, some surrogates are making up for past acts, like abortion, or giving up a child for adoption. (Evidently, research shows that a high proportion of surrogate mothers at one time either gave children up for adoption or had abortions [Guinzburg 1983].) From the perspective of the recipient couple, stories dwell on the psychologically painful, heart-wrenching ordeal of couples who, through "hiring" a surrogate birth mother, are trying to have a child partly sharing their genetic inheritance. Narratives stress the "torture" such couples endure while waiting for their surrogate to be pregnant, and the tension suffered during the period of the pregnancy. Legal and ethical issues are sometimes noted in popular stories (e.g., Mingay 1982; McKay 1983; Thom 1988; Malcolm 1988), although such issues are largely reserved for formidable, specifically legal literature (e.g., Pateman 1988).

Commentary and Discourses

I have always been suspicious of the sisterly pronouncements in my first set of narratives, and equally troubled by the polemical, self-righteous tone of the negative narratives. Clearly, the two kinds of narrative set up a false binary that is inadequate for dealing with the actual psychological, political, scientific, economic, and racial aspects of the increasing

surrogacy phenomenon. The multiplicity of positions is lost in the polemical arguments being made in both sets of stories. Also troubling is
the amazing *similarity* among the popular stories—the repetition of
motifs of the gift, of doing something for infertile couples, of frustration,
pain, ultimate joy to the adoptive parents, and so on—from as early as
1983 through 1989, after which time popular magazines seemed to
finally sense that enough was enough. The story gradually acquires the
status of myth, with fixed characters, set verbal exchanges, and similar
language and tone. It seems that Mary Beth Whitehead's 1989 book, *A
Mother's Story,* provided the full mythic account so that, once articulated, more cases did not need citing.

In commenting briefly, let me begin with the glaring absence of reference to the economic, class, and race issues in positive surrogacy narratives, since this absence is clearly an important structuring element. Just
because money is rarely mentioned in these narratives, one might suppose that financial gain (usually $10,000 with all medical and related
expenses paid) is the real, repressed motive. When the fee is mentioned,
it is as enabling the surrogate mother to buy necessities or to pay bills
when a husband has been laid off; these comments are accompanied by
statements that claim the main motive is "to make infertile couples
happy" (Gelman and Shapiro 1985). The financial surrogate arrangement may account for the class difference between surrogate and adoptive mothers, so why can this not be more readily mentioned? Presumably, the women need to show higher motives for their surrogacy than
financial ones; and perhaps this is a need produced through religious or
community values. Once again, Mary Beth Whitehead's story provides
the prototype for such feelings and values: "I have always been religious," she says, ". . . and I certainly prayed that if I did this for another
childless couple, God would reward me by giving my sister a baby"
(Whitehead 1989: 8). Although the women rarely mention the financial
part of the contract, I do not assume conscious duplicity. My future
research will aim to discover, through interviews and other strategies,
what prevents women from mentioning finances.

Something more complex, psychologically and socially, is at stake
than what emerges from either women's stories or my cynical questions.
First, it is important that most of the surrogate mothers seem to be white
and lower middle class, adoptive ones apparently white and middle
class, with the rare exception of Anna Johnson, a black surrogate mother
involved in a custodial suit with the white biological parents ("Psychia-

trist Testifies" 1990; "Surrogate Mother Sues for Baby's Custody" 1990). Research on profiles of surrogate mothers is difficult because such profiles are difficult to obtain. Few narratives talk about either class or race, but rarely are the surrogate or recipient mothers touted in the media as minority women.[2]

Also intriguing in narratives is why surrogate mothers do not anticipate the separation from the child, which they describe as "heart-wrenching," or realize that they may desire to keep the child, despite their having had other children. Why does the adoptive mother also not anticipate such struggle on the part of the surrogate mother? Increasing desire to keep the child produces the unsisterly practices—the hostility and the violence on both women's parts. Surrogates suddenly, and violently, declare that they want to keep the child they have just given birth to, while the adoptive mother—having anticipated receiving the child for the previous nine months—equally violently demands the child be handed over. It is as if the surrogates and adoptive mothers have started a story whose ending they have forgotten, or as if they step into positions of women-fighting-women so common in film melodrama and television soaps, as will be suggested below. Clearly, neither woman is self-consciously aware of the discursive forces shaping their experiences and of how their stories are linked. Indeed, the surrogate mother's violent desire to *keep* the child may be provoked precisely by the adoptive mother's urgent desire to *claim* the child. A symbiotic process may be at work.

I have wondered at my skepticism about the sisterly narratives I began with: is it really so impossible for one woman to want to do something as disruptive of her own life as bearing and giving birth to a baby for another woman? What does sisterliness of these dimensions really mean? Perhaps I am missing something about what childbirth actually means to many women and simply do not understand the discursive frameworks within which surrogate mothers live; after all, having children is the main or only identity and/or life preoccupation for many women. Perhaps, as one narrator suggested, women are motivated by the idea of contributing in some way analogous to making scientific discoveries.

But it is also possible that the decision to become a surrogate is partly produced through media stories still stressing the self-sacrificial mother—such stories image self-sacrifice as what mothering is all about! The idealized self-sacrifice function has become harder and harder to fulfill for many reasons: modern household devices give the appearance of mitigating housework, as does the new entry of fathers into domestic chores and even child rearing, and so perhaps women are reaching for ways to perform this function. But desire for this self-sacrifice wills into being its binary opposite, the jealous, competitive mother, who wants to possess the child. Surrogacy provides a unique situation where the binary mothers so common in North American stories can be made to merge—or where each woman can constitute herself alternately as the "angelic" and the evil "witch" mother. The visual fictions to be discussed below will, I hope, make clear how "sisterly motives" (the angel ideal mother) quickly turns into "unsisterly practice" (the negative witch mother).

THE MINISERIES AND ROSLER'S *BORN TO BE SOLD*

The traditional angel/witch–mother figures in Western culture are obviously reworked in the metaphors and allusions in some stories outlined above. But one can isolate two main, linked strands through which this discursive mother-formation arrives back in surrogacy narratives. A possible religious formation for the sisterliness (the angelic paradigm) may be found in the way some narrators, as noted above, refer to "God"; others imply religious discourse by referring to the "gift" or by generating rituals as part of the surrogacy project. Is it possible that select forms of Christian fundamentalism partly produce the sisterly discourse and apparent genuine emotions that go with it? Could the biblical precedent put surrogacy in an entirely different category than other technologies?

The second formation, which has implications for the "women-at-odds" paradigm, seems more obvious to me: many of the stories outlined above are close to the material of melodrama and soap opera, as I noted above and as Linda Gordon once pointed out.[3] In order to explore this formation, I discuss two divergent, deliberately fictional (as against apparently autobiographical) examples of the most well-known surrogacy narrative, that of Mary Beth Whitehead, to see how the melodrama "genre" may be differently constitutive in both cases. I may then be in a position to return to the opening supposedly "factual" narratives in order to assess how far they too have been shaped by prior nineteenth- and twentieth-century literary narratives long in popular circulation through fiction, film, and television.

The ABC commercial narrative represented in the television miniseries *Baby M* focuses most on the problem of *giving up the child,* as it is the child that causes rivalry between the mothers: "women at odds," then, forms the traumatic part of the surrogacy story. It is here that the story links up with nineteenth-century stage—and then film—melodrama. The adulterous mother in such nineteenth-century narratives is punished by having to give up her children. Such narratives (*East Lynne* [1861] is a well-known model; see Kaplan 1992) dwell on the painful separation from the children—the years-long yearnings for them in exile, the tears over their loss, the poverty the mother succumbs to, her guilt. The surrogacy situation, it seems, very much evokes this convention regarding mothers and children in the commercial stories.

The miniseries follows the old classical Hollywood melodrama realism that television soaps have adopted. It claims to be a window on the world, on reality, and conceals its processes of selecting which images to show, which to ignore, and on the illusory constructions at play. The series attempts to get viewers to identify with the characters as with historical people, and even in *Baby M* gives the characters the name of their real-life equivalents. What is of interest in this connection is exactly what identifications the miniseries solicits, and what repressed perspectives are able to emerge, unawares.

As already noted, the television miniseries genre is always ultimately *melodrama:* that is, it is a film about the domestic sphere, dealing with families, children, and conflicts within this terrain. The genre has potentially both liberatory and regressive aspects, the latter being limits on what can be said and what is excluded. But unconscious desires are often at work, and the genre may provide a space for articulation of what cannot be said, what has to be repressed, but is conveyed implicitly in the drama (Gledhill 1987).

The first episode opens with revealing title shots taken from the whole series. These isolate the most dramatic parts of the narrative—the most sensational—and they stress the fictional Bill Stern's bonding to the child. Arguably, the title shots show what is self-consciously at stake for the filmmakers, which is not the same as what ultimately is communicated.

The "women at odds" (or the women-to-be-at-odds) are established in deliberately contrasting ways in the opening sequences through careful selection of clothes, body language, and physical location—signs that convey culturally loaded meanings. Betsy Stern (a doctor as well) is represented as stiff, proper, professional, well-dressed, and in control of her emotions. Early scenes indicate that Dr. Stern cannot have a child and, despite her emotional control, make clear how upset she is about it.

Second, the motivation for Bill Stern's desire for a biological, not adopted, child is stressed with the loss of his mother and his being "all alone." Stern's Jewishness is focused on at some length, perhaps to underscore his need for heritage. While male figures are usually remote authorities or lovers in the melodrama convention, in this case both husbands (Stern and Rick Whitehead) show the impact of the women's movements and see themselves as quite involved with domestic life. But this is especially so for the middle-class Mr. Stern.

The first image of Mary Beth Whitehead is in loud contrast to that of Betsy Stern. Again, stereotypical class signs predominate: Mary Beth is shown in an unattractive manner lying in bed, eating chocolates (sign of decadence, boredom?), watching television in the afternoon. It is while watching that she hears about a surrogacy case, which gives her the idea of becoming a surrogate—something mentioned frequently in the women's popularized narratives. The following scene in which she persuades her husband is the only one in which money is mentioned (and then it's the last thing, an aside). Her main weapon is sex, and again this seems to be a class sign: Betsy's "virgin" to Mary Beth's "whore," in a return to weary melodrama female types.

Indications of Mary Beth's unreliability mesh with her sexual seductiveness (the whore is always unreliable!). Mary Beth wears the wrong color suit to the restaurant (she changes her mind at the last moment, prefiguring her change of mind about the baby); and she brings her child, Tuesday, to an insemination session, which the narrative seems to agree, with Bill, is inappropriate. In the car, Mary Beth's radio plays loud rock music, and the structure of the scene invites the viewer to identify with Bill Stern's dislike and disapproval of the music.

The miniseries, then, all but puts Betsy and Mary Beth into the old, classic virgin/whore binary in terms of body types and emotional valence. Mary Beth is flirtatious with Bill, fun-loving, and emotional, while Betsy is stiff, unsexy, and emotionally controlled. Betsy has fair hair, Mary Beth dark black hair. Mary Beth is plump and well contoured; Betsy thin and plain.

Narratively, Mary Beth becomes the witch when frustrated and when she wants her own way. Within dominant gender codes, violent emotion in women still connotes inability to function in the public sphere—irresponsibility, unreliability. Within the miniseries discourse, where motherhood is now part of a legal contract, a hired job, this turns into unreliability as wife and mother. The discourse assumes old notions, namely that the mother is to be the calm, transcendent presence over the emotional turmoils of the children, and then to succor and nurture her husband who returns from the brutal battles of the public sphere. But in neither case is she herself allowed to be emotionally out of control.

Betsy, as career woman, perhaps paradoxically, also exemplifies the best emotional life needed to be mother. She wins both in terms of class and emotional timbre. Presumably because Bill is such a devoted father, Betsy's career is not seen to render her an inadequate mother. Indeed, given that she is a pediatrician, it seems to actually help!

But while the miniseries apparently upholds Betsy as the best mother, some aspects of Mary Beth's own account reappear in the somewhat ambivalent depiction of Betsy. In telling her own story in the ghostwritten book, Mary Beth depicted Betsy as cold, unfeeling, and selfish—the fifties' Hollywood stereotype of the career woman. Does the miniseries unconsciously collude in a sort-of critique of the yuppie Stern couple? Certainly, the scene in which Betsy finds Mary Beth's dog distasteful could be cited as one critique of middle-class uptightness and inability to let go and have fun, in contrast to the loose, fun-loving working-class family. Bill's middle-class attitudes are stressed through the scenes of the funeral: interestingly, however, there seems something too pretty about Bill, something too Waspish about Betsy. A subtle critique underlies their representations.

The women-at-odds, high-strung emotionality predominates in the miniseries once the baby is born and it is clear that Mary Beth will not relinquish her. Mary Beth becomes more and more hysterical, wild, and unreasonable; Betsy more and more despondent, depressed, silent, tortured. Their intense rivalry, competition, and even hatred override any consideration for each other, let alone the child. Bill, and to some degree Rick, Mary Beth's husband, show some ability to distance themselves, but for the most part the series portrays the two women as locked in an intense competition to win the baby from the other. The baby is reduced to a "thing," standing in for all loss, absence, desire—the breast, the phallus. At some point, this raw female emotion becomes out of control and the authorities move in: the police, social agencies, and finally the Father, the Law. Hysteria and jealous rivalry are now mitigated through, or displaced onto, the series of institutions the women have to move through in order to win each one's desire: the baby-breast-phallus.

While I have put psychoanalytic labels on the women's desire in an effort to understand its intensity, the text itself, of course, does not produce concepts to understand the intensity of the jealous female rivalry over the baby. Such jealous rivalry in traditional melodramas is usually over the male lover: think of Betty Davis in *Jezebel,* Vivien Leigh in *Gone with the Wind,* or Olivia de Havilland in *The Heiress,* all competing to the death for their man! The similarities in the structure of the jealous competition in stories about male lovers and now about babies is significant and invites psychoanalytic explanations. (A full exploration of the similar structures of these women-at-odds jealousies will be taken up in future work.)

Ultimately, the miniseries is more complex than some of the surface details—the surface semiotics—might make it seem. In line with feminist film critics' theorizing that melodrama is a form that can permit articulation of complex emotional dilemmas and of conflicts culture does not want to address, the miniseries does represent a range of positionalities vis-à-vis surrogacy: it allows viewers to experience the kinds of complications that arise within a given culture, like that of the contemporary U.S. While one can read the images of Betsy and Mary Beth as falling into conventional witch/angel polarities, the narrative does not automatically favor one over the other—as traditional melodramas may do. The varying depictions of the women, and the varying positions spectators are invited to occupy throughout the drama, enable the kind of complexity that results from multiple perspectives.

Ironically, such complexity is less evident in Martha Rosler's *Born to Be Sold: The Strange Case of Baby S/M* (Paper Tiger Videos). The video is produced in the alternate sphere, outside the obvious constraints of commercial institutions like Hollywood and commercial television. Nevertheless, its genre and context of production offer different kinds of constraint: the video is asked to be explicitly didactic, since that is the mission of the production company. Typically in these videos an expert "reads" a media text from a specific, polemical position.

In this case, Rosler "reads" the Mary Beth miniseries, and in so doing she puts herself under yet another constraint: responding within the forms that the miniseries first sets forth. Rosler's unconventional aesthetic form is determined by the need to break the conventional realist codes of the commercial series. She does this by inserting herself as speaker in the text, first by reading a paper on camera, and then by using her own body, in various disguises, to image the various characters of the melodrama she is deconstructing—Mary Beth, the baby, Betsy, Bill's sperm, the doctors, the judge in the case. She also uses a familiar "collage" technique, in which she inserts clips from Hollywood films and television news programs to make her polemical points.

For instance, she stages scenes from a Hollywood film about adoption, *Lucky Junior,* which would fit into the first set of "positive" surrogacy stories, even though the baby was not "commissioned" or genetically linked. Rosler uses the film to bolster her point that dominant culture demands that lower-class women serve the middle class by producing babies for them.

But most of the time, Rosler comments on the television miniseries. Hers is not a video about the actual case, as Maureen Turim seemed at times to indicate (Turim 1991). The figures Rosler acts out are meant to mimic not the historical people but the miniseries versions of those people. The specificities of the clothes and hairstyles mimic those in the miniseries, not the historical figures.

As in Agit-Prop street theatre, Rosler acts out the various key moments in the miniseries melodrama with minimal props, and comic, deliberate exaggeration.[4] With no attempt at verisimilitude, Rosler's body, dressed as a character, is usually seated in a room with wall paintings behind it. Rosler presents a didactic, classical class analysis of the case and critiques the media as "bourgeois" for supporting the middle-class Sterns all along. Images from the miniseries are repeated in the background to prove Rosler's case about dominant media. This direct-camera address by the filmmaker avoids any attempt to hide the video's production or producer.

In this way, Rosler's piece breaks the realist illusion of commercial melodramas and makes impossible identification with any of the characters as such. In place of the multiple and alternating identifications of the miniseries, the spectator is lectured to even more deliberately than in most Brecht works. Basically, Rosler's is a radical feminist reading of the case. Turim points out that there is no discussion of the baby as baby anywhere in the video. And while this is true, it may miss the point of Rosler reading a particular representation of the Whitehead case (in the miniseries), not the case itself or the historical figures. The miniseries also ignores the baby and thus does not draw attention to her.

Turim's second point has more strength: namely, that while the video means to mark feminist consciousness regarding the solidarity of women, it in fact reinforces separation in its simplistic class denunciation of Betsy. Rosler wants to show solidarity with the working-class Mary Beth, but this is at the expense of differently positioned women. The only good women are the lower-class women! The video makes the infertile woman the brunt of ridicule in a simplistic reduction of the complexity of things—a complexity that, ironically, is present in the commercial text.

I find this the most surprising: in the name of a critique of the position in the miniseries, Rosler's video simply reverses the stereotypes. It does not attempt to move beyond them. The video repeats what I pointed out regarding Mary Beth's own volume (Kaplan 1992), namely an anticareer woman stance that is, paradoxically, close to right-wing positions.

Further, in inserting the *Lucky Junior* clips, is Rosler using anti-adoption arguments to make the case against surrogacy? This is certainly how Harold J. Cassidy, Mary Beth's lawyer, presented the case against the Sterns, namely arguing for the harmful effects of adoption on the child. As much as the miniseries, the video ironically sides with the stance that the birth mother will "naturally" want to keep her baby, as if biological urges are paramount and cannot be transcended. As Turim points out, prohibition of either surrogacy or abortion relies on a repressive idea of the pregnant woman's body and on legitimating state control over these bodies (Turim 1991).

Rosler's video does make important points about class privilege and the imbalance between those able to buy surrogacy and those able to provide it. Such discussions are completely avoided in popular and commercial materials. But a main problem is the concept of the central speaking subject—Rosler herself—on which the video relies, and that is not problematized or questioned at all. In this sense, *Born to Be Sold* is a very modernist, as against postmodernist, work. It does not argue for the plurality of voices that feminists are currently looking for and that many feminist texts try to produce.

CONCLUSIONS

The two films I discussed were both made shortly after the Mary Beth Whitehead case in direct relation to it. I offer them as diverse examples of how the Whitehead case was used to make imaginary productions, and how it figured in different kinds of imaginations, different fiction making processes. Interesting are the different meanings the different textual strategies produce: the Rosler video is in part a direct critique of the television Whitehead film and included its footage to makes its points. While the miniseries does not draw attention to values of any kind, it is clear that discourses about class, race, and "family values," ongoing in U.S. culture, structure how surrogate mothering is conceptualized. The unavoidable genre of melodrama that constructs the *Baby M* commercial production, in turn, governs how the two women are categorized and the type of drama that is shown. Meanwhile, Martha Rosler's deliberately provocative, didactic video on the miniseries and other media treatment of the case, made from a classical Marxist perspective, partly critiques dominant media treatment of the case, by focusing on representations of Mary Beth versus the Sterns from a theory of working class versus bourgeois relations. It also critiques the medical establishment in ways now quite predictable in some feminist quarters. Simple antimedicine perspectives too easily degenerate into antitechnology stances that assume there is an unmediated "nature," that "biology" is discursively neutral. The antimelodrama narrative is, then, still constituted by melodrama forms.

It is easy to see how close some of the women's positive and negative narratives, explored earlier on, are to genres like melodrama, or to the soaps Gordon mentions. Indeed, the traditions of the melodrama genre may construct or shape the form that women's stories take in the first place, including sisterliness becoming unsisterly: women at odds. What is important for my purposes is how the melodrama form oversimplifies the actual psychological, political, social, and economic contexts of surrogacy. I have argued that the prevalence of the melodrama form in women's lives itself conditions the modes through which women think their lives. Women need to find forms more subtle—ones that enable multiple perspectives, ambiguities, contradictions, the yes/but, and the no/and/yes possibilities that are crucial as feminisms enter the nineties and attempt to grapple with difference on new levels.

NOTES

This essay will be developed and published in a 1994 issue of *Postmodern Occasions,* edited by Susan Squier, Michael Sprinker and E. Ann Kaplan, called "Reproductive Technologies, Gender and Culture." Papers in the volume were first delivered at a Stony Brook Humanities Institute conference on the same topic.

1. Research is still in progress and results of what I have been able to do are therefore tentative. I selected popular articles listed under the heading "Surrogacy" in the *Reader's Digest* index throughout the 1980s. Materials quoted came from many magazines, including *Redbook, Good Housekeeping,* and *Women's World*. In addition, I reviewed approximately twenty books about surrogacy, ranging from those aimed at quite a broad market to those more highly specialized, addressing legal or medical experts.

2. Indeed, minority women and their use of reproductive technologies seems a taboo subject: this is why the film *Made in America* was so interesting. In the film, the heroine, played by Whoopi Goldberg, has conceived her daughter by artificial insemination. The plot dwells on the consequences of the daughter finding out about her AI birth and discovering that her father was apparently white, for its comic effect.

3. However, Gordon was complaining about what she called "the soap-opera approach to surrogacy" and to the fact that this approach obscured the politics and the litigation. I believe she had the media accounts in mind more than the surrogate mothers' actual narratives. I am here more interested in how the availability of a form like melodrama in itself conditions the forms in which women think of their lives and tell their stories. The genre may be constitutive of the experience as much as the other way around.

4. I was most reminded of the agit-prop techniques in a little-known early British feminist film, *The Amazing Equal Pay Show,* which Rosler may well have had in mind. This film, however, did mimic actual historical political figures and was not a reading of a commercial text, as is Rosler's piece.

REFERENCES

Butzel, Henry M. 1987. "The Essential Facts of the Baby M Case." In Richardson, *On the Problem of Surrogate Parenthood.*

Chesler, Phyllis. 1988. *Sacred Bond: The Legacy of Baby M.* New York: Times Books.

Deegan, Mary Jo. 1987. "The Gift Mother: A Proposed Ritual for the Integration of Surrogacy into Society." In Richardson, *On the Problem of Surrogate Parenthood,* 93.

"Elizabeth." 1983. "A Surrogate's Story of Loving and Losing." *U.S. News and World Report* (June 6): 77.

Gelman, David, and Daniel Shapiro. 1985. "Infertility: Babies by Contract." *Newsweek* (November 4): 74–76.

Gledhill, Christine, ed. 1987. *Home Is Where the Heart Is: Studies in Melodrama and the Woman's Film.* London: British Film Institute.

Gordon, Linda. 1987. "Some Policy Proposals: Reproductive Rights for Today." *Nation* (September 12): 230–32.

Grogan, D. 1989. "Little Girl, Big Trouble." *People* (February 20): 36–41.

Growe, S. J. 1982. "The Furor over Surrogate Motherhood." *Maclean's* (July 5): 48.

Guinzburg, Suzanne. 1983. "Surrogate Mothers' Rationale." *Psychology Today* (April): 79.

Gupta, Nelly E., and Frank Feldinger. 1989. "Brave New Baby." *Ladies Home Journal* 106 (2): 140–41.

Kane, Elizabeth. 1988. *Birth Mother*. New York: Harcourt Brace Jovanovich.

Kaplan, E. Ann. 1992. *Motherhood and Representation: The Mother in Popular Culture and Melodrama*. London: Routledge.

King, Sherry, and Elaine Fein. 1986. "'I Gave Birth to My Sister's Baby.'" *Redbook* (April): 34–38.

Lacayo, Richard, and Wayne Svoboda. 1986. "Is the Womb a Rentable Space?" *Time* (September 22): 36.

Malcolm, Andrew H. 1988. "Steps to Control Surrogate Births Stir Debate Anew." *New York Times* (June 26).

Markoutsas, Elaine. 1981. "Women Who Have Babies for Other Women." *Reader's Digest* (August): 71.

McKay, Shona. 1983. "A Media Judgement on Surrogate Birth." *Maclean's* (February 14): 41.

Mills, Karen. 1985. "'I Had My Sister's Baby.'" *Ladies Home Journal* (October): 20–23.

Montgomery, Peter. 1988. "Should Surrogate Motherhood Be Banned?" *Common Cause Magazine* (May/June): 36–38.

Murphy, Julie. 1984. "Egg Farms." In R. Arditti, R. Dueilli Klein, and Shellen Minden, eds., *Test Tube Women: What Future for Motherhood*. London: Pandora Press.

Neff, David. 1987. "How Not to Have a Baby." Editorial. *Christianity Today* (April 3): 14–15.

"Psychiatrist Testifies in Black Surrogate Mom's Favor." 1990. *Jet* (October 29): 9.

Richards, Louise. 1989. "Giving the Gift of Life." *Ladies Home Journal* 106 (2): 22–23.

Richardson, Herbert, ed. 1987. *On the Problem of Surrogate Parenthood: Analyzing the Baby M Case*. Symposium Series 25. New York/Ontario: Edwin Mellen Press.

Stanworth, Michelle. 1990. "Birth Pangs: Conceptive Technologies and the Threat to Motherhood." In M. Hirsch and E. Fox-Keller, eds., *Conflicts in Feminism*. New York: Routledge.

"Surrogate Mother Sues for Baby's Custody." 1990. *New York Times*, August 15.

Thom, Mary. 1988. "Dilemmas of the New Birth Technologies." *Ms Magazine* (May): 70–72.

Turim, Maureen. 1991. "Viewing/Reading *Born To Be Sold: Martha Rosler Reads the Strange Case of Baby S/M* or Motherhood in the Age of Mechanical Reproduction." *Discourse* 13, no. 2: 32.

Turner, Victor. 1969. *The Ritual Process*. Chicago: Aldine.

Whitehead, Mary Beth. 1989. *A Mother's Story*. New York: St. Martin's Press.

III.

WOMEN IN THE HOUSE OF THE FATHER

10.

WOMEN AT ODDS: BIBLICAL PARADIGMS

JUDITH R. BASKIN

The Hebrew and Greek Bibles (the Old and New Testaments), themselves literary works of overwhelming power, are essential foundation texts for understanding a wide variety of themes and motifs in Western literature and art. Indeed, many argue that reinterpretations of the characters, situations, and concerns of biblical literature constitute the most significant component of the European and American cultural tradition.[1] Given this overwhelming resonance of biblical subject matter and language in prose, poetry, and imaginative representations of all kinds, it is not surprising that feminist critics have returned to biblical texts in search of the originals of some of the women who appear and reappear in our literary tradition. This essay, sharing in that endeavor, analyzes some of the Hebrew Bible's paradigmatic portrayals of women in conflict with other women.

The Hebrew Bible, a heterogeneous collection of documents reflecting a variety of attitudes and environments, was written and redacted over a thousand-year period by numerous authors and editors.[2] Composite in its makeup, the Hebrew Bible does not provide a consistent or accurate mirror of everyday Israelite life in any particular time and place. Nor does it purport to offer an objective or complete record of the history of ancient Israel, or its rulers, laws, and customs. Rather its component documents reflect the social, religious, and class-based views both of its various authors and of the group of editors who shaped the final form of the biblical canon.

Yet the Hebrew Bible is an ideologically united text, concerned with expounding and exploring the meaning of the relationship between the people of Israel and their single deity. Thus, the dominant dichotomy in the literature of the Hebrew Bible is that between creation and Creator, most specifically between human beings and God. Certainly, other distinctions exist, including those between human beings and other creatures, Israel and the other nations, priestly and nonpriestly Israelites, and men and women, but these are distinctions of power and status, not distinctions that imply essential difference.

Thus, the two sexes share a common humanity. Moreover, the Hebrew Bible maintains that both men and women were created in the divine image (Genesis 1:27). From this statement it seems clear that gender is irrelevant to what makes a human being similar to God: since both women and men are created in the divine image, women are not essentially other than men in their qualities, abilities, or characters.[3] Rather, as Tikva Frymer-Kensky writes, "Gender is a matter of biology and social roles . . . not a question of basic nature or identity."[4] Biblical women, like biblical men, are portrayed as noble and contemptible, brave and cowardly, wise and foolish, stalwart and abject. As Frymer-Kensky notes, "The circumstances of [women's] lives are different from those of *some* men (those with power), but there are no innate differences that preclude women from taking men's roles or men from taking women's roles should the occasion arise and circumstances warrant it. There is nothing distinctively 'female' about the way women are portrayed in the Bible."[5]

But at the same time it also important to reiterate that the men and women depicted in biblical texts did not share the same status or social roles. The narrative portions of the Hebrew Bible delineate a patriarchal society in which women were subordinate to male authority and were expected to function primarily in the domestic sphere as wives, mothers, and nurturers, while men provided for their family's sustenance, and, in some cases, acted in the public domain. Certainly this gender-based division of power and labor has its origins far back in the ancient Near Eastern past, and it was accepted as an unquestioned norm by all biblical authors and editors. Thus, the concept of an equal creation in Genesis 1 presents a surprising vision of female-male sameness, which coexists uneasily with the female subordination implicit in the details of women's real life, however partial, which biblical narratives reveal. As Susan Niditch notes, "While such an exalted view of human equality in the presence of their Creator might seem to be a positive and liberating force in Israelite religion, the statutes preserved in Scripture present the image of a strongly patrilineal culture in which women are in some instances highly marginalized and fenced out, and in others neatly fenced in, enclosed, and safely bound."[6] This culture may have believed that females and males shared intrinsic human qualities and abilities, but it sharply circumscribed the options and opportunities available to women.

Most scholars would agree that the authors of the various documents which comprise the literature of the Hebrew Bible were male,[7] as were the redactors who selected the narratives that make up the canon and edited them in their final form. As Niditch has noted, the Hebrew Bible "is an explicitly edited work from which many women's roles and important aspects of women's lives have been excluded."[8] She cautions that the reader must be as alert to what has been left out as to what is included. Nor should the contemporary reader of the Hebrew Bible forget that the many layers of exegetical tradition through which we read biblical texts may also distort our vision. As Frymer-Kensky notes, the biblical view of "a unified humanity was eventually overlaid with new concepts that entered Israel at the end of the biblical period," especially from Greek and Hellenistic sources.[9] "The stories about women were reinterpreted, and these later reinterpretations, masquerading as the biblical message, were used to import sexist ideology and practice."[10] Thus, our readings of biblical women, from Eve onwards, are often unconsciously modified, if we are not on guard, by our assimilation of later Jewish and Christian interpretive recastings of the texts before our eyes, often to the detriment of their female characters.

Women in the Hebrew Bible are generally represented in terms of their relationships to men. A woman's predominant roles were as a wife loyal to her husband's cause, and as a mother anxious to advance the ambitions of her sons. An admirable woman is one who wishes to further her family's interests, as in the "woman of valor" of Proverbs 31; occasionally a woman, like Deborah, takes on the role of mother of the nation (Judges 5:7). We hear a fair amount about husbands and wives and fathers and daughters, but almost nothing about mothers and daughters. Although we should not imagine that such relationships were not important to the women involved, we must conclude that they were not of particular interest to the messages biblical authors were trying to convey, probably because daughters married out of the patrilineal household and became part of someone else's lineage. Mothers-in-law and daughters-in-law, on the other hand, are a matter of significant import when their relationship affects Israel's history.

Biblical writings preserve several accounts of conflicts between women, usually reflecting situations in which one woman has power over another, or is struggling with a rival for male attention.[11] These biblical models of women at odds fall into three general categories: the competition between co-wives for the affection of their husband; the persecution of a maidservant by her mistress; and enmity between women of Israel and the women of other nations. In some cases the boundaries among these categories are blurred. The one striking exception to this pattern, a positive relationship between a mother-in-law and her foreign daughter-in-law, is paradigmatic simply in its surprising reversal of expected patterns, and there, too, the women share the ultimate goal of ensuring the continuation of the male line.

Biblical society was polygynous, and rivalry between or among the co-wives of one man must have been both common and unpleasant. In fact, the Hebrew word for co-wife means "trouble."[12] Even worse was the situation, depicted several times in biblical texts, where one wife was fertile and the other was not. In fact, in many cases, infertility of a first wife may have been the factor prompting the addition of a second wife to the household. For instance, in I Samuel 1, the favorite of Elkanah's two wives, Hannah, is childless, while the less beloved Peninnah has sons and daughters. "Moreover," the text continues, Peninnah, "her rival, to make her miserable, would taunt her that the Lord had closed her womb. This happened year after year: Every time she went up to the House of the Lord, the other would taunt her, so that she wept and would not eat. Her husband Elkanah said to her, 'Hannah, why are you crying and why aren't you eating? Why are you so sad? Am I not more devoted to you than ten sons?'" (I Samuel 1:6–8). Despite her husband's attempts to comfort her, Hannah is distraught, and certainly she has reason, even beyond Peninnah's cruelty. In ancient Israel, a woman's social position was secured by her fertility, and since women did not inherit property, they depended on their sons to provide for them in their declining years.[13] As a widow, without sons to support her, Hannah would be in a parlous position indeed when Peninnah's sons inherited Elkanah's property. Yet Hannah's desire for a son transcends her own personal needs, and she promises God that should she conceive she will pledge her son to divine service. Sure enough, she does become pregnant, and when he is weaned, Samuel, Hannah's son, enters the service of the Lord. Hannah herself is rewarded with the further births of three sons and two daughters.

This narrative is really about the miraculous birth of Samuel. A number of major figures in biblical history are born to apparently barren mothers. From a theological vantage point, this motif demonstrates the active and omnipotent presence of God in history. The births of Isaac, Jacob, Joseph, and Samuel all follow this pattern, yet before these marvelous events occur the Hebrew Bible also lets us see the misery of the barren wife and describes the suffering she endures at the behest of other women.

Perhaps the most prominent example of the co-wife scenario is found in the matriarchal narratives concerning Leah and Rachel, the two sisters the patriarch Jacob married in Haran (Genesis 29–30). In the case of Jacob's wives the rivalry is heightened because Leah, the unloved and unattractive wife, is fertile, while Rachel, her beautiful and beloved sister, is barren. In fact, in this instance, it is hard to decide which wife is more miserable—the slighted but fecund Leah, whom her husband was tricked into marrying, or the childless but cherished Rachel.

In this narrative Leah's fertility is seen as divine compensation for her neglected status. The names she gives each of her sons become explanations of her situation:

Leah conceived and bore a son, and named him Reuben; for she declared, "It means: 'The Lord has seen my affliction'; it also means 'Now my husband will love me.'" She conceived again and bore a son, and declared, "This is because the Lord heard that I was unloved and has given me this one also"; so she named him Simeon. Again she conceived and bore a son and declared, "This time my husband will become attached to me, for I have borne him three sons." Therefore he was named Levi. She conceived again and bore a son, and declared, "This time I will praise the Lord." Therefore she named him Judah. Then she stopped bearing. (Genesis 29:31–35)

During this time the self-absorbed Rachel remains infertile, and becomes increasingly envious of her sister. In pain at her situation, she impetuously cries out to her helpless husband, "Give me children, or I shall die." Jacob, incensed, declines to become involved in women's quarrels: "Can I take the place of God, who has denied you fruit of the womb?" (Genesis 30:1–2). Resorting to a customary ancient Near Eastern remedy to her situation, Rachel offers her maidservant Bilhah to her husband as a concubine, commanding him, "Consort with her, that she may bear on my knees and that through her I too may have children" (Genesis 30:3). It is understood that any children Bilhah bears Jacob will be considered Rachel's. Indeed, when Bilhah, whose own feelings about these events are neither considered nor revealed, gives birth to a son, Rachel proclaims, "God has vindicated me!" (Genesis 30:6). For Rachel, the drama of childlessness takes place on two planes—the divine and the human. Giving birth through Bilhah reassures Rachel that God has not abandoned her. She has been divinely justified as a worthy wife.

The human terms of the contest are made clear when Bilhah again gives birth to a son, and Rachel exults: "A fateful contest I waged with my sister; yes and I have prevailed" (Genesis 30:8). For the spoiled and narcissistic Rachel the competition against her sister for Jacob's full attention is the real battle. Yet how has Rachel prevailed? Her sister Leah has given birth to four sons at this point; Rachel is only the surrogate mother of her maidservant's children. But the birth of Bilhah's children apparently convinces Rachel that she has not merited unmitigated divine disfavor, while her surrogate motherhood is enough to secure the smitten Jacob's total devotion. Already confident in the love of her husband, her power struggle with her sister had come down to proving that she too is worthy of being a mother, even if only at second hand. It is no accident that Leah offers Jacob her own handmaid, Zilpah, who also bears him two sons, as the next move in the rivalry between the sisters.

Yet Rachel has not really fulfilled her wifely role in the way her culture most esteems, while Leah, despite all her sons, has still not gained her husband's love. This standoff is epitomized in the story of the mandrakes. Reuben, Leah's oldest son, has found some mandrake plants and brought them to his mother. These plants, which resemble human limbs, were believed to have both fertility-enhancing and aphrodisiac qualities. When Rachel asks Leah for some of the mandrakes, Leah refuses, setting out their quarrel in its simplest terms: "Was it not enough for you to take away my husband, that you would also take my son's mandrakes?" (Genesis 30:15). Of course, Rachel has not taken Jacob from Leah; he has always loved Rachel best. What Leah is expressing is the frustration of the good wife who has borne her husband sons, fulfilled all her duties admirably, and is still unloved. Rachel, secure in her power over her husband, if in little else, responds with an offer the ever-hopeful Leah cannot refuse: "I promise, he shall lie with you tonight, in return for your son's mandrakes." The passage continues, "When Jacob came home from the field in the evening, Leah went out to meet him and said, 'You are to sleep with me, for I have hired you with my son's mandrakes'" (Genesis 30:16). It is revealing of women's power in ancient Israel to see that Jacob's sexual choices are not always his own; apparently the master of the household submits to the wishes of his wives in the domestic sphere. Leah conceives as a result of this encounter, and bears a fifth son; subsequently she is rewarded with the birth of one more son and a daughter while Rachel still remains childless, unaided by the mandrakes. Only at this point does God remember Rachel, heed her pleas, and open her womb. When she conceives and bears a son, she rejoices that, at last, "God has taken away my disgrace." Yet still unsatisfied in her desire to better her sister once and for all, Rachel names her son Joseph, "which is to say, 'May the Lord add another son for me'" (Genesis 30:24).

Once again this story concludes with the miracle birth of a great hero. Rachel does not conceive and give birth in the normal course of events, nor because of the extraordinary aid of mandrakes; she conceives when, and only when, God opens her womb. Her son Joseph will grow up to be a most significant figure in the destiny of the people of Israel, saving his brothers and their families from famine, and bringing his entire clan to live in Egypt where the next necessary chapter of their relationship with God will unfold.

But what do we learn about conflict between women? Certainly we learn that a co-wife relationship was a constant struggle for power. Barrenness was seen as a sign of God's disfavor while fertility was understood as divine approbation. Though a beloved wife had considerable power over her husband, she was always weak without the support of sons. The biblical authors have no illusions that life is fair. God's disposal of human events is beyond human understanding. Rachel, who prayed for children or death, dies in her next childbirth and is buried alongside the road to Canaan. Leah endures, surrounded by sons, presumably always uncherished by the husband with whom she is buried in the family tomb. The deeper meaning of Rachel and Leah's mutual jealousy and competition is murky: does the narrative of this bitter rivalry exist simply to account for the birth of Jacob's sons, who become the progenitors of the twelve tribes of Israel? Are the details depicted here of life for co-wives in a polygynous household simply an accidental result of this larger goal, or do they constitute an endorsement of monogamy? Is there a lesson here about pride humbled and humility exalted? If so, it is decidedly ambivalent. The only thing we are sure of from this story is the biblical conviction that God acts in history in order to execute a divine plan of larger meaning and consequence than the life and experiences of any one individual. Meanwhile, women's lives are represented as taking place in the margins, where they are preoccupied with the personal, and subsumed in domestic detail.

Another connection between women of particular interest to biblical writers is the relationship between mistress and maidservant, particularly when that maidservant becomes a sexual partner of the master of the house. The most striking example of such a situation is the story of Sarah and Hagar, where the jealousy of the mistress for her fertile servant is played out against the tension of Sarah and Abraham's childless marriage (Genesis 16–21). Here, as elsewhere in biblical narratives, reprehensible human actions, driven by the most elemental emotions, are seen to work to fulfill a larger predetermined plan.

Sarah first enters the biblical narrative in Genesis 12 when, as Sarai, she joins her husband and half-brother Abram in fulfilling the divine command to leave behind homeland and kin to go to an unknown land and destiny. Abram is encouraged to make this drastic change because of God's promise to make him a "great nation" (Genesis 12:2). Moreover, when Abram enters the land of Canaan, the Lord appears to him and says, "I will assign this land to your offspring" (Genesis 12:7). Yet the great irony and tragedy of Abram's and Sarai's life at this very time when God is assuring Abram that his offspring will be as numerous as the stars in the sky (Genesis 15:2–9) is that, despite the divine promises, they are childless.

It is at this point that Sarai decides to take action on her own to ensure that she and her husband will have offspring. According to Genesis 16:1, Sarai had an Egyptian maidservant whose name was Hagar. "And Sarai said to Abram, 'Look, the Lord has kept me from bearing. Consort with my maid, perhaps I shall have a son through her.' And Abram heeded Sarai's request. So Sarai, Abram's wife, took her maid, Hagar the Egyptian—after Abram had dwelt in the land of Canaan ten years—and gave her to her husband Abram as concubine" (Genesis 16:2–3). This passage makes clear that Hagar is Sarai's property to bestow as she pleases. The contact between Abram and Hagar is initiated and orchestrated by Sarai, as Abram's wife. Abram must be willing to acquiesce to Sarai's request, but Hagar has no choice in the matter; as a possession she is simply an object through which the desire of her mistress for a child might be fulfilled.

Many scholars who have studied this passage, and the somewhat similar narratives of Rachel and Leah's bestowal of their maidservants upon Jacob (Genesis 30:3–12), have been interested in the legalities of such domestic arrangements in the larger context of the ancient Near East. They have found that analogous cases of surrogate motherhood through a maidservant were quite common across a large geographical area and over at least a thousand-year period. P. Kyle McCarter, Jr., for example, notes that "the responsibility of a barren wife to provide a slave woman to her husband for the purpose of bearing children is cited in Old Babylonian, Old Assyrian and Nuzi texts (all from the [second millennium B.C.] Middle Bronze Age), but also in a 12th-century Egyptian document and a marriage contract from Nimrud, dated 648 B.C." [14] Sarah's stratagem to give her husband a child, then, was not unique to her own situation, or to the milieux that produced the Hebrew Bible.

Yet while ancient Near Eastern parallels illuminate our knowledge of the social dynamics at work in this passage, far more interesting for the modern reader is the way in which the biblical author demonstrates how human passions can undermine the best laid plans. Genesis 16:4 informs us that when Hagar realized that she had become pregnant, "her mistress was lowered in her esteem"; undoubtedly, Hagar found ways to let Sarai sense her disdain. Suddenly Hagar, by virtue of pregnancy, has become an empowered individual whose very presence is an oppressive reminder to Sarai of her own infertility. Sarai turns to her husband in despair, but he dissociates himself from the conflict, telling Sarai: "Your maid is in your hands. Deal with her as you think right." "Then," the text tells us, "Sarai treated Hagar harshly, and she ran away from her" (Genesis 16:6).

What is at issue here is power and status. Sarai, who thinks she has acted for the good of her husband and herself, finds that Hagar's pregnancy has upset her ordered household; the fertile maidservant, Sarai's possession, threatens to displace the barren mistress. Yet the text makes clear that Abraham does not collude in this effort. The conflict is between Sarai and Hagar, and Hagar, pregnant or not, remains the slave who must submit to the inexcusably harsh treatment of her mistress. Even when Hagar flees to the wilderness, she encounters an angel of the Lord who addresses her as "slave of Sarai" and tells her she must return to endure Sarai's unkindness. The divine messenger does provide some comfort to Hagar by informing her that she will bear a son, Ishmael, who will be the father of many children, "for the Lord has paid heed to your suffering" (Genesis 16:7–12).

This story serves many purposes in the biblical narrative. For one thing, it accounts for Abraham's paternal connection to the children of Ishmael. It is also a cautionary tale about meddling with the divine purpose. Sarai sought to hurry God's plan by acting on her own to ensure offspring for Abraham. Although she acted within the legalities of her time and place in giving her maidservant to her husband, and although her motive was good, the punishment for her lack of faith was to feel the scorn of her servant. The envious Sarai cannot refrain from oppressing her pregnant maidservant, who was, at least initially, the innocent victim of her mistress's whims. Biblical women, as biblical men, often behave badly. Yet the mystery in the story is why Hagar's pregnancy is so upsetting to Sarai. In the similar situation discussed above, the barren Rachel gave her maidservant Bilhah to her husband Jacob, ordering him, "Consort with her, that she may bear on my knees and that through her I too may have children" (Genesis 30:3). When Bilhah gives birth, Rachel exults, "God has vindicated me; indeed He has heeded my plea and given me a son" (Genesis 30:6). In that story, Bilhah, who came from the household of Rachel's father, Laban, remains a cipher; she is simply an instrument through whom the desire of her mistress is fulfilled. Why is this not the case with Sarai and Hagar?

One answer may lie in Hagar's ethnic status as an Egyptian. From the perspective of the biblical authors, Israel, at the very moment of its birth as a nation, appeared to be threatened with pollution from an outside source. Hagar does not fit into the divine plan for Abram and Sarai and their descendants. In Genesis 21, following the crucial covenantal scene in which Abram and Sarai are renamed Abraham and Sarah, God again affirms that Sarah, despite her advanced age, will bear a son through whom the covenant will be eternally preserved (Genesis 17). Only then, when all hope has been abandoned, does the long-awaited birth of Sarah's son, Isaac, occur. Almost immediately, Sarah, powerful once more, demands that Hagar and Ishmael be expelled: "Cast out that slave-woman and her son, for the son of that slave shall not share in the inheritance with my son Isaac" (Genesis 21:10). Although Abraham is distressed to treat his own son so cruelly, God reassures him, "Do not be distressed over the boy of your slave; whatever Sarah tells you, do as she says, for it is through Isaac that offspring shall be continued for you. As for the son of the slave-woman, I will make a nation of him, too, for he is your seed" (Genesis 21:12–13).

In this narrative Sarah's rather natural antipathy to her husband's scornful concubine and the irritation occasioned by the concubine's son take on a larger significance. In protecting her son's inheritance, Sarah is acting to fulfill the divine plan that Isaac, not Ishmael, will carry on the everlasting covenant that God has established with Abraham. The authors of these particular texts are also making some significant comments about the importance for Israel of marrying within the group. It is no accident that the final biblical comment on Ishmael in this episode is that when he was grown his mother took a wife for him from the land of Egypt, her own homeland. Similarly, when Abraham remarries after Sarah's death, and fathers more sons, Abraham makes clear that these children are not his heirs, for their mothers were not of his kin. As the text recounts, "Abraham willed all that he owned to Isaac; but to Abraham's sons by concubines Abraham gave gifts while he was still living, and he sent them away from his son Isaac eastward, to the land of the East" (Genesis 25:5–6). Again, the themes of overriding importance for the biblical editors are the covenantal relationship and the unimpeachable lineage of Israel's mothers and fathers. At a level of deep structure, the story of ancient Israel is one of a lineage and succession constantly in jeopardy and miraculously preserved by the intervention of God.

Another biblical example of women at odds, revealed in the Song of Deborah (Judges 5), takes place against the larger political backdrop of the ancient Near East in which the tribes of Israel wage battle against their enemies. Women in such biblical texts identify with the goals of their husband or of their nation. The Song of Deborah, and the prose narrative that precedes it (Judges 4), tells a story in which women figure prominently, and in unexpected ways. Deborah, a prophetess and Israel's leader in the period prior to the establishment of a monarchy (Judges 4:4), designates her general, Barak, to lead Israel's forces against their Canaanite enemies, led by the commander Sisera. When Sisera's forces are defeated, he flees in panic to the tent of Jael, the wife of Heber the Kenite, where he expects to find safety. But Jael is loyal to Israel, and when Sisera falls asleep from exhaustion she kills him, driving a tent pin through his temple. As Niditch observes, "In language and imagery richly dripping in eroticism and death, Jael partakes of a wider ancient

Near Eastern and more universal archetype of the seductress-exterminator. Jael is an unlikely heroine, a self-appointed female soldier, who reverses the normal fate of women in battle. She is not seduced, taken, or despoiled but herself seduces, marginalizes and despoils a man."[15]

That capture and humiliation would have been women's expected fate in the event of defeat is evident in the Song of Deborah, which retells this story in poetic form. Here Sisera's mother is depicted, anxiously waiting for her son to return from battle: "Through the window peered Sisera's mother,/ Behind the lattice she whined:/ Why is his chariot so long in coming?/ Why so late the clatter of his wheels?" (Judges 5:28). She comforts herself by imagining that he is delayed in dividing the plunder, including the captured women: "They must be dividing the spoil they have found:/ A damsel or two for each man,/ Spoil of dyed cloths for Sisera, Spoil of embroidered cloths,/ A couple of embroidered cloths/ Round every neck as spoil" (Judges 5:30). In this passage, Sisera's mother equates the women of Israel, coarsely described in Hebrew as "wombs," with dyed and embroidered cloths. They are valuable and desirable objects, but objects nonetheless. In fact, the reader knows that Sisera, her son, is dead, murdered by Jael. Mieke Bal has observed that Sisera's mother, "who borrows masculine language to designate other women as wombs, richly deserves such a lesson" as her son's death at the hands of a woman in an act of sexually reversed violation.[16] But in this powerful and ironic poem, as Frymer-Kensky writes, Deborah expects this hostility from her enemy's mother and returns it in full. First and foremost, "Deborah (and her projection of Sisera's mother) are conscious of the separate identities of Israelites and Canaanites."[17] In biblical thinking, this is the norm; women, as men, are devoted to advancing their own cause—favored offspring first, followed by loyalty to family, tribe, and nation. There is no notion of a female solidarity, whether within Israel itself or transcending ethnic affiliation and loyalty.

Perhaps some sense of resolution can be found in a final example that does not seem to fit the rules. From the perspective of the male biblical authors, the family is a source of both strength and turmoil. With mother-in-law and daughters-in-law, for example, as with co-wives, the expectation is that women who compete for the attention and love of one man will be in conflict. Just as Rachel and Leah, and Peninnah and Hannah, are far from allies, so Rebekah complains of her son Esau's Canaanite wives, fearing that her younger son Jacob will also marry outside the family's ethnic group (Genesis 27:46) and bring her additional grief. Israelite women have a strong antipathy for the women of neighboring hostile cultures and feel no sense of solidarity with those of their own gender who live beyond their boundaries. It is both the expected hostility between a mother and her son's wife and the anticipated enmity between a woman of Israel and a woman of the despised Moabites that are reversed so strikingly in the story of Naomi and Ruth.

In this biblical narrative, which begins in the land of Moab, the divine plan synchronizes with human action as the widowed Moabite Ruth, an outsider, unexpectedly pledges her future with her equally bereft Israelite mother-in-law and the people of Israel. With her fateful words to Naomi—"For wherever you go, I will go; wherever you lodge, I will lodge; your people shall be my people, and your God my God. Where you die, I will die, and there I will be buried. Thus and more may the Lord do to me if anything but death parts me from you" (Ruth 1:16–17)—Ruth makes clear that her love for Naomi transcends her ties to her own parents and people. Settled back in the land of Israel, Naomi and Ruth work together to secure their futures and the continuation of the male line of Ruth's deceased father-in-law and husband. Ultimately they succeed, as through their strategems Ruth becomes the wife of her dead husband's kinsman, the wealthy and kind Boaz. Boaz announces publicly that he is undertaking this marriage, "so as to perpetuate the name of the deceased upon his estate, that the name of the deceased may not disappear from among his kinsmen and from the gate of his home town" (4:10). The townspeople who serve as witnesses applaud his actions with the following prayer: "May the Lord make the woman who is coming into your house like Rachel and Leah, both of whom built up the House of Israel" (4:11). Ruth is able to fulfil this preeminent requirement that an Israelite wife "build up" her husband's house; the story concludes with the birth of Ruth's son and happiness all around as Naomi becomes the child's foster mother. The townswomen approve of Naomi's joy and pray that the child will "renew your life and sustain your old age; for he is born of your daughter-in-law, who loves you and is better to you than seven sons" (4:14). Indeed, this child, Obed, does prosper; the son of a Moabite woman, Obed becomes the father of Jesse and the grandfather of King David. Thus, the story of Ruth also achieves its narrative interest on human and divine grounds. This narrative of a loving mother-in-law and daughter-in-law is as surprising and compelling, and perhaps as instructive, as God's choice of a despised Moabite woman to be the forebear of Israel's greatest king.

The male-constructed biblical paradigms discussed in this essay of women in conflict or, by rare contrast, in unexpected harmony reinforce the ideology of biblical narrative that finds God's marvelous purposes in every human action. Women's conflicts, as with the many instances the Hebrew Bible records of hostility and despicable behavior between men, advance Israel's destiny in unexpected ways. Such representations offer only partial glimpses of the actual lives and concerns of women in biblical times; female characters appear in the story only when their activities are seen by the biblical authors or editors to reveal a larger divine purpose or message. Still, these powerful and psychologically complicated portraits of women at odds resonate far beyond the Hebrew Bible in two millennia of representations of women and their encounters with others of their sex.[18]

NOTES

All biblical quotations are from *Tanakh: A New Translation of the Holy Scriptures according to the Traditional Hebrew Text* (Philadelphia: Jewish Publication Society, 1985).

1. See, for example, Robert Alter and Frank Kermode, "General Introduction," in their edited volume, *The Literary Guide to the Bible* (Cambridge, Mass.: Harvard University Press, 1987), 2–3.
2. On the history of the writing and redaction of the Hebrew Bible's component parts, see Richard Elliott Friedman, *Who Wrote the Bible?* (New York: Harper and Row, 1987).
3. In fact, the Hebrew Bible contains two accounts of the creation of human beings. In the first (Genesis 1:1–2:4), human beings, male and female, are created together, by the divine word, in the divine image. In the second account (Genesis 2:5–3:24), the first human being is a man shaped by God from the dust of the earth. Only later is a woman formed out of the sleeping man's rib. This second view, in which the female is subsequent to and subordinate to the male, predominates in post-biblical Jewish and Christian thought and exegesis.
4. Tikva Frymer-Kensky, *In the Wake of the Goddesses: Women, Culture, and the Biblical Transformation of Pagan Myth* (New York: Free Press, 1992), 141.
5. Ibid., 120.
6. Susan Niditch, "Portrayals of Women in the Hebrew Bible," in Judith R. Baskin, ed., *Jewish Women in Historical Perspective* (Detroit: Wayne State University Press, 1991), 29.

7. Friedman, in *Who Wrote the Bible?* (86), suggests reasons why "J," one of the authors represented in Genesis, could have been female. Similar arguments are made at greater length by Harold Bloom, "The Author J," in Harold Bloom and David Rosenberg, *The Book of J* (New York: Grove Weidenfeld, 1990), 9–10, 36–48.
8. Niditch, "Portrayals of Women," 28.
9. Frymer-Kensky, *Wake of the Goddesses*, 143, 203–12.
10. Ibid., 143.
11. This is not to imply that all relationships between women were negative, but rather that biblical authors are only interested in portraying women's interactions when it fits their own ideological agenda. References to positive contacts between women are most frequently found in oblique comments. Similarly, wives and mothers, whose roles in narratives about their husbands or sons are portrayed as minor, are often mentioned but not named.
12. Frymer-Kensky, *Wake of the Goddesses*, 127.
13. Ibid., 125.
14. P. Kyle McCarter, Jr., "The Patriarchal Age: Abraham, Isaac and Jacob," in *Ancient Israel: A Short History from Abraham to the Roman Destruction of the Temple*, ed. Hershel Shanks (Washington, D.C.: Biblical Archaeology Society; Englewood Cliffs, N.J.: Prentice-Hall, 1988), 11.
15. Niditch, "Portrayals of Women," 33.
16. Mieke Bal, *Murder and Difference: Gender, Genre, and Scholarship on Sisera's Death,* trans. Matthew Gumpert (Bloomington: Indiana University Press, 1992), 134.
17. Frymer-Kensky, *Wake of the Goddesses*, 127.
18. Three quite disparate examples of literary works by women that make extremely interesting use of the biblical themes discussed in this essay are George Eliot, *Daniel Deronda*; Willa Cather, *Sapphira and the Slave Girl*; and Margaret Atwood, *The Handmaid's Tale*.

REFERENCES

Alter, Robert, and Frank Kermode. *A Literary Guide to the Bible*. Cambridge: Harvard University Press, 1987.
Bal, Mieke. *Murder and Difference: Gender, Genre, and Scholarship on Sisera's Death*. Translated by Matthew Gumpert. Bloomington: Indiana University Press, 1992.
Bloom, Harold, and David Rosenberg. *The Book of J*. New York: Grove Weidenfeld, 1990.
Friedman, Richard Elliott. *Who Wrote the Bible?* New York: Harper and Row, 1987.
Frymer-Kensky, Tikva. *In the Wake of the Goddesses: Women, Culture, and the Biblical Transformation of Pagan Myth*. New York: Free Press, 1992.
McCarter, P. Kyle, Jr. "The Patriarchal Age: Abraham, Isaac and Jacob." In

Ancient Israel: A Short History from Abraham to the Roman Destruction of the Temple, edited by Hershel Shanks, 1–29. Washington, D.C.: Biblical Archaeology Society; Englewood Cliffs, N.J.: Prentice-Hall, 1988.

Meyers, Carole. *Discovering Eve: Ancient Israelite Women in Context.* New York: Oxford University Press, 1988.

Newson, Carol A., and Sharon H. Ringe. *Women's Bible Commentary.* Louisville: Westminster/John Knox Press, 1992.

Niditch, Susan. "Portrayals of Women in the Hebrew Bible." In *Jewish Women in Historical Perspective,* edited by Judith R. Baskin, 25–42. Detroit: Wayne State University Press, 1991.

11.

POST-FEMINIST AND ANTI-WOMAN: THE REVOLUTIONARY REPUBLICAN WOMEN IN FRANCE, 1793–1794

WILLIAM THOMPSON

Over the course of the French revolutionary era, which witnessed the creation of a staggering number of revolutionary clubs and organizations, it is hardly surprising that a political group composed entirely of women should make an appearance. Such is the case of the Société des Citoyennes Républicaines Révolutionnaires (who will be referred to here as the Revolutionary Republican Women, or the Society). The founding of this group, a radical faction initially aligned with the Jacobins and later with the Enragés, marks the beginning of a unique enterprise in revolutionary France: a society formed for women and by women who wished to serve the Revolution by regulating and policing the behavior of their fellow citizens, both male and female. Founded in the agitation which preceded the official Terror of 1793, this women's group established itself firmly within the political activism and rhetoric of the exclusively male domains of the Convention and the Commune of Paris. Its members engaged in a variety of activities intended to defend the revolution: they complained about indecision and corruption in government, petitioned the Paris Commune to arrest the wives of émigrés and to place prostitutes in national homes for rehabilitation, reported food hoarding, and forced the market women of Paris to wear the tricolor cocarde, the ribbon symbolic of revolutionary patriotism.

Although the actual founding of the Society is not exceptional, since women frequently and actively engaged in protest throughout this period, the existence of this Society presents a difficulty to any attempt to comprehend the breadth of the role of women in the Revolution, as well as the extent to which the actions of women during this period can be considered "feminist." How can we discuss and qualify, within the parameters of the term "feminism," the actions of a group of women, acting as women, attempting to solidify and guarantee their status as citizens within a particular society, yet who at the same time *oppressed* other women, and favored a Terror that led to the execution of thousands of women and men? In an attempt to answer this question, this essay will consider: (1) the history of the Society, in particular its platforms that infringed on the rights of other women; (2) the implication of these activities in the context of a feminist discourse; and (3) the possibility of introducing and utilizing the term "post-feminism" to describe this Society and its actions, including those both benefitting and oppressing women.

Amidst the chaos and constant change that characterized the political and social scenes in revolutionary France between 1789 and 1794, and during which the notion of "citizen" underwent constant redefinition, it is not surprising that women should play an increasingly prominent role. The era of the French Revolution would see many women, through both individual and collective endeavors, achieve a fame (or notoriety) of sometimes mythic proportions: Marie Antoinette, Charlotte Corday (the assassin of Marat), women in need of bread marching to Versailles, would-be women soldiers volunteering to take up arms to defend the Revolution, and isolated "feminist" activists such as Olympe de Gouges and Théroigne de Méricourt. Yet while some of the actions by women were not without precedent (such as protesting about the lack of food), new areas such as political activism were being explored for the first time.

Even before the actual commencement of revolutionary activities, women had participated in the composition of the "cahiers de doléances," the pamphlets written to complain about the various inequalities in French society. Women both wrote and were the subject of these tracts, as the challenge to the old order made discussion possible about issues such as marriage laws, the legalization of divorce, and the lack of education for girls.

Yet it is evident from the nature of these topics that in the opinion of many of the citizens of the new France, a woman's place should remain in the home, or at the very least she should continue to preoccupy herself with traditional, socially acceptable activities: care giving, child rearing, perhaps shopkeeping. Few of the dramatic events of the revolutionary era actually allowed women to alter in a significant manner their status within French society. The women who marched on Versailles in 1789, after all, were not revolutionaries; they only wished to complain about the lack of bread to a king they believed sympathetic to their situation. Olympe de Gouges's treatise on the rights of women was only written as a response to the insufficiencies of the *Declaration of the Rights of Men,* which was published at the beginning of the revolutionary period and which ignored the status of women. And although the new government was eager for women to contribute to national defense (both against counterrevolutionaries and against France's neighbors), it was assumed that they would fulfill supportive roles such as rolling bandages and knitting. Such, however, was not to be the case of the Revolutionary Republican Women.

Already active in an unofficial capacity in February of 1793, a group of women made a formal application to the Paris Commune on May 10 of the same year, asking for permission to form a club (such a request being required by law). In the application, the women expressed "their intention of assembling and forming a society which admits only women" (Levy et al. 149),[1] which was in itself unique for the revolutionary period, as other women either joined men's clubs already in existence or formed clubs that allowed both men and women as members. The women of the new Society also stated that their aim was "deliberation on the means of frustrating the projects of the republic's enemies" (Levy et al. 149), in itself a most acceptable activity for a revolutionary club during a period of great fear of counterrevolution.[2]

There are few accounts of the meetings of the Society, but the written Regulations of the Revolutionary Republican Women have survived and provide some indication of the initial goals of these women. By their very existence, the Regulations demonstrate the seriousness with which the Society's members approached their work, as well as their desire to legitimize the Society and its activities, and indeed most of the articles cover such issues as correct procedure for meetings, the keeping of minutes, and the protocol for the signing of correspondence. In spite of its popular origins in the lower echelons of Parisian society, the club wished to convey a sense of respectability and propriety; Article XII, for example, states, "The Society, believing that people should join together only for mutual honor, support, and encouragement in virtue, has decreed that it will receive in its midst only those *citoyennes* of good habits" (Levy et al. 163).

More important for understanding the aims of the Revolutionary Republican Women are the general goals, as stated in the introduction to the Regulations, which elaborate on the statement of objectives made in the original application to the Commune:

Convinced that there is no liberty without customs and principles, and that one must recognize one's social duties in order to fulfill one's domestic duties adequately, the Revolutionary Republican *citoyennes* have formed a Society to instruct themselves, to learn well the Constitution and laws of the Republic, to attend to public affairs, to succor suffering humanity, and to defend all human beings who become victims of any arbitrary acts whatever. They want to banish all selfishness. (Levy et al. 161)

It is imperative to note that no specific mention is made of *women's* rights, suffering, and victimization. The Society in no way dedicated itself to what we might call "feminist issues." In fact, there is an acknowledgment of the importance of women's traditional role as homemaker and care giver in the references to "domestic duties" and "succor suffering humanity," although such efforts are considered only one component of a broad range of possible activities.

The rather vague goals of the introduction ("attend to public affairs" in itself will come to represent a seemingly endless list of enterprises on the part of the Society) dissimulate the truly radical nature of the Society's intentions, some of which will inevitably lead to the oppression of other women. For example, Article I of the Regulations clearly reveals the Society's wish to incorporate women thoroughly into the defense of the republic in a manner that moves far beyond the role of care giver and nursemaid: "The Society's purpose is to be armed to rush to the defense of the Fatherland; *citoyennes* are nonetheless free to arm themselves or not" (Levy et al. 161). (In spite of the Society's apparent claim to the right to bear arms, women were in fact forbidden to do so, although some did fight alongside men in the war against Austria, and it was rumored that some of the Society's members carried pistols.) Yet

Article XV, the only other article to mention the patriotic mission of the Society, declares, "All newly received *citoyennes* will be summoned by the President, in the name of the Society, to take the following oath: 'I swear to live for the Republic or die for it'" (Levy et al. 163), demonstrating again the assumption on the part of the Society that women as well as men could and must give their lives for the cause of the Revolution.

After their formation, the Revolutionary Republican Women wasted little time in making themselves known at the meetings of the Jacobin Society with which they wished to be associated. On two occasions, within days of their official application, they expressed to the Jacobins their resolution to protect the internal affairs of France, a particularly important activity considering that many men had gone to the front to combat France's external enemies. The women promised to "protect the interior" and requested that women be formed into armed corps, be entitled to arrest and disarm "suspects," and be allowed to wear the cocarde, the ribbon then worn only by men to prove one's patriotism. A call was also made to establish revolutionary armies in the cities, to punish speculators and hoarders, even to set up workshops where iron could be converted into weapons (Levy et al. 150–51). The demands in these petitions clearly situate the Revolutionary Republican Women on the side of those parties favoring an all-out Terror within France to purge counterrevolutionaries (or at the very least those accused of counterrevolutionary activities, whether guilty or not). At the same time the petitions again demonstrate that the Society, although composed exclusively of women, had no interest at this point in women's issues per se, any references to women being situated within a discussion of what was best for the republic at large.

The Revolutionary Republican Women were presented with the opportunity to back up their words with action at the end of May 1793 during the attack led by the Jacobins, which led to the ousting of the Girondin faction from the Convention. The women of the Society positioned themselves outside the entrance to the Convention and prevented supporters of the Girondins from entering. They were responsible for the whipping of Théroigne de Méricourt, a supporter of the Girondins and ironically an advocate of women's rights. The Society was able to claim a great deal of the credit when the Girondins were purged from the Convention, and they received considerable praise from the Jacobins, as well as scorn from the defeated Girondins, one of whom described them as "abandoned women, escaped from the gutter, monstrous females with all the cruelty of weakness and all the vices of their sex."[3]

In late August of 1793, the Society presented yet another petition demanding that the Convention implement the Constitution, call for a general mobilization, and arrest all suspects (Levy et al. 172–74). Angered by the laxity of the Convention, the Society advocated harsh measures to guarantee the survival of the Revolution: "Ruin all the nobles without exception; if there are any of good faith among them, they will give proof of it by voluntarily sacrificing themselves to the good fortune of their Fatherland" (Levy et al. 173). They also joined in the call for a purging of corruption in the government, advocating the inception of the Terror: "No, it will not be said that the people, reduced to despair, were obliged to do justice themselves; you are going to give it to them by ruining all guilty administrators and by creating extraordinary tribunals in sufficient number so that patriots will say, as they leave for the front: 'We are calm about the fate of our wives and children; we have seen all internal conspirators perish under the sword of the law'" (Levy et al. 173–74). This speech would be followed in the month of September by further petitions calling for the arrest of various political figures whom the Society considered suspect, as well as the confinement and rehabilitation of prostitutes, the arrest of the wives of aristocrats, and the searching of the homes of suspected hoarders.

These petitions demonstrate that within the context of their patriotic fervor, the Revolutionary Republican Women were indeed preoccupied with the status of women, both "bonnes citoyennes" and enemies to the revolutionary cause. That they showed no hesitation in promoting the condemnation of aristocratic women demonstrates their adherence to a generally accepted line of thought: aristocrats, whether actively counter-revolutionary or not, were to be considered a danger to the revolution by their very presence in France. The attack on aristocratic women could, therefore, be put forth as the perfect example of the Revolutionary Republican Women's success in including all women within any discussion of a revolutionary nature. Yet at the same time, this hostility is a strikingly ironic moment, witnessing the successful participation of one group of women in society at the tragic expense of other women.

In spite of the apparent patriotism manifested by the Revolutionary Republican Women (with violent undertones, indeed, but not extraordinary for the period), the Jacobins were becoming increasingly alarmed and irritated by their constant demands and criticism. Thus, on September 16, Claire Lacombe, the president of the Society at the time, found herself under verbal assault at a meeting of the Jacobin Society. Several citizens, both male and female, came forward to denounce Lacombe for having challenged the authority of the various Committees and of the Convention, for lodging an alleged counterrevolutionary (the Enragé Leclerc), and for having dared to call Robespierre "Monsieur" (an aristocratic term of address offensive to the revolutionary spirit). After an attempt to defend herself, Lacombe was briefly arrested, released only when the officials detaining her discovered that she had nothing in her possession to incriminate her. In fact, they declared that they "found nothing but correspondence of fraternal societies, which breathes the purest patriotism, and different personal letters where the public good and patriotism were beautifully expressed" (Levy et al. 196).

The eventual fate of the Society, however, seemed apparent. The press loyal to the Convention continued to ridicule the efforts by women to participate in matters of government, demonstrating the increasingly dominant conservative traditionalism that envisaged women as homemakers and mothers. The Revolutionary Republican Women were described as "immodest monsters, public leeches, hideous sluts, and pretentious ugly women." [4] It was clear that the concept of the "citoyenne" adopted by the Revolutionary Republican Women differed radically from that acceptable to the governing Jacobins: "Interpellated as 'citoyennes,' a minority of women began to act as if they too were expected to conform to the model of the republican 'citoyen.' But in Jacobin ideology, the stern and vigilant model of the citoyen was in fact predicated on a soft, loving, totally domestic model of the 'citoyenne'—on a 'citoyenne' that preserved nothing of the meaning of the term except the feminine ending." [5]

Shortly after the denunciation of Claire Lacombe began the episode with which the Society is most often associated: the so-called "war of the cocarde." The cocarde (or cockade) was the tricolor ribbon worn by those wishing to demonstrate their patriotism and devotion to the revolutionary cause. However, while all "citoyens" were obliged to wear it by government decree, it was not clear if this also applied to women.

The Revolutionary Republican Women, with their enthusiastic patriotism and their desire to monitor the behavior of *all* citizens, no matter how demeaning and oppressive their tactics, strongly supported the wearing of the cocarde, and some took to policing the streets of Paris to assure that all men and women were conforming to the dress code. They confronted great resistance from the market women of Paris, who were generally opposed to political activism for women, and who were already antagonistic toward the Society because of the latter's support of price controls, which the market women considered excessive (yet another form of oppression, this time economic). Tensions grew to the point that women on both sides of the issue were verbally abused and physically attacked, with the market women claiming that "only whores and Jacobin Women wear it [the cocarde]," [6] and that women should occupy themselves with their household and not politics. The Convention, however, did pass a decree on September 21 requiring all women to wear the cocarde. Yet what appeared to be a victory for the patriotic forces, including the Revolutionary Republican Women, was merely an attempt to restore order, as the Convention was only reacting to the complaints of a nervous Parisian police force alarmed by the attacks by women on other women.

Following the battle of the cocarde, yet another conflict involving dress arose toward the end of October 1793, and proved to be the fatal blow for the Society of Revolutionary Republican Women. Members of the Society were among a group of women who had taken to wearing not only the cocarde, but also the "bonnet rouge," the red wool cap symbolic of liberty worn by male revolutionaries. The adoption of the cap inevitably led to conflict between women who advocated wearing the bonnet and their opponents. Women wearing red caps were insulted, assaulted, and had the caps knocked from their heads. For the male authorities as well, the image of women wearing the red bonnet, until then an exclusively masculine item of clothing, was cause for alarm. If the cocarde was merely a symbol of patriotism, the red bonnet was, apart from its symbolic connotations, ostensibly masculine apparel, and therefore inappropriate for women. Convention member Fabre d'Eglantine would generate further fear by warning his colleagues that "today they ask for the red bonnet, but they will not be satisfied with that; soon they will ask for a belt and pistols, and you will see women going for bread as if going to the trenches." [7]

Although there is only slight proof that any women in Paris ever carried firearms, and although the cocarde and bonnet rouge held purely symbolic value for the women who wore them, Joan Landes points out that within the context of the dominant bourgeois republican discourse, the rhetoric and activities of the Revolutionary Republican Women appeared unnatural and entirely incompatible: "What ought to have been a symbol of patriotism—women dressed in the tricolor cockade, trousers, red bonnets, and donning swords—became instead a public statement of women's collective interest against the harmonious familial symbolism and masculinist practice of the virtuous republic."[8] Yet equally alarming is the dual process of oppression operating here: the Revolutionary Republican Women were to be suppressed by the male-dominated government for the notoriety they had gained through their sometimes violent attempts to oppress other women.

The red bonnet affair reached a climax on October 28 when the Revolutionary Republican Women were attacked during a ceremony commemorating two martyrs of the Revolution: Marat and Lepeletier. A number of women hostile to the Society interrupted the ceremony, shouting: "Down with red bonnets! Down with Jacobin women! Down with Jacobin women and the cockades! They are all scoundrels who have brought misfortune upon France!" (Levy et al. 209). Ironically, the Revolutionary Republican Women were vilified on this occasion in part for their association with the Jacobins, who themselves had attacked the Society the month before, and who were waiting for the opportunity to rid themselves permanently of a group they considered an annoyance. In spite of attempts on the part of authorities to restore order to the ceremony, the Revolutionary Republican Women were physically attacked, some of them seriously wounded, and only with the assistance of armed troops were the Society's members able to escape further harm. The Society thus found itself, in essence, isolated from all components of republican society: "The Revolutionary Republican Women were particularly vulnerable to the extent that within the revolutionary movement they were women, while within the women's movement they held political positions that were becoming increasingly isolated."[9]

The incident provided the Convention with sufficient material to be convinced of the instability and danger of the participation of women in the political sphere, and on October 30 the Society of Revolutionary Republican Women and all women's political groups were banned. The law enforcing the wearing of the cocarde was subsequently repealed, and arguments about the red bonnet were declared counterrevolutionary. Perhaps not coincidentally, several prominent women of the revolutionary era were guillotined during this same period: Marie Antoinette on October 16, Olympe de Gouges on November 3, and Manon Roland on November 8.

What avenues were left to women following the ban on club activity?

A prominent newspaper of the time offered some advice: "Women! Do you want to be republicans? Love, follow and teach the laws which recall your husbands and children to the exercise of their rights; honor the great deeds that may be done for your country, to show that they will be done for you; be simple in your dress, hardworking in your home; never go to popular assemblies with the wish to speak there, but so that your presence may sometimes encourage your children."[10] Thus women were encouraged (if not explicitly forced) to return to a role that the events of the Revolution had never fully succeeded in altering, abandoning the changes in dress and political activism the Revolution, many believed, had made their right. In terms of visible, long-lasting achievement, the Society of Revolutionary Republican Women had accomplished very little; in fact, they had a lengthy list of achievements only in the domain of oppression.

What we might address at this point, as suggested in the introduction to this essay, is the position of the Society within a completely different context: that of feminist discourse. In short, were the Revolutionary Republican Women feminists, and if not, how can we characterize their actions as women within the context of the French Revolution? It seems to me that Joan Landes is accurate when she states that the Revolutionary Republican Women were *not* feminists, if we understand the term feminist to mean anyone who seeks a positive change in the status of women in society: "If feminism is construed only very narrowly to be the organized struggle for women's rights, then it may be that the Society does not fit under this rubric. Women's issues were not foremost on its agenda, and its downfall was precipitated by clashes with market women, religious women, and former servants. Nonetheless, its members were caught up in a scenario of gender politics."[11] These women, by engaging in activities which, however oppressive, did parallel the activities of their male counterparts, had in fact achieved some form of emancipation and equality for themselves, but only at the expense of other women.

The paradoxical situation of the Revolutionary Republican Women is perhaps best exemplified by the donning of the red bonnet that symbolized the Revolution, and by the reports that some members carried pistols and wore trousers. These women had, in effect, reaffirmed a male/female opposition in a new female versus female conflict via transvestism. Dressed in the same outfits as the men of the Revolution, the members of the Society, while stressing their integral role in the defense of the Revolution, had perpetuated the subordination of women in general, and had demonstrated that only by adopting a patriarchal code of conduct and appearance could they enact their radical program.

Given the ironic status of the Society, how can one accurately place the endeavors of these women within a feminist discourse? And within what confines of the term "feminism" are we analyzing their activities? A discussion of women's political efforts, and of the use of the term "post-feminist" to describe them, which will be addressed in this essay, might benefit from a brief consideration of the definition of "feminism." In recent years even feminist theorists have acknowledged the difficulty of composing a precise definition of the term. Rosalind Delmar, in a 1986 essay entitled, appropriately enough, "What Is Feminism?," states: "Many would agree that at the very least a feminist is someone who holds that women suffer discrimination because of their sex, that they have specific needs which remain negated and unsatisfied, and that the satisfaction of these needs would require a radical change (some would say a revolution even) in the social, economic and political order. But beyond that, things immediately become more complicated."[12] On the basis of Delmar's definition, which implies the need for the sort of revolution that late eighteenth-century France certainly experienced, we might reexamine the case of the Revolutionary Republican Women, and consider how some historians have attempted to interpret the Society's activities within the parameters of the term "feminist."

These historians, in fact, suggest the inappropriateness of the term in any discussion of the Society. Harriet B. Applewhite and Darline Gay Levy write, "These women were active not because they translated 'feminist' demands into revolutionary petitions, riots, and other popular manifestations but because they claimed that the sovereign people, male and female, had rights to act on that sovereignty on a daily basis where government touched their lives."[13] Revolutionary, and not feminist, ideals were the motivation for their actions. The Revolutionary Republican Women were not fighting as women and for women; they were fighting as citizens on the behalf of (and at times against) their fellow citizens and the latter's rights, although the validity and status of the "citoyenne" within the new societal order was constantly being tested by their actions.

Dominique Godineau, while questioning the appropriateness of the term, does demonstrate to what extent we might consider the Revolutionary Republican Women "feminist": "Can we speak of feminism?

The word is anachronistic, but we cannot deny that the Revolutionary Republican Women were aspiring to an equality of the two sexes. They considered that women were indeed citizens, active members of the sovereign people. If we can speak of feminism, it is a feminism expressing itself in the political language of the Revolution. 'Feminism' and politics were, for these women, inseparable."[14] Godineau continues, interestingly enough, with this description of the Society, which complicates any discussion of their feminist activities even further: "a club that in the beginning declared itself to be a political force composed exclusively of women, it later asserted itself as a sexually neuter political force,"[15] suggesting that although gender was the crucial factor in the Society's founding and demise, and thus might encourage a feminist-oriented appraisal, the political agenda of the Revolutionary Republican Women remained generally untouched by gender-based concerns.

These women were not feminists for the simple reason that they had little concern for the emancipation and equality of women in the new societal order. But by the very fact that women were able to organize, to carry out a plan of action both resulting from and independent of the concurrent activities of the male-dominated revolutionary government, this women's group had, however briefly, moved *beyond* feminism, beyond an effort at establishing equality and emancipation, and had accomplished what we might call a postfeminist endeavor: one where the ability of women to initiate and participate in a politically and socially significant manner is presumed, not sought after or defended. If "feminism is usually defined as an active desire to change women's position in society," as Rosalind Delmar states,[16] the Revolutionary Republican Women assumed that this change had, in fact, already occurred, and that a preoccupation with the issue of gender politics was no longer necessary.

Postfeminism, unlike feminism, is not concerned with the tension between women and men, with the couple woman/man within which woman is the subordinate, oppressed half. Postfeminism moves beyond this couple, investigating instead the position of women in a situation or a society, however isolated, in which they are able to function, still as women, but outside the restrictions of a stereotypical, sexually coded binary opposition. Rather than strive for equality, women in a postfeminist society or endeavor would be able to presume that this equality has previously been achieved. It is no longer a question of women forging ahead in pursuit of equal rights; it is a question of women acting as women, yet under the assumption that they are already the social and political peers of men.

Yet postfeminism is far from an idealistic move beyond typical feminist efforts. It simply provides for the possibility of considering isolated events and situations in which feminist concerns are no longer of capital importance because they have been addressed and solved. Such cases would be, admittedly, rare, ephemeral, even questionable in their presumption of true equality and emancipation for women in a particular situation, as the example of the Revolutionary Republican Women amply illustrates. At best, these scenarios would offer the *possibility* of women carrying out acts that no longer depend on their status as women.

The term postfeminist is not new, yet in the past it has been used with rather little explanation or attempt at a definition. Most references to the term have occurred in sociological discussions of women in the late 1980s, in particular within the context of issues such as abortion rights, women in the workplace, and the decline of the nuclear family. For example, Judith Stacey, in an analysis of women in the Silicon Valley, employs the term "not to indicate the death of the women's movement but to describe the simultaneous incorporation, revision, and depoliticization of many of the central goals of second-wave feminism."[17] Stacey considers feminism a highly charged political movement, whereas postfeminism is more individualized; while feminism had broad goals for general social improvement, postfeminism is amorphous, defined only by the social conditions of the individual(s) to whom the term is applied, incorporating feminist ideology, yet based on vital social conditions that cannot be ignored: marriage, work, family.

Suzanna Danuta Walters, using Stacey's analysis as a point of departure, identifies two distinct postfeminist discourses. Walters situates popular postfeminism within the antifeminist discourse of the late 1980s and early 1990s, in which feminism is considered "dead, victorious, and ultimately failed," a movement that "promised more than it put out,"[18] and she deftly supports her use of the term with numerous examples from television and film. Here, postfeminism is a postmortem on and backlash against recent feminist endeavors and is not far removed from antifeminism.

Walters also defines an academic postfeminism, which operates "through a denial of the category of 'woman' altogether."[19] In a postmodern and poststructuralist era, the need for such gender-based categorization can be challenged and eliminated, and feminism subsequently loses its raison d'être. Ultimately, Walters questions any application of the term "postfeminist" to our own era: "Isn't it premature to declare a social movement/social theory 'post' when we have yet to achieve even a modicum of egalitarian goals? How can we possibly speak of 'post-feminism' when a woman is still raped or beaten every 20 seconds?"[20]

The definition that we might apply to the case of the Revolutionary Republican Women lies somewhere between the two categories devised by Walters. Using this Society as a model, we might justify the application of the term postfeminism to a situation in which the goals and platforms of feminism have already been (or appear to have been) achieved. The Revolutionary Republican Women themselves assumed that women had attained an equality of status with men. Although the ultimate demise of the Society demonstrates that this was far from true, the Revolutionary Republican Women had, in theory at least, adopted a postfeminist stance to their position in French society. And although the group was composed exclusively of women, they generally excluded all questions of gender from their petitions and discussions, considering themselves not women, but citizens, charged with the duty of monitoring the behavior of all other citizens.

Evidently this postfeminism is by no means necessarily pro-woman or pro-feminist, nor does it require a distinguishable feminist predecessor. The Society of Revolutionary Republican Women would not have existed without women, but this certainly does not imply that it is pro-feminist or the direct result of feminist achievements. If anything, the activities of these women were *anti*-woman: the consolidation of their own position in revolutionary society depended to a great extent on the oppression of their fellow countrywomen (through imprisonment, censorship, or enforced code of dress). In moving beyond a concern with the needs of women, this group ignored demands for equality by other women, confidently assuming that these demands had been satisfied, and that any dissent could be condemned as counterrevolutionary. It is evident that, in this scenario at least, postfeminism by no means suggests the universal equality of women nor their ability to act in a society not as women but as individuals with full and equal rights. Indeed, as the example of the Society demonstrates, the ability of some women to enact a postfeminist program may result in an increase of the oppression of other women (and even men), and in a perpetuation of previously existing inequalities.

In fact, the fanaticism of the Revolutionary Republican Women would result in even greater oppression: the suppression by the male-dominated government of *any* women involved in public affairs, and eventually the elimination of *all* popular societies. As the Terror subsided in 1794, the women of Paris again returned to the streets to protest the lack of bread, just as they had at Versailles at the beginning of the Revolution. The ephemeral presence in France of the Revolutionary Republican Women would have no lasting positive effect, and their disappearance would coincide with the restoration of women to a role they had occupied before any group had attempted to involve them in the political sphere.

Although small gains were made for women's rights over the course of the revolutionary era—the legalization of divorce, the right of women to inherit, improvements in education—little had been accomplished to achieve the basic civil rights the Revolutionary Republican Women had assumed were theirs. The proposed concept of postfeminism to describe these women does not denote some kind of utopian situation that has eliminated the need for concern about the oppression of any one group of people on the basis of their gender, religion, race, or sexual orientation. On the contrary, postfeminism, in this definition at least, can only refer to ephemeral, isolated, and largely (if not exclusively) unsuccessful attempts at moving beyond an endlessly necessary confrontation with the subordination of women and other individuals and groups in society.

NOTES

1. Darline Gay Levy, Harriet Branson Applewhite, Mary Durham Johnson, eds., *Women in Revolutionary Paris* (Urbana: University of Illinois Press, 1979).
2. For further information about the Revolutionary Republican Women and about women during the Revolution, the reader is referred in particular to Marie Cerati, *Le Club des Citoyennes Républicaines Révolutionnaires* (Paris: Editions Sociales, 1966), and Dominique Godineau, *Citoyennes tricoteuses: Les femmes du peuple à Paris pendant la Révolution Française* (Aix-en-Provence: Alinéa, 1988), as well as to the works cited in the present study.

3. Quoted in Linda Kelly, *Women of the French Revolution* (London: Hamish Hamilton, 1987), 89.
4. Maité Albistur and Daniel Armogathe, *Histoire du féminisme français du moyen âge à nos jours* (Paris: des femmes, 1977), 236. All translations from French texts are my own.
5. William H. Sewell, Jr., "Le citoyen/la citoyenne: Activity, Passivity, and the Revolutionary Concept of Citizenship," in *The Political Culture of the French Revolution*, ed. Colin Lucas (Oxford: Pergamon, 1988), 121.
6. Godineau, *Citoyennes tricoteuses*, 164.
7. Ibid., 349.
8. Joan Landes, *Women and the Public Sphere in the Age of the French Revolution* (Ithaca: Cornell University Press, 1988), 165.
9. Godineau, *Citoyennes tricoteuses*, 175.
10. Quoted in Ruth Rendall, *The Origins of Modern Feminism: Women in Britain, France and the United States, 1780–1860* (New York: Schocken, 1984), 52.
11. Landes, *Women and the Public Sphere*, 141.
12. Rosalind Delmar, "What Is Feminism?," in *What Is Feminism: A Reexamination*, ed. Juliet Mitchell and Ann Oakley (New York: Pantheon, 1986), 8.
13. Harriet B. Applewhite and Darline Gay Levy, "Women, Democracy, and Revolution in Paris, 1789–1794," in *French Women and the Age of Enlightenment*, ed. Samia I. Spencer (Bloomington: Indiana University Press, 1984), 67.
14. Godineau, *Citoyennes tricoteuses*, 176.
15. Ibid., 177.
16. Delmar, "What Is Feminism?," 8.
17. Judith Stacey, "Sexism by a Subtler Name? Postindustrial Conditions and Postfeminist Consciousness in Silicon Valley," in *Women, Class, and the Feminist Imagination*, ed. Karen V. Hansen and Ilene J. Philipson (Philadelphia: Temple University Press, 1990), 339.
18. Suzanna Danuta Walters, "Postfeminism and Popular Culture," *New Politics* 3 (Winter 1991): 106, 107.
19. Ibid., 110.
20. Ibid., 112.

REFERENCES

Albistur, Maité, and Daniel Armogathe. *Histoire du féminisme français du moyen âge à nos jours.* Paris: des femmes, 1977.
Applewhite, Harriet B., and Darline Gay Levy. "Women, Democracy, and Revolution in Paris, 1789–1794." In *French Women and the Age of Enlightenment,* edited by Samia I. Spencer. Bloomington: Indiana University Press, 1984.

Cerati, Marie. *Les Club des Citoyennes Républicaines Révolutionnaires.* Paris: Editions Sociales, 1966.

Delmar, Rosalind. "What Is Feminism?" In *What Is Feminism: A Re-examination,* edited by Juliet Mitchell and Ann Oakley. New York: Pantheon, 1986.

Godineau, Dominique. *Citoyennes tricoteuses: Les femmes du peuple à Paris pendant la Révolution française.* Aix-en-Provence: Alinéa, 1988.

Kelly, Linda. *Women of the French Revolution.* London: Hamish Hamilton, 1987.

Landes, Joan. *Women and the Public Sphere in the Age of the French Revolution.* Ithaca: Cornell University Press, 1988.

Levy, Darline Gay, Harriet Branson Applewhite, and Mary Durham Johnson, eds. *Women in Revolutionary Paris.* Urbana: University of Illinois Press, 1979.

Rendall, Ruth. *The Origins of Modern Feminism: Women in Britain, France and the United States, 1780–1860.* New York: Schocken, 1984.

Sewell, William H., Jr. "Le citoyen/la citoyenne: Activity, Passivity, and the Revolutionary Concept of Citizenship." In *The Political Culture of the French Revolution,* edited by Colin Lucas. Oxford: Permagon, 1988.

Stacey, Judith. "Sexism by a Subtler Name? Postindustrial Conditions and Postfeminist Consciousness in Silicon Valley." In *Women, Class, and the Feminist Imagination,* edited by Karen V. Hansen and Ilene J. Philipson. Philadelphia: Temple University Press, 1990.

Walters, Suzanna Danuta. "Postfeminism and Popular Culture." *New Politics* 3 (Winter 1991): 103–12.

12.

THE BURDEN OF MYTHIC IDENTITY: RUSSIAN WOMEN AT ODDS WITH THEMSELVES

NANCY RIES

Matushka

"Matushka,[1] Matushka, what are those distant clouds of dust?
Sudarynia, Matushka, what are those distant clouds of dust?"
　"Ditiatko, dear child, that's just horses playing."
"Matushka, Matushka, strangers in the courtyard!
Sudarynia, Matushka, strangers in the courtyard!"
　"Ditiatko, dear child, don't fear, don't be frightened."
"Matushka, Matushka, they're coming onto the porch,
Sudarynia, Matushka, they're coming onto the porch!"
　"Ditiatko, dear child, I won't let them have you!"
"Matushka, Matushka, they're sitting at our table,
Sudarynia, Matushka, they're sitting at our table!"
　"Ditiatko, dear child, don't fear, don't be frightened!"
"Matushka, Matushka, they're taking down the icons,
Sudarynia, Matushka, they're blessing me with the icons!"
　"Ditiatko, dear one, *what can I do?* God be with you."

The fetish of female powerlessness and suffering was the symbolic centerpiece of the elaborate marriage ritual of prerevolutionary peasant Russia. A young woman's poignant passage from the freedom of girlhood to the enslavement of marriage formed a pivotal image around which the entire wedding complex revolved. Above all, Russian wedding rituals stressed the inexorability of female destiny and the inevitability of female suffering and travail.

One of the most notable aspects of Russian wedding rituals was the extensive lamentation of the bride. Through the singing (or wailing) of these laments, brides marked the pathos of their imminent separation from relatives and friends and the decline in status that would accompany their taking up residence in the husband's family's household. Wailing these laments, which followed a traditional form but could vary in detail,[2] the bride would beg her dear mother and father not to give her away to a household of cruel strangers; her relatives would then, by tradition, instruct her to hide her tears and prepare to respect her new in-laws and do their bidding.

The lyrics of the Russian folksong cited above depict the ceremonial claiming of the bride by the groom's representatives on the wedding day. In the folksong, which is meant to be sung plaintively, the bride's mother deceives her daughter as to the events taking place, until the last moment when the meaning of the visitation by strangers becomes fully clear. Once the prospective bride was blessed by the icon, the marriage contract was sealed, despite whatever reluctance the bride might feel.

These ritual elements of the Russian wedding should not necessarily be taken as literal expressions of the feelings or situations of the persons involved. By the nineteenth century, the mother-daughter drama depicted in the text of "Matushka" would in most cases have been more ritual than real. In other words, a girl was likely to have been at least somewhat actively involved in the choice of a husband, and she would certainly have known about the negotiations that were taking place. Even so, the perpetuation of these ritual texts signals that marriage still meant a woman's passage into a life of subservience to her husband and his family. For a young Russian woman marriage did entail becoming the lowest member of her new husband's household where, according to custom, she could be exploited and abused, and where she was expected to endure without rebellion or complaint.[3]

What is more significant, however, is the way in which these texts highlight the active participation of mothers—and indeed of all adult women—in the subordination of daughters to the structures of patriarchal Russian society. That maternal acquiescence to the sacrifice of daughters can be explained as a function of the protection of rural society and peasant solidarity in general; Worobec, for one, explains it this way, claiming that "Russian peasant women chose not to rebel because the survival of their families and communities depended on the balancing of the finely tuned patriarchal system."[4]

However, these rituals and texts seem actually to *celebrate* the subordination and suffering of women, and to mark the significant role of mothers and mothers-in-law in that oppressive system as a whole. The wedding laments, and indeed the entire cycle of the peasant wedding ritual, elevate female unhappiness and servitude to the level of religious spectacle. They transform the idea of the inevitability of female social subordination and marital unhappiness into a sacred cultural fetish.

Whether or not this sacralization of female suffering was necessary to the maintenance of the peasant community one hundred years ago, it might be expected that by the 1990s, with all the social transformations the past century has wrought in Russian life, this fetish would have lost its power and its indispensability. However, while doing anthropological fieldwork in Moscow in 1988, 1989–90, and 1992, I found the opposite to be true: the idea of womanly suffering is still a central fixation in the Russian world. The tribulations of the twentieth century have, if anything, made female suffering an even more magnificent object of cultural worship and fascination.

Young Russian girls are still pampered, still marked with the oversized gauze bows that signify their innocence of suffering and travail, and still thoroughly instructed in all the intricacies and delicacies of male-female role differentiation. Russian mothers and schoolteachers (almost all female) continue to offer instruction in the essential female arts of sewing, cooking, cleaning, nurturing, laboring, serving, and enduring. Brides-to-be still lament (although now in conversational prose) the wifely fates that await them. As one American undergraduate, having spent four months on a homestay in Moscow, said, "I was surprised that my Moscow girlfriends didn't look forward to their weddings as big occasions. They kept talking about how awful their lives would be after marriage! But they were all planning to marry, anyway, which I couldn't understand."[5] This student's observation captures the essence of a seeming contradiction in Russian women's lives today: despite their deep dissatisfaction with the customs and structures of Russian marriage, Russian women are, on the whole, strongly committed to maintaining the status quo of gender relations and ideals.

Women and men both almost unanimously acknowledge and lament the unenviable difficulty of Russian women's lives. The plight of Russian women is a topic that frequently occupies private conversations and public discussions, where the conditions with which women have to cope are decried in terms like "appalling," "inhuman," "frightful." Calls are constantly and widely made for "something to be done to help women." The main source of women's suffering is said to be the "double burden" of their duties as women: full-time employment and full-time housekeeping.

At the same time, however, to question the ubiquitous essentializing of gender distinctions and the faithful reinforcement of customary gender roles that underlies the position of women in Russian society is to summon derision from both women and men, who immediately declare with scorn or mockery, "Ah, you must be a feminist, yes?" The very word "feminist-ka" is pronounced with a highly derogatory ring in almost every context. Feminists are supposedly part of a movement against *nature* itself, presumably desiring to turn women into men and men into women, something seen as being as illogical, absurd, brutal, and ruinous as the worst follies of the communist world-remaking project.[6] Even the most progressive members of the intelligentsia are usually scornful of the entire feminist project and worldview, as the following statement by Yunna Morits, a poet and human rights activist, illustrates: "There is no such thing as a feminist consciousness. . . . Our problems are in no way different from men's. I refuse all associations with such silliness as your women's movement."[7]

This paper concerns the question of why Russian women seem to be so at odds with themselves: why they so resent examination of the cultural practices and ideologies that make their lives so difficult. I would like to make some sense of the contradiction between women's fervent complaints and their equally fervent avoidance of critical questions about the gender hierarchies and norms that pattern their lives and their society.[8]

THE GENERAL SITUATION OF WOMEN IN CONTEMPORARY RUSSIAN SOCIETY

Thanks to the titanic efforts of Soviet women, a simple, functioning system is maintained in stable condition. Normal human life goes on, however poorly.

These titanic efforts are the cement that holds society together, preventing its total collapse.

—Alla Sariban, a Leningrad feminist, 1984[9]

The emancipation of women was a cherished ideal of the 1917 revolution and of the communist social programs that followed it.[10] As part of the larger reformation of society, women were to be released from domestic concerns and drawn into the workforce, while childcare and housework were to become collectivized in communal nurseries, kitchens, and laundries. The first part of this vision was realized, if only because perennial labor shortages necessitated the recruitment of women into labor; by the 1980s, over 85 percent of able-bodied adult women in the Soviet Union were employed, the majority full-time, outside of the home.[11] Women remained employed full-time within the home, as well, however: hence the meaning of the "double burden." For a variety of social, political, economic, and ideological reasons, public funds were consistently allocated to the development of heavy industry and the military instead of to the consumer goods sector, and so the vision of publicly provided household and family services was never fulfilled. Therefore, although their labors outside of the home kept Soviet production going (by 1987, women made up 51 percent of the total Soviet work force),[12] through their domestic labors women also shouldered most of the burden of caring for and reproducing that society.[13]

The pattern of official neglect for the needs of families was facilitated by the very fact that women *could* be relied on to take care of their families regardless of the difficulties involved. As Alla Sariban put it, "Housework is truly a matter of survival. After all, if I, as a woman, do not do all the essential things—the shopping, the cleaning, the laundry—who will do them? And if nobody does them, what are you going to do—die? So, like it or not, you do them."[14] In the most trying of times, such as during the war, families (many of which were headed by women) often quite literally fed themselves from garden plots.[15] Even through the 1980s and into the 1990s, the private resources of family sustenance have included childcare provided by grandmothers; fruits, vegetables, eggs, dairy and even meat products grown, raised, gathered, and preserved for winter on plots of land or dachas outside of urban areas; domestic production and repair of clothing and other textile items; and a wide variety of goods and services procured through the complex networks of barter, sharing, and mutual support that have been developed between friends, neighbors, and colleagues, and most especially among women. The degree to which my female acquaintances in Moscow provisioned their families independently of governmental (or "market") distribution always surprised me.

Because of all this "grey market" activity, the development of consumer goods and services could remain a secondary concern for central planners (chiefly male), who were able to count on the self-sustaining ability of the population (and particularly of the female population). An intricate correspondence thus existed between the ability and willingness of women to "make do" and the central government's inability or lack of will to dedicate itself to the fulfillment of consumer needs. This dynamic persisted throughout the Soviet period. It manifested in the well-known long lines for every basic commodity, the constant shortages in every type of product, from cheese and sugar to aspirin and anesthesia, the paucity of time-saving and convenience items or services, and the extreme overloading of many human service sectors, such as medicine and day care.

The post-perestroika period of rapid marketization has altered but not diminished this situation; in many ways it has exacerbated it, as runaway inflation has reduced the purchasing power of many salaries to the point where average families can afford little beyond the most basic food supplies: milk, butter, potatoes, cabbage, bread. While modern services and a wide variety of never-before imagined products are now widely marketed throughout Russia, they are affordable only to those who have managed to enter the new business class.

Every Soviet citizen, female or male, was affected by the overall structure of the economic system and the quotidian difficulties it imposed, but it was on the backs of women that the system really rested. Since Russian domestic life is, by custom, organized and managed by women, it has largely been Russian women who have coped with and found ways to bridge the gulf between public supply and family requirement.

Russian women's "double burden" must be viewed within the context of the specific economic conditions of Soviet/Russian society. While women in most industrialized societies bear the double burden of working outside the home while being the primary caretakers within it, in Russian families this burden is exacerbated by the sheer difficulty of maintaining the household and caring for children in the context of the insecurity of constant scarcity and the competition—often with other women, other mothers—for what resources there are.[16] Many even talk of the "triple burden," saying women have three full-time jobs: work, housework, and shopping.

The idea that domestic responsibilities could be shared equally by men and women has rarely arisen in public debate; in part it has been preempted by the very idea of—and all the utopian talk about—collective support for domestic functions. While waiting for a balanced world to be created from on high, Russian families have gone about their business with archaic divisions of domestic labor more or less intact.

Those divisions are maintained because strong cultural ideologies, which Russians rarely question or doubt, dictate that everything related to the home belongs, both symbolically and functionally, to the female domain. Male participation in domestic activities (including childcare) is termed "help" and is regarded as generous assistance offered to aid women in fulfilling their wifely and motherly (and grandmotherly) responsibilities. In my own fieldwork, I observed how school curricula and classroom teachers unquestioningly divided girl's and boy's lessons in gendered ways: sewing classes for girls and carpentry for boys. Russian television shows and publications for women are centered around cooking, needlework, beauty, proper (gender-enforcing) childcare, and social graces.[17] The everyday discourses of both women and men are peppered with affirmations of the naturalness of gender roles in the home and in society. Remarks such as "all women can bake," "men are by nature inept in the kitchen," "men think with their heads, women with their hearts," "women are born knowing how to care for others," "men are like boys, you have to take care of them," are heard constantly, and are passively accepted by both women and men. Such expressions about gender are so commonplace among Russians that they are hardly noticed. The very casualness with which they are tossed off, however, masks a passionate commitment to the sacredness of distinct gender identities and roles—a passion exposed when such commonplaces are questioned.

The official sociological view has rarely deviated much from the indigenous ideology that home and children are, by nature, the responsibility of women.[18] This ideology was also unquestioningly enshrined in much of medical, educational, and juridical practice. Widely shared and continuously expressed ideas about gender differences have thus been embodied so deeply in Russian life practices that they do finally appear objective or "natural." As long as women's role as nurturer is enforced in this way, the concomitant double burden of women is ensured.

Several other factors add further dimensions to women's burdens in Russian society. First, although they were recruited into the workplace in vast numbers through the Soviet period, women have occupied the lowest rungs of the employment ladder, in terms of both salary and work status. Gender ideologies dictated that women should fill "caring" roles in employment, thus most doctors, nurses, teachers, store clerks, secretaries, food service workers, and so on were women.[19] In other, symbolically masculine-identified fields, such as manufacturing, agriculture, and construction, women have filled many of the more physically challenging or menial jobs, because, most Russians agree, women have less aptitude for the more technically advanced jobs (such as operating tractors or cranes, or managing equipment). What this means is that in many spheres of employment, women have been the servitors of men. I observed that in professional spheres, where women held the same status as their male colleagues, when it came to getting the tea or fulfilling a similar service function (typing, organizing, filling out forms, keeping the office clean), it was often the women who performed these tasks. Female bosses can be just as bad as male bosses in expecting their female subordinates to fulfill such "womanly" functions around the office. Supporters and facilitators of family life at home, women's "instincts" or "natural abilities" for maternal nurturing are utilized in the workplace as well. Doubly employed in society (as workers and as wives/mothers), women are also often doubly employed in their jobs. And, as many critics of the Russian division of labor have pointed out, women are so overwhelmed by the difficulties of their domestic burden that they have little energy or inclination to "move up" the employment ladder; they have no time for extra schooling or for the extra investment in their work that might bring promotions. They do not even necessarily want to be promoted, since that might entail added responsibilities and longer working hours, which would make the burdens of home and shopping that much more difficult.

During perestroika there was much debate about the need to improve the situation of Soviet women. In 1987, in what was meant as a critique of the overreliance on women's labor, Gorbachev reaffirmed gender divisions when he wrote of society's responsibility to better support women in their "everyday duties at home—housework, the upbringing of children and the creation of a good family atmosphere. . . . We are now holding heated debates . . . about the question of what we can do to make it possible for women to return to their purely womanly mission."[20] Gorbachev's comment is indicative of the direction those debates usually took. Very widespread was the idea that women would be better off in the home, and that society as a whole would be "healthier" if women could fully devote themselves to their family duties and their maternal missions. The economic reforms of perestroika were accompanied by a new wave of collective dreaming about social utopia, but this time around it was no Bolshevik utopia being imagined, but rather a cozy bourgeois world of working dads and apron-clad moms.

The economic realities that had developed by the late 1980s, and especially those that have ensued since the collapse of the Communist system, have, however, shoved those fantasies way over the horizon for most families. Sheer survival now demands that most women work even harder, which often entails taking second (or third) jobs. Inflation devours most salaries even before payday, and one after another, services and provisions that used to be free or very inexpensive (housing, transportation, communications, health care, education, vacations, entertainment) have begun to cost dearly; the incentive, therefore, for women to keep working outside the home or to work even more has increased rather than diminished.

It must be said that the changes of the past several years have allowed many women opportunities for career development that never previously existed; entrepreneurial women have been able to start businesses, consulting firms, and organizations, and many women trained in foreign languages, law, accounting, and other professions have parlayed their skills into lucrative careers. The reflorescence and relegitimation of traditional bourgeois attitudes has, however, meant that many more women are faced with prejudices against females as managers and professionals—prejudices which, paradoxically, were less openly expressed in the Soviet era. Finally, many more women are being left behind in today's Russian economy because of the new bourgeois aesthetic in the marketplace, an aesthetic in which youth, physical attractiveness, and even a willingness to provide sexual favors are the most important criteria for the employment of women.[21]

An even darker trend toward the attempted enforcement of the bourgeois model exists, even despite its economic impossibility. Some legislators, concerned about growing unemployment among men and the low birth rate among Russian women, have called for mandatory laws to restrict mothers from working or to restrict all females to part-time employment.[22] Offering women more flexible or shorter working weeks is, of course, not a negative thing in itself, and it is clear that many women would be delighted to have such a range of working options. But the overall restrictions on the employment of women that are touted by many conservative, pro-natalist political factions would have catastrophic effects on Russian women's lives—not to mention the insidious effects it would have on the progress of democratization itself.

WHY NO FEMINISM IN RUSSIA? WOMEN'S DISCOURSES AND THE MAINTENANCE OF IDENTITY

Widespread cultural attitudes about "women's place" limit women's sense of collective oppression; disparate treatment does not necessarily generate moral indignation. . . . The total responsibility of women for childcare and domestic chores is never questioned.

—Ol'ga Lipovskaia[23]

In private conversations in Moscow, I have often brought up the subject of feminism, asking women to consider whether a critical view of Russian gender ideas might not lead to a useful opening up of the continuing debate about women's lives and hardships. Women commonly answer that it is not feminism that was needed to make women's lives easier, but rather a general improvement in economic conditions. Presumably, in five, ten, or twenty years, in an era of more plentiful goods and services, women's situations will be so much improved that feminism wouldn't be needed. "It's easy for you to spend time thinking about such things as feminism," my middle-aged friend Maria told me,[24] "you are economically one hundred years ahead of us, you have time to daydream about some niceties." I have found it impossible to convince my friends and acquaintances that a feminist perspective might actually lead to improvements in women's day-to-day lives; many consider such reformative enterprises as frivolous frosting on the cake of prosperity, not as basic ingredients.

Many others, in fact most of the people I have spoken with, however, react to the entire project of feminism with distaste bordering on horror. "Why should we ever want to turn women into men?" is the key question asked whenever the subject of feminism is raised—and it is exactly this fear of "masculinizing women and feminizing men" that seems to be at the root of the Russian fear of feminists.[25]

The passion with which Russian women defend their traditional gender classifications and images against even the mildest feminist introspection (or cultural inspection) suggests that they are protecting something very important and useful to them, both individually and collectively.

While listening to and recording the stories they told about their lives in everyday conversations, I have tried to understand what lay at the heart of women's refusal to critically examine the patriarchal aspects of the Russian worldview and social practice. Three kinds of discourse "genres"—which I call "shopping tales," "husband tales," and "saints' lives"—stand out in women's talk, and these give important clues to deep structures of value and systems of identity-creation that shape and anchor Russian women's ideas about themselves.

"Shopping Tales"

Shopping in the Soviet Union was always a heroic endeavor, entailing standing in lines, sometimes for hours, trudging long distances for various basic items, which were never sold conveniently in one location or even one area, and which were often merely unavailable. Shopping meant shoving through dense and aggressive crowds to reach the sales displays in stores, and then shoving through even denser crowds to pull oneself onto a bus or push into a subway car, all the while laden with purchases.[26]

There is a Russian word, *podvig,* which means a heroic feat or extraordinary achievement. Inspired to explain how they acquired this or that desirable commodity, Russians tell stories about their shopping expeditions, stories that have the quality of epic tales about outstanding *podvigs.*

Over tea one day in 1990, my friend Tania described how she traveled far and wide over the city of Moscow looking for medicine for her ailing mother. She named the far-away metro stations she visited in different regions of the city in hopes of getting the pills she needed.

First, I went way up to Medvedkovo, there was nothing. Then down to Leningradskii Prospekt, they also had absolutely nothing, then I finally tried Tushinskaya, just as the pharmacy was about to close. They had one pack of tablets left. I got it, thank god, but I practically died from exhaustion, running around the city from one end to the other. This is our life now, scouring the city, here and there, there and here, wearing ourselves out to get every little thing.

Through the dramatic tone she adopted, and the long pauses she used to convey suspense while evoking the distant, unfamiliar neighborhoods of Moscow, Tania's story came across as an ordeal, a quest, a mythical search. Stories such as this one are a significant part of conversations among Russian women; I have heard them mainly in the workplaces I visited, where groups of female co-workers share their daily joys and troubles,[27] or in people's kitchens, over tea and sweets. The more poignant such stories concern searches for medicines, clothes, shoes or school supplies for children, bottles of champagne for a birthday, cheese, sausage, sugar, or precious laundry detergent, always in short supply. With the development of the open market, the terrifying inflation of prices has become another element in these stories, another hurdle in the epic battle of shopping.

Wound into the fabric of one of many long kitchen-table talks we had in 1990 was this rather mythical story told by my friend, Irina, a poet:

One day last week, I went to meet a woman, a stranger, in a subway station, to pick up a package of poems. Over the phone, I asked "How will I know you?" and the woman told me, "I will be wearing a bright blue coat." Having waited on the platform a few minutes, suddenly I saw a blue apparition walking toward me. Nancy, you cannot imagine. This woman wore blue, a sort of bright azure blue from head to toe: azure coat, with a perfectly matching wool hat, azure gloves, handbag, and even her boots: azure. Looking at her, so well coordinated, I felt such a deep sense, feeling—the image of that woman remains indelibly inscribed on my mind: it was the image of a woman, can you imagine this, Nancy, a woman who must have spent literally years assembling that brilliant outfit, you know what it is like shopping for clothes here, you take what you can get and women work so hard to assemble a fashionable outfit or two, it was so poignant to see this woman; she told me she had found the purse in a store on her one trip to East Germany. Her grandmother somehow found some perfectly matching blue yarn and made the hat. That is our Russian woman.

This story is mundane but also magical. Resonant with the form and force of tradition, it is a tale about the mystery of a woman's self-creation, about the magic symbolism of dress, about powerful helpers like grandmothers who can spin perfect hats out of found skeins of yarn. In the telling, it is also about the self-creation of the narrator: as Russian woman, as poet, as cultural witness, as articulate teller (and embroiderer?) of tales. As Sandra Stahl commented, the successful teller of personal narratives engages the listener in an adventure—not simply the plot of a story, but rather the shared activity of exploring the teller's world, the teller's identity.[28]

Indeed, the more of these "personal narratives" about shopping and taking care of self and family I heard from women, the more I felt that what was being spoken of was, at heart, not really the burden of shopping at all. It was, rather, the identity of the speaker that was at issue. Whatever the ordeal described—standing in line for hours for sugar or bananas, scouring the city for medicine, pulling together an arresting outfit—the ordeal was only context; the true nucleus of the story was the protagonist herself, and her stoic endurance of whatever difficulties Moscow invented for her. Not every story my Russian interlocutors told was as colorful as the azure lady story, but each one highlighted in some way the important facets of Russian female identity.

In Russian culture, suffering, self-sacrifice, endurance, and magical productivity have come to be seen as integral elements of femaleness.[29] The function of provisioning home and family in the direst economic circumstances provides the primary situation through which this femaleness can develop and assert itself. In other words, Russian women utilize the very difficulties of their lives as material for their construction of selfhood and identity.

This epic female endurance is a widely relished theme. In a recent article, "A Nation Begins with Its Women," Yevgenii Yevtushenko poeticizes and reiterates the mythic quality of the Russian female's shopping *podvig*:

Nobody is saying, of course, that men do not suffer from the continuous shortages. But women obviously bear the brunt. It is they after all who are constantly searching and improvising to cope with the situation. Foreigners are surprised at how smart many Soviet women look these days. How much ingenuity is behind every detail of a Soviet woman's costume. Foreigners admire the hospitality and culinary talents of our women. They have no idea to what lengths they must go to find all those little tidbits (which incidentally would grace a royal banquet). A Russian woman shops for the home, for the children, for her husband, and only then for herself. Try getting a kilo of frankfurters, half a dozen boxes of detergent, a pack of disposable diapers, some razor blades and a pair of nice looking shoes that do not cost the earth—all in one round of shopping![30]

Yevtushenko's main point in the essay from which this is excerpted is not that men should participate in "woman's work" but that women should be freed from outside work, so they can dedicate themselves to their natural domestic tasks and be spared the "double burden." His text thus stems from and perpetuates the Russian essentializing of gender and gender roles. But it also shows the subtle fetishizing of female endurance and the conviction that female suffering and travail are a magical "yeast" in the culture. Not too surprisingly, this theme structures many traditional Russian folktales. Most of the ordeals of female heroines in Russian folk literature are trials of faith, tests of the endurance of brides coercively married to animals or monsters or cruel tsars; these husbands become handsome, wealthy, kind, and human once the heroine has shown her abiding faith and her ability to magically produce desired objects from impossibly meager materials. The parallel between this folkloric icon of womanliness and the structure of contemporary women's lives should be clear; I do not think it is incidental.

My poet friend, Irina, rendered another tale over tea one day, several months after the "Woman in Blue" story; this story vividly echoes Yevtushenko's seemingly sympathetic text about women, shopping, and self-sacrifice. Irina had just returned from a three-day trip to Hungary, her first trip abroad to read her poetry. She forged a mythic scene out of a moment's window-shopping.

I stood in front of a shop window and could not help weeping. . . . They had given me enough Hungarian currency that I could have gone in and bought myself a pair [of boots], but then I thought of all the people here, all my friends, poor little things, and I knew that I could not buy boots for myself when everybody is so poor—so I used my money to buy small presents instead, just small change, pencils, soap, tea, and so on. But I wept because our Russian women will never have boots like those.

Each of the texts above shows this mythic "genre" of the feminine feat of tragic or at least poignant self-sacrifice and endurance running through personal narratives about shopping. In many ways, these are tales of the moral self-proving of women, so much like the recurrent "trials" of Russian fairy tales—where the heroine proves her spiritual purity by choosing to absorb difficulty and torment, not by choosing that object or path which would most benefit herself.[31]

"Husband Tales"

One of the most common ways Russian women define themselves is through the narrative genre I term "husband tales." These are the stories and anecdotes about husbands' habits that the women of my acquaintance frequently related. More amusing than tragic—at least in the telling—these tales provide a glimpse of a more intimate aspect of the "double burden" of women.

In Russian women's stories, men in general and husbands in particular are cast not as solid patriarchal figures, but as childish, mischievous, irresponsible creatures. Expressing a range of attitudes—affection, amusement, condescension, indulgence, irony, frustration, weariness, resignation—women's stories about their spouses almost invariably depict them as dependent, spoiled, and inept. One young, newly married woman described her married life thus:

Aliosha likes his life very much; he wants nothing to change! In the morning his mother, who lives upstairs in our same building, makes his kasha [porridge]. I go up in the elevator and get it and bring it down for him. His mother does his laundry; I do all the shopping and cook dinner for him. I go on errands for him all over town—he is too busy building his career in the theater. He has the psychology of a little boy: he looks at his life as if from the side, not really attached to it, almost a nonparticipant in his own existence. He is like a little boy.

This account was told to me cheerfully and even with pride, perhaps in her own just-discovered "maternal" abilities and capacities. Another woman, in her late forties, laughingly depicted her husband's ways about the house:

He has excellent tricks; he has it all worked out so that in the end he does nothing. One day he rages and scolds and yells if I ask him to do the slightest errand, go to the store for instance; I end up doing it myself instead of facing that abuse. His more common technique is just not to do anything—he just waits and ignores everything, does not even feed himself, so that in the end I start in and do it because I cannot stand it. Another good trick he has—he starts doing something, peeling potatoes for example, but he does it so haphazardly, peels are flying around the kitchen, half the potato ends up being wasted . . . that I cannot stand it and I end up taking over. He is so clever! He knows how to get everything exactly as he wants it, so that he is the tsar and I am his servant who does everything for him.

A feminist scholar, also in her forties, offered this little fable, both joking and complaining:

We were a progressive couple, it was in the 1970s and we lived together for about a year before we got married. He was generous; he did almost all the cooking, he kept the house immaculately clean, he was a real darling. Then we got married and the very next day he somehow completely forgot how to boil water or fry an egg—and to this day he has not remembered how.

Finally, another woman's account came across as pure complaint, though it was couched in historical perspective:

You have to understand, you have to grasp the history here. The generation that is adult now, my generation, was raised by women who went through the war, and lost lots of men. For them men are utterly precious beings, who they raised as little gods, investing all in them, spoiling them terrifically, appreciating their very presence on the earth. Now these same men are husbands, they demand the same from their wives that their mothers gave them. Even though he goes to work very early, and I work late at night, my husband demands that I get up at six in the morning to fix his morning coffee. If I refuse, if, for instance, I just sleep through, he will be mad at me the whole day, refuse to speak, go around pouting, etc. We have discussed this a thousand times. I have explained that it is unfair, impractical. I have offered to organize everything the night before so that he can fix his own coffee easily himself. He refuses to even heed my argument.

Having met this husband and found him to be a progressive, intelligent, and calm professional, I felt surprise (though not disbelief) to hear this story about his demands for morning coffee served by his wife.

All of these stories reflect and reproduce a structure of relations between spouses that is defined less by "patriarchal" principles (said to be the defining principles of the Russian family) than by maternalism (to call this matriarchy would hardly do). These stories turn patriarchy upside-down via mini-exposés of intrafamilial relations: in them the "patriarch" is merely a spoiled little boy (albeit one who can make life miserable) in domestic orbit with the all-controlling, all-managing, all-giving mother. The question of whether this circle of relations is objectively true in these families is beside the point. These stories—be they cultural clichés, yarns, fairy tales—do exist, and they are extensively and constantly circulated, serving to reproduce certain expectations regarding male and female behavior and relationships. Even the mourning or mocking of this norm is a key to its reproduction in society over time, to the extent that the norm is made to appear a natural, inevitable part of existence.

While lamenting these structures and striving to explain them via historical reference, many narratives actually validate and even valorize them, by constructing Russian men as "the victims of history" in one or another form, with women as the eternal attendants and caretakers of sacrificial males. A social scientist in her late thirties offered this explanation:

Soviet life has made human beings absurd. Soviet life is absurd life, we have had seventy years of absurdity. The men are especially abnormal here, they are totally warped by the system—women, after all, have their domestic lives, a woman can take pride, create a sense of herself by taking care of the house, the family, her husband, but men cannot, and they cannot provide for their families either, as in any normal society in the world, because the system will not let them really accomplish anything. So they become just pathetic, pathetic creatures. Men feel domesticated, turned into domestic pets. They want a little drama; sometimes they get it by becoming little tyrants in their families. That is the only power they can enjoy.

Many of the stories that Russian women tell, and the stances that Russian women (and men) adopt, derive from or in other ways relate to this key scenario, which casts men as desired, important, perhaps wounded (or self-wounding, alcoholic) visitors in a symbolically female society—that is, a society built by, on, and through the labors, discourses, and demands of the female.

To what extent these women's stories are expressions or signs of "real" power or status in self-proclaimedly patriarchal Russian marriage is hard to measure. There does happen to be a bountiful repertoire of jokes and proverbs that play with the cultural paradoxes entailed by the coexistence of different forms or realms of social power. A joke that I heard twice from men and once from a woman (the details each time were slightly different) satirizes this paradox and the cultural ideologies that circulate around and through it: "A wife, talking to a friend about her marriage, says, "I make all the trivial, unimportant decisions—where we will vacation, if we will move to a new apartment, if we will buy a car. . . . My husband makes the really important decisions in the family, you know: should the USSR disarm, should the two Germanies reunite. . . ."

This joke, obviously set in a particular historical moment, plays with the question of what constitutes real power in both families and nations, at the same time that it mocks male demonstrations of powerfulness and satirizes male and female representations of female subservience.

There are more solemn genres of female discourse about the relative status of men and women in Russian society. Tatiana Tolstaia, one of the leading writers of any gender in Russia today, insists that Russian society is based around matriarchal authority and structured by "feminine principles" such as intuition, myth, and irrationality. She believes that the separation of women from spheres of power has allowed women to maintain the spiritual values on which society rests. "Soviet women have been less repressed than Soviet men," she says. "Our men were driven over the edge and many of them lost any sense of ethical criteria. Women weren't; and they remained human."[32] This matriarchal argument, that women are the real rulers in Russia, is widespread. As Irina S., a Moscow feminist, put it to me, "Russian women are the very implements of totalitarianism, the tools of conservatism, the tyrants in their own families: women uphold our entire social order."

This set of ideas—that women are higher or more pure spiritually than men, that they are the repository of value, and that they hold the meaningful power in society—is sustained and reproduced through the telling of "husband tales" and other stories of male childishness. Indeed, such stories cast women as mothers to childlike men and, by symbolic extension, reaffirm the ancient cultural idea of the maternal embrace of Russia over the long-suffering population as a whole. Such ideas serve not only as sturdy ideological barriers to the consideration of women's place in society; they also romanticize and legitimate women's double burden itself. In other words, the stories that women tell about their husbands' childish, demanding, or irresponsible behaviors actually affirm the existing dynamic of gender relations. By telling such stories, women assert and celebrate the social value of their role as all-enduring supermothers; by asserting this value, however, the inequality of Russian gender relations is concomitantly insured, valorized, and entrenched.

"Litanies" and "Saints' Lives"

A third category of Russian women's discourse is perhaps most significant of all in reproducing gender relations and female identity in Russian society. It is arguably the most common identifiable genre of talk among women. I have termed this genre "litany" because it entails the voicing of long, circular, poetic inventories of suffering, sacrifice and loss, often rising into a mode of almost musical lamentation.[33] Russian men seldom speak in litanies; it is a woman's mode, which those who have spent time in Slavic cultures will probably recognize. I recorded numerous examples of litanies, some tragic, some absurd, some ironic.

Russian women's litanies do not necessarily concern only the suffering of women; they frequently address and lament the suffering of the entire Russian (or Soviet) people, posing key questions about Russian existence: how can this be, why are we so burdened, why is our life so full of suffering, why are we such victims, where is our salvation?

One day I visited a woman in her fifties for an interview. She insisted on feeding me something after our talk, and we went into her small kitchen, where she made some toast with melted cheese and a little salad. I sat at her kitchen table as she chopped vegetables and spoke; she would not let me help. In the midst of a long litany about the various difficulties facing Russia—shortages, corruption, crime, inefficiency, pollution—she stopped cutting cabbage for a moment, and wielding her knife dramatically, she lamented, "Such a life we have, a real theater, theater of the absurd. The things that happen here could never happen anywhere else, they could never happen in a civilized country like America. Do you understand what it means for people that there is no aspirin, no insulin? The last meat I saw was nearly rotten and so overpriced at that, who can afford it? This motherland of ours is so unfortunate, so unfortunate."

This is a paradigmatic litany, of the type reeled off by the millions on any given day in Russia. Other litanies focus more specifically on a woman's personal tribulations or those of people in her life. I have heard litanies about family members lost during the war, about life in prison camps in the Stalin era, about the general poverty of Russia. I have heard others about how hard it is to get apartments painted, about the rigidness of schoolteachers, about the tortures that bureaucrats put people through. In the years after the fall of Communism, the most common litanies have concerned inflation, the growing crime rate, and—the favorite topic—shortages of basic commodities.

As in the example above, women's litanies symbolically link the individual speaker to the Russian land as a whole, to the entire Russian people, and to all of Russian history. Litanies often begin in the first person singular with a story about personal travail, difficulty, or loss; then the speaker switches into the first person plural, into a lament about "our" general difficulty, the "our" implying Russian, Soviet, or one of many other fields of identification. Through the litany, women's private travails are incorporated within a collective saga, a sacred cultural saga about "the motherland" and her thousand years of suffering and loss.

There is a subcategory of litanies I call "Saints' Lives." These tales are the pinnacle of the litany genre, indeed of the entire corpus of Russian women's discourses. In "Saints' Lives" the protagonist (at times the teller herself) endures hardships of such epic proportions as to transcend mere human identity. The poet Anna Akhmatova, who suffered great personal losses during the Stalin era, is a public figure whose endurance stands as a familiar paradigm of this genre. But I heard numerous stories about other such women, who, though not famous, had endured terrific hardships and come through transcendent.

The clearest example of this genre of life history I heard while visiting a Moscow school. In the familiar intonations of the litany, the vice principal, Natalia, told me the following story over tea in her office.

There was a woman, Irena Ivanovna, who was connected to our school through the Veteran's Committee. Before she died in 1987, she had constantly shared her life with our students and especially shared her tales of the war. Irena Ivanovna had two sons and a husband. After her husband and her elder son died at the front, she went with her second son, born in 1925, to the occupied territories; they became partisans working together against the Nazis. One day Irena Ivanovna was wounded and her son carried her for three weeks through dense forests to safety behind the front. [Here Natalia's voice rises into litany.] For three weeks, he carried her on his back, through woods, over small rivers, he fed her and tended her wounds—until finally, miraculously, they crossed into safe territory. Then, he went back to fight. He was killed right before the end of the war.

At this point, Natalia took a large book down from her shelf. It was an album commemorating Irena Ivanovna's life, which had been put together by a group of schoolgirls. Elaborately embellished with calligraphic labels, arrows, and ribbons, it was like a sacred object in Natalia's hands. In the album were photos of Irena Ivanovna's natal family, Irena Ivanovna as a middle-aged woman before the war, Irena Ivanovna with her son during the war, dressed in improvised camouflage. After that came maps and charts of the front zone, one of them marked with an arrow and a ribbon to show the place where the son had died (which was now part of Poland). On the next page, surrounded by more ribbons, was a photographic copy of the son's last letter. A separate section held pictures of a visit Irena Ivanovna made in the late 1950s to her son's grave in Poland; living on meager means, she had only been able to make this trip because she studied Polish and placed first in a regional language competition, whose prize was a four-day trip. After the war, Irena Ivanovna had adopted an orphaned teenager, and there were photographs of her with this daughter. The last image in the book showed Irena Ivanovna with the children of the school, shortly before her death. As we looked at this photograph, Natalia said, with trembling voice:

Her life was so difficult, so unimaginably full of tragedy. But if you ever saw her . . . she was such an energetic woman, and so kind. She loved our students. Every year for her son's birthday Irena Ivanovna baked *one thousand* cookies, she baked cookies for the whole school, and she came here and we held a birthday party. . . . The kids just ate the cookies, as you can understand, but to Irena Ivanovna they were cookies for her son.

This story capsulizes the central symbolic and functional elements of Russian female identity and sacrifice. Indeed, as Natalia's emotion and the schoolgirls' album attest, Irena Ivanovna's story is a paradigm of the kind of identity that Russian women honor and inculcate in their daughters and female students.

RUSSIAN WOMEN AT ODDS WITH THEMSELVES

The cultural/discursive systems that Russian women have developed for imagining, creating, valuing, and sustaining their own identities (as individuals, as women, and as Russians) depend to a very great extent on key constituent elements: suffering, loss, hardship, the endurance of outrageous burdens and the acceptance of sacrifices so enormous they enter the realm of the mythic. I do not wish to imply that there is anything deterministic about these systems, that they are in any way inherent to the structure of Russian culture. Suffering, sacrifice, and loss have, for many reasons, been the historical context of women's lives in Russia for many centuries. Like people everywhere, Russian women have utilized the facts of their social context—their pain, their burdens, their powerlessness—as the material for their creation of selfhood and value. In their talk, Russian women keep ancient value and identity formations alive; through the stories they tell they reproduce both themselves and their culture as a whole.

There is no question that Russian women desire improvements in their lives and that many people—women and men—are trying hard to find ways to bring about a general amelioration of the conditions under which Russian women live and work. But their efforts are undermined by the very discourses they employ for talking about their lives, discourses that fetishize and valorize women's hardships at the same time they lament and deplore them. The pragmatic, progressive vision that most Russian women share, of an easier, more secure, more comfortable society is thus at odds with the ancient, mythic system by which they establish their value in society.

Russian women create their social identity by exercising their power of endurance against the many weights, constraints, and pressures their society poses for them. Like athletes subjecting themselves to arduous workouts, women develop the "muscles" of their social identity through interaction with a difficult system. Removing those difficulties would seem to mean removing the very material through which Russian women create themselves as women. When seen in this light, perhaps it is possible to understand why, in Russia, the ideas and ideals of feminism are encountered with such disdain.

NOTES

1. *Matushka* is an affectionate diminutive that can be translated "dear mother." *Sudarynia* is a term of address denoting respect. *Ditiatko* is an affectionate diminutive meaning "dear little child." This text is my translation of a traditional Russian folk song. There are several variations of this song; I have used that sung by Zhanna Bichevskaia in a 1985 recording. A slightly different version appears as "*Matushka, chto vo pole pyl'no,*" in *Russkaia Pesennaia Lyrika* (Moscow: Sovietskaia Rossiia, 1992), 96.

2. Traditional laments are reproduced in numerous Soviet-era ethnographies and folklore collection. See, for instance, *Goi esi vy dobry molodtsy: Russkoe narodno-poeticheskoe tvorchestvo*, eds. P. S. Vykhodtseva and E. P. Kholodovoi (Moscow: Molodaia Gvardiia, 1979), 91–134.

3. Christine Worobec provides a fairly detailed account of the young bride's situation in "Victims or Actors: Russian Peasant Women and Patriarchy," in *Peasant Economy, Culture, and Politics of European Russia, 1800–1921*, ed. Esther Kingston-Mann and Timothy Mixter (Princeton: Princeton University Press, 1991), 177–206.

4. Ibid., 206.

5. Personal conversation, Colgate University, September 1993.

6. In a recent issue of the liberal paper *Moscow News*, the Russian writer Viktor Erofeev (well known for his outrageous sexual fiction) draws an explicit analogy between feminism and Marxism in a mocking essay about Marilyn French's newest book, *War against Women*. By calling French "the latest Engels" and making other snide references to now-despised Communist icons, his essay is designed to scare readers away from any engagement with feminist ideas, which are supposedly nothing more than "utopian half-truths," Moskovskie Novosti, March 21, 1993, B-4.

7. This comment by Morits was reported by Francine du Plessix Gray in *Soviet Women: Walking the Tightrope* (New York: Doubleday, 1989). Morits is a leading poet and humanist writer; she was an outspoken and courageous critic of the Soviet regime for many years.

8. Though central planning insured that there were many similarities in the experiences of women throughout the Soviet Union, there are also many differences in ideologies about gender and gender roles among the many cultures of the former USSR. I want to specify that this paper addresses the experiences of Russian women in the Soviet period and in the years following the dissolution of the USSR, and does not presume to speak about gender relations in the other republics.

9. Alla Sariban, "The Soviet Woman: Support and Mainstay of the Regime," in *Women and Russia: Feminist Writings from the Soviet Union* (Boston: Beacon Press, 1984). *Women and Russia* appeared as an underground (samizdat) publication in the Soviet Union in 1979.

10. See Gail Lapidus, *Women in Soviet Society: Equality, Development and Social Change* (Berkeley: University of California Press, 1978), 54–94, for a concise overview of revolutionary programs to define women's role in socialist society.

11. David Lane, *Soviet Society under Perestroika* (Boston: Unwin Hyman, 1990), 217. As comparison, Lane points out that the female labor participation rate in the U.S. and Britain stands at around sixty percent. See V. G. Kostakov, "The Development of Female Employment," in *Women, Work, and Family in the Soviet Union,* ed. Gail Warshofsky Lapidus (Armonk, N.Y.: M. E. Sharpe, 1982), 33–68, for a summary of the history of female labor development in the USSR.

12. Lane, *Soviet Society under Perestroika,* 217.

13. Many surveys have measured the respective domestic contributions of men and women in Soviet and post-Soviet Russian society. As Porokhniuk and Shepeleva report, a survey in Odessa in the early 1970s showed, for example, that in only 8.6 percent of families did men and women share housework and childcare equally. In 48 percent of families women performed all of the household work. See Jo Peers, "Workers by Hand and Womb: Soviet Women and the Demographic Crisis," in *Soviet Sisterhood,* ed. Barbara Holland (Bloomington: Indiana University Press, 1985), for a stark rendering of women's working and domestic lives. Natalya Baranskaya's novelette, *A Week Like Any Other* (Seattle: Seal Press, 1989), published in Russian in the Soviet journal *Novy Mir* in 1969, is a poignant literary representation of women's double burden.

14. Sariban, "Soviet Woman," 208.

15. William Moskoff, *The Bread of Affliction: The Food Supply in the USSR during World War II* (Cambridge: Cambridge University Press, 1990).

16. The extreme scarcity of certain commodities that could ease the burden of women should be viewed as signs of the degree of official disregard for women's problems and concerns. For example, condoms were always scarce

and other forms of birth control even scarcer; Russian women were thus forced to use abortion as a primary form of family planning, and ten or more abortions per woman were the norm. Sanitary supplies for menstruation were unheard of until they were introduced (by foreign firms) in the late 1980s.

17. Of course this is also true of the media in the West, but even the most conservative Western women's publications feature stories on nondomestic themes and on other women's concerns such as rape, equal opportunity, sexual health, and so on.

18. Lynne Attwood explored the gender assumptions of Soviet social science in detail in *The New Soviet Man and Woman: Sex-Role Socialization in the USSR* (Bloomington: Indiana University Press, 1990). For revealing examples of official ideologies concerning gender roles and "female duties," see E. E. Novikova, V. S. Iazykova, and Z. A. Iankova, "Women's Work and the Family," and V. Porokhniuk and M. S. Shepeleva, "How Working Women Combine Work and Household Duties," both in *Women, Work and Family in the Soviet Union*, ed. Gail Warshofsky Lapidus (Armonk, N.Y.: M. E. Sharpe, 1982). See also the interviews by Mary Buckley in *Soviet Social Scientists Talking: An Official Debate about Women* (London: Macmillan, 1986).

19. For a statistical breakdown of women in the Soviet labor force, see Lane, *Soviet Society under Perestroika*, 219.

20. Mikhail Gorbachev, *Perestroika: New Thinking for Our Country and the World* (New York: Harper and Row, 1987), 117.

21. See Yelena Khanga, "No Matryoshkas Need Apply," *New York Times*, November 25, 1991.

22. There is a tendency in Russian political thinking to assert common solutions for the entire populace, that is, to enact laws or design social programs that will affect all members of a group equally. This tendency toward centralized social engineering was, of course, a marked feature of Communism, but it hardly began or ended with the Soviet political system.

23. Ol'ga Lipovskaia, "New Women's Organizations," in *Perestroika and Soviet Women*, ed. Mary Buckley (Cambridge: Cambridge University Press, 1992), 72. Lipovskaia is one of a handful of active feminists in Russia today. Her essay gives an excellent overview of the kinds of women's groups—mostly not feminist at all—that developed during perestroika.

24. In keeping with anthropological guidelines, my interview subjects and informants remain anonymous.

25. This fear has been carefully kindled, it must be noted, by a regular stream of newspaper essays and articles that ridicule the women's movement via the clichéd half-truths and misrepresentations long familiar to feminists. These essays appeared with such regularity in the media that there seems to be an organized campaign to keep any discussion of feminist issues at bay.

26. Although the number of private shops and kiosks has grown during the post-Soviet years, this has had scant impact on the availability of the basic

necessities of life. The prices in private (nonstate) shops are too high and the goods on sale are mostly luxury items such as imported liquor, chocolates, cigarettes, garments, and electronics.

27. As Colette Shulman writes, most accurately, I think, "If I had to select one satisfaction most widely felt by the working woman at all levels of society, I would say that it is the work-collective as a source of community and communication and of mutual support in coping with the daily problems of life." See "The Individual and the Collective" in *Women in Russia,* ed. Dorothy Atkinson, Alexander Dallin, and Gail Warshofsky Lapidus (Stanford, Calif.: Stanford University Press, 1977), 380.

28. Sandra Stahl, *Literary Folkloristics and the Personal Narrative* (Bloomington: Indiana University Press, 1989), x.

29. See Joanna Hubbs, *Mother Russia: The Feminine Myth in Russian Culture* (Bloomington: Indiana University Press, 1988), and Vera Sandomirsky Dunham, "The Strong-Woman Motif," in *The Transformation of Russian Society: Aspects of Social Change since 1861,* ed. Cyril Black (Cambridge: Harvard University Press, 1960), for perspectives on the historical evolution of feminine ideals in Russia.

30. Yevgenii Yevtushenko, "A Nation Begins with Its Women," in *Perestroika: The Crunch Is Now,* ed. L. Krishtoff and Eva Skelley (Moscow: Progress Publishers, 1990), 318.

31. There are myriad complications to this topic. What the Russian woman is giving up by not buying those craved boots is not simply "nice new boots." Dressing, fashion, the cultivation of whatever charm or style or beauty can be created from the materials at hand—this is the Moscow woman's artistry, her poetry, her motion picture, her montage, her communication, which functions on many simultaneous planes of semiosis, says volumes about the era, about shifts in politics or spirituality, about household economics and creativity. In Russia, a winter culture, not to have the right boots is to be missing a crucial element, a building block for the rest of the story of "self." This emphasis on footwear has a long (and class-based) history: witness the old proverb that "the peasant wears bast [straw] shoes so the master can wear soft leather boots."

32. Tatiana Tolstaia, in an interview with Irena Maryniak, *Index on Censorship,* No. 9, 1990, 29–30.

33. Nancy Ries, "The Power of Negative Thinking: Russian Talk and the Reproduction of Mindset, Worldview, and Society," in *The Anthropology of East Europe Review* 10: 2 (Autumn 1991).

REFERENCES

Anisimov, V. I., and A. A. Tselishchev, eds. 1992. *Russkaia Pesennaia Lyrika.* Moscow: Sovietskaia Rossiia.

Attwood, Lynne. 1990. *The New Soviet Man and Woman: Sex-Role Socialization in the USSR.* Bloomington: Indiana University Press.

Baranskaya, Natalya. 1989. *A Week Like Any Other.* Seattle: Seal Press.

Buckley, Mary. 1986. *Soviet Social Scientists Talking: An Official Debate about Women.* London: Macmillan.

Dunham, Vera Sandomirsky. 1960. "The Strong-Woman Motif." In *The Transformation of Russian Society: Aspects of Social Change since 1861,* edited by Cyril Black, 459–82. Cambridge: Harvard University Press.

Erofeev, Viktor. 1993. *Ochen' Zhenskoe 'Shto Delat'?* [A Very Female 'What is to be Done?'] Moskovkie Novosti, March 21, 1993, B4.

Gorbachev, Mikhail. 1987. *Perestroika: New Thinking for Our Country and the World.* New York: Harper and Row.

Gray, Francine du Plessix. 1989. *Soviet Women: Walking the Tightrope.* New York: Doubleday.

Hubbs, Joanna. 1988. *Mother Russia: The Feminine Myth in Russian Culture.* Bloomington: Indiana University Press.

Khanga, Yelena. 1991. "No Matryoshkas Need Apply." *New York Times,* November 25, 1991.

Kostakov, V. G. 1982. "The Development of Female Employment." In *Women, Work and Family in the Soviet Union,* edited by Gail Warshofsky Lapidus, 33–68. Armonk, N.Y.: M. E. Sharpe.

Lane, David. 1990. *Soviet Society under Perestroika.* Boston: Unwin Hyman.

Lapidus, Gail. 1978. *Women in Soviet Society: Equality, Development, and Social Change.* Berkeley: University of California Press.

Lipovskaia, Ol'ga. 1992. "New Women's Organizations." In *Perestroika and Soviet Women,* edited by Mary Buckley, 72–82. Cambridge: Cambridge University Press.

Maryniak, Irena. 1990. "The Human Spirit is Androgynous." *Index on Censorship* 9:29–30.

Moskoff, William. 1990. *The Bread of Affliction: The Food Supply in the USSR during World War II.* Cambridge: Cambridge University Press.

Novikova, E. E., V. S. Iazykova, and Z. A. Iankova. 1982. "Women's Work and the Family." In *Women, Work, and Family in the Soviet Union,* edited by Gail Warshofsky Lapidus, 165–90. Armonk, N.Y.: M. E. Sharpe.

Peers, Jo. 1985. "Workers by Hand and Womb: Soviet Women and the Demographic Crisis." In *Soviet Sisterhood,* edited by Barbara Holland, 116–44. Bloomington: Indiana University Press.

Porokhniuk, V., and M. S. Shepeleva. 1982. "How Working Women Combine Work and Household Duties." In *Women, Work, and Family in the Soviet Union,* edited by Gail Warshofsky Lapidus, 267–76. Armonk, N.Y.: M. E. Sharpe.

Ries, Nancy. 1991. "The Power of Negative Thinking: Russian Talk and the Reproduction of Mindset, Worldview, and Society." *The Anthropology of East Europe Review* 10 (2): 38–53.

Sariban, Alla. 1984. "The Soviet Woman: Support and Mainstay of the Regime." In *Women and Russia,* edited by Tatyana Mamonova, 205–13. Boston: Beacon Press.

Shulman, Colette. 1977. "The Individual and the Collective." In *Women in*

Russia, edited by Dorothy Atkinson, Alexander Dallin, and Gail Warshofsky Lapidus, 375–84. Stanford: Stanford University Press.

Stahl, Sandra. 1989. *Literary Folkloristics and the Personal Narrative.* Bloomington: Indiana University Press.

Vykhodtseva, P. S., and E. P. Kholodovoi, eds. 1979. *Goi esi vy dobry molodtsy: Russkoe narodno-poeticheskoe tvorchestvo.* Moscow: Molodaia Gvardiia.

Worobec, Christine. 1991. "Victims or Actors: Russian Peasant Women and Patriarchy." In *Peasant Economy, Culture, and Politics of European Russia, 1800–1921,* edited by Esther Kingston-Mann and Timothy Mixter, 177–206. Princeton: Princeton University Press.

Yevtushenko, Yevgenii. 1990. "A Nation Begins with Its Women." In *Perestroika: The Crunch Is Now,* edited by L. Krishtoff and Eva Skelley. Moscow: Progress Publishers.

13.

THE WONDERFUL-TERRIBLE BITCH FIGURE IN HARLEQUIN NOVELS

SUSAN OSTROV WEISSER

"Harriet?" Sharn said, and Caryn felt her heart sink a little. "I can't see what it is you don't like about her."

Caryn fell silent. How obtuse men were! But then it always took a woman to read another woman effectively. Men were influenced by the veneer, especially if it were as charming and polished as that possessed by Harriet. And men were also easy to deceive when a clever woman set out to exert her charm as Harriet had done. Watching her with Sharn, Caryn could well understand his being taken in by her, for she even changed her voice for his benefit, purring like a kitten being lovingly fondled. She used her beautiful eyes in a way that surely would hold him spellbound; she could smile like an angel. Her figure was slender yet voluptuously tempting because of the affected manner in which she would swing her hips or bend suddenly, so that her low-cut neckline revealed curves which brought hot color surging into Caryn's cheeks. But Sharn never turned away as she did; no, he, like any other man, would always look his fill.

—Anne Hampson, *Unwanted Bride*

The Bitch figure, a staple of Harlequin novels as well as other popular romances, is not only wonderfully terrible, the woman the reader loves to hate; she is also terrible *because* she is wonderful, in ways that the heroines of these novels most decidedly are not, and which I will suggest the female reader herself might long to be. This is why, in the quotation above, only women are said to be able to read and correctly understand other women. The two figures, good and bad women, constitute a couple system orbiting around the male as if by nature, exhibiting and concealing the secret traits that make them "who they really are" by turns. But in fact another sort of triangle is hidden within the woman-man-woman configuration of the text, namely the triangular relation of the Bitch, the Heroine, and the female reader, who is made to contemplate the consequences of bad and good female behavior in its extremes through these two fictional character types. It is the nature of these ways of being terrible and wonderful that this essay will attempt to explore.[1]

As can be seen in the excerpt from a Harlequin novel above, in which we see a Bitch viewed through the eyes of the good girl, this antiheroine's effectiveness as a literary type depends on the device of doubling. Not only is she an exact inversion of the heroine herself, she is also always involved in a duplicity of her own, in which she pretends to outdo the heroine in sweet, soft, pleasing ways, while deliberately manipulating the hero to her own advantage. She is, in other words, meant to be read against the heroine as a nightmare version of assertive, aggressively sexual, and non-nurturant womanhood. This is the literary analogue to what the psychoanalyst Jessica Benjamin refers to as the "splitting into complementary forms: subject and object, idealization and repudiation, good and bad, doer and done-to."[2] However, Benjamin sees the split primarily in terms of "gender opposition," rather than between forms of womanhood. For her purposes, such splitting is an explanation of the development of sadomasochistic female sexuality in relation to a powerful male, since, according to her theory, the power of the father is the "gendered process of defensive idealization." By contrast, I would note that the pervasiveness of the Bitch figure (in other venues, as well, of course, such as soap opera, melodrama, and everyday gossip) suggests its importance among women themselves.

While Harlequin romances are all about the essentialism of male and female, purporting to illustrate their inevitable opposition and necessary complementarity, the excesses of the Bitch figure suggest that being female is more than mere femininity can encompass. The heroine conforms to a quite rigid set of conditions (though not unchanging in response to standards of acceptable behavior)[3]—for example, she no longer has to be unwilling to bed the hero before marriage, but she must never sleep with a man for pleasure only—whereas the Bitch is both fluid in identity and outrageous in her behavior. Because she is willing to pretend, that is, to be anything she needs to be, or act in any way at all to get the man in question, she encompasses all things women are capable of—except for the Good, a small nugget of gold standard behavior reserved for the heroine alone.

One conventional representation of heroinism in Western literature identifies the domestic heroine with virginity, if not asexuality, but as every reader of Harlequin novels knows, their romantic heroines are surprisingly passionate "by nature" and are described as experiencing a great deal of desire in explicitly "sensual" language.[4] "Good" and "bad" women are therefore not so simply distinguished by the whore/madonna structure that pervades other popular forms; the split is far more subtle and interesting. Rather, the good girl, who is defined by her fitness to adapt to the hero, is pitted against the bad woman who represents an element in the gendered universe that, although capable of chameleonlike disguises, ultimately cannot be transformed (unlike the wild male who can be tamed and domesticated), and so must be punished and finally expunged from the range of possibilities open to the heroine. In the end the Good must be proven the only way to be Real as a woman, through the ancient plot mechanism of a final reward in an ultimately just universe.[5]

The device of doubling can also be found in a typical plot (sometimes separate and sometimes concurrent) of the popular romance in which the heroine chooses between two contrastive men.[6] This narrative structure has, of course, a long and distinguished pedigree in the conventions of the traditional British novel—think of *Jane Eyre, Wuthering Heights, Mill on the Floss.* But unlike the heroine's Bitch-rival, the alternate male lover has *two* different modes of sexuality. He comes in basic and distinctive types: either too brutal to reform, or else dull, dull, dull next to the hero. The former is simply uncontrollable by the heroine and very frequently is put in his place by a sock in the jaw from the true love; the latter, the tedious, bland, stable but asexual rejected male lover (i.e., The Wimp), functions primarily to underline the heroine's right to her sexuality, which the hero alone evokes. The point is that we don't want her to "settle" for Mr. Dull. She deserves more, as we know—the best in fact: all other characters are there to reveal either that She is the most deserving or that He is the best that can be deserved.

The *heroine's* rival, however, is rarely another good girl like herself, and her sexuality is always underlined. Indeed, the Bitch figure attracts to herself all the negative aspects of sexual assertion, aligning it with aggression, "masculine" unemotionality in general, and, significantly, an emphasis on materialistic values. She belongs, in other words, very much in the category of signs constructed by the text as *male*. But the constellation of traits identified as alluring in a male is then in turn reconstructed as a kind of hyperfemale, "capable of anything" a "woman" might do. We might speculate that the excess of emotion and power left out of real women's lives by the repressive and limiting constraints of being "feminine" in relation to the male and to the public world finds its way into an inhuman and distorted version of womanhood that is the heroine's hated Other, i.e., the Bitch.[7]

This too has a very old literary tradition: Blanche Ingram in *Jane Eyre* used her looks and social status to sneer at our heroine Jane while trying to catch her prize, Mr. Rochester, whom she did not, needless to say, "really" love. The modern Bitch usually has what the heroine ought to have but is too humble to acquire: beauty (always identified as artificial and cold), ego, status, money, material goods, men at her feet. Interestingly, the Bitch often has "a cap of very short hair," unlike the heroine, whose mane is much more frequently long and lustrous as a sign of her traditional femininity.[8] As in the tale of Cinderella, the defeat of the antiheroine(s) is as much of the fun as catching the boring Prince himself.

Here, by way of illustration of the Bitch as both super-feminine and dangerously masculine, are the descriptors of the Bitch-Rival Harriet in Anne Hampson's *Unwanted Bride*,[9] quoted above: Harriet, we note, is "beautiful," like the heroine, but unlike either hero or heroine, she is blonde, "fair as a lily, with eyes like blue stars and the figure of an angel" (30). Her looks are both quintessentially feminine, defined according to popular traditions as blonde, blue-eyed, delicate, and angelic, and also associated with the modern equivalent of the nineteenth-century Lady figure, with her social status and conspicuous consumption. Thus she is said to be "elegant," "glamorous," doing "little besides make herself pretty," unlike the useful, frugal and efficient heroine, Caryn, who has the modest virtues of bourgeois domesticity in her favor.

The rival, Harriet, though physically perfect and extremely desirable, like Caryn herself, has an overt sexuality not permitted to the heroine, who would never dream of bending over on purpose so the hero could see down her dress. Significantly, the female sexuality of the Bitch, in sharp contrast to that of the heroine (which expresses itself as nameless, unfulfilled longing), is associated with the lust for material gain, the "masculine" ethic of the marketplace in a capitalist and traditionally patriarchal social order. Most interestingly, we never see Harriet herself as actually sexually desirous of the hero; we only see her *inviting* desire, "tempting" the hero as a conscious means to a material end. Conversely, the true heroine's (sexual) desire is the engine that runs the novel, yet she is never allowed to be conscious of her own power to "get what she wants," much less go after it.[10] The heroine has all the subjectivity, since the novel allows us to eavesdrop on her thoughts and adopt her point of view, while the Bitch never gets a chance to think or dream or even feel in the reader's hearing. She appears very much as men do to the heroine, which is to say she seems all surface, all power, all action.[11]

But in addition to epitomizing femaleness as pure object of male lust, without desire of her own, the Bitch-rival figure also is herself aligned with desirably "masculine" traits such as aggression, authoritativeness, self-assertion, autonomy, and emotional aloofness. Oddly, the same adjectives that praise the typical Harlequin hero in his early phase (in which he is either mistaken by the heroine for cold, aloof, or arrogant, or really is so and therefore in need of her reformation through romantic love) are applied with great derogation to the Bitch-rival. Harriet, for example, is extremely aggressive verbally, rude and unfriendly in her gestures and remarks: she "sneers" at the heroine, she has a "supercilious" expression, she makes such "scathing remarks" that the heroine may justifiably retaliate, to the reader's delight. Thus "Caryn excused her own conduct by remembering how very bitchy Harriet had always been with her" (111). Very often the heroine herself is quite "bitchy" in response to the rival's verbal cuts, but we cheer her on—because the Bitch went first.

The very confidence, assertiveness, and coolness that make the hero an alluring and challenging figure to the young, warm, self-doubting heroine are the signature vices of the Bitch: thus Harriet is variously cited for her "insolence," her "lack of friendliness," her "edge of arrogance and skepticism," qualities that in a good-looking and high-status male would have the heroine panting at his feet. Just as a hero's eyes are frequently said in these novels to "rake the body of the heroine" (with *raking* a displacement for visually *raping*), so Harriet's eyes "rake the clothes" of the heroine, insulting her for their plainness, which of course it turns out the hero secretly prefers. Moreover, Harriet's "tones ring with confidence," she is (as we saw in the opening quotation) "clever" (with *clever* used in binary opposition to *innocent*) and "sharp," which is contrastive to the heroine's feminine softness and vulnerability. This penetrating cleverness and sharpness steals some of the hero's masculinity and makes the Bitch unripe for his own penetration; though he may look down her dress, he will never have intercourse with her. She is too much his double; such a union would be homoerotic. Harriet, in fact, in contrast to the soft, melting heroine, is even said to "sit up stiffly."

The heart of the matter, so to speak, is reached in *Unwanted Bride* when Caryn, our heroine, tries to picture the marriage she fears between her Bitch-rival and the man she loves. This is her conclusion:

Sharn was there, helping and *leading and giving out instructions*. He noticed Caryn, but his glance passed indifferently through her. His work was his life, she thought, and wondered if Harriet would eventually become resigned to this. Harriet had declared [note the self-confident assertion in the verb] . . . he would give more work to his employees and take time off himself for leisure. So confident the girl had been, and yet, looking at Sharn as he stood for a moment, his eyes narrowed in that characteristic way, directing operations, she could not see Harriet—or any other woman for that matter—*telling him what he must do*. (100; my emphases)

The arrogance, coldness, and bossiness of the Bitch is therefore not only an effect of rivalry with the heroine or a measure of the heroine's greater worth; more than this, it is a counter in the power game with men, aligned with the values of feminism itself, which champions assertiveness and authority in women. Thus while hero Sharn and heroine Caryn both are said to "love old things," namely the antique furniture and decorative knick-knacks of the ancestral mansion they jointly inherited from a distant relative, the Bitch Harriet wants to replace all the old traditional furniture with new and make a grotesque addition to the lovely old homestead "in the modern style." "The very thought of this addition," adds the narrator, "made by a girl who had no real connection with the property whatsoever . . . strengthened Caryn's sense of possession" (60). You are either in the nexus of patriarchy and property or you're out, the text is informing us; and the Bitch who wants to modernize and tell her husband what to do is not going to possess either land or man.

Why, one might well inquire, include a Bitch figure in the romance novel at all? We might first speculate that such a triangle allows cultural ambivalence about women's assertive (sexual and economic) self to be bifurcated and expressed in a gendered negative model. Femininity as the core of a novelistic universe that is defined through the permutations of gender is itself made coherent by the play of same-sexed/differently-sexed bodies within a small circle of "good" and "bad" social traits. These traits appear encoded in nature, while the natural is defined by the effect of these traits in the social world: thus the Bitch is a manlike, unnatural woman, because she is more beautiful and exciting than the good girl; the Wimp is a deformed and inadequate "feminine" man, and so on.

By comparison with the Bitch-Rival, the heroine has traits clearly marked off and aligned with one another as the *only* coherent form of femininity: i.e., erotic needs tempered with innocence and self-denial, and assertion tempered by a kind of economic innocence that clears her of the charge of "acting like a man" in the marketplace. By comparison, the Bitch figure is a kind of dumping ground for anxiety and discomfort in gender roles and the desires they do and do not legitimize. Both women intensely desire the hero, but the Bitch is never "truly" in love and never suffers for her man, since her reasons for wanting him are construed as superficial, materialistic, and "selfish." The heroine, by contrast, who of course suffers a great deal, would never simply marry for money, unless it is for the selfless reason of giving a home to an orphaned nephew, or some such windy device; her desire is therefore legitimated, and Desire itself found natural and unproblematic in its "pure" form.

The overt subject of the Harlequin romance is the "power" of love as a force; the covert message of the text is that love is an operation of power as an end in itself, since it pits the unworthy rival in a struggle against the underdog heroine to see who wields the greater attraction for the hero. In the marketplace of desire in these texts, power is therefore disguised as the natural reward for true womanhood, rather than displayed as the real coin of exchange for the prize of the coveted male.

Romantic love, like all gender relations, is essentially a field of play for domination and control, in which all kinds of seemingly good bargains are negotiated and struck: her body for his promise, his strength for her nurturance, the renunciation of his wildness for the safety of her domesticity, and so on. The basic pattern of the Harlequin novel is the humiliation of powerlessness (the weak position of the bad bargain) revenged: the heroine frequently knows she is in love before she knows her own power over her lover, so she textually "experiences" her helplessness and passivity while the reader enjoys the irony of the certain ending. The much-remarked-upon certainty of the closure is all-important here, and marks off the mass-market romance novel from other genres of romance.

Humiliation, as critics have noted, is a constant feature of the Harlequin genre. Female masochism is sometimes cited to explain this troubling aspect of a text that is otherwise assumed to provide pure pleasure and "escape" to female readers.[12] But humiliation and powerlessness is a predominant theme of many women's *lives*, and therefore represents an issue of some urgency that should not be surprising to find in a fantasy about short-circuiting women's problems through the efficacy of romantic love. In the Harlequin novels, the problem of male domination is very frequently rendered as an effect of misreading: the hero is misjudged, for example, or the heroine assumes her value is low, whereas we know that her value (for the hero, which is to say her value in the world) is very high and steadily increasing. Because of the certainty of comfort in the formulaic closure, I would speculate, the female reader can safely experience that which is fearful yet limited and controlled temporally and textually, the equivalent of a pleasurable scream during a roller coaster ride.

The comfort of Harlequin novels is that they render a quick dose of terrible discomfort within a safe frame that provides an expectation of ultimate comfort and mastery of anxiety. The world of love is terribly, even agonizingly, vexed and uncertain because that makes certainty all the more gratifying when restored. Or another way of putting this is that the fears and anxieties of powerlessness are allowed to surface because the genre creates a secure and stable space in which to present and frame them.

This effect is accomplished by several devices that, to use the language of romance, have "withstood the test of time": first, the social context of a Harlequin is strictly prescribed by rigid convention, delineating a narrative world that appears immutable, ahistorical, and universal in its meanings; second, the clues to the "meaning" of characters' language and gestures are utterly predictable and eminently interpretable; and finally, if all else fails, the ending is absolutely certain—there never was a Harlequin yet in which the heroine wound up poor, unhappy, and loveless.[13] Thus the reader is free to enjoy the subject position of humiliation, as well as the object position of irony at the expense of the heroine (and of the hero, who will himself be subject to love).

Where a Bitch figure appears in the text, therefore, she provides a stabilizing effect, like the third leg of a tripod, by grounding the reader's fears in a known target. As the disruptive element, the Terrible Third, she defines and delineates "the problem" in terms of the binary gender system and the romantic couple system. If she can be extruded, all will be well. Yet the unhappy couple formed by the Good and Bad Women are the secret subtext of female sexuality. We might even say that women appear to be at odds in these novels, while in fact they are working different sides of the same street. Trapped in these stilted, inflexible, and highly stylized representations, thorns in each other's sides, defined each by what the other does not have or do, the reader sees the Good Girl and the Bad Girl humiliate each other, depend on each other, deploy strategies on each other, spend endless energy on undermining each other, but never understand each other. It is as if they were an old married pair, in fact, perhaps a mirror for the reader's own or feared marriage.

It has been frequently observed that there is an astonishing amount of violence in a Harlequin novel, most obviously in the physical forceful-ness of the hero, sometimes culminating in rape or near-rape. Most often the heroine "understands" this fierceness to be an effect of passion, if not the sign of its intensity and value; in this way the principles of coercion and domination are accommodated within the narrative by affixing them to a natural "force" of romantic passion outside the "will" and control of the protagonists. The Bitch figure fits well into this scheme as a magnet for the instability of aggression that floats unnamed around the text. First, male aggression and privileged access to material wealth is displaced onto a figure that can be hated and disposed of, unlike the necessary male; and secondly, the reader's own desire for outright pursuit of *and* revenge against the male can be projected onto the Bitch. The Bitch is Who I Am Not, a defining force of the heroine's identity, which is She Who Can Be Loved—at the price of her absolute fidelity and devotion to the hero.

Thus in another Harlequin novel, *Heart on Fire,* by Charlotte Lamb,[14] the heroine is insulted and humiliated by the hero more than by the Bitch-Rival who we are falsely led to believe is his lover. Ellis, the "dynamic head of an multinational corporation," announces to the heroine Claudia, whom he hires as a temporary secretary, that he is going to lock her in his hotel suite until she types a report he needs. Her response to this move is to be resentful and flash her green eyes, but she does not seem to consider that this is in fact an illegal act of physi-cal coercion, if not outright slavery. Her explanation is that "Ellis was a very powerful man. . . . He was rich and used to his own way" (17). He also questions her "insistently" in the first moments of their acquaintance as to whether "she was married or had a boyfriend . . . lived alone or with others" (12). But she is, mysteriously, neither "threatened [n]or alarmed" by this strangely intrusive behavior.

When the rival Estelle is introduced (note the similarity of names between the male prize and the female rival), it is clear that she too colludes in oppressing the heroine, treating her rudely and emphasizing her own class privilege, demanding, "Who's that? . . . She's one of your girls [secretaries]!" (22). . . . "Didn't you explain that the meal was only for your secretary?" (24). Estelle is, not surprisingly, beautiful and sexy, purring "Darling" to the hero in every scene, "icy" and peremptory ("Tell him I want to talk to him!") (43). Yet though her treatment of the heroine is less horrendous than that of the hero Ellis—he sneers, for example, "Are you so stupid that you can't understand a simple explanation?" (29)—the "dynamic head of the multinational corporation" is soon forgiven for his trespasses, whereas Estelle is not.

What Ellis does, in fact, to place himself on the side of the angels is to make love to the heroine immediately following all this nasty degradation. The Bitch Estelle also likes to make love: "It was easy to guess how Estelle felt about him. She made no secret of it, kissing him lingeringly, her arms clasping his neck, her body leaning towards him. . . . She couldn't have been more obvious if she had tried, Claudia thought sourly" (133). But the assertive sexuality of the rival does not mitigate her aggression, as it does the hero's; on the contrary, it plays the role of defining the relation between gender and sexuality, since in women such behavior can only have a "bad" intent. This motive for both sexuality and aggression on the part of the Bitch is later identified as "husband-hunting"—as though the heroine herself finds one by just tripping over him.

The plot of the Harlequin novel, then, makes good use of the sexuality of difference *within* gender, pitting innocent sex against knowing sex, humility against (female) arrogance, cold upper-class beauty, taste, and luxury against warm, modest, middle-class domestic uprightness. The good heroine and her wonderful/terrible rival push or clash against one another but never talk to each other about their situation with anything like interest or curiosity, never work together to accomplish a goal, never imagine for each other the possibility of a female-female relation outside a narrative centered on a man as the coveted prize.

While the Bitch appears in the narrative to be the obstacle to the heroine's freedom to choose what she desires, in fact the rigidity of these roles is the unacknowledged source of oppression. It is not only that the shape they give to desire and to the "feminine" directs the pleasure to one object only, as is frequently remarked; more subtly than this, these narratives set up categories of identity that shut off the flow of pleasure between women, who can occupy only one oppressive position at the expense of the other.[15] The *only* scenario that can be imagined is that a reversal of positions should occur, in which the one-down heroine must climb over the body of the Bitch to take her place. Furthermore, this exchange must transpire without the heroine ever playing the sex/gender game, since her "natural" goodness and innocence presume she cannot knowingly act in her own interest (as can the Bitch and the male). In the end the figure of the Bitch constructs a stable, reassuring picture of a world rigidly hierarchical yet structured as a kind of emotional meritocracy: one (deserving) wins only at the loss of the other (alluring but, fortunately, undeserving). Bad riddance to good rubbish, says the Harlequin novel.

One reason why the Bitch is hated is that she exposes the terms of inequality in the world: she demands without being willing to return, striking a good bargain for herself, which the heroine (and not unlikely the reader) cannot do. As in all fairy tales, it is the humble who do not ask who are supposedly the most rewarded. The Bitch, on the other hand, seems to get away with murder, sexually or romantically speaking—until she herself is murdered by being expunged from the plot at the novel's end. You will want to know what the fate of the rude, insolent, cold, beautiful, short-haired, sexy, haughty Harriet of *Unwanted Bride* is: she is forced, in the final pages, to sit passively on a sofa, watching with impotently hostile eyes, as the heroine is asked outside on the terrace for her marriage proposal from the dominating-but-good hero—who has finally, after 180 pages, caught on as to who would *really* make the better wife.

Whether she sat stiffly or not is not recorded.

NOTES

My thanks to Paul Mattick, Jr., for his comments, and for stimulating conversation on the subject of this paper.

1. The title of my paper was suggested by an essay by Caesara Arbatis, "The Ugly-Pretty, Dull-Bright, Weak-Strong Girl in the Gothic Mansion," *Journal of Popular Culture* 13 (1979): 257–63, which points to the paradoxical traits that produce the heroine of the Gothic novel.

280 Susan Ostrov Weisser

2. Jessica Benjamin, *Bonds of Love: Psychoanalysis, Feminism and the Problem of Domination* (New York: Pantheon Press, 1988).

3. Several works usefully trace the history and variety of women's popular romances: Kay Mussell, *Fantasy and Reconciliation: Contemporary Formulas of Women's Romance Fiction* (Westport, Conn.: Greenwood Press, 1984); Jean Radford, ed., *The Progress of Romance: The Politics of Popular Fiction* (London: Routledge and Kegan Paul, 1986); Carol Thurston, *The Romance Revolution: Erotic Novels for Women and the Quest for a New Sexual Identity* (Urbana: University of Illinois Press, 1987).

4. The relation between women's sexuality and the form of the genre is examined by both Ann Douglas, "Soft-Porn Culture," *New Republic*, 30 August 1980, 25–29; and Ann Snitow, "Mass Market Romance: Pornography for Women is Different," in *Powers of Desire: The Politics of Sexuality*, ed. Ann Snitow, Christine Stansell, and Sharon Thompson (New York: Monthly Review Press, 1983).

5. One thinks of Samuel Richardson's *Pamela: or, Virtue Rewarded* as the type of this standard plot in the British novel, for example.

6. Jean Kennard has written about the "convention of the two suitors" in the British novel in *Victims of Convention* (Hamden, Conn.: Archon Press, 1978), as has H. M. Daleski, *The Divided Heroine: A Recurrent Pattern in Six British Novels* (New York: Holmes and Meier, 1983).

7. Women's romantic fantasies have been explored in contrasting ways by Rosalind Coward, whose *Female Desires* (New York: Grove Press, 1985) is interesting and provocative, and Janice Radway, *Reading the Romance: Women, Patriarchy and Popular Literature* (Chapel Hill: University of North Carolina Press, 1984). Coward points out that the power of men is fearfully adored and is marked by their greater age, emotional detachment, social status, and control over others (190). Where Radway's important study implies that women fantasize domesticating men into nurturing figures as the most important element of the plot, Coward emphasizes that women do acquire power in the novels, rendering men "the helpless slaves of passion," disciplining and humbling them (196), though at the price of ignoring the damage inflicted by patriarchal relations.

8. Lois Banner's *American Beauty* (Chicago: University of Chicago Press, 1984) studies the stereotypical power of female beauty to attract wealth and status.

9. Anne Hampson, *Unwanted Bride* (Ontario: Harlequin Presents, 1982).

10. This is a point made at length by Tania Modleski, *Loving with a Vengeance: Mass-Produced Fantasies for Women* (Hamden, Conn.: Archon Books, 1982).

11. Jan Cohn's excellent *Women and the Erotics of Property* (Durham, N.C.: Duke University Press, 1988) sees Harlequins as fantasies of "power," which she defines rather narrowly, in my view, as control over property and authority. She says disappointingly little about the power of female rivals, however.

12. The pleasures and "positive, life-affirming values" of Harlequins are argued

for in Jayne Ann Krentz, ed., *Dangerous Men and Adventurous Women: Romance Writers on the Appeal of the Romance* (Philadelphia: University of Pennsylvania Press, 1992). For a complex refutation of the "escape" theory of motivation, see Radway, *Reading the Romance*.

13. On the conventions of reading popular genre fiction, see Thomas J. Roberts, *An Aesthetics of Junk Fiction* (Athens: University of Georgia Press, 1990); Tony Bennett, ed., *Popular Fiction: Technology, Ideology, Production, Reading* (London: Routledge, 1990); and Jerry Palmer, "Reading as a Woman," in *Potboilers: Methods, Concepts and Case Studies in Popular Fiction* (London: Routledge, 1991).

14. Charlotte Lamb, *Heart on Fire* (Toronto: Harlequin Presents, 1992).

15. Kay Mussell notes that very few heroines in popular romances have close female friends their own age, leaving women dependent on men for emotional support (*Fantasy and Reconciliation*, 107). Tania Modleski also remarks that "this fantasy . . . ensures the impossibility of women ever *getting together* (as women) to form a 'subculture'" (*Feminism without Women: Culture and Criticism in a "Postfeminist" Age* [London: Routledge, 1991]).

REFERENCES

Arbatis, Caesara. "The Ugly-Pretty, Dull-Bright, Weak-Strong Girl in the Gothic Mansion." *Journal of Popular Culture* 13 (1979): 257–63.

Banner, Lois. *American Beauty.* Chicago: University of Chicago Press, 1984.

Benjamin, Jessica. *Bonds of Love: Psychoanalysis, Feminism and the Problem of Domination.* New York: Pantheon Press, 1988.

Bennett, Tony, ed. *Popular Fiction: Technology, Ideology, Production, Reading.* London: Routledge, 1990.

Cohn, Jan. *Women and the Erotics of Property.* Durham: Duke University Press, 1988.

Coward, Rosalind. *Female Desires.* New York: Grove Press, 1985.

Daleski, H. M. *The Divided Heroine: A Recurrent Pattern in Six British Novels.* New York: Holmes and Meier, 1983.

Douglas, Ann. "Soft-Porn Culture." *New Republic,* 30 August 1980: 25–29.

Hampson, Anne. *Unwanted Bride.* Toronto: Harlequin Presents, 1982.

Kennard, Jean. *Victims of Convention.* Hamden, Conn.: Archon Press, 1978.

Krentz, Jayne Ann, ed. *Dangerous Men and Adventurous Women: Romance Writers on the Appeal of the Romance.* Philadelphia: University of Pennsylvania Press, 1992.

Lamb, Charlotte. *Heart on Fire.* Toronto: Harlequin Presents, 1992.

Modleski, Tania. *Feminism without Women: Culture and Criticism in a "Postfeminist" Age.* London: Routledge, 1991.

———. *Loving with a Vengeance: Mass-Produced Fantasies for Women.* Hamden, Conn.: Archon Books, 1982.

Mussell, Kay. *Fantasy and Reconciliation: Contemporary Formulas of Women's Romance Fiction.* Westport, Conn.: Greenwood Press, 1984.

Palmer, Jerry. *Potboilers: Methods, Concepts and Case Studies in Popular Fiction*. London: Routledge, 1991.

Radford, Jean, ed. *The Progress of Romance: The Politics of Popular Fiction*. London: Routledge, 1986.

Radway, Janice. *Reading the Romance: Women, Patriarchy and Popular Literature*. Chapel Hill: University of North Carolina Press, 1984.

Roberts, Thomas J. *An Aesthetics of Junk Fiction*. Athens: University of Georgia Press, 1990.

Snitow, Ann. "Mass Market Romance: Pornography for Women is Different." In *Powers of Desire: The Politics of Sexuality*, edited by Ann Snitow, Christine Stansell, and Sharon Thompson. New York: Monthly Review Press, 1983.

Thurston, Carol. *The Romance Revolution: Erotic Novels for Women and the Quest for a New Sexual Identity*. Urbana: University of Illinois Press, 1987.

IV.

FAMILY LIKENESSES

14.

THE PROBLEM OF SPEAKING
FOR OTHERS

LINDA ALCOFF

Consider the following true stories:

Anne Cameron, a very gifted white Canadian author, writes several semifictional accounts of the lives of Native Canadian women. She writes them in first person and assumes a Native identity. At the 1988 International Feminist Book Fair in Montreal, a group of Native Canadian writers decided to ask Cameron to, in their words, "move over," on the grounds that her writings are disempowering for Native authors. She agrees.[1]

After the 1989 elections in Panama are overturned by Manuel Noriega, President Bush declares in a public address that Noriega's actions constitute an "outrageous fraud" and that "the voice of the Panamanian people have spoken." "The Panamanian people," he tells us, "want democracy and not tyranny, and want Noriega out." He proceeds to plan the invasion of Panama.

At a recent symposium at my university, a prestigious theorist was invited to give a lecture on the political problems of postmodernism. Those of us in the audience, including many white women and people of oppressed nationalities and races, waited in eager anticipation for what he had to contribute to this important discussion. To our disappointment, he introduced his lecture by explaining that he could not cover the assigned topic, because as a white male he did not feel that he could speak for the feminist and postcolonial perspectives that have launched the critical interrogation of postmodernism's politics. He went on to give us a lecture on architecture.

These examples demonstrate the range of current practices of speaking for others in our society. The prerogative of speaking for others remains unquestioned in the citadels of colonial administration, while among activists and in the academy it elicits a growing unease and, in some communities of discourse, it is being rejected. There is a strong, albeit contested, current within feminism that holds that speaking for others—even for other women—is arrogant, vain, unethical, and politically illegitimate. Feminist scholarship has a liberatory agenda that almost requires that women scholars speak on behalf of other women, and yet the dangers of speaking across differences of race, culture, sexuality, and power are becoming increasingly clear to all. In feminist magazines such as *Sojourner,* it is common to find articles and letters in which the author states that she can only speak for herself. In her important paper, "Dyke Methods," Joyce Trebilcot offers a philosophical articulation of this view. She renounces for herself the practice of speaking for others within a lesbian feminist community, and argues further that she "will not try to get other wimmin to accept my beliefs in place of their own" on the grounds that to do so would be to practice a kind of discursive coercion and even a violence.[2]

Feminist discourse is not the only site in which the problem of speaking for others has been acknowledged and addressed, however. In anthropology there is also much discussion going on about whether it is possible to adequately or justifiably speak for others. Trinh T. Minh-ha explains the grounds for skepticism when she says that anthropology is "mainly a conversation of 'us' with 'us' about 'them,' of the white man with the white man about the primitive-nature man . . . in which 'them' is silenced. 'Them' always stands on the other side of the hill, naked and speechless . . . 'them' is only admitted among 'us,' the discussing subjects, when accompanied or introduced by an 'us.' "[3] Given this analysis, even ethnographies written by progressive anthropologists are *a priori* regressive because of the structural features of anthropological discursive practice.

The recognition that there is a problem in speaking for others has followed from the widespread acceptance of two claims. First, there is a growing awareness that where one speaks from affects the meaning and truth of what one says, and thus that one cannot assume an ability to transcend one's location. In other words, a speaker's location (which I take here to refer to their *social* location, or social identity) has an epistemically significant impact on that speaker's claims and can serve either to authorize or disauthorize one's speech. The creation of Women's Studies and African American Studies departments were founded on this very belief: that both the study of and the advocacy for the oppressed must come to be done principally by the oppressed themselves, and that we must finally acknowledge that systematic divergences in social location between speakers and those spoken for will have a significant effect on the content of what is said. The unspoken premise here is simply that a speaker's location is epistemically salient. I shall explore this issue further in the next section.

The second claim holds that, not only is location epistemically salient, but certain privileged locations are discursively dangerous.[4] In particular, the practice of privileged persons speaking for or on behalf of less privileged persons has actually resulted (in many cases) in increasing or reinforcing the oppression of the group spoken for. This was part of the argument made against Anne Cameron's speaking for Native women: Cameron's intentions were never in question, but the effects of her writing were argued to be counterproductive to the needs of Native women because it is Cameron who will be listened and paid attention to. Persons from dominant groups who speak for others are often treated as authenticating presences that confer legitimacy and credibility on the demands of subjugated speakers; such speaking for others does nothing to disrupt the discursive hierarchies that operate in public spaces. For this reason, the work of privileged authors who speak on behalf of the oppressed is coming more and more under criticism from members of those oppressed groups themselves.[5]

As social theorists we are authorized by virtue of our academic positions to develop theories that express and encompass the ideas, needs, and goals of others. However, we must begin to ask ourselves whether this is ever a legitimate authority, and if so, what are the criteria for legitimacy? In particular, is it ever valid to speak for others who are unlike me or who are less privileged than me?

We might try to delimit this problem as only arising when a more privileged person speaks for a less privileged one. In this case, we might say that I should only speak for groups of which I am a member. But this does not tell us how groups themselves should be delimited. For example, can a white woman speak for all women simply by virtue of being a woman? If not, how narrowly should we draw the categories? The complexity and multiplicity of group identifications could result in "communities" composed of single individuals. Moreover, the concept of groups assumes specious notions about clear-cut boundaries and "pure" identities. I am a Panamanian-American and a person of mixed ethnicity and race: half white/Angla and half Panamanian mestiza. The criterion of group identity leaves many unanswered questions for a person such as myself, since I have membership in many conflicting groups but my membership in all of them is problematic. On what basis can we justify a decision to demarcate groups and define membership in one way rather than another? For all of these reasons it quickly becomes apparent that no easy solution to the problem of speaking for others can be found by simply restricting the practice to speaking for groups of which one is a member.

Adopting the position that one should only speak for oneself raises similarly difficult questions. For example, we might ask, if I don't speak for those less privileged than myself, am I abandoning my political responsibility to speak out against oppression, a responsibility incurred by the very fact of my privilege? If I should not speak for others, should I restrict myself to following their lead uncritically? Is my greatest contribution to *move over and get out of the way?* And if so, what is the best way to do this—to keep silent or to deconstruct my discourse?

The answers to these questions will certainly differ significantly depending on who is asking them. While some of us may want to undermine, for example, the U.S. government's practice of speaking for the "third world," we may *not* want to undermine someone such as Rigoberta Menchu's ability to speak for Guatemalan Indians.[6] So the question arises as to whether all instances of speaking for should be condemned and, if not, how we can justify a position that would repudiate some speakers while accepting others.

In order to answer these questions we need to become clearer on the epistemological and metaphysical issues involved in the articulation of the problem of speaking for others, issues that most often remain implicit. I will attempt to make these issues clear, and then I will turn to discuss some of the possible responses to the problem before advancing a provisional, procedural one of my own. But first I need to explain further my framing of the problem.

In the examples used above, there may appear to be a conflation between the issue of speaking for others and the issue of speaking about others. This conflation was intentional on my part. There is an ambiguity in the two phrases: when one is speaking for another one may be describing their situation and thus also speaking about them. In fact, it may be impossible to speak for another without simultaneously conferring information about them. Similarly, when one is speaking about another, or simply trying to describe their situation or some aspect of it, one may also be speaking in place of them, i.e., speaking for them. One may be speaking about another as an advocate or a messenger if the person cannot speak for herself. Thus I would maintain that if the practice of speaking for others is problematic, so too must be the practice of speaking about others, since it is difficult to distinguish speaking about from speaking for in all cases.[7] Moreover, if we accept the premise stated above that a speaker's location has an epistemically significant impact on that speaker's claims, then both the practice of speaking for and of speaking about raise similar issues. I will try to focus my remarks in this paper on the practice of speaking for others, but it will be impossible to keep this practice neatly disentangled from the practice of speaking about.

If "speaking about" is also involved here, however, the entire edifice of the "crisis of representation" must be connected as well. In both the practice of speaking for as well as the practice of speaking about others, I am engaging in the act of representing the other's needs, goals, situation, and in fact, *who they are*. I am representing them *as* such and such, or in post-structuralist terms, I am participating in the construction of their subject positions. This act of representation cannot be understood as founded on an act of discovery wherein I discover their true selves and then simply relate my discovery. I will take it as a given that such representations are in every case mediated and the product of interpretation (which is connected to the claim that a speaker's location has epistemic salience). And it is precisely because of the mediated character of all representations that some persons have rejected on political as well as epistemic grounds the legitimacy of speaking for others.

And once we pose it as a problem of representation, we see that, not only are speaking for and speaking about analytically close, so too are the practices of speaking for others and speaking for myself. For, in speaking for myself, I am also representing my self in a certain way, as occupying a specific subject-position, having certain characteristics and not others, and so on. In speaking for myself, I (momentarily) create my self—just as much as when I speak for others I create their selves—in the sense that I create a public, discursive self, a self which is more unified than any subjective experience can support, and this public self will in most cases have an effect on the self experienced as interiority.

The point is that a kind of representation occurs in all cases of speaking for, whether I am speaking for myself or for others, that this representation is never a simple act of discovery, and that it will most likely have an impact on the individual so represented.

Although clearly, then, the issue of speaking for others is connected to the issue of representation generally, the former I see as a very specific subset of the latter. I am skeptical that general accounts of representation are adequate to the complexity and specificity of the problem of speaking for others.

Finally, the way I have articulated this problem may imply that individuals make conscious choices about their discursive practice free of ideology and the constraints of material reality. This is not what I wish to imply. The problem is a social one, the options available to us are socially constructed, and the practices we engage in cannot be understood as simply the results of autonomous individual choice. Yet to replace both "I" and "we" with a passive voice that erases agency results in an erasure of responsibility and accountability for one's speech, an erasure I would strenuously argue against (there is too little responsibility-taking already in Western practice!). When we sit down to write, or get up to speak, we experience ourselves as making choices. We may experience hesitation from fear of being criticized or from fear of exacerbating a problem we would like to remedy, or we may experience a resolve to speak despite existing obstacles, but we experience in many cases having the possibility to speak or not to speak. On the one hand, a theory that explains this experience as involving autonomous choices free of material structures would be false and ideological, but on the other hand, if we do not acknowledge the activity of choice and the experience of individual doubt, we are denying a reality of our experiential lives.[8] So I see the argument of this paper as addressing that small space of discursive agency we all experience, however multilayered, fictional, and constrained it in fact is.

The possibility of speaking for others bears crucially on the possibility of political effectivity. Both collective action and coalitions would seem to require the possibility of speaking for. Yet influential postmodernists such as Gilles Deleuze have characterized as "absolutely fundamental: the indignity of speaking for others,"[9] and, as already mentioned, important feminist theorists such as Joyce Trebilcot have renounced the practice for themselves, thus causing many people to question its validity. I want to explore what is at stake in rejecting or validating speaking for others as a discursive practice. But first, we must become clearer on the epistemological and metaphysical claims implicit in the articulation of the problem.

A plethora of sources have argued in this century that the neutrality of the theorizer can no longer, can never again, be sustained, even for a moment. Critical theory, discourses of empowerment, psychoanalytic theory, post-structuralism, feminist and anticolonialist theories have all concurred on this point. Who is speaking to whom turns out to be as important for meaning and truth as what is said; in fact what is said turns out to change according to who is speaking and who is listening. Following Foucault, I will call these "rituals of speaking" to identify discursive practices of speaking or writing that involve not only the text or utterance but their position within a social space that includes the persons involved in, acting upon, and/or affected by the words. Two elements within these rituals will deserve our attention: the positionality or location of the speaker and the discursive context. We can take the latter to refer to the connections and relations of involvement between the utterance/text and other utterances and texts as well as the material practices in the relevant environment, which should not be confused with an environment spatially adjacent to the particular discursive event.

Rituals of speaking are constitutive of meaning, the meaning of the words spoken as well as the meaning of the event. This claim requires us to shift the ontology of meaning from its location in a text or utterance to a larger space, a space that includes the text or utterance but also includes the discursive context. And an important implication of this claim is that meaning must be understood as plural and shifting, since a single text can engender diverse meanings given diverse contexts. Not only what is emphasized, noticed, and how it is understood will be affected by the location of both speaker and hearer, but the truth-value or epistemic status will also be affected.

For example, in many situations when a woman speaks the presumption is against her; when a man speaks he is usually taken seriously (unless his speech patterns mark him as socially inferior by dominant standards). When writers from oppressed races and nationalities have insisted that all writing is political, the claim has been dismissed as foolish or grounded in *ressentiment* or it is simply ignored; when prestigious European philosophers say that all writing is political, it is taken up as a new and original "truth" (Judith Wilson calls this "the intellectual equivalent of the 'cover record'").[10] The rituals of speaking that involve the location of speaker and listeners affect whether a claim is taken as true, well reasoned, a compelling argument, or a significant idea. Thus, how what is said gets heard depends on who says it, and who says it will affect the style and language in which it is stated, which will in turn affect its perceived significance (for specific hearers). The discursive style in which some European post-structuralists have made the claim that all writing is political marks it as important and likely to be true for a certain (powerful) milieu; whereas the style in which African-American writers made the same claim marked their speech as dismissable in the eyes of the same milieu.

This point might be conceded by those who admit to the political mutability of *interpretation*, but they might continue to maintain that *truth* is a different matter altogether. And they would be right that the establishment of locations' effect on meaning and even on whether something is *taken* as true within a particular discursive context does not entail that the "actual" truth of the claim is contingent upon its context. However, this objection presupposes a particular conception of truth, one in which the truth of a statement can be distinguished from its interpretation and its acceptance. Such a concept would require truth to be independent of the speakers' or listeners' embodied and perspectival location (except in the trivial case of a speaker's indexical statements, e.g., "I am now sitting down").

Thus, the question of whether location bears simply on what is taken to be true or what is really true, and whether such a distinction can be upheld, involves the very difficult problem of the meaning of truth. In the history of Western philosophy, there have existed multiple, competing definitions and ontologies of truth: correspondence, idealist, pragmatist, coherentist, and consensual notions. The dominant view has been that truth represents a relationship of correspondence between a proposition and an extra-discursive reality. On this view, truth is about a realm completely independent of human action, and expresses things "as they are in themselves," that is, free of human interpretation.

Arguably since Kant, more obviously since Hegel, it has been widely accepted that an understanding of truth which requires it to be free of human interpretation leads inexorably to skepticism, since it makes truth inaccessible by definition. This created an impetus to reconfigure the ontology of truth, or its locus, from a place outside human interpretation to one within it. Hegel, for example, understood truth as an "identity in difference" between subjective and objective elements. Thus, within the variety of views working in the Hegelian aftermath, so-called subjective elements, or the historically specific conditions in which human knowledge occurs, are no longer rendered irrelevant or even obstacles to truth.

On a coherentist account of truth, for example, which is held by such philosophers as Rorty, Donald Davidson, Quine, and (I would argue) Gadamer and Foucault, truth is defined as an emergent property of converging discursive and nondiscursive elements, when there exists a specific form of integration between these elements in a particular event. Such a view has no necessary relationship to idealism, but it allows us to understand how the social location of the speaker can be said to bear on truth. The speaker's location is one of the elements that converge to produce meaning and thus to determine epistemic validity.[11]

Let me return now to the formulation of the problem of speaking for others. There are two premises implied by the articulation of the problem, and unpacking these should advance our understanding of the issues involved.

Premise 1. The "ritual of speaking" (as defined above) in which an utterance is located, always bears on meaning and truth such that there is no possibility of rendering positionality, location, or context irrelevant to content.

The phrase "bears on" here should indicate some variable amount of influence short of determination or fixing.

One important implication of this first premise is that we can no longer determine the validity of a given instance of speaking for others simply by asking whether or not the speaker has done sufficient research to justify their claims. Adequate research will be a necessary but insufficient criterion of evaluation.

Now let us look at the second premise.

Premise 2. All contexts and locations are differentially related in complex ways to structures of oppression. Given that truth is connected to politics, these political differences between locations will produce epistemic differences as well.

The claim here that "truth is connected to politics" follows necessarily from Premise 1. Rituals of speaking are politically constituted by power relations of domination, exploitation, and subordination. Who is speaking, who is spoken of, and who listens is a result, as well as an act, of political struggle. Simply put, the discursive context is a political arena. To the extent that this context bears on meaning, and meaning is in some sense the object of truth, we cannot make an epistemic evaluation of the claim without simultaneously assessing the politics of the situation.

According to the first premise, though we cannot maintain a neutral voice, we may at least all claim the right and legitimacy to speak. But the second premise suggests that some voices may be disauthorized on grounds that are simultaneously political and epistemic. Any statement will invoke the structures of power allied with the social location of the speaker, aside from the speaker's intentions or attempts to avoid such invocations.

The conjunction of Premises 1 and 2 suggests that the speaker loses some portion of their control over the meaning and truth of their utterance. Given that the context of hearers is partially determinant, the speaker is not the master or mistress of the situation. Speakers may seek to regain control here by taking into account the context of their speech, but they can never know everything about this context, and with written and electronic communication it is becoming increasingly difficult to know anything at all about the context of reception.

This loss of control may be taken by some speakers to mean that no speaker can be held accountable for their discursive actions. The meaning of any discursive event will be shifting and plural, fragmented, and even inconsistent. As it ranges over diverse spaces and transforms in the mind of its recipients according to their different horizons of interpretation, the effective control of the speaker over the meanings they put in motion may seem negligible. However, a *partial* loss of control does not entail a *complete* loss of accountability. And moreover, the better we understand the trajectories by which meanings proliferate, the more likely we can increase, though always only partially, our ability to direct the interpretations and transformations our speech undergoes. When I acknowledge that the listener's social location will affect the meaning of my words, I can more effectively generate the meaning I intend. Paradoxically, the view that holds the speaker or author of a speech act as solely responsible for its meanings ensures their least effective determinacy over the meanings that are produced.

We do not need to posit the existence of fully conscious acts or containable, fixed meanings in order to hold that speakers can alter their discursive practices and be held accountable for at least some of the effects of these practices. It is a false dilemma to pose the choice here as one between no accountability or complete causal power. The truth, as usual, lies somewhere in between.

In the next section I shall consider some possible responses to the problem of speaking for others.

The first response I will consider is to argue that the formulation of the problem with speaking for others involves a retrograde, metaphysically insupportable essentialism that assumes one can read off the truth and meaning of *what* one says straight from the discursive context. This response I will call the "Charge of Reductionism" response, because it argues that a sort of reductionist theory of justification (or evaluation) is entailed by premises 1 and 2. Such a reductionist theory might, for example, reduce evaluation to a political assessment of the speaker's location where that location is seen as an insurmountable essence that fixes one, as if one's feet are superglued to a spot on the sidewalk.

After I vehemently defended Barbara Christian's article, "The Race for Theory," recently, a male friend who had a different evaluation of the piece couldn't help raising the possibility of whether a sort of apologetics structured my response, motivated by a desire to valorize African-American writing against all odds. His question in effect raised the issue of the reductionist/essentialist theory of justification I just described.

I, too, would reject reductionist theories of justification and essentialist accounts of what it means to have a location. To say that location *bears* on meaning and truth is not the same as saying that location *determines* meaning and truth. And location is not a fixed essence absolutely authorizing one's speech in the way that God's favor absolutely authorized the speech of Moses. Location and positionality should not be conceived as one-dimensional or static, but as multiple and with varying degrees of mobility.[12] What it means, then, to speak from or within a group and/or a location is immensely complex. To the extent that location is not a fixed essence, and to the extent that there is an uneasy, underdetermined, and contested relationship between location on the one hand and meaning and truth on the other, we cannot reduce evaluation of meaning and truth to a simple identification of the speaker's location.

Neither Premise 1 nor Premise 2 entail reductionism or essentialism. They argue for the relevance of location, not its singular power of determination. Since they do not specify how we are to understand the concept of location, it can certainly be given a nonessentialist meaning.

While the "Charge of Reductionism" response has been popular among academic theorists, a second response I will call the "Retreat" response has been popular among some sections of the U.S. feminist movement. This response is simply to retreat from all practices of speaking for and assert that one can only know one's own narrow individual experience and one's "own truth" and can never make claims beyond this. This response is motivated in part by the desire to recognize difference, e.g., different priorities, without organizing these differences into hierarchies.

Now, sometimes I think this is the proper response to the problem of speaking for others, depending on who is making it. We certainly want to encourage a more receptive listening on the part of the discursively privileged and discourage presumptuous and oppressive practices of speaking for. But a retreat from speaking for will not result in an increase in receptive listening in all cases; it may result merely in a retreat into a narcissistic yuppie lifestyle in which a privileged person takes no responsibility for her society whatsoever. She may even feel justified in exploiting her privileged capacity for personal happiness at the expense of others on the grounds that she has no alternative.

Opting for the "Retreat" response, however, is not always a thinly veiled excuse to avoid the difficult work of political resistance and reconstruction. Sometimes it is the result of a desire to engage in political work but without practicing what might be called discursive imperialism.

The major problem with such a retreat is that it significantly undercuts the possibility of political effectivity. There are numerous examples of the practice of speaking for others that have been politically efficacious in advancing the needs of those spoken for, from Rigoberta Menchu to Edward Said and Steven Biko. Menchu's efforts to speak for the thirty-three Indian communities facing genocide in Guatemala have helped to raise money for the revolution and bring pressure against the Guatemalan and U.S. governments, who have committed the massacres in collusion. The point is not that for some speakers the danger of speaking for others does not arise, but that in some cases certain political effects can be garnered in no other way.

Joyce Trebilcot's version of the retreat response needs to be looked at separately because she agrees that an absolute prohibition of speaking for would undermine political effectiveness. She applies her prohibition against the practice only within a lesbian feminist community. So it might be argued that the retreat from speaking for others can be maintained without sacrificing political effectivity if it is restricted to particular discursive spaces.

Why might one advocate such a retreat? Trebilcot holds that speaking for and attempting to persuade others inflicts a kind of discursive violence on the other and her beliefs. Given that interpretations and meanings are discursive constructions made by embodied speakers, Trebilcot worries that attempting to persuade or speak for another will cut off that person's ability or willingness to engage in the constructive act of developing meaning. Since no embodied speaker can produce more than a partial account, everyone's account needs to be encouraged (that is, within a specified community, which for Trebilcot is the lesbian community).

There is much in Trebilcot's discussion with which I agree. I certainly agree that in some instances speaking for others constitutes a violence and should be stopped. But there remains a problem with the view that, even within a restricted, supportive community, the practice of speaking for others can be abandoned.

This problem is that Trebilcot's position, as well as a more general retreat position, presumes an ontological configuration of the discursive context that simply does not obtain. In particular, it assumes that one *can* retreat into one's discrete location and make claims entirely and singularly within that location that do not range over others, that one can disentangle oneself from the implicating networks between one's discursive practices and others' locations, situations, and practices. In other words, the claim that I can speak only for myself assumes the autonomous conception of the self in Classical Liberal theory—that I am unconnected to others in my authentic self or that I can achieve an autonomy from others given certain conditions. But there is no neutral place to stand free and clear in which one's words do not prescriptively affect or mediate the experience of others, nor is there a way to decisively demarcate a boundary between one's location and all others. Even a complete retreat from speech is of course not neutral, since it allows the continued dominance of current discourses and acts by omission to reinforce their dominance.

As my practices are made possible by events spatially far from my body, so too my own practices make possible or impossible practices of others. The declaration that I "speak only for myself" has the sole effect of allowing me to avoid responsibility and accountability for my effects on others; it cannot literally erase those effects.

Let me offer an illustration of this. The feminist movement in the U.S. has spawned many kinds of support groups for women with various needs: rape victims, incest survivors, battered wives, and so forth, and some of these groups have been structured around the view that each survivor must come to her own "truth," which ranges only over oneself and has no bearing on others. Thus, one woman's experience of sexual assault, its effect on her, and her interpretation of it should not be taken as a universal generalization to which others must subsume or conform their experience. This view works only up to a point. To the extent it recognizes irreducible differences in the way people respond to various traumas, and is sensitive to the genuinely variable ways in which women can heal themselves, it represents real progress beyond the homogeneous, universalizing approach that sets out one road for all to follow. However, it is an illusion to think that, even in the safe space of a support group, a member of the group can, for example, trivialize brother-sister incest as "sex play" without profoundly harming someone else in the group who is trying to maintain her realistic assessment of her brother's sexual activities with her as a harmful assault against his adult rationalization that "well, for me it was just harmless fun." Even if the speaker offers a dozen caveats about her views as restricted to her location, she will still affect the other woman's ability to conceptualize and interpret her experience and her response to it. And this is simply because we cannot neatly separate off our mediating praxis that interprets and constructs our experiences from the praxis of others. We are collectively caught in an intricate, delicate web in which each action I take, discursive or otherwise, pulls on, breaks off, or maintains the tension in many strands of a web in which others find themselves moving also. When I speak for myself, I am constructing a possible self, a way to be in the world, and, whether I intend to or not, I am offering that to others, as one possible way to be.

Thus, the attempt to avoid the problematic of speaking for by retreating into an individualist realm is based on an illusion, well supported in the individualist ideology of the West, that a self is not constituted by multiple intersecting discourses but consists in a unified whole capable of autonomy from others. It is an illusion that I can separate from others to such an extent that I can avoid affecting them. This may be the intention of my speech, and even its meaning if we take that to be the formal entailments of the sentences, but it will not be the effect of the speech, and therefore cannot capture the speech in its reality as a discursive practice. When I "speak for myself" I am participating in the creation and reproduction of discourses through which my own and other selves are constituted.

A further problem with the "Retreat" response is that it may be motivated by a desire to find a method or practice immune from criticism. If I speak only for myself it may appear that I am immune from criticism because I am not making any claims that describe others or prescribe actions for them. If I am only speaking for myself I have no responsibility for being true to your experience or needs.

But surely it is both morally and politically objectionable to structure one's actions around the desire to avoid criticism, especially if this outweighs other questions of effectivity. In some cases perhaps the motivation is not so much to avoid criticism as to avoid errors, and the person believes that the only way to avoid errors is to avoid all speaking for others. However, errors are unavoidable in theoretical inquiry as well as political struggle, and they moreover often make contributions. The desire to find an absolute means to avoid making errors comes perhaps not from a desire to advance collective goals but a desire for personal mastery, to establish a privileged discursive position wherein one cannot be undermined or challenged and thus is master of the situation. From such a position one's own location and positionality would not require constant interrogation and critical reflection; one would not have to constantly engage in this emotionally troublesome endeavor and would be immune from the interrogation of others. Such a desire for mastery and immunity must be resisted.

A final response to the problem that I will consider occurs in Gayatri Chakravorty Spivak's rich essay "Can the Subaltern Speak?"[13] In Spivak's essay, the central issue is an essentialist, authentic conception of the self and of experience. She criticizes the "self-abnegating intellectual" pose that Foucault and Deleuze adopt when they reject speaking for others on the grounds that it assumes the oppressed can transparently represent their own true interests. According to Spivak, Foucault and Deleuze's position serves only to conceal the actual authorizing power of the retreating intellectuals, who in their very retreat help to consolidate a particular conception of experience (as transparent and self-knowing). Thus, to promote "listening to" as opposed to speaking for essentializes the oppressed as nonideologically constructed subjects. But Spivak is also critical of speaking for which engages in dangerous representations. In the end Spivak prefers a "speaking to," in which the intellectual neither abnegates his or her discursive role nor presumes an authenticity of the oppressed but still allows for the possibility that the oppressed will produce a "countersentence" that can then suggest a new historical narrative.

This response is the one with which I have the most agreement. We should strive to create wherever possible the conditions for dialogue and the practice of speaking with and to rather than speaking for others. If the dangers of speaking for others result from the possibility of misrepresentation, expanding one's own authority and privilege, and a generally imperialist speaking ritual, then speaking with and to can lessen these dangers.

Often the possibility of dialogue is left unexplored or inadequately pursued by more privileged persons. Spaces in which it may seem as if it is impossible to engage in dialogic encounters need to be transformed in order to do so, such as classrooms, hospitals, workplaces, welfare agencies, universities, institutions for international development and aid, and governments. It has long been noted that existing communication technologies have the potential to produce these kinds of interaction even though research and development teams have not found it advantageous under capitalism to do so.

Spivak's arguments, however, suggest that the simple solution is not for the oppressed or less privileged to be able to speak for themselves, since their speech will not necessarily be either liberatory or reflective of their "true interests," if such exist. I would agree with her here, yet it can still be argued, as I think she herself concludes, that ignoring the subaltern's or oppressed person's speech is "to continue the imperialist project."[14] But if a privileging of the oppressed's speech cannot be made on the grounds that its content will necessarily be liberatory, it can be made on the grounds of the very act of speaking itself, which constitutes a subject that challenges and subverts the opposition between the knowing agent and the object of knowledge, an opposition that serves as a key player in the reproduction of imperialist modes of discourse. The problem with speaking for others exists in the very structure of discursive practice, irrespective of its content, and therefore it is this structure itself that needs alteration.

However, while there is much theoretical and practical work to be done to develop such alternatives, the practice of speaking for others remains the best option in some existing situations. An absolute retreat weakens political effectivity, is based on a metaphysical illusion, and often effects only an obscuring of the intellectual's power. There can be no complete or definitive solution to the problem of speaking for others, but there is a possibility that its dangers can be decreased. The remainder of this paper will try to contribute toward developing that possibility.

In rejecting a general retreat from speaking for, I am not advocating a return to an unself-conscious appropriation of the other, but rather that anyone who speaks for others should only do so out of a concrete analysis of the particular power relations and discursive effects involved. I want to develop this point through elucidating four sets of interrogatory practices meant to help evaluate possible and actual instances of speaking for. In list form they may appear to resemble an algorithm, as if we could plug in an instance of speaking for and factor out an analysis and evaluation. However, they are meant only to suggest a list of the questions that should be asked concerning any such discursive practice. These are by no means original: they have been learned and practiced by many activists and theorists.

    1. The impetus to speak must be carefully analyzed and, in many cases (certainly for academics!), fought against. This may seem an odd way to begin discussing how to speak for, but the point is that the impetus to *always* be the speaker and to speak in all situations must be seen for what it is: a desire for mastery and domination. If one's immediate impulse is to teach rather than listen to a less-privileged speaker, one should resist that impulse long enough to interrogate it carefully. Some of us have been taught that by right of having the dominant gender, class, race, letters after our name, or some other criterion, we are more likely to have the truth. Others have been taught the opposite, and will speak haltingly, with apologies, if they speak at all.[15]

    At the same time, we have to acknowledge that the very decision to "move over" or retreat can occur only from a position of privilege. Those who are not in a position of speaking at all cannot retreat from an action they do not employ. Moreover, making the decision for oneself whether or not to retreat is an extension or application of privilege, not an abdication of it. Still, it is sometimes called for.

    2. We must also interrogate the bearing of our location and context on what it is we are saying, and this should be an explicit part of every

serious discursive practice we engage in. Constructing hypotheses about the possible connections between our location and our words is one way to begin. This procedure would be most successful if engaged in collectively with others, by which aspects of our location less highlighted in our own minds might be revealed to us.[16]

One deformed way in which this is too often carried out is when speakers offer up in the spirit of "honesty" autobiographical information about themselves usually at the beginning of their discourse as a kind of disclaimer. This is meant to acknowledge their own understanding that they are speaking from a specified, embodied location without pretense to a transcendental truth. But as Maria Lugones and others have forcefully argued, such an act serves no good end when it is used as a disclaimer against one's ignorance or errors and is made without critical interrogation of the bearing of such an autobiography on what is about to be said. It leaves for the listeners all the real work that needs to be done. For example, if a middle-class white man were to begin a speech by sharing with us this autobiographical information and then using it as a kind of apologetics for any limitations of his speech, this would leave those of us in the audience who do not share his social location to do the work by ourselves of translating his terms into our own, apprising the applicability of his analysis to our diverse situations, and determining the substantive relevance of his location on his claims. This is simply what less-privileged persons have always had to do for ourselves when reading the history of philosophy, literature, etc., which makes the task of appropriating these discourses more difficult and time-consuming (and alienation more likely to result). Simple unanalyzed disclaimers do not improve on this familiar situation and may even make it worse to the extent that by offering such information the speaker may feel even more authorized to speak and be accorded more authority by his peers.

3. Speaking should always carry with it an accountability and responsibility for what one says. To whom one is accountable is a political/epistemological choice contestable, contingent, and, as Donna Haraway says, constructed through the process of discursive action. What this entails in practice is a serious and sincere commitment to remain open to criticism and to attempt actively, attentively, and sensitively to "hear" the criticism (understand it). A quick impulse to reject criticism must make one wary.

4. Here is my central point. In order to evaluate attempts to speak

for others in particular instances, we need to analyze the probable or actual effects of the words on the discursive and material context. One cannot simply look at the location of the speaker or her credentials to speak; nor can one look merely at the propositional content of the speech; one must also look at where the speech goes and what it does there.

Looking merely at the content of a set of claims without looking at their effects cannot produce an adequate or even meaningful evaluation of it, and this is partly because the notion of a content separate from effects does not hold up. The content of the claim, or its meaning, emerges in interaction between words and hearers within a very specific historical situation. Given this, we have to pay careful attention to the discursive arrangement in order to understand the full meaning of any given discursive event. For example, in a situation where a well-meaning first-world person is speaking for a person or group in the third world, the very discursive arrangement may reinscribe the "hierarchy of civilizations" view where the U.S. lands squarely at the top. This effect occurs because the speaker is positioned as authoritative and empowered, as the knowledgeable subject, while the group in the third world is reduced, merely because of the structure of the speaking practice, to an object and victim that must be championed from afar, thus disempowered. Though the speaker may be trying to materially improve the situation of some lesser-privileged group, one of the effects of her discourse is to reinforce racist, imperialist conceptions and perhaps also to further silence the lesser-privileged group's own ability to speak and be heard.[17] This shows us why it is so important to reconceptualize discourse, as Foucault recommends, as an *event*, which includes speaker, words, hearers, location, language, and so on.

All such evaluations produced in this way will be of necessity *indexed*. That is, they will obtain for a very specific location and cannot be taken as universal. This simply follows from the fact that the evaluations will be based on the specific elements of historical discursive context, location of speakers and hearers, and so forth. When any of these elements is changed, a new evaluation is called for.

Our ability to assess the effects of a given discursive event is limited; our ability to predict these effects is even more difficult. When meaning is plural and deferred, we can never hope to know the totality of effects. Still, we can know some of the effects our speech generates: I can find out, for example, that the people I spoke for are angry that I did so or appreciative. By learning as much as possible about the context of reception I can increase my ability to discern at least some of the possible effects. This mandates incorporating a more dialogic approach to speaking, that would include learning from and about the domains of discourse my words will affect.

Let me illustrate the implications of this fourth point by applying it to the examples I gave at the beginning. In the case of Anne Cameron, if the effects of her books are truly disempowering for Native women, they are counterproductive to Cameron's own stated intentions, and she should indeed "move over." In the case of the white male theorist who discussed architecture instead of the politics of postmodernism, the effect of his refusal was that he offered no contribution to an important issue and all of us there lost an opportunity to discuss and explore it.

Now let me turn to the example of George Bush. When Bush claimed that Noriega is a corrupt dictator who stands in the way of democracy in Panama, he repeated a claim that had been made almost word for word by the opposition movement in Panama. Yet the effects of the two statements are vastly different because the meaning of the claim changes radically depending on who states it. When the President of the United States stands before the world passing judgment on a third-world government, criticizing it on the basis of corruption and a lack of democracy, the immediate effect of *this* statement, as opposed to the opposition's, is to reinforce the prominent Anglo view that Latin American corruption is the primary cause of the region's poverty and lack of democracy, that the U.S. is on the side of democracy in the region, and that the U.S. opposes corruption and tyranny. Thus, the effect of a U.S. president's speaking for Latin America in this way is to reconsolidate U.S. imperialism by obscuring its true role in the region in torturing and murdering hundreds and thousands of people who have tried to bring democratic and progressive governments into existence. And this effect will continue until the U.S. government admits its history of international mass murder and radically alters it foreign policy.

CONCLUSION

This issue is complicated by the variable way in which the importance of the source, or location of the author, can be understood, a topic alluded to earlier. On one view, the author of a text is its "owner" and "originator" credited with creating its ideas and with being their authoritative interpreter. On another view, the original speaker or writer is no more privileged than any other person who articulates those views, and in fact the "author" cannot be identified in a strict sense because the concept of author is an ideological construction many abstractions removed from the way in which ideas emerge and become material forces.[18] Now, does this latter position mean that the source or locatedness of the author is irrelevant?

It need not entail this conclusion, though it might in some formulations. We can de-privilege the "original" author and reconceptualize ideas as traversing (almost) freely in a discursive space, available from many locations, and without a clearly identifiable originary track, and yet retain our sense that source remains relevant to effect. Our meta-theory of authorship does not preclude the material reality that in discursive spaces there is a speaker or writer credited as the author of their utterances, or that for example the feminist appropriation of the concept "patriarchy" gets tied to Kate Millett, a white Anglo feminist, or that the term feminism itself has been and is associated with a Western origin. These associations have an effect, an effect of producing distrust on the part of some third-world nationalists, an effect of reinscribing semi-conscious imperialist attitudes on the part of some first-world feminists. These are not the only possible effects, and some of the effects may not be pernicious, but all the effects must be taken into account when evaluating the discourse of "patriarchy."

The emphasis on effects should not imply, therefore, that an examination of the speaker's location is any way less crucial. This latter examination might be called a kind of genealogy. In this sense a genealogy involves asking how a position or view is mediated and constituted through and within the conjunction and conflict of historical, cultural, economic, psychological, and sexual practices. But it seems to me that the importance of the source of a view, and the importance of doing a genealogy, should be subsumed within an overall analysis of effects, making the central question what the effects are of the view on material and discursive practices through which it traverses and the particular configuration of power relations emergent from these. Source is relevant only to the extent that it has an impact on effect. As Gayatri Spivak likes to say, the invention of the telephone by a Euro-American upper-class male in no way preempts its being put to the use of an anti-imperialist revolution.

In conclusion, I would stress that the practice of speaking for others is often born of a desire for mastery, to privilege oneself as the one who more correctly understands the truth about another's situation or as one who can champion a just cause and thus achieve glory and praise. And the effect of the practice of speaking for others is often, though not always, erasure and a reinscription of sexual, national, and other kinds of hierarchies. I hope that this analysis will contribute toward rather than diminish the important discussion going on today about how to develop strategies for a more equitable and just distribution of the ability to speak and be heard. But this development should not be taken as an absolute disauthorization of all practices of speaking for. It is not always the case that when others unlike me speak for me I have ended up worse off, or that when we speak for others they end up worse off. Sometimes, as Loyce Stewart has argued, we do need a "messenger" to advocate for our needs.

Certainly, the key motivation of feminist scholarship has been precisely this: to provide a more accurate depiction than was ever given by male scholarship of the lives of all women, and to advocate more effectively for all women, thus enhancing the likelihood that the role of advocate will become unnecessary. Clearly this goal has been achieved in at least some instances, even across differences of power and privilege.

The source of a claim or discursive practice in suspect motives or maneuvers or in privileged social locations, I have argued, though it is always relevant, cannot be sufficient to repudiate it. We must ask further questions about its effects, questions that amount to the following: will it enable the empowerment of oppressed peoples?

NOTES

I am indebted to the following for their substantial help on this paper: Eastern Society for Women in Philosophy, the Central New York Women Philosopher's Group, Loyce Stewart, Richard Schmitt, Sandra Bartky, Laurence Thomas, Leslie Bender, Robyn Wiegman, Anita Canizares Molina, and Felicity Nussbaum.

1. See Lee Maracle, "Moving Over," in *Trivia* 14 (Spring 1989): 9–10.
2. Joyce Trebilcot, "Dyke Methods," *Hypatia* 3, no. 2 (Summer 1988): 1. Trebilcot is explaining here her own reasoning for rejecting these practices, but she is not advocating that other women join her in this. Thus, her argument does not fall into a self-referential incoherence.
3. Trinh T. Minh-ha, *Woman, Native, Other: Writing Postcoloniality and*

Feminism (Bloomington: Indiana University Press, 1989), 65, 67. For examples of anthropologist's concern with this issue see *Writing Culture: The Poetics and Politics of Ethnography*, ed. James Clifford and George E. Marcus (Berkeley: University of California Press, 1986); James Clifford, "On Ethnographic Authority," *Representations* 1, no. 2 (1983): 118–46; *Anthropology as Cultural Critique*, ed. George Marcus and Michael Fischer (Chicago: University of Chicago Press, 1986); Paul Rabinow, "Discourse and Power: On the Limits of Ethnographic Texts," *Dialectical Anthropology* 10, nos. 1, 2 (July 1985): 1–14.

4. To be privileged here will mean to be in a more favorable, mobile, and dominant position vis-à-vis the structures of power/knowledge in a society. Thus privilege carries with it, e.g., presumption in one's favor when one speaks. Certain races, nationalities, genders, sexualities, and classes confer privilege, but a single individual (perhaps most individuals) may enjoy privilege in respect to some parts of their identity and a lack of privilege in respect to other parts. Therefore, privilege must always be indexed to specific relationships as well as to specific locations.

  The term privilege is not meant to include positions of discursive power achieved through merit, but in any case these are rarely pure. In other words, some persons are accorded discursive authority because they are respected leaders or because they are teachers in a classroom and know more about the material at hand. So often, of course, the authority of such persons based on their merit combines with the authority they may enjoy by virtue of their having the dominant gender, race, class, or sexuality. It is the latter sources of authority that I am referring to by the term "privilege."

5. See also Maria Lugones and Elizabeth Spelman, "Have We Got a Theory for You! Cultural Imperialism, Feminist Theory and the Demand for the Women's Voice," *Women's Studies International Forum* 6, no. 6 (1983): 573–81. In their paper Lugones and Spelman explore the way in which the "demand for the women's voice" disempowered women of color by not attending to the differences in privilege within the category of women, resulting in a privileging of white women's voices only. They explore the effects this has had on the making of theory within feminism, and attempt to find "ways of talking or being talked about that are helpful, illuminating, empowering, respectful" (25). This essay takes inspiration from theirs and is meant to continue their discussion.

6. See her *I . . . Rigoberta Menchu*, ed. Elisabeth Burgos-Debray, trans. Ann Wright (London: Verso, 1984). (The use of the term "Indian" here follows Menchu's use.)

7. E.g., if it is the case that no "descriptive" discourse is normative- or value-free, then no discourse is free of some kind of advocacy, and all speaking about will involve speaking for someone, ones, or something.

8. Another distinction that might be made is between different material practices of speaking for: giving a speech, writing an essay or book, making a movie or television program, as well as hearing, reading, watching, and so

on. I will not address the possible differences that arise from these different practices, and will address myself to the (fictional) "generic" practice of speaking for.

9. Deleuze, in a conversation with Foucault, "Intellectuals and Power," in *Language, Counter-Memory, Practice,* ed. Donald Bouchard, trans. Donald Bouchard and Sherry Simon (Ithaca: Cornell University Press, 1977), 209.

10. See her "Down to the Crossroads: The Art of Alison Saar," *Third Text* 10 (Spring 1990): 25–44, for a discussion of this phenomenon in the art world, espec. 36. See also Barbara Christian, "The Race for Theory," *Feminist Studies* 14, no. 1 (Spring 1988): 67–79; and Henry Louis Gates, Jr., "Authority, (White) Power and the (Black) Critic; It's All Greek to Me," *Cultural Critique* 7 (Fall 1987): 19–46, espec. 34.

11. I know that my insistence on using the word "truth" swims upstream of current postmodernist orthodoxies. This insistence is not based on a commitment to transparent accounts of representation or a correspondence theory of truth, but on my belief that the demarcation between epistemically better and worse claims continues to operate (indeed, it is inevitable), and that what happens when we eschew all epistemological issues of truth is that the terms upon which those demarcations are made go unseen and uncontested. A very radical revision of what we mean by truth is in order, but if we ignore the ways in which our discourses appeal to some version of truth for their persuasiveness, we are in danger of remaining blind to the operations of legitimation that function within our own texts. The task is therefore to explicate the relations between politics and knowledge rather than pronounce the death of truth.

12. Cf. my "Cultural Feminism versus Post-Structuralism: The Identity Crisis in Feminist Theory," *Signs: A Journal of Women in Culture and Society* 13, no. 3 (1988): 405–36. For more discussions on the multidimensionality of social identity, see Maria Lugones, "Playfulness, 'World'-Travelling, and Loving Perception," *Hypatia* 2, no. 2, 3–19, and Gloria Anzaldua, *Borderlands/La Frontera* (San Francisco: Spinsters/Aunt Lute Book Company, 1987).

13. Gayatri Chakravorty Spivak, "Can the Subaltern Speak?," in *Marxism and the Interpretation of Culture,* ed. Cary Nelson and Lawrence Grossberg (Urbana: University of Illinois Press, 1988).

14. Ibid., 298.

15. See Edward Said, "Representing the Colonized: Anthropology's Interlocutors," *Critical Inquiry* 15, no. 2 (Winter 1989): 219, on this point, where he shows how the "dialogue" between Western anthropology and colonized people has been nonreciprocal and supports the need for the Westerners to begin to *stop talking.*

16. See again ibid., 212, where he encourages in particular the self-interrogation of privileged speakers. This seems to be a running theme in what are sometimes called "minority discourses" these days: asserting the need for whites to study whiteness, e.g., and for males to study masculinity. The need for an interrogation of one's location exists with every discursive event

by any speaker, but given the lopsidedness of current "dialogues," it seems especially important to push for this among the privileged, who sometimes seem to want to study everybody's social and cultural construction but their own.

17. To argue for the relevance of effects for evaluation does not entail that there is only one way to do such an accounting or what kind of effects will be deemed desirable. How one evaluates a particular effect is left open; premise 4 argues simply that effects must always be taken into account.

18. I like the way Susan Bordo makes this point. In speaking about theories or ideas that gain prominence, she says: "all cultural formations . . . [are] complexly constructed out of diverse elements—intellectual, psychological, institutional, and sociological. Arising not from monolithic design but from an interplay of factors and forces, it is best understood not as a discrete, definable position that can be adopted or rejected, but as an emerging coherence which is being fed by a variety of currents, sometimes overlapping, sometimes quite distinct." See her "Feminism, Postmodernism, and Gender-Skepticism," in *Feminism/Postmodernism,* ed. Linda Nicholson (New York: Routledge, 1989), 135. If ideas arise in such a configuration of forces, does it make sense to ask for an author?

15.

FEMINISM MEETS POST-COMMUNISM:
THE CASE OF THE UNITED GERMANY

NANETTE FUNK

The fall of the Berlin Wall in November 1989, symbolizing more than any other single event the end of the Cold War division of Europe into East[1] and West, ushered in contact between post-Communist women and feminists from Western Europe and the United States. In some instances, there is promise of fruitful interaction; but in the newly united Germany, where there is a direct meeting between East and West, tensions have become systematic, playing havoc with the possibility of joint action and even dialogue between East and West German women. The bitterness, anger, hostility, and suspicion on both sides that exploded to the surface between German women cannot be overestimated. Friendships that survived years of the Cold War and the divided Germany disintegrated rapidly once the Wall came down in November 1989.[2]

In the divided city of Berlin, East and West German women were at first eager and curious to meet their sisters on the other side. Quickly, the differences between them hardened into prejudices, provoking confrontations and fracturing meetings, starting almost immediately with conferences in the spring of 1990. Two years later, by the time of the meeting of women at the end of January 1991 at the Technical University in Berlin, attended by women philosophers, social and cultural scientists, and literary theorists, dialogue was strained and fraught with hostility. In May 1991 at a conference at Humboldt University in Berlin, East German women in the audience angrily demanded of a West German speaker that she speak of her own experiences, rather than talking about East German women. "Why do you talk about us when you don't even know us?" yelled one East German woman. A few months later, after a meeting held by West German women political scientists and to which East German women were invited, some West German women vowed never to work with East German women again.

In their joint research project on the differences among East and West German feminists, Ulrike Helwerth and Gislinde Schwarz, West and East German feminist journalists, respectively,[3] report the following remarks by an East German women: "Once I left an event in tears. A woman from the West had told me that my kid should shut up. Not only do they blame us for our husbands and children, but also for not being real feminists."

Helwerth and Schwarz report a West German woman saying: "I'm not really sure what kind of crash course they [East German women] would need. I only know that a lot of what we do is over their heads. And when they talk about patriarchal structures or the patriarchy, I have the feeling that they've just found out about that. There are only one or two women in the East with whom I enjoy talking. I also can't stand listening to them whine all the time."[4]

In Berlin, where the confrontation between East and West is so direct, many Eastern women do not venture into West Berlin, preferring to stay behind the Wall that once was. West German women, initially open and curious, have concluded they just don't have anything in common with East German women who continually complain and talk about *their* problems. At the 1991 conference, curiosity turned into "boredom," loss of interest, and finally avoidance. The only thing the two groups of women could agree on was that each should go their own way. And yet they could not because they were bound together in one country, governed by one set of laws and under one policy.

How did it come to such a pass? What lies at the root of these tensions and hostilities? How does this hostility express itself? Is this only a situation unique to Germany, where the citizens of a Communist state and a liberal democracy were united into one state, bringing them face to face with each other on a daily basis? An analysis of this situation will not only help to understand gender and the unification of Germany,[5] as well as the tensions latent in relations between Eastern and Western women in general, but it will also help to explore the relationship between women and the political.

The unification of Germany was not only the unification of two separate states but of two different systems of male domination within two different systems of modernization and rationalization. The German Democratic Republic was organized through a state-party political system; the Federal Republic of Germany through a democratic constitution and principles of economic efficiency and the market.[6] Each incorporated women very differently and through different political mechanisms. For instance, women's "emancipation" and first trimester abortion on demand were part of the political capital of the GDR, touted as signs of a more progressive society, more committed to women than West Germany. But in the GDR an authoritarian party-state ("father state") without a public sphere, and without much meaningful women's political participation,[7] defined women's interests and introduced a women's policy. In the West, on the contrary, feminism, a collective social movement that was part of the development of the democratic process and a more active citizenship, as well as of the expansion of the public sphere, had been the vehicle for expression of women's issues and demands.

Eastern Europe is in general being incorporated into the Western system, most clearly in the incorporation of East Germany into West Germany according to Article 23 of the Basic Law of West Germany. To be sure, the unification of Germany was not predicated on a mutual understanding between East and West Germany, on the basis of dialogue or on a substantive rationality. It was a process of unification that repressed many concerns for justice and equality, in no way more evident than with regard to women. The disinterest in the economic consequence of the transition for women, including the massive elimination of women from the labor market at all levels, invalidation of women's job qualifications resulting in their disqualification, and the consequent removal of women to lower level jobs, are all signifiers of the instrumental rationality that prevailed.[8] The prediction, already made early in 1990 by active East German feminists of the Independent Women's Association (the Unabhängige Frauen Verband)—that the unification would have these effects—did not lead the primarily male West German politicians directing the unification to modify their course. In short, the 1990 unification of Germany was structured by an instrumental rationality.⁹ As in the modernization of New York City by Robert Moses, who in building his highways rode roughshod over the cultures and communities of New York City, and in doing so destroyed them, so the unification of Germany by Herr Kohl and company rode over democratic processes and cultural and social spheres, especially in East Germany.

The German unification also brought with it a progressive orientation to the future, akin to the faith in the march of history toward a better future that characterized the former state socialist system. This attitude reinforced the German forgetting of the past, including the Nazi past and the diverging historical pasts and experiences of East and West Germany. Particularly striking is women's different standings and histories in the two Germanies; denial of this became operative in distorting communication and frustrating understanding between East and West German women at the Berlin conference.

The unification of Germany affected men and women differently. There was in general a silence in the unification agreements about the very spheres with which women were especially concerned—the domestic, cultural, and social spheres. The very absence of women in positions of power on either side during unification led to the inattention to these spheres, as they were not matters of interest to those male politicians with power at the time. The hostility that developed between women in East and West Germany must be understood as rooted in this male inattention to the issues of importance to women.

The sudden unification led both East and West German women to make hasty generalizations and adopt stereotypes of each other, especially in Berlin where there was the most direct contact between East and West Germans. Cliches starting with "East German (West German) woman are . . . ." provided categories with which each group of women conceptualized the other and coped with the massive changes. Former GDR women were stereotyped as unemancipated, having bought into sexism, subordinating themselves to the family and dependent on men and marriage, oriented only to children, antifeminist or lacking any understanding of feminism, conformist, passive, and unwilling to stand up for themselves. East German women bitterly characterized West German women as "Besserwessis": arrogant, ignorant Westerners who claim to know better than anyone else, dogmatic, aggressive feminists who thought they were bringing the feminist truth to the heathen, and women hostile to children and men.

Such antagonisms and stereotypes are not limited to West and East German women; similar if less pronounced versions can be found between Western feminists and post-communist women in general. In fact, discourse between Eastern and Western women is pervaded by such negative stereotypes. Russian, Hungarian, and women of the former Yugoslavia characterize American and Western feminists as "man-haters" and feminism as a luxury. They accuse Western feminists in general of having idealized and totally misunderstood the condition of Eastern European women under state socialism.[10]

DIFFERENCE, INEQUALITY, POWER, AND DOMINATION

At its deepest level, feminism in East and West Germany, as in Eastern and Western Europe, is confronting the issue of difference, this time not only of race and class, but of politics as well. The conflicts between Eastern and Western women reveal that not only is "man a political animal" but woman as well. The intense conflicts between women in the now-united Germany in effect provide a lab school that reveals, in the intimacy and immediacy of the contacts, and with a clarity no theory could, just how deeply political women are and how deep their political differences run. This raises the question of how feminism deals with the political. This is a major problem in post-Communism, exemplified by the growing nationalist conflicts and adding to the cultural differences and relations of power that manifest themselves in the conflicts between Eastern and Western women. An analysis of these conflicts between German women will help to shed light on these broader problems.

Identity

Women are not only political insofar as they participate in parliamentary, or even extraparliamentary activities, or insofar as all relationships and institutions are political. A woman's identity is partially defined by the political system of which she is a part. One is an East German, a West German, or an American woman, even if one has been critical of one's political system. One does not change political identities like clothes; this is reflected in the continuing identification of East

Germans as "Ossis" (slang for "Easterners") and West Germans as "Wessis." Former GDR women's status and self-respect are partially dependent on attitudes toward their past political system. Now that it has been eliminated and politically demeaned, they have been degraded in the process. Reacting to this, East German women defend that system when it is attacked by West German women, often turning to an illusory nostalgia for that system; this in turn annoys West German women.

As became apparent during the conference, West German feminists often have very strong opinions about East German women and very definite political positions on, and attitudes toward, "the other Germany" as well as about their own system, opinions that had been formed well before the "fall of the wall." This is so because for both East and West Germans, in a more obvious way than usual, self-identity had been defined relationally, in terms of the "other" Germany. Insofar as the integrity and a hold on one's identity appear to require allegiance to one's previous judgments and perceptions of that "other"—the other person and the other system—meetings between East and West women, and the unification itself, challenge not only political perceptions and judgments, but each woman's sense of integrity as well. These crises of identity on both sides, which have resulted from political dislocations, underlie the conflicts between East and West German women.

Perceptions of the Other take extreme forms. West German women who had been very deeply critical of the GDR as an authoritarian, rigid, repressive political order, often perceive former GDR women as embodying correlative nondemocratic and authoritarian styles and political norms. They cannot then support women of whom they are so deeply critical in such politically fundamental ways. Other West German women, especially on the Left, idealize the East German system, regarding East German women as having had it all—day care, employment, and abortion—and feel jealousy toward them.

East German women, in contrast, threatened in their own sense of self-worth, self-respect, and identity by the demolition of their system and its culture, feel moved to support their past society even though they had been critical of it before. They retaliate by criticizing West German women and West German feminism for its participation in, and ineffective struggles against, a capitalist system that keeps women at a low employment level, without adequate day care, or a strong right to abortion. In meetings between East and West women, these attacks against women also serve as criticisms of their political systems themselves, which further provokes irritation. Accepting "the Other Woman" is seen as an acceptance of "the Other political system" (which in many ways the other woman does embody); this in turn threatens the first woman's identity. Similarly, praise of the other in any way (of the day care available to GDR women or the space for a woman's movement in West Germany) is experienced as dangerously close to praise for that system, and again a threat to the women's senses of identity and their firmly entrenched, often mutually critical worldviews.

Difference in Experiences and Interests

East and West German women had, and continue to have, different experiences, and the two groups of women have different and sometimes conflicting interests. For former GDR women the "Wende"—the political transition of 1989—meant radical autobiographical ruptures, with disorienting experiences of dislocation and radical changes in daily life, loss of status and self-respect, and intensified stresses and demands. East German women are filled with a sense of insecurity and uncertainty, and a profound sense of the loss of meaning in their lives. Those who are among the most respected often have to insert themselves in a world with different standards, one that plays by different rules, where different skills and know-how are called for, and a world that comes complete with its own entrenched networks, status, and power hierarchies. One result has been the strong public attacks on the literary merits of the most renowned East German writers, who were mainly women, including the well-known author Christa Wolf.

After the Wende, East German women came to joint East-West women's meetings with urgent existential problems of survival and unemployment; those meetings were a means to integrate into the dominant system, to get support and recognition of their experiences and circumstances. They hoped to get a piece of the pie of the rich Western state. Instead, they were confronted with West German women whom they envied for having it so much "easier" than they did and who did not seem to grasp their situation.

Usually ignorant of the radical changes East German women are experiencing daily, West German women have little compassion or empathy for them, and this infuriates East German women. In contrast West German intellectuals and feminists approached interactions between Eastern and Western women with curiosity, a desire to extend feminism to the East, and a hope that East German women would provide an impetus to the much subdued West German feminist movement. When the latter did not happen, they blamed East German women.

West German women in 1989–91 tended to think their lives and identities were not substantially changed by the "Wende." [11] They have since come to fear that they will lose from the unification, that the sharing of the benefits of their society with East Germans will risk loss of personal opportunities and social benefits. West German feminists fear, not without grounds, that they will lose funding for women's projects and research that now must be shared with former GDR women. Indeed, German funding institutions do sometimes pit East and West German women's projects against each other. Moreover, West Germans, including women, are resentful of higher taxes, reduced benefits, higher unemployment, and growing right wing neo-Nazi groups, all of which they blame on East Germans and unification.

In fact, both East and West German women see themselves in the category of "victim"—as being victimized by the other woman. The West German women fear that the more submissive, conservative conformist attitudes they perceive in former GDR women will result in undermining the gains they have made. The East German women see themselves as being insulted, criticized, and exploited by West German women.

Legally, the interests of East and West German women also differ. The unification agreements for Germany required a joint law to be established by parliament by the end of 1992 to revise the West German abortion law, Paragraph 218. The united parliament in August 1992 voted for a compromise law, which was immediately challenged and appealed to the Supreme Court by conservatives; the Court rejected that law in May 1993. Every stage in these legal developments had a different meaning for East and West German women. The 1992 proposed compromise law meant a loss of rights for former GDR women, but a gain for West women. Since that law would have imposed obligatory counseling, the proposed law would have meant East German women had lost their GDR right to a first trimester abortion. For West German women, the proposed law meant that for the first time they had the legal right to decide for themselves whether to have a first trimester abortion. But the effect of the Supreme Court decision in May 1993—since such a law was not constitutional, health insurance could not pay for abortions (although abortions would not be criminalized)—was to create a two-tier system that negatively affected East German women, who are more likely to be poor and unable to afford abortions. These are among the differences that inform meetings and result in resentments and misunderstandings, poisoning contacts between East and West German women. Under these conditions, constructive dialogue, to the extent there is any such dialogue between East and West German women, is difficult.

Power and Inequality

The meetings between East and West German women also highlighted the fact that women are also in positions of power and domination over other women, as African-American women have made so clear to white feminists in the U.S. Power relationships between women have often been a problem for feminism, a movement that arose in part from an understanding of women as all victims of male domination. How does feminism constitute itself in the face of oppressive relationships between women? As in the case of race and class, differences of political and socioeconomic systems mean that interactions between East and West German women are asymmetrical relationships of power, inequality, and domination. Such relations exist both at the level of society and at the level of discourse.

Social Inequality and Domination. West German women, coming from the dominant political and cultural system, have greater freedom and opportunity than East German women in the united Germany; they have readier entrée into that system and to the power that comes from experience and entrenchment within it. After a great deal of struggle against sexism, some West German women have acquired positions of status and respect. Obviously, none of this is true for East German women, who must first learn to navigate in a new system and struggle for any place at all in there. Furthermore, West German women even hold dominant positions in workplaces involved with promoting the interests of East German women, and they may have decision-making powers about funding East German women's research projects. In administrative positions in the eastern half of Germany, in Offices for the Equality of Women (akin to Affirmative Action offices in the U.S.), in offices collecting data on women and the transition in Germany, West German women often outrank and outnumber East German women.

West women's qualifications are deemed more appropriate for these higher positions, but East German women accuse West women of insensitivity to East German women's issues and see them as uncommitted to working on behalf of East German women. Moreover, West German women ignore East German women's judgments, even in matters concerning them; they are in subordinate positions and simply not sought out.

Significantly, West German women are frequently oblivious—sometimes in the name of feminism—or insensitive to all these structural inequalities. They assume that, after twenty years of a Western women's movement, they know best the "real women's issues" or "what is to be done" politically and individually. West German women have told former GDR women what feminism is, that they shouldn't have men in their organizations, and how they should deal with the German political system. Such arrogance prevents West German women from hearing the valid criticisms by East German women. In one case, at a meeting of a predominantly East German woman's group, a former GDR woman voiced doubts about accepting government funding for positions in a woman's organization, fearing it would create dependency on the state. Instead of taking this hesitation as grounds for critical self-reflection on standard West German feminist practices, a West German woman at the meeting immediately dismissed the East German woman's doubts as another sign of unfamiliarity with the West German system. Similar problems, in a less intense way, have surfaced in relations between post-Communist women and West European and American women in general.

Power and Inequality in Discourse. Power imbalances also exist at the level of discourse where Western feminist discourse is hegemonic in feminism. This threatens to suppress and distort post-Communist women's concerns. In speaking their own language of feminism, Western women in general, and West German women in particular, risk imposing on Eastern women the standards of discourse, provoking intellectual and political resentment, and sometimes shattering the possibilities of political cooperation.

West German women often have more facility with and are better read in the Western feminist discourse, which may even be accepted as the standard of discourse by East German women themselves. The West German women are also often better educated in the methodology of the social sciences, which they may bring to bear on feminist research. When East German women participate in those discourses they are simply swamped by the West German women, who set the pace and direction of the discussion. The agreement or nonagreement of the East German women ceases to be a relevant consideration. The relative advantages of the West German women in the discourse leads them to submerge and ignore important insights, critiques, and differing interests of East German women, who may not get an effective opportunity to articulate them. Moreover, some of the questions that West German women pose are inappropriate to East German women's concerns.

In the united Germany, language, as the articulation of a lifeworld, is itself a contested issue. West German women are resentful and irritated by East German women's use of linguistic forms that West German women fought long and hard to overcome. At issue is the East German woman's use of the male grammatical form when referring to herself, for example, as a teacher, *Lehrer* (a common occupation of women in both East and West Germany), while the West German woman's movement instituted the use of the female form, *Lehrerin*. This is equivalent to the American feminist fight to reject the use of "he" or "man" as a neutral linguistic form.

Oppressive relations usually seen between men and women exist between East and West German women. Irene Dölling, a long time East Berlin feminist researcher, noted that at one meeting, West German women took on the role of men in relation to East German women: while East German women talked about their experiences, West German women "theorized." East German women were the objects to be studied (a position, of course, they resent), while West Germans remained in the role of subjects who conducted the study. Being represented as the "other" raises problems for East German women, who also resent the ignorance and lack of understanding West German women have of their lives, their daily problems, their present, and their past. They feel that West German women use categories and concepts that do not speak to their concerns, that are not their own, that they do not understand, and in which they cannot recognize themselves. East and West German women, in effect, have not been mutual partners in a dialogue between feminists; the issues, problems, and questions, as well as answers, are often posed by West German women, and East German women—even those active on behalf of women—are often discredited as not understanding feminism.

Competition. East and West German women compete for the same goods—funding for women's projects and research, jobs in the newly reorganized East German university system, in business, administration, and in government. Yet West women have better connections and more appropriate skills, making them structurally better positioned and better able to succeed in that competition. Moreover, the standards by which women are being evaluated, both political and intellectual, are Western standards. East German women often feel unwelcome in the universities by the few West German women there, whom they regard as having their own closed networks. Ironically, West German women themselves are not well represented in German universities, being present in much smaller percentages than women in the U.S. This is due to a much smaller, more hierarchical university system and a women's movement that initially focused on "autonomous" extra-institutional positions. Their lean numbers mean that, in contrast to U.S. feminist academic women, West German women and feminists have developed weaker academic networks, models of behavior, or institutional styles; their style is more likely to be an imitation of the male aggressive style.

Eastern European women intellectuals generally, and former GDR women in particular, experience themselves as exploited by Western feminist intellectuals who come to collect Eastern European women's experiences, stories, and insights, then tell them in their own voice, building careers on those stories and accounts, sometimes without citation or acknowledgment. This provokes resentment that is compounded when the Western woman beats the Eastern woman to the publication or the job in the West.

Culture, Beliefs, Socialization, and Personality. There are tremendous differences in what Habermas has referred to as the "lifeworld" and the stock of taken-for-granted unreflected beliefs and worldviews that East and West German women hold. Women's pre-reflective, philosophical categories of thought, such as conceptions of the individual and equality, and normative principles, such as a commitment to equality, are all profoundly political. In the meetings of Eastern and Western women, and of East and West German women in particular, political differences pervade women's consciousness, their normative, philosophical presuppositions and categories of thought and belief systems. Eastern women, if not Eastern feminists, often believe they had equality and that they certainly don't want that in the future; some Western feminists claim to want equality, but do not yet have it. Eastern European women see themselves much more as part of a totality, while Western women see themselves in more individualist ways. In addition, different attitudes toward autonomy, self-development, the family, and in the understanding of emancipation and feminism itself divide these women. Women in state socialist countries, even those active on behalf of women, appear to be more oriented than Western feminists toward children and the family, more skeptical of the benefits of paid work, and have different attitudes toward men's or to women's collective action. In public presentations or in biographies in books, intellectual East German women identify themselves by how many children they had and whether they were married or not, as well as by their professional accomplishments; West German intellectual women usually do not mention their children—in fact, generally, much more so than American academic women today, they do not have children.

Different habits of behavior also characterize the women. Women (as well as men) in East Germany are much less accustomed to putting themselves forward, or to bringing attention to themselves and to what is distinctive about them, than are West Germans. Being different was not an asset in an authoritarian state; it was destined to get one in trouble, so one was socialized against self-assertion or self-destruction. If one insisted nevertheless on being different, an "Andersdenken" (one who thinks differently), the best thing to do was to find a community of like-minded persons—a niche—and disappear into it. West German attitudes are just the reverse.

Differences in dealing with conflicts and with authority have, not surprisingly, emerged. East Germans in general, and women in particular, had little experience dealing with conflicts in the workplace or in the public sphere; and after unification they did not understand the new rights and freedoms they had as workers and citizens. Coupled with the fear since 1990 of losing their jobs (not surprising given that women are two-thirds of the East German unemployed and about 50 percent have lost the jobs they held in 1990), East German women tend to withdraw from conflicts with employers or the state, even when their rights are being violated. Expectations that the "father-state" would do it all, the absence of a tradition of democratic institutions and a public sphere, and the fact that they are overwhelmed by the dislocations of their personal lives mean they are unlikely to assert themselves against authority. This has become an issue between women in the ongoing struggle over abortion rights: East German reluctance to join in demonstrations for abortion rights have further alienated Western women. All this, in turn, annoys West German women.

In the face of all these differences,[12] there is a risk of Western women's moralistic rejection of post-Communist cultural differences. This moralism can be predicated on a nonunderstanding of the meaning and origin of these practices: [13] for example, that a family orientation in state socialism was also an escape from the even greater state control in other spheres. Western moralism itself risks provoking resentment, defensiveness, and hardened suspicion of Western women by East women.

Even Western standards of style, dress, and cosmetics have been imposed on post-Communist women: these are the standards that Eastern women aspire to, or are being judged by. This is especially true in Germany, where East German women find themselves newly self-conscious or resentful. Thus Ina Merkel of the former GDR wrote:

I suddenly begin to wonder whether I shouldn't dress differently, whether it wouldn't be useful for me to color my hair, go on a diet, go to a health club, and to reach deeper into my wallet to dress more elegantly or femininely or who knows what.

. . . New demands arise totally anew. In order to successfully sell oneself, to compete with others, one has to understand how to trump and exclude the other, to charm and to make oneself pleasant. These mechanisms work in particular ways on me as a woman. They pressure me to a new externalization and presentation of my sex, which up to now hadn't been expected of me.[14]

As an American woman at the Berlin conference, I was also sensitive to these differences, but unlike East German women who felt they had to "dress up" when they went to West meetings or parties, I felt I had to "dress down" in meetings with East German women for fear of flaunting the West.

Such East German women's experiences and the stories others pass on structure future interactions, making Eastern women suspicious of all Western women. This is not unlike the assumptions blacks and women bring to their interactions with whites and men, respectively. Constrained by the need to accommodate themselves to the new hierarchies into which they are plunged and to the new people with whom they must deal, many post-Communist women become defensive or resentful.

Post-Communist women in general do not want to be dominated by the priorities of Western women or to be swamped by the debates among Western feminists that do not resonate for them.

DIFFERENCE, DIALOGUE, AND SOLIDARITY

How does one recognize difference and yet preserve solidarity? Feminism was conceived as a system of support among "sisters" based on sharing a common oppression, and therefore on being a "we," an undifferentiated united subject. But the latter was readily elided into a "unitary" subject, one in which there were no fundamental disagreements and differences. In the German unification, this was expressed by early conversations between East and West German women, who in listening to each other's stories said, "Yes, it's just like that for us." But when it became clear that it was not "just like that" for Eastern and Western women, that there are important differences and real conflicts and disagreements, there has been no model for how to go forward.

In some ways, women have not completely regarded each other as full subjects who can be in solidarity but still be individuated. The problems in the meeting of Eastern and Western women are not only sociological problems of differences in socialization but expose the problem of what it is to be united with those with whom one disagrees, and of whom one has criticism. How can there be solidarity when there is criticism and conflict, when the validity claims of one threaten the identity of the other, when the integrity of one seems to depend on criticism of the other? What is revealed at the deepest level is the need for a model of feminism and solidarity that does not require agreement on all things and that recognizes differences, a feminist model of constructive disagreement, a model of solidarity that can also be constituted by engagement in dialogue among those who differ. Working through the differences, East and West can provide such a model.

Such a model of collective political action and constructive disagreement through dialogue requires as a first step an acknowledgment and analysis of the conflict, in this case between Eastern and Western women, and its roots. But for such recognition and dialogue to occur, there must be an acknowledgment of the existence of power and domination, of competition and structural inequality, and acknowledgment of the fear of dialogue itself. Those who enter into dialogue with each other must also expect that there will be disagreement, some of which will not be readily resolved, and that there will be misunderstanding and mistakes. Dialogues should be set up so as to best promote openness, fairness, and equality in the discourse, limited to those who share the goal of promoting the good for women, women's mutual support and respect, and to the elimination of prejudices. The precondition of that dialogue must be a commitment to understand each other, a commitment to achieve mutual recognition, rather than a battle to prove the other wrong and make moralistic judgments. There must be a commitment to discussing unspoken assumptions and resentments, an openness to engage in critical self-reflection, and a preparedness to change heretofore unexamined assumptions if they cannot withstand critical examination. The process of engaging in such a difficult dialogue with the goal of mutual understanding and recognition itself creates a common experience and can help to bridge differences and disagreements. Dialogues constituted procedurally as interactions between equals will help to create a new atmosphere and more positive experiences between women and help to change prejudices that pervade present contacts.

To this end, the facilitators of such dialogues should be both Eastern and Western women, in equal numbers where possible, who agree on the circumstances in which that dialogue takes place and the procedures it follows. Not only must it be possible for each to establish the agenda and pose challenges, but enabling conditions that facilitate former GDR women to exercise these rights effectively must be incorporated. East German women must have a central role in determining what those enabling conditions are. The topics of such discourse must be not only East German women, but West German woman as well. Such dialogues can be part of joint political activities by feminists and women active on behalf of women. Those activities must be predicated on joint leadership under conditions mutually agreed upon, with equal participation by both East and West German women and under conditions that promote the possibilities for equal effective participation by both groups.

To these ends, several East and West German feminists have proposed meeting in small groups to exchange personal experiences—in effect, a cross cultural consciousness-raising, not only to see the ways in which they are the same, but also how and why they differ. Others are attempting to work together in more sensitive, self-reflective political structures.

The meeting of East and West German women potentially creates new opportunities for critical feminist reflection on the political systems of which they are and were a part, the different systems of male domination in East and West, the unification of Eastern and Western systems of male domination, and the significance of the male-directed nature of the unification of Germany and its willingness to sacrifice women. A feminist self-understanding of these phenomena and the role of women in the unification of Germany as well as on the political strategies now possible could be encouraged by these interactions. It could also provide an opportunity and incentive for a critical self-reflection of both East and West German women on their normative and political beliefs and worldviews. For West German women it could provide an opportunity to reflect on their conception of feminism, their past focus on alternative structures that left many institutional structures intact. East women could reflect on the "patriarchal emancipation" of the state socialist system, on its day-care, abortion, and employment policies for women, on what is and is not of value in that past, and whether the GDR had really provided gender equality. Finally, such a meeting could give both sides a way of confronting the changed reality that they both have to master to achieve individual life plans and to be able to act on behalf of women. The energy created from new perspectives, new possibilities, and new insights could invigorate both sides. It would be a shame if missteps up to now created a permanent impasse.

NOTES

1. Throughout this essay the term "East" or "Eastern" refers to the countries of the former Eastern Bloc and the former Soviet Union.
2. Ulrike Helwerth and Gislinde Schwarz, "Estranged Sisters: Eastern and Western Feminists and Their Differences" (unpublished manuscript).
3. Ulrike Helwerth worked for the alternative Berlin newspaper *Die Tageszeitung* and has also studied sociology. Gislinde Schwarz is a free-lance journalist from East Berlin and previously worked for what was the only women's magazine in the German Democratic Republic, *Für Dich.*
4. Helwerth and Schwarz, "Estranged Sisters."
5. Christine Kulke, "Ferne Nähe: Zum Dialog unter Frauen im rationalisierten Einigungsprozess," in *Wider Das Schlichte Vergessen. Der deutsch-deutsche Einigungsprozess: Frauen im Dialog,* ed. Christine Kulke, Heidi Kopp-Degethoff, and Ulrike Ramming (Berlin: Orlanda Frauenverlag, 1992), 20.
6. Ibid., 21.
7. There was the Demokratische Frauenbund Deutschland (Democratic Women's Organization of Germany), the official women's organization, but like most such organizations in state-socialist countries since the 1950s, they

did not play an independent role representing women, but were much more the instrument for the transmission of state policy to women.

8. "Instrumental rationality" refers to emphasis, at the exclusion of other considerations, to find the most efficient means to the desired goal—in this case, unification.

9. Kulke, "Ferne Nähe," 16–30; Jürgen Habermas, "Vergangenheit als Zukunft," in *Vergangenheit als Zukunft,* ed. Michael Haller (Zürich: Clausen and Bosse, Leck, 1990), 56–59.

10. Olga Toth, "No Envy, No Pity," in *Gender Politics and Post-Communism: Reflections from Eastern Europe and the former Soviet Union,* ed. Nanette Funk and Magda Mueller (New York: Routledge, 1993), 213–14; Larissa Lissyutkina, "Soviet Women at the Crossroads of Perestroika," in *Gender Politics and Post-Communism,* 274–80, 286.

11. According to some psychologists, West German women and men repress feelings of change, and other strong feelings, out of a desire not to threaten their self-assured sense of control over themselves and their world.

12. In Germany the differences even extend to how one takes leave of another person. Former GDR women shake hands, which West German women consider unduly formal, a practice they rejected in 1968, substituting simply a verbal acknowledgment of greeting among friends.

13. West German women see these family-oriented practices as the very same ones they had rebelled against in 1968, but they ignore the different cultural meaning these practices had in state socialism.

14. Ina Merkel, . . . *und Du, Frau an der Werkbank: Die DDR in den 5oer Jahren* (Berlin: Elephanten Press, 1990), 7–8.

16.

REHABILITATING MARY CRAWFORD: *MANSFIELD PARK* AND THE RELIEF OF "THROWING RIDICULE"

EILEEN GILLOOLY

Miss Crawford was glad to find a family of such consequence so very near them, and not at all displeased either at her sister's early care [in choosing a husband for her], or the choice it had fallen on [Tom Bertram]. Matrimony was her object, provided she could marry well, and having seen Mr. Bertram in town, she knew that objection could no more be made to his person than to his situation in life. While she treated it as a joke, therefore, she did not forget to think of it seriously.

—*Mansfield Park* (75)[1]

No matter how highly acclaimed it sometimes is—Lionel Trilling, for example, ranked it among the greatest of English novels—*Mansfield Park* is famous for being the least well-liked of Austen's novels.[2] Dominated by the moral correctness of Fanny Price, it generally leaves its readers with an impression of earnestness and sobriety that even partisans of Austen have at times found hard to appreciate. As Claudia Johnson has noted, "Janeites confessed and unconfessed" lament its "ungratifying humorlessness."[3]

Mansfield Park, however, is home not only to Fanny Price but Mary Crawford as well, whose laughing comments and quick wit pervade and animate the novel. No other female character in Austen, with the possible exception of Elizabeth Bennet, approaches the comprehensiveness of Mary's humorously ironic perspective, and certainly no other poses such a threat to the moral and epistemological order of the narrative community. Yet perhaps because she is limited to a supporting role and banished from the novel before closure, Mary's importance as a competing textual presence is generally ignored. If seriously considered at all, Mary is judged to be seductive but superficial, amusing but morally impoverished, the "bad" girl against whom Fanny's goodness is defined.

Narratively pitting Mary against Fanny in this way—making them "women at odds," so to speak—forces the reader to choose between them; and no matter how much we may regret having to do so, we must on moral grounds side with Fanny. Yet once our moral allegiance to Fanny is assured, the narrator is free to align herself with Mary in a number of other ways. Her discourse, for example, at times uncannily resembles Mary's, and despite her expressed maternal affection for "My Fanny" (446) (she alone of Austen narrators claims such singular possession of her heroine), she rarely participates fully in Fanny's opinions or perspective.[4] On the other hand, however, the narrator shares with Mary Crawford an ironic sense of humor that challenges not only the morally conservative (Fanny-associated) tone dominating the novel, but cultural values like feminine passivity and dutifulness that are embodied by the heroine and at least apparently supported by the plot.

Narratologically, then, Mary functions as a counterpart to Fanny: the narrator, while associated with Fanny's ethics, nevertheless shares Mary's epistemology and sensibility. This splitting of the heroine-object has particularly significant consequences for the disposition of humor in *Mansfield Park*. For despite Mary's obvious lack of sisterhood, and despite whatever plot functions her temperamental antagonism toward Fanny performs, Mary Crawford's presence in the text also serves to disguise (and to support) the narrator's own subtle humorous assaults upon the patriarchal construction of nineteenth-century femininity that Fanny has (so to speak) internalized—a construction that forcibly restricts and reductively defines female opportunities, identity, and agency. The "relief" of "throwing ridicule" (256) is, as I hope to suggest in the following pages, a tactic equally common to them both.

Of all the women of *Mansfield Park,* Mary Crawford clearly presents the greatest challenge to phallocratic control. She not only displays a tremendous sexual energy that captivates even an improbable wooer like Edmund Bertram, but she is completely unintimidated by authority, and, next to the narrator, is the sharpest wit in the novel. She frankly points out the hypocrisies of others—the lasciviousness of her uncle the admiral and the dangerous flirtation "of those indefatigable rehearsers" (188), Maria Bertram and Henry Crawford—and laughingly demystifies cultural myths of both gender and class. In response to Edmund's query about the size of her naval acquaintance, Mary replies, " 'Among Admirals, large enough; but,' with an air of grandeur; 'we know very little of the inferior ranks. Post captains may be very good sort of men, but they do not belong to *us*' " (91). And in response to Fanny's rather pietistic exclamation that "a whole family assembling regularly for the purpose of prayer, is fine!," Mary, "laughing," exposes the paternalistic results such evangelical notions often breed: "It must do the heads of the family a great deal of good to force all the poor housemaids and footmen to leave business and pleasure, and say their prayers here twice a day, while they are inventing excuses themselves for staying away" (115).

She is particularly shrewd on the subject of marriage, avoiding its overromanticization and accepting the materialism of marital negotiations as de rigueur among the leisured middle class: for both sexes, marriage simply boils down to "a manoeuvring business" (79). And while she believes that "every body should marry as soon as they can do it to advantage" (76) and not "throw themselves away," her class allegiance is limited; she is personally "not displeased" with her brother Henry's wishing to marry one who, like Fanny, is "a little beneath him" (296) and even appreciates its symbolic feminist value: "'the glory of fixing one who has been shot at by so many; of having it in one's power to pay off the debts of one's sex!'" (358). Furthermore, Mary is the only character who recognizes how fully Maria has been victimized by her upbringing. While the others view Maria's decision to marry Rushworth with varying degrees of approbation or apprehension, Mary suggests that Maria has little real say in the matter, having been reared from birth by Sir Thomas to be a sacrificial lamb at the altar of Hymen: " 'Don't be affronted,' said she laughing; 'but it does put me in mind of some of the old heathen heroes, who after performing exploits in a foreign land, offered sacrifices to the gods on their safe return'" (135).

Mary's views on feminine agency and daughterly duty are as potentially radical as her views on marriage and class. She holds that financial independence, not marriage, "is the best recipe for happiness I ever heard of" (226), and betrays a decidedly unfeminine ambition both in becoming "angry with Edmund for adhering to his own notions and acting on them in defiance of her" (290) and in wistfully longing for a more constructive activity than flirting: " 'I often think of Mr. Rushworth's property and independence. . . . A *man* might represent the county with such an estate; a *man* might escape a profession and represent the county' " (182; emphasis added). Like Maria's, her sense of duty is unsentimental and self-interested (" 'It is every body's duty to do as well for themselves as they can' " [293]); yet unlike Maria's, it is explicitly held and shamelessly masculine.

Precisely because Mary Crawford is not the heroine of *Mansfield Park*, she has narrative permission to scandalize her fellow characters, and often her readers, with relative impunity. Fanny and Edmund may condemn Mary for her weak morality and lack of "feminine loathings" (441), but the narrator shows considerably more mercy.[5] When Fanny thinks Mary undeserving of Edmund and fears that "his worth would finally be wasted on her," the narrator comes to Mary's defense: "Impartiality would not have denied to Miss Crawford's nature, that participation of the general nature of women, which would lead her to adopt the opinions of the man she loved and respected, as her own" (362). In other words, Mary's love for Edmund would, in the narrator's opinion, lead to her behavioral reformation rather than his vitiation.

Moreover, no matter how ethically unsound it may be, almost everyone finds Mary's witty volubility irresistible. The reader thanks her for it; Edmund falls in love with her at least partially because of it; and even the relentlessly somber Fanny has to admit to being amused: " 'I like to hear her talk. She entertains me' " (94); and, wonder of wonders, " 'She made me almost laugh' " (95). Mary's "lively mind" (95) and "playful manner" (412) are so appealing, in fact, that in order for the lackluster Fanny to rise to the stature of romantic heroine and for her moral severity to win our sympathy (if not our allegiance), Mary must ultimately be exiled from the novel. As D. A. Miller has noted, Mary, whose language makes up "so much of the text," suddenly "disappears from direct view" in "the last hundred or so pages of *Mansfield Park,*" being "represented only by her letters to Fanny and by Edmund's report of his last meeting with her."[6]

The most damning evidence against Mary for immorality, then, consists of interpretive accounts of her speech and letters by Edmund and Fanny—two of the least impartial of character witnesses. (Were her own humorous reporting of the facts admitted as testimony, we might, regardless of our better judgment perhaps, acquit her.) Despite her denunciation by the Mansfield moralists, Mary is allowed to escape the novel not simply without punishment, but with her charm, though somewhat tarnished, still largely intact. And, thanks to the destabilizing, elusive character of humor, Mary evades definitive interpretation and labeling as well. Though she cannot possibly be called a heroine, Mary is no villainess either.

Indeed, Mary functions as nothing so much as a narrative analogue to Fanny. Edmund is simply love-blind in asserting that there is "so much general resemblance in true generosity and natural delicacy" (270) between his cousin and his would-be lover, but the narrator, too, notes that, although some of the difference between them belongs to "disposition and habit . . . still more might be imputed to difference of circumstances" (290). That is, their cultural and domestic upbringing has marked them more decidedly than any disparity in temperament; for like Fanny, Mary has "really good feelings by which she was almost purely governed" (170). Consequently, an examination of "some points of interest [upon which] they were exactly opposed to each other"— namely, their sense of propriety and appropriate feminine conduct— throws into high relief not only the nature of their differences, but indeed how very far our acceptance of Mary and her ideas actually goes: point for point, we find the witty disruptor of the patriarchal status quo more sympathetically engaging than its ideal woman.[7]

Mary's profuse and sometimes brazen talk, for instance, is consistently more agreeable than Fanny's even more profuse feminine silence (arguably, Fanny speaks demonstrably less than any other Austen heroine because she has in Mary a double who speaks so much). Her failure to internalize an upper-middle-class code of feminine conduct exposes Mary to Edmund's charge of unwomanliness (a lack of "feminine loathings"), but it doesn't paralyze her as Fanny's successful internalization does; indeed, Fanny's strict sense of propriety prohibits her from directly expressing desire of any sort, which, among other things, makes her hostage to Henry's sexual advances.[8] Furthermore, Mary's interpretation of Maria's conduct as mere folly, which so infuriates Edmund, proceeds from a standard of judgment that recognizes no gender distinction in moral culpability: Mary reasonably concludes that Maria, being no more to blame than Henry for their elopement, deserves no severer labeling or punishment. Fanny reacts more to Edmund's liking: "If there was a woman of character in existence, who could treat as a trifle this sin of the first magnitude, who could try to gloss it over, and desire to have it unpunished, she could believe Miss Crawford to be the woman!" (429). But the hysterical intensity of her response to the news of Maria's elopement—her "sleepless" "misery," her "feelings of sickness" and "shudderings of horror," her "hot fits of fever" and "cold" (429), as well as her feeling that "the greatest blessing to every one of kindred with Mrs. Rushworth would be instant annihilation" (430)—suggests that such a response owes as much to Fanny's intrapsychic conflicts as to her high-minded morality.[9]

The surest sign of the narrative object-splitting that operates with regard to Mary and Fanny can be found in the presentation of laughter, for in *Mansfield Park* as in none of Austen's other novels, laughter and patriarchal principle are internalized in the text as mutually exclusive traits. Nowhere else in Austen, indeed, does a narrator so frequently gesture to a character's suppression of laughter; it rivals similar gesturing to Marianne's violent suppression of speech in *Sense and Sensibility*.[10] Although Fanny comes close at a number of points (she "almost laugh[s]" at Mary [95]; she "could hardly help laughing at" Tom [145]; "in spite of herself, she could not help half a smile, but she said nothing" [340]; "Fanny could not avoid a faint smile, but had nothing to say" [358]), she never actually manages an outright show of amusement. Tellingly, her only approach to a witticism is a temptation to allude to Dr. Johnson, the most famously moral of wits (385).

Mary, on the other hand, habitually inclines to laughter. In her last dramatized appearance in the novel (as reported by Edmund), she answers his vituperative attack on her for "faults of principle, of blunted delicacy and a corrupted, vitiated mind" (442) with "a sort of laugh" (444), and she exits the scene with "a saucy playful smile" that Edmund interprets as a sexual come-on. In charging Mary with both sexual and gender misconduct (her laughter, to his mind, is not simply femininely indecorous under the circumstances, but lewd), Edmund unwittingly associates her with the adulterous Maria. As Maria's adultery transgresses the law governing male ownership of female bodies, so Mary's irreverent laughter defies phallocratic injunctions against female speech. Unlike Maria, however, who is castigated for her crime, Mary finds sanctuary from censure in her doubleness. Not only is she "double" to Fanny (her function as heroine-counterpart, narratologically speaking, prevents her moral condemnation), but her doubly indecent laughter (because both sexually suggestive *and* of female origin) proceeds from her (doubly determined) humor. That is, being an expression of humor, Mary's laughter evades fixed meaning and, in so doing, she escapes punishment.

Edmund finds Mary's "habit" of mocking serious principle and her "impudence in wrong" (444) so repugnant that he refuses to admit having ever been in love with her: "It had been the creature of my own imagination, not Miss Crawford, that I had been too apt to dwell on"— an observation that, given Edmund's stuffiness, is probably correct. The narrator, however, judges Mary less harshly and far less prejudicially, reproaching not her femininely impertinent laughter, but rather her disingenuous "intentions to please" (282) and her near-cynical insouciance (which is most clearly seen in her crass joke about Tom's illness).[11] And yet even these faults are lightly rebuked in the narrative, largely because Mary is held only limitedly responsible for them. Despite their differences, Mary is, like Fanny, a product of her upbringing, femininely educated (like the Bertram sisters) in "manners" but not in "active principle" (448) and morally abandoned to the "vicious" example of her guardian uncle, the Admiral (74). Her impoverished moral education consequently grants her an excuse for speaking indecorously and sometimes insensitively, which in turn permits her—so long as she speaks under cover of laughter—both to disparage patriarchal practices and to challenge, by her own enormous appeal, cultural notions of feminine ideality.

Despite her reserved disapproval of Mary's moral character, the narrator not only tolerates Mary's laughter, but actually participates in it herself. For while she may ultimately judge according to the lights of Fanny's morality, the narrator characteristically responds to the inhabitants of Mansfield with an ironically inflected humor that matches Mary's. For example, when Mary (unlike Fanny, who gravitates to Dr. Johnson) quips on Sir Thomas in a parody inspired by Pope—" 'Blest Knight! whose dictatorial *looks* dispense / To Children affluence, to Rushworth sense' " (182; emphasis added)—she merely concentrates in two lines the narrative opinion of Sir Thomas's closed-fistedness (and of Mr. Rushworth's intelligence) that is dispersed throughout the text in comments like these:

[Sir Thomas] would not have wished her [Mary Crawford] to belong to him, though her twenty thousand pounds *had* been forty. (439; emphasis added)

[Mr. Yates] was not very solid; but there was a hope of his becoming less trifling—of his being at least tolerably domestic and quiet; and, at any rate, there was comfort in finding his estate rather more, and his debts much less, than he had feared. . . . (447)

[B]y looking . . . most exceedingly pleased with Sir Thomas's good opinion, and saying scarcely any thing, he [Mr. Rushworth] did his best towards preserving that good opinion a little longer. (202)

Similarly, the narrator's assessment of Dr. Grant not only resembles Mary's, but employs the same tone and sometimes the same language:

[Narrator:] It delighted Mrs. Grant to keep them [the Crawfords] both with her, and Dr. Grant was exceedingly well contented to have it so; a talking pretty young woman like Miss Crawford, is always pleasant society to an indolent, stay-at-home man [like Dr. Grant]; and Mr. Crawford's being his guest was an excuse for drinking claret every day. (80)

[Mary:] "And though Dr. Grant is most kind and obliging to me, and though he is really a gentleman, and I dare say a good scholar and clever, and often preaches good sermons, and is very respectable, *I* see him to be an indolent selfish bon vivant who must have his palate consulted in every thing, who will not stir a finger for the convenience of any one, and who, moreover, if the cook makes a blunder, is out of humour with his excellent wife." (137)

[Narrator:] They lived together [Mary and Mrs. Grant]; and when Dr. Grant had brought on apoplexy and death, by three great institutionary dinners in one week, they still lived together. . . . (453)

The humor that Mary and the narrator share is as alike in strategy as in perspective. Both rely upon word-play, italics (or emphasis, in Mary's case), litotes, periphrasis, and occasionally hyperbole to give their humor form, and both fix upon targets that are consistently, if not exclusively, "feminist": for example, Sir Thomas's oppressively paternalistic treatment of Fanny and his daughters (" 'Advise' was his word, but it was the advice of absolute power" [285]); the vitiating practices of the marriage market (Sir Thomas was "happy to secure a marriage which would bring him such an addition of respectability and influence, and very happy to think any thing of his daughter's disposition that was most favourable for the purpose" [215]); or the gender-bias of the dominant cultural attitude toward adultery.[12] On the issue of sexual inequality in the punishment of adultery, indeed, not only is the narrator at her most explicitly (proto)feminist, but her moral judgment is notably closer to Mary's than at any other time: "That punishment, the punishment of disgrace, would in a just measure attend his [Henry's] share of the offence, is, we know, not one of the barriers which society gives to virtue. In this world, the penalty is less equal than could be wished" (452).

Mary and the narrator's humor is so alike that its main distinction lies in their preferences for particular rhetorical strategies. Mary favors hyperbole (what she calls " 'the *never* of conversation' " [120]) and word-play (" 'Certainly, my home at my uncle's brought me acquainted with a circle of admirals. Of *Rears*, and *Vices*, I saw enough. Now, do not be suspecting me of a pun, I entreat' " [91]). The narrator, on the other hand, inclines to periphrasis and litotes.[13] Periphrasis, by burying the target of her humor (and often the humor itself) in an excess of words, allows the narrator to make her joke without incurring explicit responsibility or even lasting notice. Consider the following passage:

As a general reflection on Fanny, Sir Thomas thought nothing could be more unjust [than Mrs. Norris's complaint of Fanny's having a "little spirit of . . . independence"], though he had been so lately expressing the same sentiments himself, and he tried to turn the conversation; tried repeatedly before he could succeed; for Mrs. Norris had not discernment enough to perceive, either now, or at any other time, to what degree he thought well of his niece, or how very far he was from wishing to have his own children's merits set off by the depreciation of hers. (323)

Although easily overlooked in a sentence devoted to Sir Thomas's compensatory appreciation of Fanny, the narrative comment—that "he had been so lately expressing the same sentiments himself"—clearly distinguishes the narrator's opinion of Sir Bertram from Fanny's hopelessly idealized version. For like Mary Crawford, the narrator realizes that the man who is responsible for Maria's education—and indirectly for her outcome—cannot possibly be, as Fanny describes him, "all that was clever and good" (397). Litotes, on the other hand, which works by negation, permits the narrator to exercise a linguistic form of denial that, like denial in its psychoanalytic sense, obliquely confirms the validity of what it denies:

[Sir Thomas was now] at leisure to find the Grants really worth visiting; and though infinitely above scheming or contriving for any the most advantageous matrimonial establishment that could be among the apparent possibilities of any one most dear to him, and disdaining even as a littleness the being quick-sighted on such points, he could not avoid perceiving in a grand and careless way that Mr. Crawford was somewhat distinguishing his niece—nor perhaps refrain (though unconsciously) from giving a more willing assent to invitations on that account.

. . . [He] began to think, that any one in the habit of such idle observations *would have thought* that Mr. Crawford was the admirer of Fanny Price. (247)

As Mary Crawford's humorous remarks scandalize the inhabitants of Mansfield Park, so the narrator's ironic humor dialogically destabilizes—through periphrasis—and "unsays"—through litotes—the dominant, sober discourse of the text, which consistently aligns itself with Fanny's morality. In so doing, the narrative humor constitutes an instance of "feminine lawlessness" (122) as surely as does Mary's more overt subversion of prescribed feminine values and behaviors. Furthermore, because laughter—to which the humor gives rise—has its origins and expression in the prelinguistic (or the Lacanian presymbolic), it not only disrupts the symbolic (paternal) discourse of the text, but establishes an affective, prediscursive (maternal) connection between narrator and reader as well—a connection that essentially imitates the bond between the narrator and heroine of *Mansfield Park*. More importantly, however, from a narratological viewpoint, the textual blurring of the maternal narrator's humorous perspective with Mary Crawford's implicates Mary—with her dubious ethics and apparent lack of sisterhood—in the narrator's protective attitude toward Fanny. Consequently, Mary's humor, while it functions as a cover for the narrator's, participates as well in protecting Fanny when it attacks the constructions of femininity that constrain both characters.

Both Mary and the narrator seek to avoid a "too harsh construction" of their "playful manner" (412)—a detection of their "feminine lawlessness"—not only by adopting indirect strategies of humor, but sometimes by simply diverting attention from their own humorous utterance. Like the narrator, who draws notice away from her mockery of Sir Thomas by thrusting Mrs. Norris before us, Mary either abruptly "turns the subject" (117; 294) when the point of her remarks becomes too apparent or else insists that she is "merely joking" (135). Unlike the narrator, however, Mary is only partially successful in disguising the tendency of her wit. Largely because she is more obviously gender-marked than the narrator—because she has a female body and name as well as an identifiable "voice" and a "laugh" (130)—Mary is more often cited and more severely judged for her unfeminine opinions (by readers as well as fellow characters), even when those opinions are virtually identical to those of the narrator.[14]

Finally, humor provides both Mary and the narrator with a linguistic outlet for the frustration that arises when their desires and opinions conflict with internalized cultural definitions of femininity and external demands for conformity. Although in the following passage Mary's access to such an outlet is blocked, the manner by which it is normally achieved throughout the novel is indicated:

> [Mary,] startled from the agreeable fancies she had been previously indulging on the strength of her brother's description, no longer able, in the picture she had been forming of a future Thornton, to shut out the church, sink the clergyman, and see only the respectable, elegant, modernized, and occasional residence of a man of independent fortune—was considering Sir Thomas, with decided ill-will, as the destroyer of all this, and suffering the more from the involuntary forbearance which his character and manner commanded, and from not daring to relieve herself by a single attempt at throwing ridicule on his cause. (256)

By "throwing ridicule" on the patriarchal organization of nineteenth-century culture (its customs, hypocrisies, and phallocentrism) and on those who represent it (Sir Thomas and, to some degree, the masculinely constructed feminine such as Fanny typifies), both Mary and the narrator find temporary relief from the contained aggression (the "involuntary forbearance") they suffer on its account. And by granting them a means of expressing frustration (provoked when Mary's desires are thwarted by her cultural limitations or when the narrator's judgment conflicts with reigning practices of daughterly education), humor not only alleviates that frustration but indeed profitably transforms it into both a derivative means of instinctual gratification and—for us as readers—a primary source of literary satisfaction.

NOTES

1. Jane Austen, *Mansfield Park* (Harmondsworth: Penguin, 1966).
2. See Lionel Trilling's enormously influential essay *"Mansfield Park,"* in *The Opposing Self* (New York: Harcourt, 1955), 181–202.
3. Claudia L. Johnson, *Jane Austen: Women, Politics, and the Novel* (Chicago: University of Chicago Press, 1988), 94.
4. See Tony Tanner, "Introduction," in *Mansfield Park*, 7–36. Tanner writes that Fanny "is never, ever, wrong. Jane Austen, usually so ironic about her heroines, in this instance vindicates Fanny Price without qualification" (8). As I hope to demonstrate, this is rather too strongly put. Although Fanny may well be treated less ironically than any other Austen heroine, there are moments when even she, no matter how affectionately, is made fun of (as the undesiring object of Henry's romantic plot, for example). Moreover,

Elinor Dashwood of *Sense and Sensibility* is very seldom treated ironically either, though being a wit herself, she is implicated in the narrative humor in ways that Fanny is not. On Austen's irony toward Fanny, see Martin Price, *Forms of Life: Character and Moral Imagination in the Novel* (New Haven: Yale University Press, 1983).

5. D. A. Miller points out in *Narrative and Its Discontents: Problems of Closure in the Traditional Novel* (Princeton: Princeton University Press, 1981) that the narrator's ambivalent feelings toward Mary are evidenced by the fact that Mary's expulsion from the Mansfield Park community is presented "through a character's narration of it, that it is from a point of view that she [the narrator] has never fully embraced" (86). Similarly, Mary Poovey, in *The Proper Lady and the Woman Writer: Ideology as Style in the Works of Mary Wollstonecraft, Mary Shelley, and Jane Austen* (Chicago: University of Chicago Press, 1984), while noting the power of Mary's seductive appeal, suggests that the narrator not only permits such appeal but is susceptible to it herself: Mary "constantly threatens to escape narrative control" (220).

6. Miller, *Narrative and Its Discontents*, 77; 83. Miller also argues that "if the categories of moral knowledge are to be brought to bear on her effectively, then the linguistic polyvalency that has made up her empirical reality in the novel must be forcibly reduced. The closure that Mary is subjected to involves a necessary simplification of her discourse and the implication it has sustained" (87). In other words, Mary's appeal must be neutralized (by reducing the instances of her witty talk) in order for Austen to assert Fanny's moral authority (and thereby to achieve closure). It is only after closure is effectively achieved that Mary is "allowed to recover (in the narrator's final wrap-up) some of her earlier complexity" (87).

7. Paul Pickrel, "Lionel Trilling and *Mansfield Park*," *SEL* 27 (1987): 609–21, catalogues a number of other points of comparison between Fanny and Mary; both women are reared in the homes of their uncles; both are companions to a brother; one is "spoilt" by her upbringing, the other "made" by hers; one has the advantages of nature (Mary), the other of nurture; one is inspirited by the city, the other by the country; one is reared in domestic privilege, the other in inconsequence. We could add that while Fanny is the slave to all, Mary is not even "the slave of opportunity" (353) and that whereas Fanny is persistently asexual despite being eroticized by her male admirers, Mary, precociously inducted into sexuality (thanks to her exposure to the Admiral), is overwhelmingly sensual.

8. Poovey points out that "Fanny's embrace of propriety . . . is intimately bound up with her defense against rejection, and . . . linked to her ideas about love" (*Proper Lady*, 217). In the case of Henry, however, Fanny's propriety expresses her gratitude rather than her love. Fanny, who is repulsed by Henry's selfishness, his unprincipled behavior, and his insensitivity to the feelings of others, nevertheless softens under the pressure of his persistent courting ("Would he have persevered, and uprightly, Fanny must have been his reward" [451]), partly in *gratitude* for his considerate blind-

ness to her Portsmouth family's gaucheness, partly as a consequence of emotional blackmail: "[H]e approached her now with rights that demanded different treatment. She must be courteous, and she must be compassionate. She must have a sensation of being honoured, and whether thinking of herself or her brother, she must have a strong feeling of gratitude" (327). See Poovey (15–30) on the titillating aspect of feminine propriety (some men find it irresistible).

9. Miller argues in a similar vein (*Narrative and Its Discontents*, 60).

10. Angela Leighton, "Sense and Silences: Reading Jane Austen Again," in *Jane Austen: New Perspectives* [*Women & Literature*, n.s., vol. 3], ed. Janet Todd (New York: Holmes & Meier, 1983), 128–40, discusses the suppression of speech in *Sense and Sensibility*, particularly Marianne's, as overdetermined silence; the suppression of laughter in *Mansfield Park*, I want to suggest, may similarly be read as complexly significant.

11. Mary writes in a letter to Fanny with regard to the news of Tom's sudden illness:

> "I need not say how rejoiced I shall be to hear there has been any mistake, but the report is so prevalent, that I confess I cannot help trembling. To have such a fine young man cut off in the flower of his days, is most melancholy. Poor Sir Thomas will feel it dreadfully. I really am quite agitated on the subject. Fanny, Fanny, I see you smile, and look cunning, but upon my honour, I never bribed a physician in my life. Poor young man!—If he is to die, there will be *two* poor young men less in the world [i.e., Edmund will inherit Tom's property as first son]. . . . It will be but the loss of the Esquire after his name. With real affection, Fanny, like mine, more might be overlooked." (423)

Miller points out that this is the most damning evidence against Mary, largely because, being her own text, and free from even narrative commentary, it comes to us and our judgment unfiltered and undistorted by another's interpretation.

It is worth noting that this epistolary joke of Mary's, though perhaps less funny, is not dissimilar in topic and tone to some of Jane Austen's jokes in letters to her sister, Cassandra: for example, "Mrs. Hall, of Sherborne, was brought to bed yesterday of a dead child, some weeks before she expected, owing to a fright. I suppose she happened unawares to look at her husband." In *Jane Austen's Letters to Her Sister Cassandra and Others*, ed. R. W. Chapman, 2d ed. (London: Oxford University Press, 1952), 24.

12. Others have noted stylistic similarities between Mary Crawford and the narrator. Poovey, for example, notes that the narrator's "vitality is far closer to Mary Crawford's energy than to Fanny's passivity" (*Proper Lady*, 203), and Miller finds that the narrator often sounds like Mary, though he sees the phenomenon as a recurring aberration rather than a sign of essential sympathy in their voice and perspective: "The tones of Mary's self-irony have once more [near closure] been allowed to infiltrate the narrator's discourse about her" (*Narrative and Its Discontents*, 87).

13. The narrator's humor also relies heavily on linguistic and syntactic repeti-

tion, emphatic punctuation (such as dashes), apophasis, subjunctive constructions, and, as Louise Flavin and Zelda Boyd have pointed out, respectively, free indirect speech and modal auxiliaries for its expression. See Louise Flavin, "*Mansfield Park:* Free Indirect Discourse and the Psychological Novel," *Studies in the Novel* 19 (1987): 137–59, and Zelda Boyd, "Jane Austen's 'Must': The Will and the World," *Nineteenth Century Fiction* 39 (1984): 127–43.

14. Mary, like the narrator, is most identifiable as a voice and laugh. Fanny, for example, detects Mary's unseen presence at Sotherton audially: "Getting quite impatient, she resolved to go in search of Henry and Mary, when the voice and laugh of Miss Crawford once more caught her ear" (130). Yet unlike the narrator (and to her own undoing), she has an obvious bodily presence as well. See Claire Kahane, "Seduction and the Voice of the Text: *Heart of Darkness* and *The Good Soldier*," in *Seduction and Theory: Readings of Gender, Representation and Rhetoric*, ed. Dianne Hunter (Urbana: University of Illinois Press, 1989), 135–53, for a compelling discussion of the narrative voice as "the presence of the body in writing, or that which gives the illusion of presence in the midst of absence, an illusion which is the primary pleasure of the text" (136).

REFERENCES

Austen, Jane. *Jane Austen's Letters to Her Sister Cassandra and Others.* Ed. R. W. Chapman. 2d ed. London: Oxford University Press, 1952.

———. *Mansfield Park.* 1814. Harmondsworth: Penguin, 1966.

Boyd, Zelda. "Jane Austen's 'Must': The Will and the World." *Nineteenth Century Fiction* 39 (1984): 127–43.

Flavin, Louise. "*Mansfield Park:* Free Indirect Discourse and the Psychological Novel." *Studies in the Novel* 19 (1987): 137–59.

Johnson, Claudia L. *Jane Austen: Women, Politics, and the Novel.* Chicago: University of Chicago Press, 1988.

Kahane, Claire. "Seduction and the Voice of the Text: *Heart of Darkness* and *The Good Soldier*." In *Seduction and Theory: Readings of Gender Representation, and Rhetoric,* edited by Dianne Hunter, 135–53. Urbana: University of Illinois Press, 1989.

Leighton, Angela. "Sense and Silences: Reading Jane Austen Again." In *Jane Austen: New Perspectives,* edited by Janet Todd, 128–40. New York: Holmes and Meier, 1983.

Miller, D. A. *Narrative and Its Discontents.* Princeton: Princeton University Press, 1981.

Pickrel, Paul. "Lionel Trilling and *Mansfield Park.*" *SEL* 27 (1987): 609–21.

Poovey, Mary. *The Proper Lady and the Woman Writer: Ideology as Style in the Works of Mary Wollstonecraft, Mary Shelley, and Jane Austen.* Chicago: University of Chicago Press, 1984.

Price, Martin. *Forms of Life: Character and Moral Imagination in the Novel.* New Haven: Yale University Press, 1983.

Tanner, Tony. "Introduction." In *Mansfield Park,* by Jane Austen, 7–36. Harmondsworth: Penguin, 1966.

Trilling, Lionel. *"Mansfield Park."* In *The Opposing Self: Nine Essays in Criticism,* 181–202. New York: Harcourt, 1955.

17.

LOST IN SPACE BETWEEN "CENTER" AND "MARGIN": SOME THOUGHTS ON LESBIAN-FEMINIST DISCOURSE, BISEXUAL WOMEN, AND SPECULATIVE FICTION

ROBIN ANNE REID

In volume one of *The History of Sexuality* Foucault argues that the "psychological, psychiatric, medical category of homosexuality was constituted . . . less by a type of sexual relations than by a certain quality of sexual sensibility. . . . The sodomite had been a temporary aberration; the homosexual was now a species" (43).[1] Thus, in the nineteenth century, important changes occurred in the discourses of sexuality, as the previous category of homosexual acts was replaced by the creation of the homosexual individual. The creation of the homosexual individual was accompanied by a proliferation of discourses that functioned as mechanisms to analyze, dissect, and control aberrant sexualities (42–49).

And yet this earlier proliferation of discourses about sexualities has been mythologized as "repression" by twentieth-century discourse, which has constructed a contemporary myth of personal and erotic liberation by means of the confession, often regarding our (essential) sexual identity. In our current myth, discussing our sexual identities is the primary means of overcoming past repression and silence. Foucault also notes that although the historical origins and development of the confessional mode focused on controlling sexuality, the appearance of discourses to control "perversity" did make possible "reverse discourses," or sites of resistance. As a result, "homosexuality began to speak in its own behalf, to demand that its legitimacy or 'naturality' be acknowledged, often in the same vocabulary, using the same categories by which it was medically disqualified" (101).

Strategically speaking, the construction of "the homosexual" as an essential category based on its difference from the norm, the married, heterosexual couple, can be simultaneously a site of institutionalized oppression and one of resistance. Reading Foucault's analysis of such discursive formations reveals that underlying the perceived binary opposition of such rhetorical structures as *repression vs. liberation, heterosexual vs. homosexual,* and *dominant vs. oppressed* are complex, interconnected networks of power relations. Awareness of these networks means that now, during the last decade of the twentieth century, few individuals or groups can construct themselves as purely and simply oppressed, if by oppressed they mean their identity is always that of "victim of oppression" and never that of "oppressor." Constructing "homosexuals" as always victims of oppression ignores, among other things, the power relations of race and class hierarchies in this country; additionally, the ways in which homosexual discourses and institutions have excluded or denied the existence of individuals of other "alternate sexualities" or other "sexual minorities" complicates the stance of gays as always only oppressed.

My specific focus in this essay is the exclusion of bisexual women by lesbian and feminist discourses. This exclusion, which is often ignored in a discourse focused primarily on the heterosexual/lesbian binary, seems to have, as its basis, the belief in an essential "lesbian" identity and the concurrent marginalization of the "bisexual woman." I would argue instead for the possibilities of reconceptualizing "sexuality" as process/oscillation/textuality, a project carried out with some success by a few women writing speculative fiction (SF) in the eighties.[2] Beginning to reconceptualize sexual identity in this manner would open up new strategies for relationships between women which, while not attempting to ignore "differences," would, I hope, undercut the belief that differences in sexuality, sexual behavior, or sexual choices must be divisive in nature and thus somehow be "policed" in or by feminism.

Gays and lesbians, in basing a political movement for liberation upon the construction of an essential homosexual self or identity, opposite/ opposed to heterosexuality, have reversed the dominant binary structure: homosexuality is constructed as natural and good (as opposed to naturally depraved).[3] But that reversal means that a new "center" has been created, and "the bisexual" has been marginalized or demonized, made to fit the "evil" position that "the homosexual" has rejected. This exclusion occurs in various discourses: academic writing, the activist press, and even general conversation.[4] In 1987, a white, married friend of mine shared a secret with me: she had rented a post office box and joined a letter-writing club for lesbians. She showed me the magazine that stated, clearly, that bisexual women were not encouraged to join the club. Furthermore, any bisexual women who decided to join despite this lack of encouragement had to identify themselves beforehand. What with, I wondered, a red "B" on our foreheads? My friend was open about her marriage to a man, but since she did not identify herself as a "bisexual," she was warmly accepted as a member and, apparently, as a "lesbian."

Locating "sexual identity" in something other than specific sexual behavior (my friend, after all, continued to make love with her husband during this time) is based in our current historical and cultural matrix. The lesbian who told me that she would rather sleep with a "married woman" than a "bisexual woman" is operating on the same assumptions about what constitutes identity as the lesbian letter-writing club: there are heterosexual women and lesbians. Heterosexual women may have lesbian encounters; lesbians may have sexual encounters with males. But these experiences do not change their "essential" identities. And there is nothing in between. Such essentializing of a binary system of identity is exclusive at best, oppressive at worst. For if only two essential identities exist, individuals must be either heterosexual or homosexual.[5] As a result, lesbian discourse has been telling bisexual women more or less what the straight world has been telling homosexuals: bisexuals *really* do not exist; or, bisexuals are *really* homosexual and are just "choosing" to be difficult about it.

Beginning to redefine identity as multiple identities, rather than static or essential, or to refigure identity as a process, leads me to complicate my declaration that I am a bisexual woman. My skin color is that pinkish-tan categorized as "white"; my own ethnic identification is as a fourth-generation Welsh-American whose family history and tribal genealogy have been transmitted orally. Born and raised in northern Idaho, I rarely mention that my hometown is Moscow since most people react by commenting how well I have learned English. Although there are eight "Moscows" in the world that I know of, most people in America equate Moscow with Russia. As a child and adolescent, I benefitted from my father's middle-class income and access to health care, but as an adult who has rarely held a job that includes benefits, I live with ulcerative colitis, a chronic illness that may not be covered by any insurance I may eventually get. Identifying as a Republican for the first twenty years of my life, I went straight to declaring myself a radical in my twenties without even a stopover as a liberal. Yet in my thirties I tend to get along much better with those conservatives who have a sense of humor than with many liberals I meet in the academy. I have a Ph.D. in English, but thirty years of reading SF and my involvement in SF fandom (a subculture that relegates the rest of the world to the status of "mundanes") makes me a bit of a renegade in the "field" of English, although most fans are surprised to find an English teacher in their midst.[6] I live with the contradiction of growing up in the academic culture as an insider, a faculty brat whose father is a white male professor; yet, as a white woman, I had to overcome strong feelings of exclusion before starting a Ph.D. program in my thirties (although I had no problems with completing master's programs in English). On my left shoulder is a tattoo of a rose, a souvenir of a summer spent studying at Oxford. All these identities overlap with and inform my "sexuality" which, in fact, I rarely think of as an essential or static identity, but as a series of attitudes, proclivities, emotions, behaviors, and choices that have changed through time and no doubt will continue to do so, both in terms of the different levels of energy involved and in terms of preferences.

In 1989, soon after I began work on my Ph.D., I found myself sitting in a graduate seminar on feminist theories and narratives listening to white lesbian separatists and white heterosexual women debate issues of sexuality, politics, and oppressions. "I" never could get a word in as a bisexual woman. Furthermore, "I" did not exist in any of the theoretical or narrative texts we were reading. These feminist texts complicated "gender" in a number of ways, in terms of the intersections of gender with ethnicity and class.[7] But most texts took the lesbian/heterosexual division of identities for granted. Lesbian and heterosexual feminists have had an uneasy relationship with each other, especially in regard to feminist organizing, methods, and goals. But at times both "groups," or, more accurately, their dominant discursive practices (I know full well that ethnic, class, religious, and age differences mean that constructing all lesbians or heterosexual feminists as "similar" is impossible) have operated to exclude, ignore, or deny the existence of bisexual women.[8]

The various rejections I have experienced from lesbians were more painful than the ignorance I have seen exhibited by heterosexuals: most heterosexuals' response to my declaration of bisexuality involves some insistence on *percentages*. I was told by one woman that I could not claim to be a bisexual unless I had slept with exactly 50 percent men and exactly 50 percent women. Since she had slept with a few women during her life and still defined herself as heterosexual, her need to insist upon some specific boundary lines between heterosexuals, bisexuals, and lesbians was clear. Most heterosexuals tend to class "bisexuals" as "queer" in the same sense that they class "homosexuals" as "abnormal." "Queer" sexual identity is often constructed, by heterosexuals, as willed and specific sexual behaviors, not as an essential ("natural") identity, a category reserved for the heterosexual identity exclusively.[9] While I believe moving away from seeing sexuality as an essential identity could be strategically useful, I would question the dominant contemporary attitude that sexual identity exists only in individuals who are sexually active in certain (socially approved) ways. I also want to avoid setting up "bisexual" as a third static/essential identity. One solution is to shift from conceptualizing sexuality as an essential identity that must be maintained by excluding all deviant "others," or limiting sexuality as dependent on specific sexual activity, to considering the idea of sexuality as oscillation/process, as Pamela L. Caughie does in her essay, "Virginia Woolf's Double Discourse."

Although her essay is primarily focused on analyzing an important aspect of Woolf's writing, Caughie's argument is based on defining androgyny as a process, linking it to the the "double discourse" (Jane Gallop's term) of Woolf's novel, and to playfulness. Androgyny is oscillation, ambiguity, a process that should be understood as "not so much a psychosexual category as a rhetorical strategy, less a condition than a motive. Androgyny does not *substitute* for anything."[10] Androgyny and bisexuality have been seen as two separate and distinct categories; the more reading and thinking I have done, the more I wonder why. In my own experience—personal, social, professional, and literary—the two concepts often overlap. Caughie defines androgyny as "constructing lives, histories, identities, and fictions" (42). Woolf's androgynous statement, argues Caughie, is "not a metaphysical or feminist theory, not . . . a resolution to or a synthesis of contrarities, but . . . a way to remain suspended between opposed beliefs"; androgyny is vacillation, ambiguity, the "refusal to choose" (44). Redefining sexuality as process / oscillation / textuality need not be limited to bisexuality; extending this definition to all and any sexualities would overcome the difficulties in conceptualizing sexuality as an essential identity, or as predicated upon overt and specific behaviors.

Such an expanded definition of sexual identities may leave more room for the coalitions necessary in the era of AIDS. Since lesbians have allied with gay men to work on a number of issues, forming some coalitions across gender and class boundaries at least (I am not aware of multiracial coalitions, but I assume those also exist), I do not see why the possibility of coalitions with bisexuals is denied; nor do I see that my identifying as a bisexual woman takes anything away from lesbians. Several essays in *Bi Any Other Name*, an anthology of writings by bisexuals, argue that bisexuals can work with gays and lesbians under the rubric of "Queer Politics," and that such coalitions are necessary, especially given the social and cultural constructions of AIDS, a phenomenon that has made bisexuals more visible in the media.[11] Currently, bisexuals are often blamed as primarily responsible for transmitting AIDS. Robert Neveldine, a friend who works with Queer Theory, notes that bisexual men are either excluded from categories of queerness or are considered conduits of corruption and contagion between straight and gay people, especially in various AIDS discourses where bis get represented as the route of transmission from "fags" to "nice straights" (usually women).[12] Such a construction of bisexual equates bisexuals with men; women are invisible in this discourse (as are lesbians, when "homosexual" means men). Two other friends, Katherine Cummings and Leslie Donovan, have informed me that lesbians (in magazines and in conversations) have blamed bisexual women for carrying AIDS into the lesbian community; the claim is often made that lesbians would never have experienced AIDS except for those (bisexual) women who sleep with men and women.[13] The straight community casts bisexual men as the means of transmitting AIDS from the gay to the straight community, and the lesbian community sees bisexual women as the means of transmitting AIDS from the straight to the lesbian community. Both groups are falling prey to the prejudices first exhibited at the start of the AIDS epidemic: blaming a marginalized group. All the work by AIDS activists to focus on specific at-risk behaviors instead of demonizing a marginalized group seems to have been ignored.

I have only recently learned of the accusations concerning AIDS transmission; my previous experiences concerned a lesser series of accusations. For example, as a bisexual women, I have been accused of being wishy-washy, of sitting on the fence, of masquerading as a lesbian just to meet women, of leaving lesbian lovers for male lovers, and of "passing" in the straight world to maintain my "heterosexual privileges." Stripped of the tone of accusation often used by lesbians, some of these constructions tend to critique the idea of essential sexual identity: the idea of a "masquerade" undercuts the idea of an essential and clear-cut lesbian identity that cannot be "counterfeited." I would also question why the practice of bisexuals passing as straight or gay is any more suspect than the practice of gays and lesbians passing as straight. While being in closets is not necessarily a "good" for any number of reasons, being in the closet and passing for straight should be considered no less acceptable an option for bisexuals than for gays and lesbians. I have begun to suspect that bisexuals "passing" as "homosexual," as a number apparently have for years in various gay and lesbian communities, is considered the most problematic. The accusation of "heterosexual privilege" would carry more weight with me had feminism succeeded in more of its goals for all women: but privilege in the material sense is probably based more on gender, class, and racial status than some blanket heterosexual "privilege."

The need to consider the possibilities of coalitions between gays, lesbians, and bisexuals is clear, and I have the sense that a good deal of work is being done in various activist and community groups. Perhaps the pressure to deal with such an overwhelming threat as AIDS serves as an incentive to overcome issues of exclusion among heterosexuals, homosexuals, and bisexuals. My concerns are with the discourses of those who may not face such pressures and thus see any need to change.

Examining the paradigms that affect relations between women in feminism reveal a pattern of attempts to ignore or exclude difference in the interests of reducing conflict, based on the belief that "women" are naturally (i.e., biologically and essentially) nonhierarchical and cooperative.[14] This belief has been critiqued and questioned by feminists but still holds sway in various forms and strengths (i.e., many feminists believe women are culturally conditioned to be nonhierarchical and cooperative).

Handling conflict by means of exclusion of difference is obviously a problem for feminism.[15] Yet one possible strategy to deal with this problem involves restructuring relations between women by constructing sexuality differently. Such restructurings of sexuality, conflict, and resolution occupy SF novelists Diane Duane and Lynn Abbey, who publish mostly in the genre of fantasy, and Janet Kagan and Vonda McIntyre, who publish mostly in the genre of science fiction. Keeping in mind Caughie's definition that links the construction of "lives, histories, identities, and fictions" (42), I would like to discuss briefly the ways these texts restructure relations between women and how feminist discourse would benefit by including some of those constructions.

Written in the eighties, the texts above are among the few that work with both the ideas of androgyny and (to some extent) bisexuality in unusual ways. They speculate on the possibilities of androgyny/bisexuality and fill the gaps in other texts. Categorized as speculative fiction, they create different worlds—that is, different cultures. SF, like mainstream literature, evidences many of the dominant culture's values and assumptions; in fact, since SF in this country started with a pulp tradition written mostly by white males trained in the sciences, the genre can circulate the worst patriarchal assumptions.

But a subgenre of recent SF novels explores the ways cultures construct identity, sexual, erotic, and otherwise, and those books are worth noting for their construction of the erotic.[16] Interestingly, most of these novels separate "sex" from procreation and the presence of children who must be raised. Yet others, such as the ones I analyze here, attempt to reconstruct cultures from the "bottom" up, including the erotic and social lives of adult characters, as well as familial structure and child-rearing practices. Such reconstructions necessarily result in critiquing the ways in which female identity is constructed and maintained. As Joanna Russ points out in her essay analyzing the feminist utopias of the seventies, sexual permissiveness in those texts is there "not to break the taboos but to separate sexuality from questions of ownership, reproduction and social structure." [17] The earlier utopias separated child-rearing from sexuality by showing cultures where people other than the biological mother are responsible for children, but did not exclude children entirely. The novels I discuss here are not utopian by design, nor would many people label them "feminist" (with the possible exception of Abbey's trilogy).[18] And yet in presenting cultures where rigid gender roles have disappeared (or never existed), where androgyny and bisexuality are more the norm than the exception, and where child-rearing is included in the expectations for adults of both genders (while not being required by state or religious institutions as the sole culturally approved reason for sexual activity or marriage), these writers start to shift from accepting sexual identity as essential to conceptualizing the idea of multiple sexualities and sexuality as process and to critiquing the role culture plays in constructing identity and the "erotic." As a result, relationships between women, involving sexual love and conflict, become exceedingly complex.

These novels extend the possibilities for eroticism and intimacy beyond the homogeneous heterosexual norm (in which two lovers are presumed to be of the same species, race, class, and age). Women both love and are sexually involved with other women, but not necessarily exclusively. Duane's and McIntyre's female characters tend to be what most people today would categorize as "bisexual." In Duane's novel, *The Door into Shadow,* people have a committed emotional relationship with a "loved" of the same or the opposite gender, but monogamy seems to be rare. (A person may have more than one beloved.) Marriage is possible with "any man or woman or group" (*Shadow,* 61). Child-rearing and living arrangements are personal choices. McIntyre's trilogy has protagonists who are in contracted marriages. But these characters are seen as old-fashioned by others: this African-Canadian woman, Japanese-American man, and Anglo-American man are criticized not for their bisexuality, but for actually committing to a legal relationship. Two other main characters, an Anglo-American woman and a "diver" (a human being genetically modified to live underwater with the orcas of Puget Sound), work with and eventually become involved with the marriage, which can change and grow over time. Abbey's trilogy describes "bisexual" women, although the protagonist in the third novel is primarily "lesbian." Kagan's protagonist is sexually involved with a man and finally decides to marry him, but one of her primary emotional relationships is with a woman who, it turns out, is raising the protagonists's children. In fact, even using the terms like "bisexual" and "lesbian" to discuss these novels is difficult because the cultures created by these writers do not split up and label sexual identities in this way. The novels emphasize the spectrum of relationships possible when women do not see themselves in competition for men, or do not need to base their identities on excluding others.

Yet significantly, conflicts among and between women structure plot in many of these novels. The shift in cultural constructs of gender and sexuality allows for much more complex plotting of conflicts: the spectrum ranges from verbal disagreements all the way to physical violence resulting in death. Women are not in conflict with other women over a "scarce" commodity—men—nor with each other over some approved sexuality. But neither are the women weighed down with essentialist traits, such as nurturing, selflessness, or passivity as far as acting on their desires or needs (as opposed to acting to further the needs of a male figure). In some ways, constructing sexuality differently opens the way for more and different kinds of conflict among women, and also between women and men. For example, in these cultures, military training or service is not limited to men, nor is there the belief that men are "naturally" aggressive and women "naturally" pacifistic. Women in these novels can choose to be trained and to defend themselves or their country against aggression; not all women (or men) make this choice, nor is it required of them to do so. None of these novelists are interested in glorifying or eroticizing physical violence, or in supporting the belief that military power justifies actions taken by a government against another nation.

The spectrum of conflicts ranges from disagreement and debate to fighting in self-defense. Abbey, McIntyre, and Kagan show women training with a variety of weapons, fighting in self-defense, and disagreeing with each other over various courses of action. In McIntyre, women debate the question of arming a spaceship and the courses of actions possible once the ship leaves Earth; the reason the spaceship is hijacked is to keep the U.S. government from arming it and making it into an orbiting arsenal. Kagan presents discussions of ecological issues. Physical conflict is most notable in manifestations of the goddess: some are shadows perceived as evil, denying life and presenting death as seductive. Segnbora fights one of these goddesses and a Nightmare (a carnivorous winged horse that only a woman can kill), in *The Door into Shadow*. In these narratives, conflict demands resolution, and most of these novels tend toward resolving conflicts, but without "totalizing" happy endings in which dissenting voices are expelled.[19]

These novels provide me with a way of conceptualizing my life and problematizing the essential pattern of identity I have so often been presented with. Personal choices I have made—such as my decision not to marry or have children—have all been ones that result in my feeling outside the mainstream of contemporary American society. Yet my early involvement with SF fandom, which categorizes the rest of world as "mundanes," kept me from succumbing to the pressure to conform during my twenties.[20] Fen (the proper plural of fan) of different classes, ideologies, and philosophies (if not often enough, different races) generally bond around two issues: the mundane rejection of SF as trash and the belief in the superior intelligence of fen. SF images of the alien give that fan identification a good deal of scope. Discovering in my thirties novels such as the ones described above has made me feel as if I have come home in ways difficult to describe. I only know that I have not found such a feeling in other texts, no matter how enjoyable, and have been motivated to begin writing more and differently in order to share that particular sense of community.

In writing about these texts, I hope to extend knowledge of them beyond the bounds of "fandom" (and to break down the perception that an SF novel is by definition only a fun read for an academic's off-time). Perhaps their time is now: the past few years have witnessed a definite increase in the level of bisexual activism and a move toward inclusion of bisexuals (and others of "alternate sexualities") in formerly gay/lesbian groups. And recent resistance to inclusion of those "others" in gay pride marches and events indicates that bisexuality is finding its place. SF is in a good position to communicate feminist views to those outside the academy. Looking at new ways of constructing relationships between women and dealing with conflict can be valuable; beginning to reconstruct sexuality as oscillation/process may address some of the problems I have experienced with lesbian-feminist discourse: specifically, the marginalization, demonization, or exclusion of bisexual women.

NOTES

1. Michel Foucault, *The History of Sexuality, Volume 1: An Introduction,* trans. Robert Hurley (New York: Vintage Books, 1990).
2. The term "speculative fiction," often abbreviated as SF, can be used as an umbrella term encompassing the subgenres of horror fiction, science fiction, and fantasy. Two of the writers I discuss in this essay write primarily "fantasy," and two write primarily "science fiction."

3. Karla Jay and Allen Young, eds., *Out of the Closets: Voices of Gay Liberation* (New York: New York University Press, 1972; reprint, 1992). The majority of essays are based on the split between the heterosexual and the homosexual (world, culture, personality). A few mentions of bisexuality or bisexuals exist: Karla Jay's essay, "A Gay Critique of Modern Literary Criticism," references Michelangelo's bisexuality as an example of how homosexuality is presented as a flaw in an artist; John Murphy, in "Queer Books," mentions a bisexual character as being "an acceptable partner in the eyes of the liberal straight reader" (78). Thus, bisexuality is constructed as *really* homosexuality, or as a way to maintain heterosexual privilege. The anthology attempts to deconstruct the perceived "naturalness" of sex/gender roles, and one editor argues that the impulse in the gay liberation movement of the late sixties and early seventies to question "natural" categories of homosexual and heterosexual was lost by the mid-seventies, when the ideas reverted to pre-Stonewall form: "fixed identities, determined early in life (if not at birth), but natural, good, and healthy rather than unnatural, bad, and sick" (xxvi).

4. The new "discipline" called "Gay and Lesbian Studies" still tends to exclude bisexuals, but my focus in this paper is elsewhere.

5. And, often, in a racist society, "homosexual" means "white homosexual." The false universalization in terms such as "Americans and minorities" carries over: the fact that Anglo-European feminists rarely feel the need to identify their ethnicity, while African-American and other feminists of color do, shows the way the false universalization works. The same dichotomy seems to be operating in the gay community: Anglo-European gays and lesbians, in the texts I have read, do not foreground their ethnicity as part of their identity.

6. Only recently has SF started to be included in the "field" of literary studies since many academics once dismissed it all as "trash" unworthy of serious study, an attitude I often encountered as an undergraduate.

7. I believe that, among white feminists at least, more work needs to be done on issues of generational differences and age discrimination (which goes both ways).

8. Even groups that foreground the need for inclusion and acceptance of diversity in their organization reveal that this problem still exists. When I joined the National Women's Studies Association, I received a registration form with a list of caucuses and task forces that I could join, if I wished. Although the various groups included a category of "Lesbian Women," various ethnic identifications, and even a category for "Fat Oppression," which interested me, there was no category for "Bisexual Women." I wrote a note on the bottom of the form asking if they would consider forming such a category.

9. The tendency to define "gay sexuality" as primarily sexual behavior is clearly seen in the rhetoric against "gays" in the military, which denies the comparison with past exclusion of African Americans by insisting that being gay is a choice (and an immoral one), unlike skin color. While there are

problems with comparing "homosexuals" with "blacks" in civil rights discourse, the response to the analogy by heterosexuals reveals their belief in homosexuality as chosen behavior, not identity.

10. Pamela L. Caughie, "Virginia Woolf's Double Discourse," in *Discontented Discourses: Feminism/ Textual Intervention/ Psychoanalysis,* ed. Marleen S. Barr (Urbana: University of Illinois Press, 1989), 49.

11. Loraine Hutchins and Lani Kaahumanu, eds., *Bi Any Other Name: Bisexual People Speak Out* (Boston: Alyson Publications, 1991). This anthology has a number of essays that speak directly to the issues of coalitions between bisexuals and gays and lesbians, and the possibilities of the linguistic shift to terms like "Queer Theory" and groups like "Queer Nation," since bisexuals can identify as queers in a straight world. While the collection asserts an identity based on a shared sexuality, the mixture of essays breaks down any sense that bisexuals are identical (in terms of politics, philosophy, life choices).

12. My thanks to Robert Neveldine for his help in clarifying this issue. He also notes that several writers in AIDS analysis/activism have begun to critique this representation, especially Paula A. Treichler, Alexis Danzig, and Mariana Valverde.

13. Conversations in July 1992 with Leslie Donovan and Katherine Cummings.

14. This belief may be strongest among white, middle-class women, but that does not mean it is completely missing among women of color. The contradictory belief that "women" do compete for the sexual attentions of men, but in covert (i.e., nonmasculine) ways, also seems to be specifically downplayed in many heterosexual feminist groups as well.

15. My analysis of the discursive formations surrounding "differences" between women and how those differences (of race, class, and sexuality) operate appears in chapters 1–3 of my doctoral dissertation, *A Genealogy of North American Feminism, 1963–1991: Competing Narratives of "Gender," "Race," and "Ethnicity,"* University of Washington.

16. Diane Duane's four-volume novel, *The Tale of the Five,* with three volumes published so far (*The Door into Fire, The Door into Shadow,* and *The Door into Sunset*), draws on goddess-based pagan beliefs to create a culture where people sleep with (and marry) people but monogamy seems to be rare. Lynn Abbey's trilogy, *The Chronicles of Tornor,* is not as specifically linked as Duane's multivolume novel. The three novels, *Watchtower, Dancers of Arun,* and *The Northern Girl,* describe the history of a family "line" rather than an individual. Each novel is set at a different time and has a different protagonist: the first, a male; the second, a disabled male; the third, a female; but all three are in the same family line. Janet Kagan's *Mirabile* describes a multiethnic population of humans who are "marooned" on a planet when the computers in their generation-starship crash. After four or five generations on Mirabile, the colonists have evolved a culture that values genetic (and individual) diversity over all, where child-rearing is an honored profession among many others, and where the sense of oneself as a sexual being and shared passion are maintained well into what mainstream

America would call "old age." A recent trilogy by Vonda McIntyre *(Starfar-ers, Transition,* and *Metaphase)* describes how a solar spaceship designed for research and the search for intelligent life must be "hijacked" by the academics and support crew to keep it away from the United States government, which has decided to turn it to military purposes.

17. I am indebted to Russ's discussion of pornography and erotica in *Magic Mommas, Trembling Sisters, Puritans, and Perverts* (Trumansburg, N.Y.: Crossing Press, 1985) and to her essay, "Recent Feminist Utopias," in *Future Females: A Critical Anthology,* ed. Marleen S. Barr (Bowling Green, Ohio: Bowling Green State University Popular Press, 1981), 76, for points made in this paragraph.

18. While the issue of naming or labeling is a complex one, depending on different definitions of "feminist," these books are, in general, published primarily as trade paperbacks by mainstream SF publishing companies; only Abbey's trilogy has any blurbs by or references to "feminism," and, finally, all include males as protagonists and important characters. Too often "feminist" is understood to mean "lesbian" or "separatist," although I have argued elsewhere that writers publishing after the seventies utopias are expanding the definitions of feminism.

19. I do not intend to celebrate women's violence in these novels, nor do I believe these novels do so. The issues raised are complicated ones, the more so in a year in which the National Rifle Association has begun to use the feminist rhetoric of "choice" and "empowerment" to argue for women in America arming themselves with guns. These writers are beginning to explore questions of how we are trained to accept the limits of current gender roles (for men and women) in various ways, one of which is how conflict and violence are handled. Showing women able to fight in self-defense is one means of doing that.

20. I am no longer sure I identify as a "fan." Not only am I writing "academic" analyses of SF, which would horrify many fen, but I dropped out of most of the organized groups in fandom when I became tired of the increasing professionalization of what had been a purely amateur activity performed out of love.

REFERENCES

Abbey, Lynn. *The Dancers of Arun.* New York: Berkley Books, 1979.
———. *The Northern Girl.* New York: Berkley Books, 1980.
———. *Watchtower.* New York: Berkley Books, 1979.
Caughie, Pamela L. "Virginia Woolf's Double Discourse." In *Discontented Discourses: Feminism/Textual Intervention/Psychoanalysis,* edited by Marleen S. Barr and Richard Goldstein, 41–53. Urbana: University of Illinois Press, 1984.
Duane, Diane. *The Door into Fire.* 1979. New York: Tor Books, 1985.
———. *The Door into Shadow.* New York: Bluejay Books, 1984.

————. *The Door into Sunset*. New York: Tor Books, 1992.

Foucault, Michel. *The History of Sexuality. Volume One: An Introduction.* Translated by Robert Hurley. New York: Vintage Books, 1990.

Hutchins, Loraine, and Lani Kaahumanu, eds. *Bi Any Other Name: Bisexual People Speak Out*. Boston: Alyson Publications, 1991.

Jay, Karla, and Allen Young, eds. *Out of the Closets: Voices of Gay Liberation.* 1972. Reprint. New York: New York University Press, 1992.

Kagan, Janet. *Mirabile*. New York: Tor Books, 1991.

McIntyre, Vonda M. *Metaphase*. New York: Bantam, 1992.

————. *Starfarers*. New York: Ace, 1989.

————. *Transition*. New York: Bantam, 1990.

Russ, Joanna. *Magic Mommas, Trembling Sisters, Puritans and Perverts: Feminist Essays.* Trumansburg, New York: Crossing Press, 1985.

————. "Recent Feminist Utopias." In *Future Females: A Critical Anthology,* edited by Marleen S. Barr, 71–85. Bowling Green, Ohio: Bowling Green State University Popular Press, 1981.

18.

IN THE ZONE OF AMBIVALENCE:
A JOURNAL OF COMPETITION

MURIEL DIMEN

1. New York City. Sometime at the beginning of April, 1990.

Alice Bach asks me to contribute to a feminist issue of the Union Seminary Quarterly Review, which she edits. The issue's topic is to be "competition between women"; authors may write about it in any way they please as long as they also refer to a relevant scriptural text. Since the volume is to be interdisciplinary, Alice says that I, as a psychoanalyst and anthropologist, cover ground others don't. I'm intrigued—I know a lot about competition not only in theory but in practice (what feminist doesn't?); I've even written about it.[1] I feel weird about the religious part.

As you will see, the "religious," or at least spiritual, part comes to seem less weird.

2. New York City. May 17, 1990.

This morning, I dig out my old King James Version to scan the suggested tales of competition between women meant to provide continuity for this diverse issue of USQR. I'm drawn to the story of Rachel and Leah; their rivalry over fecundity reminds me of my late friendship with (I'll call her) Linda.

This evening, at the restaurant where I'm eating dinner with (amazingly enough) *a date, who should I see striding out from some recess in the dining room with a hurt and angry mien but* (also amazingly enough) *Linda? Her husband, following close behind with a determined step, looks equally distraught. I feel slightly embarrassed for them.*

When I arrived home that night, I began officially to keep a journal, excerpted and periodically extracted here, in a notebook purchased for that special purpose.

3. New York City. May 18, 1990.
This morning, I dream that Linda telephones me. Now that she's turning fifty, she says, she wants to bury the hatchet. I'm moved to agree this is a good idea; an old friendship is worth resuscitating even if you haven't spoken to each other for five years (except when you can't avoid each other at a book party). Then she tells me she's having an affair. "Was that why you looked so, um, worried in the restaurant?" I wanted to know. "No," she replies.

My unconscious, having turned the merely embarrassing into potential disaster, an ordinary public quarrel into marital betrayal, was, it would appear, out for blood. Now, it seemed to be saying, I can settle the score. Now I can get even with Linda for what she got before me, as Leah got Jacob even when he was to have been Rachel's. I can retaliate for the literary grace and style, and the ruthless self-interest, that permitted her to borrow some of my less attractive qualities and lend them to those odd characters in her sardonic, avant-garde novels. For now, you see, I can write as well as she, and she, no longer my friend, is fair game. I can tell on her, make her look as bad as I want. Ah. Revenge is sweet, not only because of the mean things she said and did to me in act and in print, but because she has a second husband and I don't.

Not only literary and sexual power but intellectual productivity was at stake in our friendship. When my first book was published, I brought it to a party at a friend's house in the country. I wanted to show it to them, in the same spirit, I suppose, as you would show off for your parents, parade an accomplishment before them. I thought my friends would take pleasure in my pleasure, identificatory pride in my achievement; I had no consciousness of competing (which doesn't mean I wasn't).

I can't remember if Linda said it right there and then, or waited until we were back in Manhattan: "I feel like I have to eat crow." I was stunned. After all, she explained, her manuscript had just been rejected by her publisher, which meant that I'd finished my book first. I hadn't been aware there'd been a race. I think I thought we were sister feminists together, together letting our different spirits fly, together making our separate ascents, she climbing the literary ladder, I, the academic one. How naive. Still, it was only 1977; Evelyn Fox Keller and Helene Moglen wouldn't publish their article on competition among feminists (which was the original stimulus for *USQR*'s special issue) until ten years later.[2]

Not too long afterward, at a feminist conference we'd both participated in organizing, a prestigious American publisher approached Linda to write a new book based on the paper she'd delivered. Although the same house (like half a dozen others) later rejected my next book proposal, one commercial firm did in the end give me a very large advance, much larger, indeed, than hers. Oddly enough, Linda was visiting me when my agent called with the news; while her presence was not all that kept me from tasting my triumph, my apprehension of her inevitable and painful envy certainly darkened my delight, even though, as my best friend, she was the one person with whom I'd have most wanted to share the moment. Much later, she read, and disliked, the penultimate draft of my book. About a month after that, I challenged her for the first time in our fifteen-year friendship. And soon after that she imposed a silence that has never been officially broken.

Both my books are now out of print. Whenever I poke around bookstores hoping for the small miracle that a copy of one or the other might still be on the shelves, I am compelled to look for hers (there are now two) and I always find them, still in print, sometimes even prominently displayed.

Have I conveyed to you the right combination of hurt and pride, struck the right note of ambivalence between love and hate? There seems no way to write about this matter of competition between women without anxiety, just as there is no way to think about it outside the moral(istic) question: Competition between women, is it good or is it bad? This concern pervades Valerie Miner and Helen Longino's anthology, *Competition: A Feminist Taboo?*, in which Keller and Moglen's "Competition: A Problem for Academic Women" is reprinted.[3] Some contributors think competition is a positively good thing and ought to be embraced (e.g., Lichtenstein, Lindenbaum).[4] Others, like Keller and

Moglen, argue that it sours only when denied; acknowledged, competition can be constructive and enriching for women.[5] Still others hold that competition is altogether bad not only for women, but for feminism and socialism; either it serves the oppressor by dividing the oppressed against themselves (e.g., Muse) or, as a tainted means, it spoils the ends (e.g., Ackelsberg and Addelson).[6]

At any rate, whatever their position, all the authors write in a moral discourse. For example, Keller and Moglen say that "as the doors to the ivory tower have swung open, as positions of influence and power have become available to women, we [feminists] have lost both innocence and purity."[7] The irony of their tone ("Fallen creatures now, we look at one another's nakedness in dismay")[8] only heightens the problem of morality and its slide into moralism. Being a good feminist, they remind us, has meant that we do not compete. Keller and Moglen then ask the question lurking at the back of all our minds: "But what does it mean to be a good feminist in a real world where real power, real issues of professional survival, and real opportunities to exert influence are at stake. . . ?"[9] Caught, I think, in the trap of political correctness, they offer, predictably and honorably enough, no satisfying answer. They argue that we must continue to be feminists even as we believe in "some standards of excellence—however drastically they must be revised—. . . as a necessary source of motivation,"[10] and act upon these standards in our attempt to improve our work and our positions. They ask how we can do this under conditions of political and economic inequality, and how we can keep that inequality from disrupting friendships and the feminist community. They suggest we look to other cultures for models.[11]

Whew! What burdens feminists load onto their backs! It's not only that we have to run twice as fast as men to get where we are and stay there. If men have always had more leeway to be "bad," women have always had to be good girls, which means that we always have to be better than we are.[12] And here you can see how (though not why) morality becomes moralism: Good girls are moral girls, girls who, when they become good women, privately guard the moral order contravened by public brutality; responsible for the ligatures of life, they are to make sure that what happens between people feels good so that people can also feel good about themselves, and life connects and continues. Good women are the people Carol Gilligan's girls think they are supposed to become: they reject competition, they want to make sure everyone wins; not concerned with Self at the expense of Other, they are so often concerned with Other that they forget themselves.[13]

A further irony thus emerges, unnoticed by any of the contributors to Miner and Longino's *Competition: A Feminist Taboo? In order to be a good feminist, you must conform to gender stereotype, because feminists are supposed to be good in the way that girls, and women, are supposed to be good.* If you want to be a good feminist, then be a good girl and think about everyone but yourself. Free yourself from your chains by wrapping them ever more tightly around you, trapping yourself in anxiety and guilt.

No wonder it's so hard to think about this topic. Anxiety, the psychoanalyst Harry Stack Sullivan is alleged to have said, resembles a blow on the head: it stops you from thinking. The same is true of morality-cum-moralism and the guilt with which it burdens you. I'd like to suggest one way to break these chains: Do what I did last summer. Forget about it. Drop out. Go to California.

4. Davis, California. August 14, 1990. The first day of summer vacation.

I walk my friends' dog. Or, rather, she walks me, which puts me in a most uncompetitive frame of mind. Leashed as much to her will as to her collar, I let my own desire follow hers right out of my usual mind into forgotten expanses of rest and creativity and the "unthought-known."[14] *And, as I bliss out, beginning to leave daily-life cares and woes behind for three weeks, who should pop up in my mind but Janis Joplin singing*

> *Oh lord won't you buy me a Mercedes-Benz?*
> *My friends all drive Porsches*
> *I must make amends.*
>
> *Worked hard all my lifetime*
> *No help from my friends*
> *Oh lord won't you buy me a Mercedes-Benz?*
>
> > *("Mercedes-Benz," Pearl)*

Another friend, with whom I'm in general but not direct competition (nothing at stake but success, two psychoanalysts in a field where there was at the time no institutional ladder for feminists, hence no specific place to be won or lost), openly and generously admired my having secured a book contract. In self-deprecation (the emotional equivalent of spitting three times to ward off your friends' envy), I replied, "Oh, I have a Janis Joplin complex." After she heard the following story, she concluded, "I guess I don't have enough of one."

According to the *New York Times,* Janis once bought two identical pairs of gold sandals, about which she said, "I love wearing gold shoes, it's like a breakthrough. It demands a whole kind of attitude for a chick to wear gold shoes. . . . Maybe only girls would understand, but it [feels] almost as good as singing."[15] She also told her interviewer what it felt like to bring that "whole kind of attitude" (and, I imagine, her gold shoes) back home to Port Arthur, Texas, where, although she had grown up an averagely privileged middle-class person, she nevertheless always felt deprived of respect, poor in esteem: "I read, I painted, I thought. I didn't hate niggers. There was nobody like me [there]. It was lonely, those feelings welling up and nobody to talk to. I was just 'silly crazy Janis.' Man, those people hurt me. It makes me happy to know I'm making it and they're back there, plumbers just like they were." Now, rich in money and power, she could *show* them: "People aren't supposed to be like me . . . but now they're paying me $50,000 a year to be like me."

Is that what it takes to make it—a Janis Joplin complex, a wish for victory emerging out of friendless hurt so deep it makes you want to kill? Or, at least, is that bottomless vengeance the minimum? And did Janis make it? Was the competition worth the candle she burned at both ends? Was it worth dying for, as she did the very next year? She left us a great legacy, didn't she? Don't you love her music? Don't you love her for being such a bad girl and "making it" anyway? (Or, at least, such a bad *white* girl, for there have been many black women, like Billie Holliday, who, while adulated, don't hold quite the same place in mainstream—read, "white"—cultural mythology as Janis, even if they were models for her art and life; there's another sort of competition going on here, and I'll return to it later on.)

Perhaps the most striking word in that first verse of "Mercedes-Benz" is "amends," which Webster's defines as "payment made or satisfaction given for injury, insult, loss, etc.; as, he [sic] made amends for his rudeness."[16] How puzzling. You might think that amends is what you have to make after you win, as, sort of, damage control. Yet this song suggests that you can make restitution by competing. For what offense, then, would keeping up with the Joneses compensate? It's tempting to psychologize Janis and say she felt like a bad person for being a bad girl

(or became a bad girl because she felt so bad about herself), and therefore she had to atone. But not only is she not my patient, she's dead and
can't correct me as living patients can. I'd rather listen for the more
universal connotations of her verse and suggest that the transgression
requiring amends is one we spy not only in Janis's life but in our own—
the offense of not having as much as others, of therefore not being as
"much" as they, and thus, by comparison, being "rude" and uncivilized.
The offense lies in the unpleasant feelings aroused in the "haves" by the
"have-nots," in the emotional structure of socioeconomic hierarchy:
those who have less envy those who have more, who, at the same time,
feel guilt; hence the "offense" of homeless people.

"Mercedes-Benz" was, of course, satirizing the sort of competitive
society in which having less than other people feels like, and is even
regarded as, an offense against them. Janis sets it up in that hoarse,
squeaky voice of hers: "I'd like to do a song of great social and political
import." But although she makes us laugh at the pain, she also renders
this universal scramble for dignity a far more personal than political
matter. Nor is it surprising that she does so, for her song predates our
recognition that "the personal is political," a slogan invented the same
year the article about her appeared.[17]

It's too bad that, for most people who once believed otherwise, the
political has now dwindled to the personal. Still, the inherently mutual
implication of personal and political life, which is how I understand that
now-famous motto, girds the form and informs the content of this essay:
How, I want to ask, can we understand competition between women
(between anybody, for that matter) as simultaneously personal and political, as at once in our hearts, in our friendships, and in the structure of
daily life? How can we chart the social and economic forces giving rise
to and shaping competition as we know it, and also track the intrapsychic processes infusing it?

I intend to answer these questions by what I say and how I say it.
One central disappointment of Keller and Moglen's otherwise germinal
contribution was how little they told us about their relationship. When
reading it, you really do want to know what their competition was all
about and how, or if, they resolved it. Since you never find out, you're
never entirely persuaded that the answer lies in scrutinizing other cultures. Why should we look so far afield when at least some answers
might lie rather closer to home, in the personal lives of the authors, both
of whom continue as successful professionals and feminists?

So I've chosen to take a risk here and let you in on some bits of the diary I impulsively began once I'd taken this project on. As you can tell, I'm going to interweave those bits with some thinking I've done about the matter of competition. I will be arguing, in the main, that competitiveness has an unconscious life as well as a social reality. It exists in both inner and outer dimensions, equally a graphic social drama of striving, winning, losing, and living to fight another day and a vividly felt but invisible psychic drama of desire, hate, and reparation. Like any behavior, competition is shaped doubly by emotion and politics, which is the reason that the twin demons of anxiety and political correctness plague our thinking about it. This double plague makes competition a prime arena for the struggle between love and hate, which can only be resolved by ambivalence.

To ask how we can depict the simultaneity of mind and culture is perhaps also to ask: How do we speak about an ordinary experience using the disciplinary languages that, divided, (mis)represent it? In these deconstructionist days, you might use discourse theory to cut your way out of disciplinary prisons. But still you find yourself in a moral(istic) hammerlock, because the anxious and guilty discourse in which competition between women is located keeps you from thinking straight. Is it possible to step out of this discourse? Or is the only way out to get as deeply into it as you can?

5. Tassajara Zen Mountain Monastery, Jamesburg, California.
August 16, 1990.

On the afternoon of my first workday at Tassajara, my second day here, twenty-seven hours after my arrival, plagued by hard anger and a headache that began when I arose at five-thirty A.M. *to do things I either didn't know how to do (like sitting zazen [meditating] and raking pebbles into Japanese garden–style order) or felt were beneath me (like cleaning hurricane lamps and toilets), I steamed in the sulfurous steam room, and then, lying naked on the deck, fell unknowingly into a nap. When I woke under the blue sky ringed with leaves, I found myself silently asking, "Is this, no this isn't, France? Greece?" And, then, to my horror, "Who am I? What's my name?" I did not know where I was nor could I remember my name. And that's, I guess, when I remembered why I came.*

When I went to Tassajara, I had emerged from two years of nonstop competing with close feminist friends and colleagues, more aware of my defeats than my victories, burned out, beat, mistrustful of those to whom I was closest. At Tassajara, as I swabbed toilets or made beds still smelling of the night or cleaned funky spinach in the kitchen, I felt myself losing/giving up the insignia of those losses and triumphs. As I unwillingly relinquished these signs of myself, I quickly came to feel quite humiliatingly small. To my surprise, I found myself reaching for my accomplishments, my status markers—"I have a Ph.D., I used to be a full professor of anthropology before I bravely gave it all up to become the psychoanalyst I am now," etc.—as if to remember who I was.

I'm not going to say, either, that I left Tassajara restored, trusting, and hopeful, or cleansed of desires for prestige and power, cured of competitiveness and its discontents, and certainly not of the desire for its rewards. Zen, I came to understand, is (at least in the American context) about being where you are. And if competition is where you are, then that's where you are.

The Zen teacher, Thich Nhat Hanh, tells the following story: There was a young man who liked to draw lotus flowers, but he did not know anything about drawing. . . . He went to a master, and the master took him to a lotus pond and asked him to sit there and look at the lotus flowers all day without doing anything, just breathing and looking at the lotus flowers. . . . He did only that for ten days, and then he went back to his master. His master asked him, "Are you ready?" He said, "I will try," and the brush and paint were given to him. He was painting like a child, but the lotus was very beautiful. He was nothing but a lotus at that time, and the lotus came out. . . . At first he wanted to paint the flower but finally he became the flower, and his intention to paint was no longer there. That is why he succeeded in painting. When I first read the story, my immediate reaction was, Well, if I'm writing about competition between women, do I have to *become* it? Do I have to live in that place of tension, anxiety, and, sometimes, horror? I don't *want* to live there.

Then the obvious became new: That is *where* I live.

Perhaps the ever-presence of competition in my life has something to do with the interface of biography and history: second-wave feminist activists and scholars are maturing into the peak of their professions; if they at first engaged politics with a (now declining) vigor, they currently find themselves at that point in their individual career paths where they must secure their positions if they are to have or retain any influence. Structure and desire, power and ambition, propel them into competition.

Conversely, as Keller and Moglen suggest, as long as feminists were marginal, they not only believed competition was counterproductive but (naively and/or ideologically) imagined they were immune to it.[18]

The competition we encounter with shock, recognition, amusement, dismay, exists not only in academia and politics. Although it's not all there is, it's everywhere. Competition is the stuff of which the social pyramid, its hierarchies founded on scarcity, is made. Look, competition appears even where we think it can't. For example, Longino and Miner describe themselves as "radical feminists and socialists [who] thus have two traditions behind us that seem antithetical to competition."[19] Their own volume constituting a rejoinder in regard to feminism, I need only mention Lenin and Trotsky, or the Prague Spring and its consequences, to remind you of socialism's putatively noncompetitive spirit.

Going even further back (in cultural imagery if not in actual time), competition is where Rachel and Leah, not to mention their husband, Jacob, and their father, Laban, live too. Indeed, Rachel and Leah's rivalry over desirability and fecundity has its partner and backdrop in the battle for wealth and power between two generations of men. After all, since God has already appointed Jacob as the founder of nations, it's not so hard to understand why the older man might play tricks on the younger one. How better to triumph over the man who is inevitably going to exceed you than by making him serve for twenty years to get what he ought to have received after only seven? The Oedipal boy, it turns out, is right: Not only in his guilt-stricken fantasy, but in lived life, the old man, in this case his father-in-law, *does* want to get him. Sons often have the opportunity to do what their fathers couldn't; *mutatis mutandis,* the same holds true for daughters and mothers, as Keller and Moglen so poignantly remind us in their recounting of intergenerational competition among feminists.

I am sure that, had I remained at Tassajara and let the total institution swallow me right up (indeed, I was tempted), the matter of competition would have resurfaced in me, and between me and others, in the pores of my mind and in the spaces of social life (in the short run, for example, I might have wondered who, on a given day, had meditated most "per-fectly"—an oxymoron—while in the long run, I might have wanted to rise in the monastic hierarchy). Competition would have come back up not only because Zen practice encourages the emergence of all experi-ence but because I've grown up where I've grown up, as have most of the monks there. You can't be anything but racist in a racist society, misogynist in a patriarchal one, and competitive in a hierarchical one. You can dislike your attitudes, and do battle with them—that's what being antiracist, nonsexist, and noncompetitive involves, struggling against that which contravenes your values. But your struggle doesn't purge you of your faults, even though it may help you figure out ways to ameliorate their political manifestations, or to imagine their ultimate undoing.

Racism, sexism, competition. Hmm. I seem to have reentered the moral domain. I'd like to take the analogy back, but I can't. Political correctness aside, I think it's right. So I'll try, at least, not to be moralistic (which, by the way, raises the question of whether it is any longer possible to speak about politics without being, feeling, or being accused of being moralistic, sanctimonious). If racism is the mark of imperialism and misogyny is the mark of patriarchy, then competition is the signature of hierarchy. Competition may beget pain that explodes into greatness, as it led to Janis's energy and music, or Billie Holliday's genius. But competitiveness between women, particularly between feminists, is, I will say without anxiety, often horribly painful and, in that sense, a bad thing, which doesn't mean we shouldn't engage in it. Here's why. (No, this isn't a detour; or rather, it is, but it's going to take us back to that most interesting dilemma, whether you can be a good feminist without being a good girl.)

6. *Tassajara. August 19, 1990.*

> *How do I hate thee? Let me count the ways.*
> *I hate thee to the depth and breadth and height*
> *My soul can reach, when feeling out of sight*
> *For the ends of Being and ideal Grace.*
> *I hate thee to the level of everyday's*
> *Most quiet needs, by sun and candlelight.*
> *I hate thee freely, as men strive for Right.*
> *I hate thee purely, as they turn from Praise.*
> *I hate thee with the passion put to use*
> *In my old griefs, and with my childhood's faith.*
> *I hate thee with a love I seemed to lose*
> *With my lost saints—I hate thee with the breath,*
> *Smiles, tears, of all the life!—and, if God choose,*
> *I shall but hate thee better after death.*
>
> *(after Elizabeth Barrett Browning)*

I cannot deny that a hatred equal in depth to love has accompanied the competitions in which I've engaged with my dearest friends. I'd like to deny it because, always inclined to be a good girl, I shrink from feeling such aggression in myself and from seeing it in other women. I'm probably not alone in this. Nowhere in the ideology of good-girl-ness is there room for the level of hatred that Janis spouted in her interview, which most of us feel, at least on occasion, but would never publicize.

Still, if we're going to talk about competition, I think we have to talk about hate because, my own experience convinces me, competition does not occur in the absence of this passionate concoction of "resentment, contempt, frustration, envy, [and] rage."[20] At its worst, this hatred between me and my women/feminist friends has threatened to unbalance me; short of that, it has, as I have told you, destroyed a friendship. What I wonder, though, is this: Would the hatred have had such destructive power if Linda and I had been able to know it, singly and together, beforehand? But could we have known it? Is there any way to discuss hatred without falling into moralism? Is there any way to let hatred be without immediately censuring the one who hates? Is it possible that politics tends to become moralistic when it encounters, without acceptance, the passionate and frightening emotion of hate?

Let's look at hate or, rather, the effects of ignoring it in one study of competition that justly became an instant classic.[21] Joyce P. Lindenbaum's psychoanalytic examination of competitiveness and envy within lesbian couples avoids moralizing, but only, it seems to me, by helping hatred to an early death. Somewhat coolly, she defines competition as "a constructive process that can evolve when an experience of 'felt difference' occurs between two separate selves in relationship."[22] Lindenbaum arrives at this definition from her psychotherapeutic treatment of lesbian couples who, she finds, often come to her because they have stopped having sex. This has happened, she argues, because their ease with the nonsexual merging of selves leaves them defenseless against the unconscious, primal, mother-child fusion that, in the extraordinariness of sexual union, permits ecstasy, but, in ordinary life, induces a terrifying loss of self. And their comfort with nonsexual merging has in part to do with their inability to distinguish, intrapsychically and interpersonally, difference from separateness. Difference, in these relationships, has come to signify separation, and separation to signify the loss of the other and of the relationship. Envy emerges as a way to defend against this "felt difference," with its signification of loss and abandonment. However, because envy causes pain and threatens intimacy, the couples Lindenbaum treats attempt to erase it by creating a "pseudomutuality" or pseudolikeness in which, unfortunately, each partner then feels she has sacrificed too much of herself. To minimize this high price, the partners next create "pseudodifference": Each, in order to reclaim herself, protests too much her own distinctiveness and consequently feels neither real nor comfortable, but is more often uneasily aware of hatred's seeds, of anger with and envy of the other.

Lindenbaum's solution is not to eliminate but to institute competition in the relationship as a means to imbue separateness and difference with a sense of safety, and to detoxify envy by giving it "benign expression." [23] If one partner envies the other's success in a particular domain, she is to determine the domain in which she herself wishes to succeed; if it's the same as her partner's, then she should go for it, try to beat her partner. This displacement of aggression from envy onto the job of creating the desired quality in oneself deflects the wish to hurt the other. [24] Thus purified, competition becomes curative and provides one "with the opportunity to become competent. It is not an easy task, nor is it one that can always be accomplished. There is still the possibility of deep disappointment. . . . In undertaking the challenge . . . one has, at the very least, the experience of developing a particular aspect of the Self and observing that the Other is not destroyed by this success. When One gets better, the Other does not have to get worse." [25]

Maybe. If the competition is about, say, cooking, there are always more meals to be prepared and eaten; if it's about tennis, then there's always next year's Virginia Slims tournament to train for. But sometimes, when one person wins and the other loses, that's it; the game's over and will never be played again. If the contest involves a job and there's only one to be had, then there's no second chance, as we learn from the anguished cases Keller and Moglen recount, [26] as well as from those with which we've had personal contact, either as winners or losers (I've been both). And without a second chance, hatred is likely to have its day.

Lindenbaum's model, while attentive to the psychosocial construction of women's personality, seems to ignore both the social underpinnings and unconscious matrix of competition. It's true that people who have experienced trauma during the first two years of life (Lindenbaum's thesis employs this preoedipal model) are likely to be threatened by the

Other's difference and to regard that difference as a sign of their own inadequacy, triggering retaliative, envious fantasies that envision the Other's destruction. And it's true that, because women's personalities form by identifying with, not differing from, (m)others, hence are marked by permeable boundaries, and are thus suited to the tasks of relatedness, women are often threatened by difference in precisely this way.[27]

But the drama of competition is not only internal, or even internal to couples. Competition is also a social process, and competitiveness is a socially meaningful feeling. In our society, the context for competition is a socially constructed scarcity, a fact recognized by Keller and Moglen, whose faith in the value of competitiveness is less naive than Lindenbaum's.[28] Under these circumstances, where the means to wealth and power are unequally distributed, not only competition but envy is inevitable. Envy is a complex emotion that feeds hatred. It consists, in part, of admiration; founded in processes of identification, it shows up in the desire to emulate the other. But it is also destructive, containing a wish to destroy anyone who has something, be it a quality, relationship, object, or situation, that one longs for, so that one no longer has to remember that one lacks it.

At the same time, however, loss has a political dimension. The losses of early childhood meet, and find echoes in, the socially constituted and unavoidable deprivations, disappointments, and failures of adult life.[29] When social losses cannot be reversed, the disappointment they entail borrows from the passions of early life, when any loss seemed irreversible (think of a frustrated toddler). Not infrequently, this helpless disillusionment finds expression in hatred of self, of others, of the Other— other races and ethnicities; women; the powers that be; or those who, like Janis, are deemed "weird" because of their sexuality, style, or beliefs. As we have seen in Janis's own life, it can, under the right conditions, also turn into self-destructive hatred of one's own Otherness.

The power of hatred to scare us all and to threaten social order is one reason for the social significance of competition. Competition rationalizes hate by institutionalizing it. As my pseudonymous friend Nathan, whom I regularly consult on matters male, told me, "We used to joke that, before basketball games, we were going to sit in a room and have a hate session." That's why there's no such thing as "true" competition, as Lindenbaum's positivism (or, perhaps, romanticism) would have it;[30] neither emotionally nor politically neutral, competition has cultural and psychological origins and functions specific to the society in which it is found.

In other words, "true" competition is only an *idea* in our own society, expressed in the familiar cheer, shouted by both liberals and conservatives: "May the best man win!" Yet we also know that sometimes the "best man" is not the one who wins the game as played, but the one who plays the game by pulling strings." [31] Even though being socially and economically well positioned doesn't mean you *can't* be the best at what you do, it can be an awfully big help to the competent and incompetent alike. And this socioeconomic differential tends to provoke hatred, both among the many, who envy and resent those who have, and among the few, who live in contempt, fear, and guilt toward those who do not.

Hate seems to negate love; perhaps that's one reason good girls eschew it. But, you know, I could not have hated my competitors so deeply had I not loved them well; as my adaptation of Browning's sonnet suggests, hate feeds on love as (and I will return to this thought toward the end of this essay) love needs hate. Hate can flourish only where illusions once held sway, only where love has blinded us. And its very presence tells of our longing to love once more.

So I wish Lindenbaum had let her patients hate each other for a while instead of trying to finesse the bad-girl emotion of hatred by instituting competition. Counter to my own impulses, I want to argue that we have got to bring hatred, and all the other bad-girl feelings, forward. If we don't, we remain locked in the good-girl model of feminism and femininity. *In other words, in order to be a good feminist, you have to be a bad girl.* [32] You have got to know everything you weren't supposed to know when you were supposed to be a good girl. You have to know everything about what you can and want to be. If you taboo one sector of passion, you stunt the rest.

In Lindenbaum's final case example, a woman envies her lover's fame as a public speaker, at first relishing a vicarious success, later wishing to be as skillful but fearing the damage such an accomplishment might do to her partner. Through therapy, however, she identifies and accomplishes her goal; she too becomes a public speaker, and now she and her partner playfully goad each other on, as part of what they regard as their benign competition.

I agree with Lindenbaum's concluding comment on this couple, but I also think it undermines her entire argument: "That one woman envies her partner's passion for public speaking does not mean that she must work to become a skilled public speaker herself. It is the passion that is envied. The capacity to be passionate about something is what must be examined and developed."[33] If, however, passion, not competition, is the point, then the clinical task becomes understanding why this particular woman cannot own, and thereby define, her passion, including her hatred. To institute competitiveness in the relationship forecloses inquiry into the inhibition of her desire. Writing about black adolescent girls, Daphne Muse makes a related point, contending that competitiveness is particularly damaging to them because it puts their lives "in a box," packaging their quest for personal fulfillment into conventional goals.[34] Or, as another aphorism puts it, "You can't get rich playing another man's game."

Or can you?

7. New York City. November 11, 1990.

Another dinner date, this time with (let's call him) *Jim. I tell Jim about the article on competition, and its problematic, the moral(istic) discourse from which it's trying to escape. "What's the mystery?" he wants to know. "Competition is nothing more complicated than a good game of tennis." "Well," I suggest, "imagine that you've got an assistant professor in your department* [Jim is an eminent sociologist of liberal persuasion] *who's a wonderful teacher, but doesn't publish, so, when tenure review comes around, it's not up but out." Jim is silent, indeed, I suspect, uncomfortable. Later, when he tells me that I shouldn't be worrying about competition, I can't figure out whether he's flirting or competing.*

Speaking of disillusionment and wanting to love again, it's hardly news that it's in men's interest that women not compete (except when they are battling over a man). After all, if we did, we would no longer be the good girls they have always needed us to be to keep house, raise their kids, and, in general, not threaten their sense of their own competence. Indeed, when we do show any sign of integrating the aggressiveness that is part of competing and that has traditionally marked the moral boundary between the sexes, men will tend to become anxious and start competing right back. Not only do they have to protect their place in the patriarchy, they have to defend themselves against what they don't want to see in themselves: When men comment, as some do, that women are far more vicious than men, they are complaining about what they suddenly perceive because it appears where it should not, the hatred they have learned to disavow in themselves and suddenly catch sight of in women.

In other words, men are as disturbed as women by the hostility embedded in competitiveness. They simply have a variety of means to disavow their distress. One way they do so is to liken all competition to competitive sports, which, as has often been pointed out and as Jim's response to me demonstrates, is the context in which men learn to compete. The sports model has several functions: As part of social ideology, it represents the meritocratic belief that, in any competition, the race goes to the swiftest; conversely, if the winners are, by definition, the best, then, also by definition, those who lose deserve to. If you believe this, then you don't have to worry about the fairness of the conditions under which competition takes place and you can, thereby, invalidate any social criticism the defeated may make. Competition, whether in the stadium, boardroom, or lecture hall, thus becomes a completely self-justifying, moral(istic) system.[35]

The metaphor of athletics also does some emotional housekeeping by clearing away the ambivalence of competition, in which you must recognize that, because your gain is usually someone else's loss, your pleasure comes at the expense of someone else's pain, and vice versa. One way boys learn to deny ambivalence, and thereby to remember the pleasure and forget the pain, is via competitive athletics. When they find out that "it's only a game," they minimize the hostility of triumph and void the shame of defeat, so that winning contains only pure pleasure, losing only stoic hope. Furthermore, if it's nothing but a game, then any blows you give or take don't really hurt because you were only playing in the sense of pretending, and so, once it's over, you need feel neither remorse for beating someone else nor hatred of the one who beats you.

I hear, however, that there's another side to the story. I hear there's an intense experience you can get from competitive athletics that you can't get anywhere else, and what I've heard makes me hunger for it. Not that I'm likely to get it; at my age, you don't begin to play field hockey or tennis, and, like many other women who are more comfortable working out alone than meeting an opponent or being responsible to a team (and team sports, I know, receive short shrift here), I go in more for individual endurance sports, like swimming or jogging.[36] Furthermore, since I'm one of those women who has always looked down on team sports as "trivial . . . orgies of violence,"[37] I've always found the interest women friends take in organized athletics slightly mystifying, amusing, and suspect (what a way to compete for men, no?).[38]

I'm beginning to understand, though, that there are four secrets women like me have never been let in on. One of these concerns the relationship between competition and self-esteem. I can't be alone among women in feeling that, if I lose the game, I am "a loser." Of course, if your narcissism is at stake every time you play a game, you can hardly take any pleasure in playing. Rather, under those circumstances, each game becomes "a life-and-death struggle." [39] If, in contrast, you know that "each game is nothing more than a game," as "the most accomplished women athletes" do, then the aphorism boys learn, "it's only a game," takes on a new meaning: winning and losing are only about that particular contest.[40] The competition is not, in other words, about you, it's about your performance, which is not, as Zen strives to teach, the same thing at all. This distinction, unstable though it may be, is taught to boys explicitly, but hardly at all to girls.

In this restricted sense, then, competitive sports is, in fact, morally neutral. While I don't believe it's particularly easy to distinguish yourself from the game you played on any given day, nevertheless I can see that competition in this arena offers you the opportunity to evaluate what you do without judging who or what you are. Surely this is a great and valuable lesson, applicable to many different parts of life. It might, for example, be exceptionally useful for women who want to resist the psychological and social compulsion to be better than they are. If you can feel that your own performance is not a matter of your own goodness, then you are freed from the anxiety that attends your attempts to improve your performance: you can work to improve what you do because you are already good, because, as psychobabble has it, "You're worth it."

Athletics can't be the only route to this capacity for dispassionately estimating one's strengths and weaknesses (a goal Lindenbaum would have her patients strive for). However, it seems to be the major one in our culture. Competitive sports nurtures this ability by carving out a sacred space from ordinary life, a space in which the normal rules of politeness are temporarily suspended and ambivalence is irrelevant. Defined as "play," athletics rationalizes hostility by splitting pain from pleasure, as I have suggested. But within the play itself, athletic competition can make room for the irrational and thereby release normally proscribed aspects of self, in particular, aggression and hatred. Play, in Winnicott's classic definition, lies somewhere between ordinary life and fantasy,[41] and the pleasure we find in it depends on nearing the poles without settling into one or the other; "indeed, play loses its piquancy when it settles into either reality or fantasy, when, for example, 'the nip becomes a bite,' to quote Bateson's famous insight."[42] I'm not ignoring the commercial side of sport, the big bucks of professional and even amateur athletics. But I am saying that, within the rules of the game, even when its frame is money and fame, anything goes.

Thus detoxified and brought under the sway of ambivalence, aggression and hatred lose their power to paralyze, and what happens next is Zen-like. Once you let these powerful emotions be, they let you be; once experienced, they can be known and managed, and hence no longer dangerous to you or anyone else. And then it becomes possible to identify aggressiveness not only between you and your opponent but within yourself. The opportunity to experience and reverse one's self-hate is the second great secret known by top women athletes, many of whom say that your most important opponent is not your competitor but "yourself, your negative internal voices."[43] Successful athletic competition allows, indeed, demands that you own, confront, and triumph over those inner voices, those "bad objects," to use the psychoanalytic jargon. Regarding these bad objects not as a sign of your intrinsic badness but as obstacles to your goodness, you can subordinate them to your goal, whether it be a prize or a poem that pleases you more than the one you wrote last. By knowing, accepting, even loving your own hatred of self and others, you can clear away the obstacles to your own competence, the goal that Lindenbaum set for her patients.

Which brings us to "the zone." The process of examining and standing up to your own internal voices confers and demands a certain toughness of spirit, which, the experts argue, is essential to success. The third secret to which the most successful women competitors are privy is that "the race . . . goes not to the swiftest, but to the toughest,"[44] that is, to those who concentrate. "[T]he ability to . . . focus so completely on this one event, moment by moment, stroke by stroke, . . . gives the athlete the tiny edge she needs to beat an equally talented rival whose attention might wander. [Chris] Evert Lloyd, a Zen Master when it comes to concentration, always cites this quality as the key to her game."[45] Athletic competence requires what in fact the Zen Buddhists call "mindfulness," absolute concentration on the present.[46] This ability, achieved only by sustained hard work, can put you into the altered state of consciousness that athletes refer to as "the zone." This ecstatic state is a seamless unity among mind, body, and the rules and tools of the game. Here's Evelyn Ashford, who holds the world record in the 100–meter dash: "Time stands still when you're racing. . . . When I'm free-flowing and just everything's working, it feels like nothing. It's effortless. You don't feel the track, you don't feel your arms moving, you don't feel the wind going by. It's just nothing. It's perfect."[47] In the zone, there's not even competition any more. And, as is well known, when Evert Lloyd could no longer be in the zone, she quit playing tennis.

Here, then, is the biggest secret of all: In order to reach this "state of grace,"[48] you have to traverse the fullness of yourself, the entire spectrum of your personality, so that you know what your capacities and desires are. This means that you have to travel into those dangerous sectors of yourself, the places of badness and pain. You must, in fact, encounter and accept ambivalence: You have to risk being a bad girl and hurting others even while trying to love them. And, in the service of self-regard and self-love, you have to tolerate being hurt yourself, hurt by losing, hurt by what you don't like in yourself.

I think this argument holds not only in the athletic arena but in, for example, writing or making art; more generally, I think it holds when it comes to doing anything well. But I also think it's hard for women to recognize these requirements because we've learned that, if something hurts, it means we're doing something wrong. I don't think we've learned what boys often do—even if it hurts and even if you're scared, you do it anyway.[49] As psychoanalysis teaches us, all growth entails anxiety. As the sports masters say, "No pain, no gain."

Janis, to return to the heroine of this story, knew all about that. When she sang, she was "in the zone." Listen to her once again: "I can't talk about my singing. I'm inside of it. How can you describe something you're inside of. I can't know what I'm doing; if I knew it, I'd have lost it. When I sing, I feel, oh, I feel, well, like when you're first in love. It's more than sex, I know that. It's that point two people can get to they call love, like when you really touch someone for the first time, but it's gigantic, multiplied by the whole audience. I feel chills, weird feelings slipping all over my body. It's a supreme emotional and physical experience." And a spiritual one, too, so precious that those who experience it become superstitious. Like Janis, "[most] ballplayers—out of confusion, or perhaps superstition, maintain silence on the subject of the zone."[50]

So, yes, you can get rich playing a(nother) man's game. I do think the traditionally male preserve of competitive sports has something to teach us, and I think the girls who now have the chance to compete will have a great advantage over those of us who came before them and did not (and I envy them for it). They will learn something about their own capacities, needs, and limits. They will have reaffirmed in their bodies the sense of empowerment we all first felt as infants when we grabbed our first toy or took our first step. They will feel powerful, not only in the sense of dominating or being dominated by others, but in the sense of being able. They will know about "power to" as well as "power over." Yes. Competition is good for women.

When the game is over, however, you still have to deal with ambivalence and the ease with which, in our society, "power to" slides into "power over."

8. New York City. November 12, 1990.

Linda reappears in another dream: I pass her in the subway. Her well-fitting white and green sweater-dress suits her curves, which I find as breathtakingly beautiful as ever. I walk quickly by, trying not to let her see me seeing her. But she does see me and, saying "Hi, sweetie," reaches to hug me. I'm just beyond her grasp. Still I turn, belatedly, thinking I should try to respond. "Oh," I say, "you seem upset." "Yes," she replies. "What—" I begin to ask. "No," she declines, hastening down the stairs with a smile that apologizes for her hurry.

Yes, it is indeed surprising that my unconscious has cooperated with this project by providing me with so much material. At the same time as I'm grateful, however, I'm nettled: how come Linda enters my dreams every time (all of twice) I have a date?

One thing I've learned in the course of reflecting on competitions with my dearest friends is that women have precious few ways to make up. When men engage in sports, they have institutionalized ways of repairing the damage they inflict or receive: They play a game of basketball or tennis, one side or person wins, the other loses, they go out and have a beer, slap each other on the backs, and go home. Women, in contrast, have no customary way to suture the wounds, their own or anyone else's. At the same time, they give each other their hearts. Men, or at least heterosexual men, let their women lick their wounds, mend their hearts. Women feed each other, they compete, but they have no ritual of reparation. They have no ceremony that, in acknowledging the need to repair the wounds, transforms hate into love and thus restores ambivalence.

In other words, I'm saying that ambivalence is a good thing. Generally used to mean the negative inability to choose between love and hate, "ambivalence" in fact refers to the simultaneity of positive and negative, to "a non-dialectical opposition which the subject, saying 'yes' and 'no' at the same time, is incapable of transcending."[51] To be capable of ambivalence is to be able to sustain the tension of paradox without falling permanently to one pole of the other, to hold love in relation to hate.

To be sure, when initially experienced, ambivalence is hellish; to recognize, for example, that you can hate the mother you love, or love the mother you hate, hurts with infinite pain until you discover that, if love always turns into hate, hate just as surely returns to love. Without ambivalence, however, hate and love destroy each other. Hate obliterates the other, love consumes the self. When you hate only, you see nothing but badness and therefore wish to wipe the other off the face of the earth. When you love and see goodness only, you can't make meaning of the other's flaws, and so, wishing to wipe those flaws off the face of the earth, you see only what you want to see, only what you can love. In a way, when you love without hating, you see only yourself, never the other.[52]

If seeing the other as the other is the trick, then seeing another woman as the other is even trickier, at least if you're a woman. Difference is not neutral; it is threatening not only because it intimates separation and abandonment, but because the other can be different in ways you don't like. Women, however, are inclined by their gendered identification with their mothers to feel comfort in being alike, which can, unconsciously, make liking one another imperative. This intrapsychic slippage from likeness to liking has its social counterpart in what I have called elsewhere an "ethic of loyalty" between women, which, at least among women of the same age, race, class, sexuality, and so on, "holds that women are, in distinction to men, the same and, therefore, peers, equals whose first obligation is to one another."[53] One component of this ethic is an emphasis on likeness and love at the expense of dis-likeness and hate, enforced by the taboo on women's anger and aggression, of which Keller and Moglen make much. Indeed, this force toward likeness is one of the main causes for conflict between the women in the examples they offer, on the basis of which they argue that "the common association made between identification and cooperation on the one hand, and between separation and competition on the other, is too simple. Under certain circumstances, cooperation may actually be facilitated by differentiation and autonomy."[54] To my way of thinking, however, differentiation and autonomy are insecure accomplishments unless you can tolerate dislikable, as well as agreeable, difference, the differences that anger as well as please you; this capacity in turn rests on the accessibility of all your emotions, from love to hate.

Nor does my dream tell how to achieve this ambivalence. It tells only of its possibility. The key to the dream lies in the multiple symbolic colors of Linda's costume. On the one hand, the combination of white and green has never appealed to me; I find it uninteresting at best and slightly repellent at worst. In the dream, then, it's a sign not so much of difference or dissimilarity or un-likeness between me and Linda as of dislike. I dislike this color combination as, in fact, I disliked certain of Linda's tastes. Not, of course, that I ever told her. No, most of our friendship was founded on being alike, not on disliking; on loving, not hating. With our selves merged, I (perhaps we) feared the chain of signifiers that goes thus: dissimilarity, dis-likeness, hatred.

At the same time, these colors possess a personal meaning having to do with sex, power, and competition: when I was in high school, I spent quite a bit of time knitting a white and green scarf for my boyfriend, whose college colors they were. That I consulted my mother frequently about this fairly simple project—how long, for example, the scarf should be—suggests to me now, as I look back, that I was in considerable doubt about whether I had the right to my own man. To interpret the dream language: that Linda wears the same colors registers my dubiety as to my own autonomy, sexuality, aggression, and power—in short, about my claim to the phallus (and how long it should be) (laugh). For me, in this dream, Linda (which is to say, the Linda/mother who is a product of my unconscious, not the Linda whom you too may know) is the phallic mother, the Dinnerstein mother who can starve as well as nurture you,[55] the sexual mother who, my dream said, may fight with her husband and sleep with another man, the Medusa with a coif of writhing snakes from whom I recoil. I am afraid of her seeing me seeing her because, if she does, that will mean I will be looking directly into the Medusa's face and thus will be at risk of being turned into stone by the aggression and competitiveness and hatred, both autochthonous and reflected, I see there. I am afraid to look straight at her and let her see my frank desire to acquire for myself the sort of sexual power she has and for her possession of which I hate her.

For her possession of which I love her. Love pervades the dream too, emotionally, sensually, sexually. I love Linda's curvaceous body even though I hate what she clothes it in. And Linda loves me too: she calls me by an endearment my real mother might have used. She loves me even though I hate her. I love her even though she hates me. The Medusa, a terrifying image of maternal hatred and destructiveness, can also be read as a passionate and utopian symbol of women's personal power. Yes, the mother has power, and "she's not deadly. She's beautiful and she's laughing."[56] As Susan Suleiman elaborates Cixous's argument, "the laughing Medusa becomes a trope for women's autonomous subjectivity,"[57] including, I would emphasize, her hatred, aggression, competitiveness, and love. For her, my, our ambivalence. I hate her for the same reason I love her, the beautiful power that ought also to be mine, could be mine if I could tolerate the ambivalence of loving and hating her, the ambivalence that made me embarrassed, both dismayed and happy to see her quarreling with her husband in public.

Life, however, is not a dream, and the longed-for phallus is awfully hard to come by if you're a woman. According to Lacanian theory, no one, not even men, can possess the phallus, because it is but a symbol representing the impossible, the desire to be the object of mother's desire.[58] But, in my view, the phallus symbolizes more. It is, in fact, overdetermined, and its condensation of the personal and the political circles back to an underlying project of this paper, the splicing of internal and external realities. This image of an erect penis, said to represent the unconscious, also stands for patriarchy. As "the [discursive] site where the social is reproduced as the biological,"[59] the phallus also refers to masculinity, which is a simultaneously cultural and psychological construction.

The phallus, then, references social power, which some people do indeed possess in greater amounts than others. Signifying the autonomous subjectivity that is traditionally the property of men, and thus representing "masculine privilege in a culture of hierarchy, the phallus comes also to signify that culture itself, the state. Other symbols of culture . . . are possible such as . . . the female jaguars worshipped by the Olmecs who lived in Mexico in 1200 A.D. . . . But when the actual configuration of power is male over female, rich man over poor man, and state over citizen, only the phallus will do."[60] Only those who possess the penis, or possess someone with a penis, may lay claim to the phallus and all it represents. However, just because you claim the prize doesn't mean you actually get it. The few who can make good on their claim are those who "really do have the sort of power that can determine the rest of our lives, [those who] control the money and jobs the rest of us need or . . . , holding the keys to the halls of state, . . . have their fingers on the nuclear buttons that can destroy human life itself."[61] They are the people with the phallus. And their power makes us want, and need, to get some of it for ourselves.

The phallus is, therefore, what we compete for. In a culture of hierarchy whose signature is competition, where possessing the phallus means that you can dominate other people, winning the game is not only about the ecstasy of being in the zone. Within the rules of the game, as I have argued, competitiveness can be a route to empowerment, competence, and self-possession. But as long as the game is played in an economy of scarcity, "power to" slides easily into "power over," and empowerment can slip under the steamroller of domination. That this elision takes place among everyone, including women and feminists, is the reason we worry about the capacity of power and its rewards to destroy feminism.

I want to argue, then, that competitiveness cannot safely proceed among women, especially feminists, unless we can do something to prevent "power over" from steamrolling "power to." As useful as competition has been for me and as much as I want and intend to go on competing, I also know, from personal experience, that the combat is deadly; I don't think the wounds of losing heal until you finally win what you want; and, although losing may help you to figure out what you're good at and what you really want to do, the connections between you and others can be damaged during the time it takes to do that.

What I really want to argue seems naive, jejune, and "girlish": Somehow, everybody has to win. But how could everyone win in a way that would not devalue the prizes? One way would be for everyone to agree to use competition only to get "power to," to enhance their own competence, sharpen their skills, know themselves, and get into "the zone." Yet, in an economy of scarcity, what would keep "power to" from becoming "power over?" How could a rule hold out against the hierarchical structure necessitating it? If one person, one woman, one feminist, sets her sights on and makes her way to the top of the pyramid, becoming, say, a media or academic star, then the game is over. "Power to" becomes forever devalued in comparison to "power over." Indeed, who of us can say she wouldn't reach for the gold ring? I myself would like this paper to be the volume's standout, even given a place of prominence. (And, as long as we're in a religious mode, should we not ask, "Let she who is without sin. . ."?)

In fact, as long as we're talking about this piece of writing, we might look here at its perhaps unavoidable participation in certain competitions between women. Each of its two main springboards, the article by Keller and Moglen and the biblical story of Rachel and Leah, differently overlooks the structures of political power that shape women's relations to each other. Keller and Moglen acknowledge the influence of politically based scarcity on competition between feminists, but they do not investigate the workings of class and race differences in the conflicts between the women whose stories they recount; their theory, located in psychoanalytic discourse and familial metaphor, weights the psychology of maternal and sororal intimacies. The story of Rachel and Leah similarly focuses on experiences of loss, power, and envy in the familial domain; insofar as its protagonists are sisters, their socioeconomic positions are as identical as any can be, and thus their competitiveness is rendered far more in personal than political terms.

While my formal and theoretical approach has been to redress the balance, so that the dialogue between the personal and the political never stops, nevertheless my focus has been women's experience of competition in its unconscious and social contexts, not the political structures dividing and joining women. It's a focus I choose not only because I like it, but because I think it leads to certain kinds of truth-telling that more "objective" approaches preclude; it allows, even, I would say, constrains us to look at both inner and outer reality. But there are other kinds of truth-telling as well, some of which may be missing here. It's in this sense that I wonder how much the essay's textual springboards have set its discourse: Having selected the story of competing sisters, for example, I chose not to talk about another suggested text, the tale of Sarah and Hagar, of the mistress and her darker-skinned slave who became a surrogate mother for her, whose political positions are as disparate and unequal as any can be. Indeed, I recall feeling overwhelmed just thinking about the challenge of analyzing competition between women of different classes, races, sexualities, and so on, and also meshing that project with the others this paper already takes on, the simultaneous dialogues between the psychological and the social, the literary and the theoretical.

One thing I've learned in writing this essay is that, in contrast to the political sanctimony to which we in feminism and on the New Left have become inured, the Bible speaks in tones that are cold and clear, but somehow unjudgmental.[62] The narrator (whose gender, a currently hot topic, I'm not qualified to discuss) looks, sees, and tells us at length about Rachel and Leah, but does not comment on this tale of love, power, and arbitrariness. For example, Rachel, it informs us, is beautiful and young, barren and dishonest, and, finally, the one whom Jacob loves. Leah, ugly and older, gets to marry first and bear her own children first, but she will never be the object of Jacob's desire. Good and bad, the story seems to say, cycle among us, alighting here, alighting there. No one deserves, no one is undeserving. Life is difficult, and life is worth it.

Not bad, and not far from Zen, wouldn't you say? And yet, also not far from Zen, the Bible accomplishes this unmoralizing stance by ignoring its own political context, thus creating the dilemma we often encounter when the political meets the spiritual. For, if the Bible does not comment on equal or unequal justice, neither does it remark the larger patriarchal and generally hierarchical structure that birthed it and that we have inherited. In effect, its lack of commentary endorses the authoritarian structure in which only some men found nations, and women never do. This silence constitutes an unacceptable acceptance, not in the Zen-like sense of recognition, but in a more complicit sense of authorization.

I think the only way to get beyond this impasse of two necessary but contradictory voices is not to fight it, but to stay right in it, to go in, as I said at the beginning, as deep as you can, to use both voices even at the cost of confusion. I believe that the nonmoralizing voice has to be juxtaposed with informed political judgment, with, you might say, morality. We have to speak in Zen-like tones of acceptance, and we have to condemn and try to change what we believe to be wrong. If you want to change what you hate, you have to love it, which does not mean that you do not struggle against it.

Once more, women's work is never done. But instead of trying to solve all the problems I've suddenly stirred up here at the end of this work, I'd like to make a modest utopian suggestion applicable to a limited sector of reality, not as a solution, but as a stimulant. And I'm going to reach for a favorite Western vision of utopia, another culture. Although contemporary college students regard anthropologists as intellectual colonialists for using Western images of other cultures to understand the West itself, to search for "the primitive" in order to recover or even invent a part of ourselves,[63] I nevertheless think it's worth the risk of political incorrectness to take up Keller and Moglen's suggestion that we let ourselves be influenced by what we see in the Other.

What I have in mind is a system of power in which, in order to get power, you have to give it away. One famous example is the potlatch practiced by the Kwakiutl and other peoples of the northwest coast of North America.[64] The potlatch is a multipurpose ceremony that individuals hold to mark momentous events in their lives, such as marriages or deaths, as well as to stake a claim to social position. As practiced before European trading systems undermined and distorted the Kwakiutl foraging economy, the potlatch also had the social function of reducing disparities of wealth within and, sometimes, between communities. In anticipation of the ceremony, an individual man or woman would accumulate a variety of goods acquired or created in the course of hunting, fishing, and trading, which, at the ceremony, she or he would give away to the assembled guests. As a result of this largess, the donor would initiate or continue a climb through the Kwakiutl ranking system, while the recipient might inaugurate or add to a stockpile that would permit him or her to do the same. The more people gave away, the greater the prestige they would obtain; hoarding, indeed, would reduce the public esteem they merited. In effect, then, the system by which prestige was acquired encouraged people to outdo one another by giving away more than they received.

The moral of this ethnographic story is that, in some cultures, one strength cannot be converted into another, but only exchanged for another. Power may be said to exist in different domains in each culture— economic, political, social, representational, personal. I am arguing that the "more difficult it is for power to be translated from one domain to another, the less power any one individual can have over another."[65] Among the Kwakiutl and other peoples, power in, for example, the material domain cannot be both retained and transformed into political or symbolic power. In other words, in order to climb in rank, the Kwakiutl had to convert the material basis for power into prestige, which in effect meant they were underwriting their own competitors.

As I said, a utopian suggestion. I'm not proposing we follow such a model; it wouldn't work in a society whose hierarchy is based on scarcity and private property. I'm proposing we think about it, think about a way in which we might be able to recycle power so that one strength could not be converted into another. Suppose, for example, that, in one very small group of feminists, someone who won the competition for "power over" couldn't keep the prestige (or money) it conferred on her unless it were exchanged for something like "power with" (and thereby became collective)? Suppose we had a ceremony in which the exchange took place? Suppose, in the ceremony, unevennesses could be smoothed? Reparations for the wounds of inequity could be made? Love could reunite with hate? And women could make up?

I can't imagine it. Can you?

9. Sag Harbor, New York. August 18, 1991.

A few days ago, I found, in that last batch of forwarded mail, a letter from Linda asking whether we might try to reconnect during her upcoming trip to the States. The penny dropped today: she's just about to turn fifty. I'm not sure I have the same desire, but I'll meet her to clear the air, and then see where we go from there.

I make no claim to prophetic dreams. But what I tell you truly happened.

NOTES

1. Muriel Dimen, *Surviving Sexual Contradictions: A Startling and Different Look at a Day in the Life of a Contemporary Professional Woman* (New York: Macmillan, 1986), 154–60.
2. Evelyn Fox Keller and Helene Moglen, "Competition: A Problem for Academic Women," in Valerie Miner and Helen Longino, eds., *Competition: A Feminist Taboo?* (New York: Feminist Press, 1987), 21–37.
3. Miner and Longino, eds., ibid.
4. Grace Lichtenstein, "Competition in Women's Athletics," ibid., 48–56; Joyce P. Lindenbaum, "The Shattering of an Illusion: The Problem of Competition in Lesbian Relationships," ibid., 195–208.
5. Keller and Moglen, "Competition: A Problem for Academic Women?," ibid., 21–37.
6. Daphne Muse, "High Stakes, Meager Yields: Competition among Black Girls," ibid., 152–60; Martha A. Ackelsberg and Kathryn Pyne Addelson, "Anarchist Alternatives to Competition," ibid., 221–33.
7. Keller and Moglen, "Competition," ibid., 22.
8. Ibid.
9. Ibid., 35.
10. Ibid.

11. Ibid., 37.
12. Ellen Willis, "Radical Feminism and Feminist Radicalism," in Sohnya Sayres, Anders Stephanson, Stanley Aronowitz, and Frederic Jameson, eds., *The Sixties without Apology* (Minneapolis: University of Minnesota Press [in cooperation with Social Text], 1984), 99.
13. Carol Gilligan, *In a Different Voice: Women's Conceptions of Self and Morality* (Cambridge: Harvard University Press, 1982).
14. This phrase, "the unthought-known," comes from Christopher Bollas, *The Unthought-Known* (New York: Columbia University Press, 1988).
15. Michael Lydon, "The Janis Joplin Philosophy: Every Moment She Is What She Feels," *New York Times Magazine*, February 23, 1969, 37.
16. *Webster's New World Dictionary of the American Language* (New York: World Publishing Company, 1956).
17. Carol Hanisch, "The Personal Is Political," in *Notes from the Second Year* (New York: Radical Feminists, 1969), 76–78; reprinted in Redstockings of the Women's Liberation Movement, eds., *Feminist Revolution* (New York: Random House, 1978), 204–5.
18. Keller and Moglen, "Competition," in Miner and Longino, 22.
19. Helen E. Longino and Valerie Miner, "A Feminist Taboo?" ibid., 1.
20. Judith Levine, *My Enemy, My Love: Man-hating and Ambivalence in the Nineties* (New York: Doubleday, 1991).
21. Muriel Dimen, review of *Competition: A Feminist Taboo?*, edited by Valerie Miner and Helen Longino, *New York Times Book Review*, October 27, 1987.
22. Lindenbaum, "Shattering of an Illusion," in Miner and Longino, 204.
23. Ibid., 205.
24. Ibid.
25. Ibid., 206.
26. Keller and Moglen, "Competition," ibid., 35.
27. Nancy Chodorow, *The Reproduction of Mothering: Psychoanalysis and the Sociology of Gender* (Berkeley: University of California Press, 1978); Jean Baker Miller, *Toward a New Psychology of Women* (Boston: Beacon Press, 1976).
28. Keller and Moglen, "Competition," in Miner and Longino, 35.
29. Muriel Dimen, "Power, Sexuality, and Intimacy," in Alison Jaggar and Susan Bordo, eds., *Gender/Body/Knowledge: Feminist Reconstructions of Being and Knowing* (New Brunswick: Rutgers University Press, 1989), 42.
30. Lindenbaum, "Shattering of an Illusion," in Miner and Longino, 206.
31. Ackelsberg and Addelson, "Anarchist Alternatives," ibid., 223.
32. Alice Echols, *Daring to Be Bad* (New York: Routledge and Kegan Paul, 1987).
33. Lindenbaum, "Shattering of an Illusion," in Miner and Longino, 206.
34. Muse, "High Stakes," ibid., 157.
35. See Adrienne Harris, "Women, Baseball, and Words," *PsychCritique* 1 (1985): 35–54.
36. Ibid.

37. Jennifer Ring, "Perfection on the Wing," in Miner and Longino, 60.

38. Lichtenstein, "Competition in Women's Athletics," ibid., 53.

39. Ibid.

40. Ibid.

41. D. W. Winnicott, *Playing and Reality* (New York: Penguin, 1971).

42. Muriel Dimen, "Deconstructing Difference: Gender, Splitting, and Transitional Space," *Psychoanalytic Dialogues: A Journal of Relational Perspectives* 3 (1991): 335–52.

43. Lichtenstein, "Competition," in Miner and Longino, 53.

44. Ibid.

45. Ibid., 54.

46. At Tassajara, the ritual schedule ensured mindfulness; for example, kitchen work was regularly punctuated not only by ceremonial chanting, but by a bell that commanded a thirty-second respite from whatever you were doing so you could bring your mind back from wherever it had wandered to where you were.

47. Ring, "Perfection," 65.

48. Lawrence Shainberg, "Finding 'the Zone,'" *New York Times Magazine,* April 9, 1989, 35.

49. Dimen, *Surviving Sexual Contradictions,* 130.

50. Shainberg, "Finding 'the Zone,'" 38.

51. J. LaPlanche and J.-B. Pontalis, *The Language of Psycho-Analysis,* trans. D. Nicholson-Smith (New York: W. W. Norton, 1973), 28.

52. The discussion of hate, love, reparation, and ambivalence originates, of course, in Freud, but really begins in Melanie Klein and Joan Riviere, *Love, Hate and Reparation* (New York: W. W. Norton, 1964) and continues in D. W. Winnicott; for example, "Hate in the Counter-Transference," in *Collected Papers: Through Paediatrics to Psycho-Analysis* (New York: Basic Books, 1958), in which he argues that the analyst must tolerate hating that patient, as the mother must tolerate her normal hatred of her baby; only in this way can the patient/infant grow to be a separate person.

53. Dimen, *Surviving Sexual Contradictions,* 170.

54. Keller and Moglen, "Competition," 27.

55. Dorothy Dinnerstein, *The Mermaid and the Minotaur: Sexual Arrangements and Human Malaise* (New York: Harper and Row, 1976).

56. Helene Cixous, quoted in Susan Suleiman, *Subversive Intent: Gender, Politics, and the Avant-Garde* (Cambridge: Harvard University Press, 1990), 167.

57. Suleiman, ibid., 168.

58. Juliet Mitchell, "Introduction—I," in Juliet Mitchell and Jacqueline Rose, eds., *Feminine Sexuality: Jacques Lacan and the ecole freudienne,* trans. Jacqueline Rose (New York: W. W. Norton, 1982), 1–26; Jacqueline Rose, "Introduction—II," in idem, 27–58.

59. Adrienne Harris, "Bringing Artemis to Life: The Role of Militance and Aggression in Women's Psychic Life and in Feminist Peace Politics," in

Adrienne Harris and Ynestra King, eds., *Rocking the Ship of State: Toward a Feminist Peace Politics* (Boulder, Colo.: Westview Press, 1989), 114.

60. Dimen, *Surviving Sexual Contradictions*, 131.
61. Ibid., 131–32.
62. At least in the translation I used, the new edition put out by the Jewish Publication Society, *Tanakh: The Holy Scriptures* (New York, 1988), and recommended to me by Alice Bach.
63. Stanley Diamond, *In Search of the Primitive* (New York: Transaction Books, 1974).
64. The classic account of the potlatch is found in Ruth Benedict, *Patterns of Culture* (New York: Houghton Mifflin, 1934). A later, ecological interpretation, rectifying Benedict's misunderstanding of the later, post-contact potlatches in which goods were not only given away but destroyed, is by Wayne Suttles, "Affinal Ties, Subsistence, and Prestige among the Coast Salish," *American Anthropologist* 62 (1964): 296–305.
65. Muriel Dimen-Schein, *The Anthropological Imagination* (New York: McGraw-Hill, 1977), 212.

REFERENCES

Ackelsberg, Martha A., and Kathryn Pyne Addelson. "Anarchist Alternatives to Competition." In *Competition: A Feminist Taboo?* edited by Valerie Miner and Helen Longino, 221–33. New York: Feminist Press, 1987.

Benedict, Ruth. *Patterns of Culture.* New York: Houghton Mifflin, 1934.

Bollas, Christopher. *The Unthought-known.* New York: Columbia University Press, 1988.

Chodorow, Nancy. *The Reproduction of Mothering: Psychoanalysis and the Sociology of Gender.* Berkeley: University of California Press, 1978.

Diamond, Stanley. *In Search of the Primitive.* New York: Transaction Books, 1974.

Dimen, Muriel. "Deconstructing Difference: Gender, Splitting, and Transitional Space." *Psychoanalytic Dialogues: A Journal of Relational Perspectives* 3 (1991): 335–52.

———. "Power, Sexuality, and Intimacy." In *Gender/Body/Knowledge: Feminist Reconstructions of Being and Knowing,* edited by Alison Jaggar and Susan Bordo, 34–51. New Brunswick, N.J.: Rutgers University Press, 1989.

———. Review of *Competition: A Feminist Taboo?* edited by Helen Longino and Valerie Miner. *New York Times Sunday Book Review,* October 27, 1987.

———. *Surviving Sexual Contradictions: A Startling and Different Look at a Day in the Life of a Contemporary Professional Woman.* New York: Macmillan, 1986.

Dimen-Schein, Muriel. *The Anthropological Imagination.* New York: McGraw-Hill, 1977.

Dinnerstein, Dorothy. *The Mermaid and the Minotaur: Sexual Arrangements and Human Malaise.* New York: Harper and Row, 1976.

Echols, Alice. *Daring to Be Bad.* New York: Routledge and Kegan Paul, 1987.

Gilligan, Carol. "In a Different Voice: Women's Conceptions of Self and of Morality." In *The Future of Difference,* edited by Hester Eisenstein and Alice Jardine, 274–317. New Brunswick, N.J.: Rutgers University Press, 1980.

———. *In a Different Voice: Women's Conceptions of Self and Morality.* Cambridge: Harvard University Press, 1982.

Goffman, Erving. *Asylums: Essays on the Social Situation of Mental Patients and Other Inmates.* Garden City, N.Y.: Anchor Books, 1961.

Hanh, Thich Nhat. "The Flute of the Buddha: Art, Practice, and Everyday Life." *Inquiring Mind* 7 (1990): 1.

Hanisch, Carol. "The Personal Is Political." *Notes from the Second Year,* 76–78. New York: Radical Feminists, 1969. Reprinted in *Feminist Revolution, An Abridged Edition with Additional Writings,* edited by Redstockings of the Women's Liberation Movement. New York: Random House, 1978, 204–5.

Harris, Adrienne. "Bringing Artemis to Life: The Role of Militance and Aggression in Women's Psychic Life and in Feminist Peace Politics." In *Rocking the Ship of State: Toward a Feminist Peace Politics,* edited by Adrienne Harris and Ynestra King, 93–114. Boulder, Colo.: Westview Press, 1989.

———. "Women, Baseball, and Words." *PsychCritique* 1 (1985): 35–54.

Keller, Evelyn Fox, and Helene Moglen. "Competition: A Problem for Academic Women." In *Competition: A Feminist Taboo?* edited by Valerie Miner and Helen Longino, 21–37. New York: Feminist Press, 1987.

Klein, Melanie, and Joan Riviere. *Love, Hate and Reparation.* New York: W. W. Norton, 1964.

LaPlanche, J., and J.-B. Pontalis. *The Language of Psychoanalysis.* Trans. D. Nicholson-Smith. New York: W. W. Norton, 1973.

Levine, Judith. *My Enemy, My Love: Man-hating and Ambivalence in the Nineties.* New York: Doubleday, 1991.

Lichtenstein, Grace. "Competition in Women's Athletics." In *Competition: A Feminist Taboo?* edited by Valerie Miner and Helen Longino, 48–56. New York: Feminist Press, 1987.

Lindenbaum, Joyce P. "The Shattering of an Illusion: The Problem of Competition in Lesbian Relationships." In *Competition: A Feminist Taboo?* edited by Valerie Miner and Helen Longino, 195–208. New York: Feminist Press, 1987.

Longino, Helen E., and Valerie Miner. "A Feminist Taboo?" In *Competition: A Feminist Taboo?* edited by Valerie Miner and Helen Longino, 1–7. New York: Feminist Press, 1987.

Lydon, Michael. "The Janis Joplin Philosophy: Every Moment She Is What She Feels." *New York Times Magazine,* February 23, 1969, 37.

Miller, Jean Baker. *Toward a New Psychology of Women.* Boston: Beacon Press, 1976.

Miner, Valerie, and Helen Longino, eds. *Competition: A Feminist Taboo?* New York: Feminist Press, 1987.

Mitchell, Juliet. "Introduction – I." *Feminine Sexuality: Jacques Lacan and the École Freudienne*, edited by Juliet Mitchell and Jacqueline Rose, 1–26. New York: W. W. Norton, 1982.

Muse, Daphne. "High Stakes, Meager Yields: Competition among Black Girls." In *Competition: A Feminist Taboo?* edited by Valerie Miner and Helen Longino, 152–60. New York: Feminist Press, 1987.

Ring, Jennifer. "Perfection on the Wing." In *Competition: A Feminist Taboo?* edited by Valerie Miner and Helen Longino, 57–69. New York: Feminist Press, 1987.

Rose, Jacqueline. "Introduction – II." In *Feminine Sexuality: Jacques Lacan and the École Freudienne*, edited by Juliet Mitchell and Jacqueline Rose, 27–58. New York: W. W. Norton, 1982.

Shainberg, Lawrence. "Finding the Zone." *New York Times Magazine*, April 9, 1989, 34.

Suleiman, Susan. *Subversive Intent: Gender, Politics, and the Avant-Garde.* Cambridge: Harvard University Press, 1990.

Suttles, Wayne. "Affinal Ties, Subsistence, and Prestige among the Coast Salish." *American Anthropologist* 62 (1964): 296–305.

Tanakh: The Holy Scriptures. The New JPS Translation According to the Traditional Hebrew Text. New York: Jewish Publication Society, 5748/1988.

Webster's New World Dictionary of the American Language. New York: World Publishing Company, 1956.

Willis, Ellen. "Radical Feminism and Feminist Radicalism." In *The Sixties without Apology*, edited by Sohnya Sayres, Anders Stephanson, Stanley Aronowitz, and Frederic Jameson, 91–118. Minneapolis: University of Minnesota Press, 1984.

Winnicott, D. W. "Hate in the Counter-transference." In his *Collected Papers: Through Paediatrics to Psycho-analysis.* New York: Basic Books, 1958.

———. *Playing and Reality.* New York: Penguin, 1971.

CONTRIBUTORS

Linda Alcoff is Assistant Professor of Philosophy at Syracuse University. Her papers have appeared in *SIGNS, Hypatia, Cultural Critique,* and numerous anthologies. She is coeditor of *Feminist Epistemologies* (forthcoming, Routledge).

Tuzyline Jita Allan is Assistant Professor of English at Baruch College, the City University of New York. She is the author of several essays on African, African-American, and English literature. Her manuscript, *Feminist and Womanist Aesthetics* (forthcoming, Ohio University Press), won the 1993 NEMLA Book Award. She recently contributed the afterword to an edition of Ama Ata Aidoo's *Changes* (Feminist Press, 1993).

Judith R. Baskin is Chair of the Department of Judaic Studies at the State University of New York at Albany. She is the author of *Pharoah's Counsellors: Job, Jethro and Balaam in Rabbinic and Patristic Tradition* (Scholars Press, 1983) and *Midrashic Woman* (Holmes and Meier, 1993), and the editor of *Jewish Women in Historical Perspective* (Detroit: Wayne State University Press, 1991). She has written numerous articles on Jewish women in late antiquity and the Middle Ages.

Rosaria Champagne is Assistant Professor of English at Syracuse University. Her book, *Crimes of Reading: Incest and Censorship in Mary*

Shelley's Early Novels, is forthcoming from NYU Press. She has published several articles on feminism and postmodernism; her current research is on the relations between "high" theory and the feminist recovery movement.

Muriel Dimen, Clinical Professor of Psychology at the Postdoctoral Program in Psychotherapy and Psychoanalysis at New York University, is the author of *Surviving Sexual Contradictions: A Startling and Different Look at a Day in the Life of a Contemporary Professional Woman* (New York: Macmillan, 1986) and *The Anthropological Imagination* (New York: McGraw-Hill, 1977), and is coeditor with Ernestine Friedl of *Regional Variations in Modern Greece and Cyprus: Toward an Ethnography of Greece* (New York: New York Academy of Sciences, Annals no. 263, 1976). She is a book review editor of *Psychoanalytic Dialogues: A Journal of Relational Perspectives,* and has written widely on theoretical and cultural issues in psychoanalysis, feminism, and anthropology. She is a Fellow at the New York University Institute for the Humanities, is on the faculty of the Derner Institute in Psychotherapy and Psychoanalysis at Adelphi University, and is a former Professor of Anthropology at Lehman College, the City University of New York. She also maintains a private practice in clinical psychoanalysis in Manhattan.

Jennifer Fleischner is Assistant Professor of English at the State University of New York at Albany. She is also a special candidate in training at Columbia University, Center for Psychoanalytic Training and Research. She has published articles on Scott, Hawthorne, female identity, slavery, and narrative. She has written and edited numerous books for children and is currently writing a book titled *Mastering Slavery: Trauma, Writing, and Identity in Women's Slave Narratives* (forthcoming, NYU Press). She was a 1993–94 Mellon Faculty Fellow in Afro-American Studies at Harvard University.

Nanette Funk is Associate Professor of Philosophy at Brooklyn College, the City University of New York. She has published essays in *Dissent, Telos, Social Text,* and philosophical journals on political and social philosophy, on recent developments in Germany, and on the German philosopher and social theorist Jürgen Habermas. She is editor of *Gender Politics and Post-Communism: Reflections from Eastern European* *and Soviet Women* (Routledge, 1993), and for the last two years has been doing research about women in the former German Democratic Republic. She is currently organizing a conference on East German women to be sponsored by the Goethe Institute in Spring 1993, and is a member of the Network of East-West Women.

Eileen Gillooly is Visiting Assistant Professor of English at Columbia University, where she is currently coordinator of its core curriculum program. She is the author of essays on humor and gender in *Feminist Studies* and *ELH* and of book reviews for a number of publications, including the *New York Times Book Review*. She is currently completing a book-length study on feminine humorous discourse in novels by Austen, Gaskell, Eliot, and Wharton.

E. Ann Kaplan is Professor of English and Comparative Studies and Director of the Humanities Institute at the State University of New York at Stony Brook. She is the author of five books on film, including *Women and Film: Both Sides of the Camera* (Methuen, 1983); *Rocking around the Clock: Music Television, Postmodernism and Consumer Culture* (Routledge, 1987); and *Motherhood and Representation: The Mother in Popular Culture and Melodrama* (Routledge, 1992). She is editor of four collections: *Psychoanalysis and Cinema* (Routledge, 1990); *Postmodernism and Its Discontents: Theories/Practices* (Verso, 1988); *Regarding Television: A Critical Anthology* (American Film Institute, 1983); and *Women in Film Noir: An Anthology* (British Film Institute, 1978). She has also published over fifty articles on film, feminism, and psychoanalysis. Kaplan is currently working on a book titled *Legacies of Slaves and Mistresses: Minority Maternal Discourse in Select Hollywood Film*.

Devoney Looser is Assistant Professor of English at Indiana State University. Her articles have appeared in *Rhetoric Review, European Romantic Review,* and *Style,* and she has published a book chapter in *Misogyny in Literature: An Essay Collection,* edited by Katherine Ackley (Garland Press, 1992). She is currently at work on a feminist investigation of genre in eighteenth-century women's writings.

Linda C. McClain is Associate Professor of Law at Hofstra University, where she specializes in feminist legal theory, property, and the law and the welfare state. In addition, she has a master's degree from the Divinity School of the University of Chicago. The author of several articles, McClain recently completed an essay called "Explicating Circumstances: Romance and Representation," which she presented as a talk at the Feminism and Legal Theory Summer Conference (June 1992) at the Columbia University School of Law.

Daphne Patai is Professor of Women's Studies and of Portuguese at the University of Massachusetts at Amherst. In addition to articles in the fields of oral history, she is the author of *Myth and Ideology in Contemporary Brazilian Fiction* (Fairleigh Dickinson University Press, 1983); *The Orwell Mystique: A Study in Male Ideology* (University of Massachusetts Press, 1984); and *Brazilian Women Speak: Contemporary Life Stories* (Rutgers University Press, 1988). She is coeditor of *Women's Words: The Feminist Practice of Oral History* (Routledge, 1991) and of *Forgotten Radicals: British Women Writers, 1889–1939* (University of North Carolina Press, 1993). She is currently coauthoring (with Noretta Koertge) a book on the problems of contemporary feminism, forthcoming from Basic Books. She has been the recipient of several fellowships, among them a Guggenheim Foundation Fellowship and a National Endowment for the Humanities Fellowship. She has also been a Fellow at the National Humanities Center in North Carolina and the Institute for Advanced Study at Indiana University.

Robin Anne Reid is Assistant Professor of English at East Texas State University. She has published poetry and review essays on fiction and poetry in numerous small journals and has presented papers on science fiction and popular culture.

Nancy Ries is Assistant Professor of Anthropology at Colgate University. Ries was one of the first Americans to do ethnographic field research in contemporary urban Russia; she spent nine months in Moscow in 1989 and 1990. She developed close connections with Russian feminists, took part in the first feminist conference ever held in Moscow (in 1990), and appeared on the popular television show *Vzglad*, in a conversation about feminism with a leading Russian feminist philosopher.

Jennifer Shaddock is Assistant Professor of English at the University of Wisconsin, Eau-Claire. She received her Ph.D. in 1993 from Rutgers

University for her work, "Culture through Anarchy: British Representations of Anarchism, 1840–1907," and edited a reprint of Helen and Olivia Rossetti's *A Girl among the Anarchists*. She has also taught extensively in feminist theory and Native American literature, and she has published on such disparate topics as the politics of naming in Conrad, the Female Gothic in popular film, and the construction of John Stuart Mill in his *Autobiography*.

Manisha Sinha was a 1992–1994 fellow at the W.E.B. Du Bois Institute for Afro-American Research, Harvard University. She recently completed her dissertation entitled, "The Counter-Revolution of Slavery: Class, Politics and Ideology in Antebellum South Carolina," which was nominated for the Bancroft Prize, at Columbia University. She has also been the recipient of a Whiting fellowship and a National Talent Scholarship from the Government of India. She is currently working on the politics of secession and the political ideology of slavery in the Old South.

William Thompson is Assistant Professor of French at Memphis State University. He has written articles on Jean Genet, the contemporary French novel, and feminism and post-feminism. He is currently editing a collection of essays entitled *The Contemporary Novel in France,* as well as two other collections: one of critical essays on Baudelaire's *Les fleurs du mal*; the other on Genet.

Susan Ostrov Weisser is Associate Professor of English at Adelphi University. She has published articles on nineteenth-century British novels and women's narratives. Her book, *A Craving Vacancy: Women and Sexual Love in the British Novel,* is forthcoming from Macmillian and NYU Press.

INDEX

Abbey, Lynn, 350–52, 355 n.16
abortion, 8, 10, 160–88; Bray v. Alexandria, 161, 162, 170; NOW, 161–63, 171, 183 nn.8, 17; Operation Rescue, 161, 162,171; prolife feminists, 8, 10, 159–88; psychological effects of, 168; rights, 159–88, 237; rights, in post-Communist Germany, 312, 315, 317–18, 323, 326; rights, in Russia, 264 n.16
aggression, 112–13, 271–73, 278, 352, 369–71, 373–74, 376, 379–80; and humor, 338; and sisterhood, 130–35, 138. *See also* oppression; victims, women as; violence
AIDS, 348–49, 355 n.12
antifeminism: in Russian press, 263 n.6, 265 n.25; of women, 5–7, 10, 64–65, 73–76, 95, 159–88, 225–41
antislavery. *See* women, and slavery
Applewhite, Harriet B., 235
Armstrong, Nancy, 108, 119
Astell, Mary, 44–46, 50, 52, 57
Atwood, Margaret, 192, 223 n.18
Austen, Jane, 10–11, 328–42
Awkward, Michael, 88–89

Baby M, miniseries, 196–203
Bal, Mieke, 220
Bass, Ellen, 146–47, 154, 156 n.5

backlash against feminism, 5, 237. *See also* antifeminism
beauty, 47–49, 96, 131, 213, 253–4, 266 n.31, 272, 278, 323
Behn, Aphra, 44
Bell, Susan Groag, 52
Benjamin, Jessica, 270
Bible, 8–9, 11; class conflict between women in, 216–19; gender roles in, 210–11; ideology of, 210–11, 222, 223 n.11; justifications of slavery in, 67–68; representations of women in, 209–24; sexual relations in, 215; surrogacy in, 192, 196, 214–19, 359, 367, 383–84
bitch figure, 11, 196–200, 269–82
body, the, 97, 147, 150; female, 2, 4, 15–16, 168, 171, 175, 177–78, 192, 198, 202, 241 n.14, 274–75, 333, 337, 341 n.14; racialized, 48, 91–92, 125–7, 129–31, 139 n.6, 218
Bordo, Susan, 309 n.18
Bourne, Jenny, 37
Butler, Judith, 57

Callahan, Sidney, 170, 175, 182 n.4, 184 n.19
Cameron, Anne, 285, 287, 304
Carey, Henry, 66–67

Fox-Genovese, Elizabeth, 63–64, 75, 139 n.9, 174
France, Anatole, 31
Freud, Sigmund, 128, 133, 137–38, 146, 156 n.7
Friday, Nancy, 142
friendship. *See* women and friendship
Frymer-Kinsky, Tikva, 210–11, 220
Fuss, Diana, 17

gender: black nationalist ideology of, 95; differences, 34, 332, 337; identity overriding class and race, 51, 127, 286; ideologies of, 8–9, 14, 248–49, 259, 265 n.18; politics, 45, 58; roles, 7, 163, 198, 210–11, 227–28, 231, 233–34, 236, 239, 244–45, 248–50, 252, 254–55, 257, 259, 264 nn.8, 13, 275, 313, 332, 351, 362. *See also* men; women
Gilligan, Carol, 170, 181 n.1, 361–62
Ginsberg, Ruth Bader, 181 n.1, 183 n.9
Godineau, Dominique, 235–36
Gordon, Linda, 196, 203, 204 n.3
Grundy, Isobel, 51–52

Habermas, Jurgen, 321
Halsband, Robert, 45, 49
Hammond, James Henry, 66
Hankiss, Agness, 34
Haraway, Donna, 302
Harlequin novels. *See* narrative, romance
Hebrew Bible. *See* Bible
Hegel, G.W.F., 292–93
Hentoff, Nat, 183 n.16
Herman, Judith, 147, 151–52
Hewitt, Nancy, 62
Hirsch, Marianne, 16
hooks, bell, 15, 17, 88, 103
Hufstader, Alice Anderson, 45
husbands, 48–49, 198, 255–59. *See also* family; wives

identity: and difference, 8, 126–40, 287–89, 299; as mothers, 190, 195, 202–3; as women, 30, 108, 119, 168, 177, 184 n.19, 211, 251–52, 254, 259, 262–63, 270, 274, 277, 279, 314–16, 322, 324, 329–30, 337, 370–71; sexual,

343–53, 354 n.3, 354 n.8. *See also* body; class conflict between women; feminism; gender; race
identity politics, 5, 15, 37
imperialism. *See* colonialism
incest, 4, 298; and abortion, 174; father-daughter, 99, 143, 149–50, 155; father's complicity, 147–48; mother-daughter incest narratives, 142–58
incestuousness and slavery, 130–31
individualism, 32, 143, 290, 296, 298–99, 322
inequality, 6, 30, 32, 36–37, 62, 64, 279, 361, 385; and abortion rights, 160, 171, 173–76; in eighteenth-century France, 226, 239; among women, 318–19. *See also* class conflict between women; colonialism; equality; race; women, and slavery
Irigaray, Luce, 2

Jacobs, Harriet, 126, 140 n.13
Jay, Karla, 354 n.3
Johnson, Claudia, 328
Joplin, Janis, 363–64, 368–69, 371, 377
Joseph, Gloria L., 94

Kagan, Janet, 350–52, 355 n.16
Kane, Elizabeth, 190, 193
Kant, Immanuel, 292
Keller, Evelyn Fox, 16, 360–61, 364, 367, 370–71, 379–80, 383–85
Kelly, Joan, 62
Kennedy, Liz, 34
Kingston, Maxine Hong, 120
Klein, Melanie, 131, 139 n.8, 388 n.52
Kristeva, Julia, 156 n.6

Lacan, Jacques, 146, 151, 337, 381
Landes, Joan, 232–34
LeGuin, Ursula, 120
lesbian-feminism, 343–57. *See also* feminist theory
lesbianism, 34, 88, 95, 143, 148–49. *See also* sexuality
lesbians and competition, 369–70, 372–73. *See also* women, and competition
Levy, Darlene Gay, 235
Lew, Joseph, 45, 51, 54, 57